ROAR
TITTER
& SNORT

Published by Prion Books Limited 2008
An imprint of the Carlton Publishing Group
20 Mortimer Street
London W1T 3JW
Copyright © 2008 Carlton Books Limited

ISBN 978-1-85375-685-6

Typeset by e-type, Liverpool
Printed in the UK by CPI Mackays, Chatham, ME5 8TD

JOKE BOOK

Hugh Jarsz

PRION

airplanes

➔ Deep into an international flight, a guy finds himself desperate to go to the toilet. It is busy for ten, then 20, then 30 minutes. He calls the stewardess and asks if he cannot just use the only free loo, the first-class ladies' toilet, just this once. She says that that will be fine, but that he mustn't use any of the buttons that he'll see on the wall. The man says that's fine and he promises not to press any of the buttons. So he goes to the bathroom and does his business, but all the time he's looking at these four buttons on the wall next to the toilet. He gets really curious and says to himself that nothing could be that bad, and that he'll just try the first button. So he presses it. There is a noise, and suddenly a warm, gentle, soothing jet of warm water sprays from the toilet, cleaning his arse. "This is fantastic," thinks the man. "I must try the second button." So he presses the second button. There is a noise and warm air comes flowing up from the toilet, drying his arse. "This really is fantastic," he thinks to himself, "I've got to try the third button." So, he presses the third button. There is a noise and some gentle, soothing powder is deposited on his arse. "Unbelievable," he says to himself. "I really have to try the last button," which has the initials "ATR" stamped upon it. So he presses the fourth button and the next thing he knows he is waking up in a hospital bed, surrounded by doctors and covered in bandages. There is blood all over the place and he is hooked up to a drip. "What the hell happened to me?" he asks the nearest doctor. "You pressed the ATR button, didn't you?" says the doctor. "Well, yes," says the man, "but I never knew what it meant!" The doctor replies, "Automatic Tampon Removal!"

It looks as if it has been dropped, piecemeal, from an aeroplane carrying rubbish.

John Gunther, 1881 – 1926, on Addis Ababa, Ethiopia

↪ Many commentators were astonished that Pan-Am could actually lose one of the engines from an aeroplane. It later transpired that the engine had a luggage sticker on it, and it was found, sad and lonely, on the baggage carousel at Karachi International.

apes and monkeys

↪ A man walks into a bar. He has a monkey with him. The man orders a drink, and while he drinks it the monkey just runs wild around the whole bar, annoying everyone, including the man. While the man is drinking, the monkey runs up to the pool table, climbs up a cue, grabs the cue ball, sticks it in his mouth and swallows it. The barkeeper walks up to the man and says, "Did you see what your bloody monkey just did?" "No, what did the little prick do this time?" replies the man. "He just swallowed the cue ball from my pool table, that's what he just did," says the barkeeper, angrily. "Well, hopefully it'll kill the little bastard, because I'm effing sick of him and his little tricks," says the man.

He then finishes his drink and leaves. A couple of weeks later the same man enters the bar with the same monkey. He orders the same drink and the monkey runs wild around the whole bar, in the same manner as the previous time. While the man is drinking, the monkey finds some peanuts on a tray on the bar. He picks one up, sticks it up his arse, takes it out again and eats it. The barkeeper finds this disgusting, so he walks up to the man again. "Did you see what your bloody monkey just did?" "No, what did the little prick do this time?" sighs the man. "He just stuck a peanut up his arse, took it out and ate it," says the barkeeper. "Well, what do you expect?" asks the monkey's owner. "Ever since he ate that sodding cue ball he has to measure everything first!"

➡ A plane crashes and five men are stranded on a desert island. They are all in their early 20s and very horny. After a month of survival John gets up and says, "I can't take it any more: I'm so horny I'm going to shag that female gorilla at the other end of the island." He grabs himself a bag and runs off. The other four guys follow him and they quickly catch the gorilla. Each of the guys grabs a limb and John pops the bag over its head, jumps on top of the animal and starts to screw it. The gorilla is pretty strong and doesn't put up with any nonsense, so pretty soon it gets an arm clear, and then another. It puts both of them around John's waist and holds on tight. Then it gets first one, then the other leg free as well. and it wraps both of them around John, too. The gorilla seems to be enjoying itself and John starts to shout, "Get it off! Get it off!" One of his mates says, "You must be joking! you're on top and she's wrapped around you tightly." John says, "Not the gorilla – I mean the bag. I want to kiss her!"

↝ A tiny zoo in Suffolk is given a very rare species of gorilla by an eccentric explorer. After a couple of weeks, the gorilla starts to go wild, it won't eat, can't sleep, becomes violent and causes all sorts of problems. The zoo owner calls the vet, determines that the gorilla is a female and, what's more, she's on heat. The only way to calm her down is to have someone mate with her. Sadly, there are no other gorillas of her species in captivity, so another solution will have to be found. It is then that the owner remembers Richard, the cage cleaner. Richard is a bit dumb, but he has a reputation for having sex with anything, so the owner decides to offer him a proposition: would he like to have sex with the gorilla for £500? Richard says he's interested, but that he'll need the night to think it over. The next day he says he'd be willing and that he'd accept the offer, but only if the owner meets three conditions. "First," he says, "I don't want to kiss her on the lips." The owner says that's fine. "Second," Richard says, "you must never, ever tell anyone about this." That's fine, the owner says again. "And third," says Richard, "I'm going to need another week to come up with the money."

The ape, the vilest of beasts – how like to us.

Quintus Ennius, 239 – 169BC

↝ It is a beautiful day and a young blonde and her husband are visiting the zoo. The blonde is dressed in a tight-fitting dress which shows quite a bit of shapely leg and boob – and there's plenty of it to show! They arrive in front of the gorillas' cage and it is obvious that her dress is impressing the male gorilla, as he starts jumping up and down staring at her. "It looks like he fancies you," the guy says. He suggests she plays a game on the poor beast and she purses her lips, wiggles her bottom and plays along for a while. The gorilla is getting wild with excitement, pounding his chest and grunting, to the amusement of the blonde and her husband. At this point, the said boy suggests she "accidentally" drops one of the flimsy straps of her dress. The blonde does that and this sends the gorilla into such a sexual frenzy that he seizes the bars of the cage, pulls them apart, grabs the girl and drags her into the cage with him, squeezing the bars back into place after him and glaring at the guy who says, a triumphant note in his voice, "Now, you tell him you have a headache!"

➻ There was a terrible bus accident. Unfortunately, no one survived except a monkey who was on board, and there were no witnesses. The police tried to investigate further, but got no results. At last, desperate, they tried to interrogate the monkey. The monkey seemed to respond to their questions with gestures. Seeing that it was trying to communicate, they started asking questions. The police inspector asked, "What were the people doing on the bus?" The monkey shook his head in a condemning manner and starts dancing around; he obviously meant that the people were dancing and having fun. The inspector asked, "Hmm, OK, but what else were they doing?" The monkey moved his hand to his mouth as if holding a bottle. The chief says, "Oh! They were drinking, eh?" The inspector continued, "Were they doing anything else?" The monkey nodded his head and moved his arms back and forth, indicating that they were having sex. "If they were having such a great time," asked the inspector, "who was driving the damn bus?" The monkey cheerfully swung his arms by his sides, as if grabbing a wheel...

↦ A little old lady had two monkeys as pets for years. One day, one of them died of natural causes. Overcome with grief, the second monkey passed away two days later. Not knowing what to do with the remains, she finally decided to take them to the taxidermist and have them stuffed. After telling the owner of her wishes, he asked her, "Do you want them mounted?" "No. Holding hands will be fine," she said, blushing.

↦ How do monkeys pick up rumours? Through the apevine.

**A demon took a monkey for his wife – the result,
by the grace of God, was the English.**

Indian saying

↦ Two young nuns, freshly inducted into their order, were visiting the zoo when they stopped in front of the gorilla cage. Something about them made the gorilla mad with desire and, after beating his chest for a while, he ran to the bars of the cage, pulled them open, jumped on one of the nuns and ravished her before going back into his cage, contented. The nun picked herself up, brushed down her clothes and said to her friend: "Promise me never to talk about this – ever." To which the other sister agreed. Twenty-five years later, the two sisters found themselves together again and went to sit on a bench in a nearby park. "I know I promised never to talk about this incident," the nun said, "but there's a question I've always wanted to ask you..." "All right: ask your question, sister." "Did it hurt?" "Did it hurt?" the nun replied in a sad voice. "Oh, yes, it hurt. He never called... he never wrote... he never sent flowers..."

➥ What's yellow and smells like bananas? Monkey vomit.

➥ Why do gorillas have big nostrils? Because they have big fingers.

aRmY

➥ A British pilot gets shot down behind enemy lines. He wakes up in a German hospital, his uniform gone, with a funny feeling in his left leg. A German doctor comes to his bed and says: "I am a doctor before I am a German, and I will treat you with the respect to which any patient is entitled. I must tell you, however, that it is quite possible we'll have to amputate your left leg." The pilot is shocked, but manages to say "Thank you for your kindness, doctor, and for agreeing to treat me, although I am an enemy." He pauses, then says "Do you think it would be possible to send my leg back to my family in England?" The doctor is a bit surprised by this request, but he agrees. Unfortunately, a month later, the second leg has to go, too, and again the pilot asks him to send it to England. The doctor agrees. Another month goes by and he is forced to admit to himself that the pilot's right arm will soon have to come off. He breaks the news very gently to him and is not surprised to hear that the pilot would like his arm to be shipped home with the rest of his bits. The doctor complies, but, when it comes to the time for the right arm to come off, he is accompanied to the unfortunate pilot's bedside by two German security officers. "So this is the pilot who gets his arms and legs sent to England," one of them says. "Tell me... you're not trying to escape, are you?"

➼ A Corporal announces: "The platoon has been assigned to unload 'luminum…'" "Er, aluminium, not 'luminum, Sir," corrects a trooper. "The platoon is going to unload 'luminum," repeats the Corporal, "and the intellectual here is going to load shit."

➼ A famous Admiral and an equally famous General were fishing together in a boat when all of a sudden a squall came up. They both fell in the water and spent some time spluttering, struggling helplessly and swallowing quite a quantity of water, until the Admiral floundered his way back to the boat and pulled himself painfully in. Then he fished out the General. Catching his breath, he puffed: "Please don't say a word about this to anyone. If the Navy found out I can't swim, I'd be disgraced." "Don't worry," the General said ruefully. "Your secret is quite safe. I myself would hate to have my men find out I can't walk on water."

The professional military mind is by necessity an inferior and unimaginative mind; no man of high intellectual quality would willingly imprison his gifts in such a calling.

HG Wells on soldiers

➼ A General visits the infirmary to check on his men. He goes to the first soldier, lying in his bed and asks: "What's your problem, soldier?" "Chronic syphilis, Sir." "I see…And what treatment are you getting?" "Five minutes with the wire brush and Dettol each day, Sir." "As it should be! And what's your ambition?" "To get back to the front, Sir."

"Good man," says the General, and he goes to the next bed. "What about you? What's your problem, soldier?" "Chronic piles, Sir." "Nasty, that... what treatment are you getting?" "Five minutes with the wire brush and Dettol each day, Sir." "What an efficient infirmary this is! And what's your ambition, soldier?" "To get back to the front, Sir." "Good man," says the General, and he goes to the next bed. "What's your problem, soldier?" "Chronic gum disease, Sir." "Unusual... And what treatment are you getting?" "Five minutes with the wire brush and Dettol each day, Sir." "This is really a top infirmary! And what is your ambition, soldier?" "To be treated before the other two, Sir!"

➳ A private who was going to be court-martialled asked the lawyer representing him for advice on what to wear. "Wear your shabbiest uniform. Let them think you are sorry and repentant," the lawyer replied. Then he asked a friend the same question, but got the opposite advice. "Don't let them intimidate you. Wear your best uniform, with all the decorations and awards you got." Confused, the man went to his chaplain, told him of the conflicting advice and requested some resolution of the dilemma. "Let me tell you a story," replied the chaplain. "A woman, about to be married, asked her mother what to wear on her wedding night. 'Wear a heavy, long, flannel nightgown that goes right up to your neck.' But when she asked her best friend, she got conflicting advice. 'Wear your most sexy negligee, with a V-neck right down to your navel.'" The private protested: "What does all this have to do with me getting court-martialled?" The priest replied, "No matter what you wear, you are going to get screwed."

➹ A guy comes to the military enlistment office. "What would you like to be?" the Officer asks him. "A pilot," he answers. "Good choice, son." The Officer enrols the guy and sends him to study flying. Unfortunately, he doesn't have what it takes to be a pilot and fails his exams. He is sent back to the military enlistment office again. "Sorry, but you can't be a pilot any more: I'm sure you can see that. Select something else." The guy thinks for a few seconds and speaks: "I want to be in the Air Defence." "First a pilot, then air defence? Why AD?" "If I can't fly, nobody will fly!" the guy answers pugnaciously.

➹ A Marine reconnaissance platoon was on patrol when the Corporal noticed a lone Special Forces soldier standing on a hilltop. As an exercise, the Corporal told two of his men to go and take out that man. They promptly ran as fast as they could toward the soldier, who disappeared over the other side of the hill. For the next few minutes, bloody screams were heard and dust flew in the air. Then, as quickly as it had started, the noise stopped and the Special Forces soldier re-appeared on the hilltop. He brushed off his uniform, straightened his beret, crossed his arms and stood there looking at the Marines. The Corporal, rather pissed off, called for a squad to go and get that arrogant soldier. They promptly ran as fast as they could towards him, and once again he disappeared over the other side of the hill just before the squad reached him. For the next few minutes there were bloody screams and dust flew in the air. Then, as quickly as it had started, the noise stopped and the Special Forces soldier came up on the hilltop. He brushed off his uniform, straightened his beret, crossed his arms and stood there looking at the Marines. This was simply too much for the Corporal. He ordered the rest of his platoon to attack the bloody Special Forces soldier, pretty sure that the supremacy in numbers would ensure victory for his patrol. They all ran up the hill screaming war cries and followed the lone soldier over to the other side of the hill. For many minutes, there were bloody screams and dust flew in the air. It continued and continued. Finally, one lone Marine crawled back to the top of the hill and towards the Corporal, all bloody and feeble, his uniform torn, cuts bleeding all over his body. The Corporal gathered the beaten-up soldier in his arms and heard him say: "Run, Corporal, it's a trick. There are two of them!"

→ A mum catches her son on the doorstep, a backpack on his shoulder. "Fred, where are you off to now?" she asks. "I'm going to join the Army," the son replies. "But you can't! You're my little baby!" "That's all right, ma. I'm going to join the infantry."

→ A Private was brought up before the unit commanding officer for a minor offence. "Here's your choice, Private," the CO said. "One month's restriction or 20 days' pay." "All right, Sir," said the bright soldier, "I'll take the money."

There are three kinds of intelligence – the intelligence of man, the intelligence of animals, and the intelligence of the military. In that order.
Gottfried Reinhardt

→ A soldier is telling his friends that his sister just enlisted, disguising herself as a bloke. "Wait a minute: she'll have to get changed and shower with the other blokes, won't she?" one of his friends points out. "So what?" "Well, won't they find out?" "Probably," replies the soldier with a wink, "but who'll tell?"

•➝ A young naval student was being grilled by an old sea captain: "What would you do if a sudden storm sprang up on the starboard bow?" "Throw out an anchor, Sir," the student replied. "What would you do if another storm sprang up after?" "Throw out another anchor, Sir." "And if another terrific storm sprang up forward, what would you do then?" asked the Captain. "Throw out another anchor, Sir." "Hold on," said the Captain, holding up his hand. "Where are you getting all these anchors from?" "From the same place you're getting your storms, sir."

•➝ After a briefing on land-mines, the Captain asked for questions. An intrepid solder raised his hand and asked: "If we do happen to step on a mine, Sir, what do we do?" "Normal procedure, soldier, is to jump 200 feet in the air and scatter oneself over a wide area."

•➝ An Army brat was boasting about his father to a Navy brat. "My dad is an engineer. He can do everything. Do you know the Alps?" "Yes," said the Infantry brat. "My dad built them." Then the naval kid spoke: "And do you know the Dead Sea?" "Yes." "Well," said the naval kid, "it was my dad who killed it!"

•➝ An F-16 was flying escort with a B-52 and the pilot was generally making a nuisance of himself by flying rolls and other silly show-off manoeuvres around the lumbering old bomber. Fed up with the smaller plane's antics, the pilot of the B-52 announced on the radio to the F-16: "Anything you can do, I can do better." Not to be outdone, the fighter pilot announced that he would rise to the challenge. "OK, then. Try this." The B-52, however, continued its flight, straight and level, apparently not having changed anything. Perplexed, the fighter pilot asked, "So? What did you do?" The B-52 pilot replied, "We just shut down two engines."

➻ During a training exercise, a commanding officer's jeep got stuck in mud. The CO, seeing some men lounging around nearby, asked them to help him get unstuck. "Sorry, Sir," said one of the loafers, "but we've been classified dead and the umpire said we couldn't contribute in any way." The CO turned to his driver and said, "Go and drag a couple of those dead bodies over here and throw them under the wheels to give us some traction."

➻ In the canteen: "Pass me the chocolate pudding, would you?" "No way, José!" "And why not?" "It's against regulations to help another soldier to dessert!"

➻ During camouflage training in a forest, a soldier is disguised as a tree. Suddenly, just as the visiting General approaches his spot, he starts shouting, lurches forward and jumps up and down a few times while spinning frantically on the spot. "You idiot!" the Officer in charge barks, quite angry at having his otherwise uneventful training disrupted right in front of the General. "Don't you know that by jumping and yelling the way you did, you could have endangered the lives of the entire company?" "Yes, Sir," the soldier answered apologetically, brushing away a branch from his brow. "But, if I may say so, I did stand still when a flock of pigeons used me for target practice and shat on my head. And I never moved a muscle when a large dog peed on my lower branches. But when two squirrels ran up the leg of my fatigues and I heard the larger of the two say, 'Let's eat one now and save the other until winter,' I couldn't take any more."

➤ Four friends in the Army were doing very well indeed – so well that they decided to have a little party before the final exams. Off they went to the local whorehouse and had a wonderful time. When they woke up the following day though, they realized that they had missed the examination by a few hours. Gutted, they went to see their teacher: "Sir, we did have a little pre-exam party yesterday, but nothing much really; only this morning, er, the car blew a tyre. That's why we were late..." one of the friends lied glibly. "Is that so?" asked the teacher. "That's unlucky indeed, especially since your results have been outstanding up until now..." After deliberation with his colleagues, the teacher agreed to let them take the exam in the afternoon. "The problem is that we can't get someone to keep an eye on you while you're sitting the exam, so you'll have to use four separate rooms," they were told. Not believing their luck and amazed that their lie had actually worked, they agreed to the conditions and each entered their own examination room. The first question counted for five points and was ever so easy. Elated, sure of passing the exam, they turned the page on their exam paper to discover that the next question, counting for 95 points, said: "Which tyre?"

➤ Four people were travelling in the same carriage on a French train. There was an old, distinguished lady wearing a fur coat and a haughty expression; what was probably her granddaughter, a stunning 20-year-old of Playboy calibre; a highly decorated General; and a soldier fresh from boot camp. They spend the time chatting about trivial things, and then entered a very long tunnel. While in the tunnel, the sound of a kiss was distinctly heard, followed by the unmistakable sound of a hand slapping a cheek. Silence followed, as all were lost in their respective thoughts: The old lady was thinking: "Isn't it wonderful that, in this day and age, there are still young people ready to defend young women's honour!" The young woman was thinking: "How strange that he would want to kiss the old hag beside me, when I am available!" The General was thinking whilst rubbing his stinging cheek: "I am outraged that any woman could think I would try to sneak a kiss in the dark." The soldier had a big grin on his face and was thinking: "Isn't it great that someone can kiss the back of their own hand, then smack a General in the face and get away with it?"

We are mad, not only individually but nationally. We check manslaughter and isolated murders, but what of war and the much-vaunted crime of slaughtering whole peoples?

Seneca, Epistle, 8BC – 65AD

➤ It was a dark, stormy night. The young soldier was on his first assignment – guard duty. The General stepped out, taking his dog, a healthy-looking, very strong German Shepherd, for a walk. The nervous young soldier snapped to attention, made a perfect salute and shouted: "Sir, good evening, Sir!" The General, out for some relaxation, returned the salute and said, "Good evening, soldier: nice night, isn't it?" Well it wasn't a nice night, as it was raining and the soldier had only the standard coat on while the General had a waterproof overcoat and a pair of gloves, but the Private wasn't going to disagree with the General, so he replied, "Sir, yes, Sir!" The General continued, "You know, there's something about a stormy night that I find soothing: it's really relaxing. Don't you agree?" The soldier didn't really agree, but he was just a soldier, and responded, "Sir, yes, Sir!" The General, pointing at the dog, said: "This is a German Shepherd, the best type of dog to train. Very intelligent, very sensitive and very faithful." The private glanced at the dog, saluted yet again and said: "Sir, yes, Sir!" The General continued, "I got this dog for my wife." The soldier simply said: "Sir, good trade, Sir!"

One observes they have gone too long without a war here.

Berthold Brecht, 1898 – 1956, Mother Courage

➠ Officer: "Soldier, do you have change for a tenner?" Soldier: "Yeah, sure, buddy." Officer: "That's no way to address an officer! Now let's try it again. Soldier, do you have change for a tenner?" Soldier: "Sir, no, Sir!"

➠ One October, during a stormy night, the following radio conversation took place off the eastern coast of Canada:

Americans: Canadian vessel, Please divert course 15 degrees to the north to avoid a collision. Over.

Canadians: Recommend you divert your course 15 degrees to the south to avoid a collision. Over.

Americans: This is the Captain of a US Navy ship. I say again, divert your course. Over.

Canadians: No. I say again, you divert your course. Over.

Americans: This is the aircraft carrier USS Lincoln, the

second largest ship in the United States' Atlantic fleet. We are accompanied by three destroyers, three cruisers and numerous support vessels. I demand that you change your course 15 degrees north – that's zero-one-five degrees north – or countermeasures will be undertaken to ensure the safety of this ship. Over.

Canadians: This is Rock Point Lighthouse, Newfoundland. Your call.

➡ Private Atkins joins the French Foreign Legion and is stationed at a remote outpost in the North African desert. After several weeks in barracks he feels a moist yearning for female companionship. He approaches the evil-looking, scar-faced sergeant, and asks him what the men do for sexual relief around here. "Zere eez only ze camel, oui?" the sergeant tells him with a leer. "I'm not desperate enough to brave that!" replies Atkins, and takes a brisk walk and another cold bath. A week later he's more desperate and asks the sergeant again. "Ze camel, I told you. Use ze camel!" comes the reply. Atkins actually has a look at the camel this time. It's like a flea-ridden carpet full of coat-hangers with camel shit matted in the hair round its rump. Atkins doesn't fancy it. Much. A week later, delirious with unvented lust, he goes to the sergeant again, only to be told: "Merde! Ze camel, I tell you, ze camel!" That night Atkins creeps out to the camel. "At least its got a pulse," he tells himself as he climbs onto a hay-rack and proceeds to roger the camel to his satisfaction. As he dismounts he sees the sergeant staring open-mouthed in horror and admiration. "How inventive and practical you Engleesh are. Ze other men, zey usually ride ze camel to ze brothel in town!"

➟ The Captain calls for the Sergeant. "I have some bad news for Private Johnson," he tells him. "His mum died last night. I'd like you to break the news to him gently, you know: he's a good guy. Tell him to come and see me." The Sergeant nods, salutes and departs for the morning roll-call. "Listen up," he says in front of the men. "The company has been assigned cleaning duties in the south yard. Douglas, you are needed at the depot and Smith, at the Mess. By the way, Johnson, your mother died yesterday: report to the Captain." Later that day, the Captain says to the Sergeant: "Sarge, that was a pretty harsh way to break the news to Johnson. Next time, be a bit more tactful when things like this happen, you know?" The Sergeant nods and says that he will. A few days later the captain receives the sad news that Private Allen's mum died of a heart attack during the night. He sends for the Sergeant and tells him to inform Allen – tactfully – of the tragedy and to send the unfortunate soldier to him. The Sergeant nods, salutes and departs. At the roll-call, when all the men are lined up, he pauses for a minute, then says: "Right, listen up! All of you who have a mother, two steps forward! Not so fast, Allen!"

Don't tell me peace has broken out – I've just bought some new supplies.

Berthold Brecht, 1898 – 1956, Mother Courage

➟ The five most dangerous things you can hear in the Army:
1. A Private saying, "I learned this in Basic..."
2. A Sergeant saying, "Trust me, Sir..."
3. A Second Lieutenant saying, "Based upon my experience..."

4. A Captain saying, "I was just thinking..."
5. A Warrant Officer chuckling, "Watch this shit..."

•• The General arrived at his office on a Sunday morning and discovered that none of his private aides was there. Grimly, he remembered it had been one aide's birthday party the previous evening and he had no doubt as to what condition they were in. At around ten o'clock, five aides arrived, unshaved and dressed in rather piteous attire. They salute as smartly as they can and brace themselves for the General's grilling. "I presume you were at Smith's birthday party last night, weren't you?" "Sir, yes, Sir," one aide answered. "And you couldn't get up early enough this morning to get to the office because you were too drunk!" thundered the General. "Er, no, Sir," the aide said timidly, looking at his friends. "So what is your excuse, young man?" the General wondered, sitting down, with a dangerous, vicious smile on his lips. "I can explain. You see, we did run a little late, I admit. We ran to the bus but we missed it; we hailed a cab but it broke down; we found a farm and bought eight horses but they dropped dead; we ran ten miles, and now we're here. It's just a logistical problem, really, General, Sir!" The General eyed him suspiciously, but as he hadn't heard such a good one for a long time, he let the men go. An hour later, the last aide showed up, in the same dishevelled state. "Sorry, Sir," he said. "I ran late; tried to catch a bus but missed it; I hailed a cab but..." "Let me guess," the General interrupted. "The cab broke down, so you bought a horse in a farm but it died on you, so you ran for ten miles. Do you really think I'm going to swallow this?" "Er, no, Sir; you see, there were so many dead horses on the way that it took forever to go around them."

➥ The physical training instructor was drilling a platoon of soldiers. "I want every man to lie on his back, put his legs in the air and move them as though he were riding a bicycle," he explained. "Now begin!" After a few minutes, one of the men stopped. "Why did you stop, Smith?" demanded the officer. "I'm freewheeling downhill," said Smith.

➥ Things to do to have the military psychiatric nurses worry over your case:

Jam tiny marshmallows up your nose and try to sneeze them out while on parade.

Use one credit card to pay off another credit card bill, then say you are under stress from the military life.

When one of your roommates says, "Have a nice day!" tell them you have other plans and remind them you are in the Army to die.

During your next roll-call, sneeze and then loudly suck the phlegm back down your throat.

Find out what a frog in a gun barrel really looks like.

Make a list of things you have done in your life and a list of the people you have ever met, then pin them on the wall and shoot them repeatedly.

Dance naked in front of the flagpole on the Winter Solstice.

Put your uniform on backwards, then go to breakfast as if nothing was wrong.

Thumb through Gun Monthly, making little cooing noises.

Drive your tank in reverse.

On parade, drop a rabbit on the ground and stop to admire its fluffy coat for 15 minutes, dragging the other conscripts around you.

•• Three soldiers come back from active duty in Afghanistan. They are all due for retirement and are all summoned before their commanding officer. He tells them that in addition to their Army pension they will be paid a premium for services rendered in the Middle East and it will be calculated in the following way: each man will be paid $100 for a measurement from two points in their body, the two points to be stipulated by the men themselves. So the first soldier, a Sergeant, walks up to the front. "Where do you want the measurements to be taken from, Sergeant?" says the CO. "From the top of my shaved head to the tip of my toes, Sir!" A Lieutenant makes the measurement and tells the Commanding Officer it is 71 inches. "Seventy-one inches!" says the Commanding Officer. "That makes $7,100 for you." So the second soldier, a Corporal, walks up to the front. "Where do you want the measurements to be taken from, Corporal?" says the Commanding Officer. "From my left fingertip to my right fingertip, Sir!" says the Corporal. A Lieutenant makes the measurement and tells the CO it is 73 inches. "Seventy-three inches!" says the Commanding Officer, "that makes $7,300 for you." So the third soldier, a Private, walks up to the front. "Where do you want the measurements to be taken from, Private?" says the Commanding Officer. "From the top of my penis to the base of my balls, Sir!" says the Private. The commanding officer is a little surprised, but gets the Lieutenant to make the measurement anyway. After a couple of seconds the Lieutenant says from down below, "Where on earth are your balls, Private?" and the private replies, "Back in Osama bin Laden's bunker, Sir!"

➻ Two military policemen were chasing a fleeing draftee from the base. The draftee ran into the courtyard of a convent where a nun was seated on a bench beneath a tree quietly reading a book. "Quick, sister; please hide me! I don't want to be drafted and the MPs are chasing me!" he said to her. "OK. Hide under my skirt." The two policemen finally entered the convent and asked the nun if she had seen anyone. "I am sorry, officers, I didn't," she replied. After they left, she told the young boy that the coast was clear. "Thank you, sister!" the boy said, very relieved. Then he felt he'd better give her some kind of compliment as a way to show his appreciation of her sacrifice. "Say," he started, "you have a nice set of legs for a nun!" "Don't get any ideas," the nun growled. "If you reach up a little farther you'll find a set of balls – I'm not going to be drafted either!"

War is nothing but a continuation of politics with the admixture of other means.

Karl von Clausewitz, 1780 – 1831, On War

➻ Two soldiers stationed in the Falklands were handed spades and told to bury a large, dead animal. While they were digging, they got into an argument about exactly what it was they were burying. "This is a bloody big mule!" "It isn't a mule, you idiot, it's a donkey." "Mule!" "Donkey!" "Mule!" "Donkey!" They went on like this for a while until the camp chef came out to see what the noise was. "What are you lads up to?" he asked. "We're diggin' a grave for this mule," said the first. "Donkey, dammit!" replied the other. The chef cut in, "Lads, this isn't either. It's an ass." An hour later, the commander of the garrison came up and said, "What are you men digging, a foxhole?" They nodded respectfully, then the first one said "No, sir! We're digging an asshole, sir!"

→ Two young men join the Army and are soon put on street patrol in an Iraqi city with a military curfew. They are given instructions to shoot anybody who's on the streets after six o'clock. So one day, they're out at twenty to six when one of them spots a man walking on the other side of the street. He lines up the man in his sights and shoots the man dead. The other soldier is shocked. "What are you doing? It's not six yet!" "I know what I'm doing," replies his companion. "I know where he lives and he wouldn't have made it!"

→ What do you get if you run over an army officer with a steam roller? A flat major.

→ What do you get when an army officer puts his nose to the grindstone? A sharp major.

→ What do you say after you've run over an army officer with a steam roller? See, flat major.

→ What do you say to an army officer while your running him over with a steam roller? Be flat, major.

AUSTRALIA

Australia may be the only country in the world in which the word 'academic' is regularly used as a term of abuse.

Dame Leonie Kramer

➥ Jake moves to Australia after working all his life in the City. He buys a farm in the remotest part of the Outback he can find. His post arrives once a week, his groceries once a month and he can call the Flying Doctor on his radio if he has an emergency. One night, after six months of this, Jake is finishing his dinner when he hears a knock on the door. He walks up, opens it and sees a huge outbacker standing in front of him. "G'day, mate," says the outbacker. "I'm your nearest neighbour, Bruce Sheldon, from 20 miles east. I'm having a party Saturday night and I thought you might like to come along, mate." "That'd be great," says Jake. "I haven't really spoken to anyone for six months. Thanks a lot." Bruce is about to turn away, but instead says, "I think I'd better warn you, though: there'll be some serious drinking going on." "Not a problem," says Jake, "I like a couple of pints myself." Bruce is about to turn away again, but instead says, "Better warn you, though, there'll probably be some fighting, too." "Not a problem," says Jake, "I know how to keep out of trouble." Bruce is about to turn away again, but instead says, "Better warn you though, there'll probably be some pretty wild sex, too." "Not a problem," says Jake, "I've been alone for six months, remember. Now, what time should I show up?" Bruce turns once more and says, "Whenever you like, mate: there's only going to be me and you there anyway!"

↦ What do you call a collection of strip-malls infested with lethally poisonous creatures? Australia.

The Sydney Opera House looks as if it is something that has crawled out of the sea and is up to no good.

Beverley Nichols, 1898 – 1983, on Sydney, Australia

↦ This Australian guy living in London went to see his GP. He walked in, and said, "Doc, it's my prick," then unzipped his fly and unfurled a thick, 12-inch penis, lovingly tattooed with a dragon, on to the doctor's desk. The doctor peered at it and asked, "And what appears to be the problem?" "Aw, there's no problem, doc," replied the Aussie. "He's a beaut, though, ain't he?"

Bad sex

↦ A man is out shopping one Saturday when he finds a new brand of condom. He is impressed by the brand: "Olympic Condoms – for winners." When he gets home he shows his wife, who asks him, "What's so special about Olympic, then?" "That's the cool thing," he says. "They come in three colours: gold, silver and bronze." "And which colour will you be wearing tonight?" the wife questions. "Well, gold, of course, darling," the man replies. Quick as a flash, the wife says, "Why don't you try silver? It'd be nice if you came second for a change!"

➤ A man dies while having sex but his erection stays hard. At the funeral parlour they discuss the situation with his wife and she gives them permission to cut it off in order to get the lid on the coffin. The wife keeps the penis, and later that night steals back and shoves it up the dead man's rear end. The next day, at the funeral, she peers over the coffin and, noticing a tear in the dead man's eye, whispers, "I told you it hurt, you heartless bastard!"

> **The terrifying power of the human sex drive is horrifically demonstrated by the fact that someone was willing to father you.**
>
> *Anonymous*

➤ A rather embarrassed man goes to see his doctor and tells him: "Well, I have this problem, you see: I can't get it up for my wife anymore, if you see what I mean." "It's quite all right," the doctor says. "Get undressed and we'll see what the problem is." He does so, but can find nothing wrong with the patient. "Come back tomorrow," he advises. "Bring your wife with you. I'd like to examine her, too." The anxious patient turns up the following day with his wife, as promised. The doctor has a quick look at the woman, then asks her to take her clothes off. "Mmm... I see... Now turn around please. Mmmm... Can you crouch down for me? That's it. Goooooood, now get on all fours on the carpet. Yes, this way... Mmmm... It's OK, you can put your clothes back on." While the wife is getting dressed, the doctor takes the husband aside and tells him: "You're perfectly healthy. Don't worry. Your wife didn't give me an erection either."

↝ A man is suffering from premature ejaculation, so he decides to see a doctor about it. The doctor says there is nothing physically wrong with the man, but that he has a mental block. The doctor suggests that to cure the problem the man should try to shock himself when he feels that he is about to ejaculate. The doctor suggests using a starting pistol: the man should fire it when he feels the need, and that this should help prevent the problem. The man thanks the doctor and runs off to the sports shop to get himself a starting pistol. He rushes home to his wife, whom he finds naked on the bed, all ready for him. Things go well, and they find themselves in the 69 position. Moments later, the man feels the urge to ejaculate, so pulls the trigger. The next day the man finds himself back at the doctor's surgery. The doctor asks, "So, how did it go? Any improvements?" "Not really," begins the man, "When I fired the pistol, my wife crapped on my face and bit three inches off my penis, and my neighbour jumped naked out of the cupboard with his hands in the air!"

↝ A therapist told a woman to use some imagination while making love with her husband to spice things up. She replied, "You mean imagine that it's good?"

↝ A woman was complaining to her best friend over lunch. "Every time my husband climaxes, he lets out an ear-splitting yell." "That doesn't sound all that bad to me," said her friend. "As a matter of fact, that would kind of turn me on." "It would me, too," said the first woman, "if it didn't keep waking me up."

➤ After making love, the woman said to the man: "So, you're a doctor?" "That's right," replied the doctor smugly. "Bet you don't know what kind of doctor." "Ummm...I'd say that you're an anaesthetist." "Yes, that's right. Good guess. How did you know?" asked the man. "Because throughout the entire procedure, I didn't feel a thing."

➤ How can a woman tell if she is having a super orgasm? Her husband wakes up.

➤ If he can't get it up, you can go down, but if he can't get it in, get out.

The pleasure is momentary, the position ridiculous, and the price damnable.

Earl Chesterfield, on sex

➤ In the distant future, a couple of humans land on a distant planet in their spaceship. They are greeted by a couple of natives of the planet, who look remarkably human and who speak the same language. They talk for hours, comparing everything on Earth and on the alien planet. Things are a lot closer than they would have all imagined and the aliens have computers, cars, television, guns and all the other things we have that make life great. Eventually the couples get on to social interaction and, in particular, how they have sex on their respective planets. It turns out that the aliens have sex pretty much the same way that Earth people do, so the two men suggest that, in order to see the differences, the couples should swap partners and see how things are done on the other planets.

The women both agree to this and they all retire for the night. The Earth woman is in the bedroom with the alien man and they both undress. She is a little worried because the alien's member is tiny: a couple of centimetres long and only about a centimetre thick, even when it's hard. "This isn't going to be easy," she says. "What's up?" says the alien, "the size bother you? Not a problem." And he slaps himself on the forehead. As he does so, his member grows longer. He continues to slap and with each hit he gets bigger until he is very impressive-looking. "That's pretty good," says the Earth woman, "but it could do with being a bit thicker." "Not a problem," says the alien again and he begins pulling his ears. With each pull, his member increases in thickness until it is even more impressive. "Amazing!" exclaims the Earth woman, and they shag wildly all night. The next day she meets her husband at breakfast. "How was it for you?" he asks her. "Well, I must admit, they've got some pretty exciting stuff over us," she replies, "but how was it for you?" "Well, I must admit I was a bit disappointed," he says, "I just got a headache. She kept slapping my forehead and pulling my ears all night!"

↦ John met Lisa down the pub one night and began buying her drinks. They got on pretty well together, and John suggested they go to his flat for a little light entertainment. Well it wasn't long before they found themselves in bed screwing passionately. As they were making love, John noticed that Lisa's toes curled up whenever he thrust into her particularly firmly. When they were done John laid back on the bed and said, "I must have been pretty good tonight. I noticed your toes curling up when I was going deep." Lisa looked over at him and smiled. "That usually happens when someone forgets to remove my tights."

➥ The Smiths were having marital problems, so they went to see an eminent sex therapist. After a couple of hours of tests he agreed to help them. The solution to their problem was for them to buy a pound of grapes and a dozen doughnuts on the way home. When they got back they were to sit opposite each other, totally naked, and Mr Smith should roll the grapes across the floor and eat the ones that ended up in Mrs Smith, while she should throw the doughnuts at him, and eat the ones that stayed on him. A couple of weeks later, the Joneses came to see the same sex therapist. "Our friends the Smiths recommended you highly," they said. After a couple of hours of tests, the therapist informed the Joneses that there was nothing he could do for them. "But you helped the Smiths, didn't you? What about us?" they said. After hours of begging, the therapist said that there was only one thing they could do and it wasn't guaranteed to work. "On your way back home, stop off and buy a pound of oranges and a packet of Polos..."

➥ The three different stages of sex in marriage: tri-weekly; try weekly; try weakly.

➥ There once was a beautiful young woman who wanted to use her good looks to get rich quick. So she started to hang around older men in the hope of netting one for herself to marry and to shag them to death on their wedding night. She pretty quickly found herself a rich 80-year-old who looked frail, and their romance went quickly and effectively. Three months later it was their wedding day. All went well and in the evening they found themselves in a five-star hotel in Paris. They both retired to their separate bathrooms and she emerged first, seductively dressed as she slipped between the satin sheets of the huge bed they were to share. The man's bathroom door opens and he walked out sporting a condom over a 12-inch erection. He was carrying a pair of earplugs and some nose plugs, too. The woman's heart sank and she began to suspect something was up. Tentatively, she asked, "Er... what are those for, dear?" The old man replies, "These take care of the two things I can't stand the most: the sound of women screaming and the smell of burning rubber!"

There comes a moment in the day when you have written your pages in the morning, attended to your correspondence in the afternoon, and have nothing further to do. Then comes that hour when you are bored; that's the time for sex.

HG Wells

↦ This guy is getting married and he is a bit nervous since he is not too experienced. So he asks his best man to come along on the honeymoon and give a few pointers. The best man exclaims, "Come on man, its your honeymoon, you're supposed to be spending time with your wife, not your best friend." To which the groom replies that he has already paid for a room next-door to his for the best man. After much coercion, the best man give in and decides to go along. They work out a system where the best man will pound on the wall and shout advice if he hears anything going wrong. So the honeymoon arrives, and the bride and groom go to the honeymoon suite of the hotel, and the best man goes to his room next door. After a few moments, the bride gets undressed, but the groom gets so nervous he runs into the bathroom and locks the door. After about five minutes of waiting, the bride says, "Honey, are you coming out? I have to go to the bathroom." The groom replies, "I will be out in a few minutes, Hon, I'll be ready soon." After a few more minutes, the bride can't take it any longer, so she rummages under the bed where all the wedding gifts are stashed, grabs a box, unwraps it, pulls out the fondue pot, shits in it, wipes with the tissue paper, closes it and shoves it under the bed. Just then the groom, having summoned his manly nerve walks out of the bathroom. The bride, being feminine and all, goes into the bathroom to stall for a few minutes so the groom won't know what she did. The groom, sitting on the bed, notices this awful smell. What can that be? He looks under the bed, finds the box, pulls it out and exclaims: "Honey, there's shit in your box." Boom! Boom! Boom! (There's pounding on the wall...) The best man yells from the other room, "Turn her over, turn her over!"

⤭ What's the difference between a turkey and a penis? It's worth waking up at five in the morning to put a turkey in, because it always lasts long enough to satisfy everyone.

⤭ You know you've been married too long when a 'quickie' before dinner now means a drink.

Banks

Switzerland has produced the numbered bank account, Ovaltine and Valium.

Peter Freedman

➦ A little old lady walked into the head branch of a respected bank holding a large paper bag in her hand. She told the young man at the window that she wished to take the £3 million she had in the bag and open an account with the bank. As it was such a large sum she asked to meet the manager of the bank first. The teller seemed to think that was a reasonable request and after opening the paper bag and seeing the bundles of £50 notes, which amounted to around £3 million, he telephoned the manager's secretary to arrange this. The lady was escorted upstairs and ushered into the manager's office. Introductions were made and the lady stated that she would like to get to know the people she did business with on a more personal level. The bank manager then asked her where she came into such a large amount of money. "Was it an inheritance?" he asked. "No," she answered. "Was it from playing the stock market?" "No," she replied. He was quiet for a minute, trying to think of where this little old lady could possibly come into £3 million. "I bet on things," she stated. "You bet?" repeated the bank manager, "as in horses?" "No," she replied, "I bet people." Seeing his confusion, she explained that she just bet different things with people. All of a sudden she said, "I'll bet you £25,000 that by ten o'clock tomorrow morning, your balls will be square." The bank manager figured she must be off her rocker and decided to take her up on the bet. He didn't see how he could lose. For the rest of the day, the bank manager was very careful. He decided to stay home that evening and take no chances; there was £25,000 at stake. When he got up in the morning and took his shower, he checked to make sure everything was okay. There was no difference; he looked the same as he always had. He went to work and waited for the little old lady to come in at ten o'clock, humming as he went. He knew this would be a good day; how often do you get handed £25,000 for doing nothing? At ten o'clock sharp, the little old lady was shown into his office. With her was a younger man. When he inquired as to the man's purpose for being there, she informed him that he was her lawyer and she always took him along when there was this much money involved. "Well?" she asked, "what about our bet?" "I don't know how to tell you this," he replied, "but I am the same as I've always been only £25,000 richer." The lady seemed to accept this, but requested that she be able to see for herself. The bank manager thought this was reasonable and dropped his trousers. She instructed him to bend over and then grabbed a hold of him. Sure enough, everything was fine. The bank manager then looked up and saw her lawyer standing across the room banging his head against the wall. "What's wrong with him?" he inquired. "Oh, him?" she replied," I bet him £100,000 that by ten o'clock this morning that I'd have the bank manager by the bollocks."

↔ In order to get a loan, you must first prove you don't need it.

BARS

↔ A baby seal walks into a bar and sits down. "What can I get you?" asks the landlord. "Anything but a Canadian Club," replies the seal.

↔ A barman is delighted when a really top bird walks up and calls him over. She's a real stunner and he's feeling lucky already. "I wonder," she begins in a low, sexy voice, "could I speak to the manager, please?" "I'm afraid he's busy right now," the barman says, not wanting to share this one with anybody or to lose the chance of such a top bird. "Perhaps I can help you instead?" he continues. "I'm not really sure," she says cautiously, stroking him gently on the shoulder. "It's quite a personal issue and I'm not sure you're in charge of the situation." "Oh, I'm in charge; I'm in charge," the barman blurts out. "I'm sure I can take care of your problem." "Well," says the woman, as she touches his face gently and begins to stroke his cheek, "it's like this..." and she slides her fingers into his open mouth, sending him into a fit of joy and excitement, "...can you tell the manager..." "Yes! Yes!" the barman is thinking, "... can you tell the manager there's no toilet paper left in the ladies'?"

One always thinks of him as a glorified bouncer engaged eternally in cleaning out bar-rooms and not too proud to gouge when the inspiration came to him, or to bite in the clinches.

Henry L Mencken, on Theodore Roosevelt

↔ A bloke walks into a pub and orders ten shots of vodka, no ice. As the landlord hands them over he crashes them down, one after the other. "Are you alright?" asks the landlord, "Why are you drinking so fast?" The bloke replies, "You'd understand if you knew what I had in my pocket." Thoroughly perplexed, the landlord asks "So what do you have in your pocket?" The bloke grimaces and says, "A grand total of 25p."

↔ A cowboy walked into a bar, dressed entirely in paper. It wasn't long before he was arrested for rustling.

➥ A circus-owner walks into a pub to see everyone crowded around a table watching a little show. On the table is an upside-down pot, and a duck tap-dancing on it. The circus-owner is so impressed that he immediately offers to buy the duck from its owner. After some haggling, they settle on £5,000 for the duck and the pot. Three days later the circus-owner comes back to the pub, furious. He goes up to the bloke he bought the duck from and says: "Your duck is a bloody rip-off! I stuck him on the pot before a whole audience, and he didn't dance a single step!" The bloke looks unimpressed. "Well," he asks, "did you remember to light the candle under the pot?"

➥ A depressed bloke turned to his friend in the pub and said, "I woke up this morning and felt so bad that I tried to kill myself by taking 50 aspirin." "Oh, man, that's really bad," said his friend, "What happened?" The first man sighed, and said, "After the first two, I felt better."

➥ A guy walks into a pub and asks for ten tequila shots. "Sorry, mate," the bartender says, "but that's too much for one go." The guy says, "I just found out that my brother is a homosexual and I'm finding it really hard to deal with," so the bartender says that's OK and that he can have his ten shots of tequila. The next day the very same man walks into the same pub and asks for 20 tequila shots. "Sorry, mate," the bartender says, "but that's too much for one go." The guy says, "I just found out that my son is a homosexual too, and I'm not coping very well," so the bartender says that's OK and that he can have his 20 shots of tequila. The next day the very same man walks into the same pub and asks for 30 tequila shots. The bartender, who's had enough, says to him, "What the hell's the matter – doesn't anyone in your house like pussy?" "Oh, yes," the guy replies, "my wife!"

↦ A man is sitting in a rough bar drinking. He orders a fresh pint, but is suddenly overcome with the urge to go to the toilet. He doesn't trust anyone in the crummy bar, but he has to go, so he scribbles on a cigarette paper, "I spat in this: don't drink it!" and he gums the paper to the side of his pint glass. He goes off to the toilet and comes back a couple of minutes later to find another cigarette paper stuck to his glass. On it is written, "So did we!"

Some of the most dreadful mischiefs that afflict mankind proceed from wine; it is the cause of disease, quarrels, sedition, idleness, aversion to labour, and every species of domestic disorder.

Francois de Salignac

↦ A man walks into a bar with a really trendy new shirt on. The bartender is a woman and she says, "Hey, nice shirt. Really suits you. Where d'you get it?" "Oh, René Kent," comes the reply and the woman is impressed. Shortly afterwards, a man walks into the bar with a really trendy new pair of trousers on. The bartender says, "Hey, nice trousers. Really suit you. Where d'you get them?" "Oh, René Kent," comes the reply and the woman is impressed. Then another man walks into the bar with a really trendy, new pair of shoes on. The bartender says, "Hey, nice shoes. Really suit you. Where d'you get them?" "Oh, René Kent," comes the reply and the woman is impressed. After a while the door to the bar suddenly bursts open and a man dressed only in his underpants runs in. "Who the hell do you think you are?" asks the bartender. "I'm René Kent!" comes the strained reply.

➡ A man walks into a bar. He has a frog attached to his forehead. He says to the barman, "I'll have a gin and tonic, please." The barman pours him the drink – all the while looking at the frog – and gives it to the man. "I'm sorry to be so curious, sir, but I was wondering how on earth you ended up with that thing on you?" he asks. Quick as a flash the frog replies, "I don't know; it started out as a wart on my bum five years ago!"

➡ A man walks into a bar. It is totally empty apart from the barman, who walks over to serve him. The man buys his beer and sits down in a corner. He then decides he'd like a chaser, so he walks up to the bar again. The barman has just gone out back for a second, but the guy hears a little squeaky voice say, "Nice shirt, mate." He looks around and he can't see anyone anywhere. He turns around to go and sit down and hears a similar voice say, "Great arse." He spins around quickly but he can't see anyone and the barman is definitely still out back. The man is a bit put-out so he decides to go and buy some smokes. As he approaches the cigarette machine he hears the most dreadful swearing, aimed at him. "You miserable wanker piece of crap; you suck, you dumbarse twat!" The insults seem to be pouring from the machine, so he retreats and goes back to the bar. The barman is back by this time, so the man asks him, "Look, pal; what's going on with the funny voices in this place?" The barman looks at him and says, "Of course, well, you must mean the complimentary peanuts; and I'm sorry, but the cigarette machine is out of order!"

➡ A man was trying to get into a town centre pub, but the doorman stopped him saying, "Sorry mate, you can't get in here unless you're wearing a tie." The man said, "Okay, I'll be right back," and popped back to his car to find something to use. All he could find, sadly, was a set of jump leads, so he tied them around his neck, went back, and asked, "How's this?" "Well," replied the doorman doubtfully, "Okay, I guess that'll do, but I'm warning you now, don't start anything."

➤ A Mexican, an Irishman, an African, a kilted Scotsman, a priest, two lesbians, a rabbi and a nun walk into a bar. The landlord looks up and says, "What the hell is this? Some kind of joke?"

➤ A small bloke is standing by the bar when he looks up and notices a really huge guy standing next to him. The huge guy glances down, sees the small bloke looking up at him and booms out "Turner Brown, I'm seven feet tall, 350 pounds, with a 20-inch dick, a three-pound left testicle and a three-pound right testicle." The small bloke faints dead away. Concerned, the big guy picks the little one up, shakes him gently and brings him back to consciousness. "What's wrong with you?" he asks. The small bloke says faintly, "Look, what did you say?" The big guy shrugs and repeats, "Turner Brown, I'm seven feet tall, 350 pounds, with a 20-inch dick, a three-pound left testicle and a three-pound right testicle." The small bloke says, "Thank God! I thought you said 'Turn around'."

➤ As Sid sat down to a big plate of chips and gravy down the local pub a mate of his came over and said, "Here, Sid, me old pal, I thought you were trying to get into shape? And here you are with a high-fat meal and a pint of stout!" Sid looked up and replied, "I am getting into shape. The shape I've chosen is a sphere."

➻ A woman walked into a bar carrying a duck under her arm. "Get that dog out of here!" yelled the landlord. "That's not a dog, stupid!" she replied, "That's a duck!" "I wasn't talking to you!" said the landlord.

➻ An old boy sits down in his local and asks the barman, an old friend, for a drink. The old boy is wearing a big, old-fashioned stovepipe hat, a black jacket and waistcoat, and a false, square beard. The barman serves him a drink and says, "You off to a party tonight, then?" "Yup," says the man, "I've come as my love life." "What are you going on about?" asks the barman. "You look like Abraham Lincoln." "Indeed I do," says the man, "my last four scores were seven years ago!"

➻ Four men are sitting in a bar when a guy comes up to them and offers them a bet. He reckons that he can place a pint glass on the bar, 25 feet away, stand behind their table and piss right into – and fill – the pint glass. The men all confer and decide that there's no way this guy can do it. They quickly stump up the £100 that he's offering. The man walks to the bar, places an empty pint glass on it and returns to where the men are. He stands there, drops his trousers and begins to piss. It goes everywhere apart from the pint glass – he doesn't even get close to it and even pisses on the men with whom he's made the bet. They can't help but laugh at his pathetic effort. When the guy has finished, he hands over the £100. One of the men turns and asks him, "What the hell made you think you could fill that glass all the way over there?" "I never thought I could," said the guy, "but I bet the bartender £500 that I could piss all over you blokes and you'd just laugh about it!"

➻ So, this dyslexic walks into a bra...

➻ There is a businessman who is not feeling well, so he goes to see the doctor about it. The doctor says to him: "Well, it must be your diet; what sort of greens do you eat?" The man replies: "Well, actually, I only eat peas; I hate all other green foods." The doctor is quite shocked at this and says: "Well man, that's your problem, all those peas will be clogging up your system, you'll have to give them up." The guy says, "But how long for? I mean, I really like peas." The doctor replies, "For ever, I'm afraid." The man is quite shocked by this, but he gives it a go and sure enough, his condition improves, so he realizes that he will never eat a pea again. Anyway, one night, years later, he's at a convention for his employer and getting quite sloshed. One of the reps says: "Well, ashully, I'd love a cigarette, coz I avn't ad a smoke in four years, I gave it up." The barman nods, and says "Really? I haven't had a game of golf in three years, because it cost me my first marriage, so I gave it up." The businessman says, "Thas nuvving, I haven't ad a pea in six years." The barman jumps up screaming, "Okay, everyone who can't swim, grab a table..."

Drinks flowed like cement...

John Mortimer

➻ Two tubs of yoghurt walk into a pub. The landlord – himself a tub of cottage cheese – says, "Get out. We don't serve your kind in here." One of the yoghurt cartons looks at him and says, "Why not? We're cultured individuals!"

BeeR

↔ Two blokes decided to open a real ale brewery in the foothills. After several months of careful work, they produced a product with a golden straw-like colour and a good strong flavour of hops. They sent it to the chemical lab at the MAFF for testing, and after waiting impatiently for three weeks, the lab analysis came back. It read, "Dear Sirs, Our analysis of the sample sent to us indicates that your horse has diabetes."

Those who drink beer will think beer.

Washington Irving

↔ A female student walks into a pub, sits up at the bar and orders a Pilsner. She drinks it down in one, her eyes roll back in her head and then she passes out. The regulars, not being ones to miss an opportunity, take her into the back room, take it in turns to fuck her, then prop her up in the alley. The next day she comes in again, sits at the bar and orders a Pilsner. Again she passes out and the lads, unable to believe their luck, take her into the back room again and take turns shagging her before putting her into the alley. The third day, the same girl walks in again and sits at the bar. "Would you like a Pilsner today?" asks the landlord. She replies, "No, no more Pilsner, thanks. Make it a draught. That bottled stuff makes my pussy ache."

BIG CATS

↦ One day a lion was walking around the jungle, sad, lonely and bored stiff, when he spotted a monkey high up in a tree. He yelled up to the monkey to come down and play, but the monkey was too scared. So the lion asked the monkey what he could do to make him feel comfortable enough to come down. The monkey said, "If you tie yourself up, I'll come down." The lion tied himself up, but as the monkey came down he started shaking. The lion said: "Hey, monkey, you don't have to be scared! I'm not going to eat you; I'm tied up real tight." "I know," said the monkey. "That's not why I'm shaking." "Why are you shaking, then?" "It's the excitement," explains the monkey. "I've never fucked a lion before."

↦ The scene is a dark jungle in Africa. Two tigers are stalking through the brush when the one to the rear reaches out with his tongue and licks the arse of the tiger in front. The startled tiger turns around and says: "Hey, leave it out, alright?" The rear tiger says, "Sorry", and they continue. After about another five minutes, the rear tiger again reaches out with his tongue and licks the arse of the tiger in front. The front tiger turns around and cuffs the rear tiger and says: "I said stop it!" The rear tiger says, "Sorry", and they continue. After about another five minutes, the rear tiger once more licks the arse of the tiger in front. The front tiger turns around and asks the rear tiger: "What is it with you, anyway?" The rear tiger replies: "Well, I just ate a lawyer and I'm trying to get the taste out of my mouth."

↦ Why don't they play poker on the African savannah? There are too many cheetahs.

47

Women, when they have made a sheep of a man, always tell him he's a lion.

Honore de Balzac, 1799 – 1850

➤ A jaguar was walking pugnaciously through the jungle, intimidating the other animals. He spotted a monkey and ran up to it, pinning it against the trunk of a tree. "Who is the fiercest animal in the jungle?" he roared. "You: you are," the monkey squeaked. Satisfied, the jaguar let him go and carried on, noticing with satisfaction that all the other animals were running away from him. He nonetheless managed to immobilize a bird and growled in a terrifying manner: "Who is the fiercest animal in the jungle?" "You: you are," the bird stammered, and the jaguar magnanimously let him go. The jaguar then spotted a lion having a siesta and, giddy with self-importance, made the mistake of running up to him. "Who is the fiercest animal in the jungle?" he roared, eyes bulging. Hearing this, the lion stood up, picked up the jaguar by the tail, swung him around faster and faster and finally released him and sent him crashing heavily into a banana tree. "All right, all right," the jaguar said, standing up groggily and shaking his head to clear it. "Even if you don't know the answer, it's no reason to get pissed off."

BIRDS

➤ A bloke walks into a pet shop and asks if he can buy a canary. The proprietor replies, "I'm sorry, we've sold out. You won't find a canary in town. I do have a parakeet, though." The bloke insists he wants a canary, so the shop owner tells him that a parakeet can be made to sound just like a canary if you file the beak down. "But you have to be careful not to file too much off, or the parakeet will drown when he goes to take a drink of water." The bloke reckons that this is complete bullshit, but thanks the shop owner politely and leaves. He goes into another pet shop and asks for a canary, but again he has no luck. "But", says the girl behind the counter, "I do have a parakeet, and if you file the beak down carefully it can be made to sound just like a canary." She, too, then goes on to explain that filing off too much beak will jeopardise the bird's life, due to the potential for drowning. The bloke decides that there might be something to it, and buys the parakeet. "Besides", he tells himself, "parakeets are much cheaper." His next stop is a hardware shop, where he wanders into the tools section, holding his recently-purchased bird. The owner wanders by and asks if he needs some help. The bloke sheepishly explains how he intends to make his parakeet sing like a canary. The hardware store owner knowingly picks up a file and hands it to him. "Here, this is what you want – a Simonson No.5 rough-edged file. But be careful not to file too much off, or the poor thing will drown." The bloke thanks the hardware store owner, pays up and leaves for home. A few weeks later, the bloke wanders into the hardware store again. The owner, recognising him, asks how it went with the parakeet. The bloke looks down and sadly reports, "Actually, the bird's dead." The hardware store owner looks sympathetic and asks, "Did you file off too much beak?" The bloke shakes his head and says, "Nope. He was dead when I took him out of the vice."

It's not only fine feathers that make fine birds.

Aesop, The Jay & The Peacock

↝ A city doctor started a practice in the countryside. He once had to go to a farm to attend to a sick farmer who lived there. After a few house calls he stopped coming to the farm. The puzzled farmer finally phoned him to ask what the matter was. The doctor said, "It's your ducks at the entrance. Every time I enter the farm, they insult me."

↝ A duck enters a grocery store and says to the man behind the counter: "Do you have any beer?" "I'm sorry, but this is a grocery store. We're not licensed to sell beer here." The duck leaves, but comes back the next day. "Do you have any beer?" he asks. "I told you yesterday! We don't sell beer here! This is a grocery store! If you come here again asking for beer, I'll nail your feet to the floor!" The duck leaves, but comes back the next day. "Do you have any nails?" The shop owner says: "No." The duck continues, "Do you have any beer?"

↝ Two tall trees, a birch and a beech, are growing in the woods. A small tree begins to grow between them. One tree says to the other: "Is that a son of a beech or a son of a birch?" The other says he cannot tell. Just then a woodpecker lands in the sapling. The tall tree asks: "Woodpecker, you're a tree expert. Can you tell if that's a son of a beech or a son of a birch?" The woodpecker takes a taste of the small tree. He replies: "It is neither a son of a beech nor a son of a birch. That, my friends, is the best piece of ash I have ever put my pecker in."

↝ Two vultures board an aeroplane, each carrying two dead raccoons. The stewardess looks at them and says, "I'm sorry, gentlemen, only one carrion per passenger."

↜ What happens when you kiss a canary? You get chirpes and it can't be tweeted because it's a canarial disease.

↜ Why do birds fly south? Because it's just too far to walk.

↜ Why do ducks have flat feet? To stamp out forest fires.

↜ Why do hummingbirds hum? Because they don't know the words.

↜ Why do ostriches stick their heads in the ground? To look for the elephants who forgot to wear their sandals.

BIRTH

Why is it we rejoice at a birth and grieve at a funeral?
It is because we are not the person involved.

Mark Twain

↜ A woman goes to her doctor, who verifies that she is pregnant. This is her first pregnancy. The doctor asks her if she has any questions. She replies, "Well, I'm a little worried about the pain. How much will childbirth hurt?" The doctor answers, "Well, that varies from woman to woman and pregnancy to pregnancy; and besides, it's difficult to describe pain." "I know, but can't you give me some idea?" she asks. "Grab your upper lip and pull it out a little..." "Like this?" "A little more..." "Like this?" "No. A little more..." "Like this?" "Yes. Does that hurt?" "A little bit." "Now stretch it over your head."

↔ A man speaks frantically into the phone, "My wife is pregnant, and her contractions are only two minutes apart." "Is this her first child?" the doctor queries. "No, you idiot!" the man shouts. "This is her husband!"

Having a baby is like watching two very inefficient removal men trying to get a very large sofa through a very small doorway, only in this case you can't say, "Oh sod it, bring it through the French windows."

Victoria Wood

↔ A native American Indian went to his father one day because his school was doing a project on how people get their names and where names come from. He first asked, "Father, why was it that you named my first sister Buffalo Grazing?" The chief looked at his son and said, "On the morning after the birth of your first sister, I walked out of the hot, sweaty tepee and I looked around the plains. I saw great beauty around me, and I saw the fields where the graceful buffalo graze peacefully. I hoped that she would know peace like these fine animals, and decided to name her Buffalo Grazing." "That's great," said the son, "and why did you name my other sister Full Moon Shining?" "Well," said the chief, "on the evening of the birth of your other sister, I walked out of the hot, sweaty tepee and looked around me. It was still dark and the only light came from the moon above. I thought of the light of life that had just been breathed into the little one and decided to name her Full Moon Shining." "That's great, dad," said the boy. And the father looked at him once more, and asked, "But why do you ask, Two Dogs Humping?"

➡ A young woman, two months pregnant, went to see her obstetrician. He was in a hurry to leave on an emergency call, so he asked her to quickly bare her stomach, then reached into his desk and took out a rubber stamp, which he pressed beside her navel. He then rushed off. At home, she and her husband tried to read the tiny words printed on her belly, but they were too small. They then found a magnifying glass and tried to read the words. The stamp read: "When your husband can read this without his glasses, it's time to get yourself to the hospital."

➡ An elderly woman went into the doctor's office. When the doctor asked why she was there, she replied: "I'd like to have some birth control pills." Taken aback, the doctor thought for a minute and then said, "Excuse me, Mrs Smith, but you're 75 years old. What possible use could you have for birth control pills?" The woman responded, "They help me sleep better." The doctor thought some more and continued, "How in the world do birth control pills help you to sleep?" The woman said: "I put them in my granddaughter's orange juice and I sleep better at night."

The end result of all that sex and marriage floating around all over the place is birth, of course. Birth hurts. It's something that men cannot really understand, and in general, they're extremely grateful for the fact. There are alternatives, but having your stomach hacked open with a sharp knife has never really been all that popular with women, for some reason...

Anonymous

➡ Max Brown, a young father-to-be, was waiting anxiously outside the maternity ward where his wife was giving birth to their first baby. As he paced the floor, a nurse popped her head around the door. "It's a boy, Mr Brown," she said, "but we think you'd better go and have a cup of coffee, because there might be another." Max turned a little pale and left. Some time later, he rang the hospital and was told he was the father of twins. "But," the nurse went on, "we're sure there's another on the way. Ring back again in a little while." At that, Max decided that coffee was not nearly strong enough. He ordered a few beers and rang the hospital again, only to be told a third baby had arrived and a fourth was imminent. White-faced, he stumbled to the bar and ordered a double Scotch. Twenty minutes later, he tried the phone again, but he was in such a state that he dialled the wrong number and got the recorded cricket score. When they picked him up off the floor of the phone box, the recording was still going strong, "The score is 96 all out, and the last one was a duck."

➡ The crofter's wife went into labour in the middle of the night, and the doctor was called out to assist in the delivery. To keep the father-to-be busy, the doctor handed him a lantern and said: "Here, you hold this high so I can see what I'm doing." Soon, a lusty baby boy was brought into the world. "Och!" said the doctor. "Don't be in a rush to put the lantern by... I think there's yet another wee bairn to come." Sure enough, within minutes he had delivered a bonnie lass. "Na, dinna be in a great hurry to be putting down that lantern, lad...It seems there's yet another one besides," cried the doctor. The crofter scratched his head in bewilderment, and asked the doctor: "Well now, doc. Do ye suppose the light's attracting them?"

↦ The new mother got out of bed for the first time since giving birth, dressed in her robe and walked down the hospital hallway to the nurse's desk where she asked for a phone book. "What are you doing out here? You should be in your room resting," the nurse exclaimed. "I want to search through the phone book for a name for my baby," the new mother replied. "You don't have to do that here. The hospital furnishes a booklet to all new mothers to assist them in picking a first name for their baby." "You don't understand," the woman said and frowned, "My baby already has a first name."

BLONDES

↦ A big-boobed waitress came up to a blonde in the café and asked her for an order. The blonde read her nametag, then said, "'Debbie.' Oh, that's sweet. What do you call the other one?"

↦ A blonde and a brunette are sitting in a pub having a drink when the brunette's boyfriend comes in with a bunch of roses. The brunette receives the flowers with apparent pleasure, but makes a face as soon as her boyfriend is off to get a drink from the bar. "Crap, he's bought me flowers again," says the brunette. "What's the matter with you? You don't like flowers?" asks her friend. "Oh, I do," the brunette replies. "It's just that when he buys me flowers it means I'll have to spend the next two or three days with my legs wide open." The blonde asks, "You don't have a vase?"

↠ A blonde and a brunette are out driving. As they've had a few beers, the brunette tells the blonde to look out for cops. They drive for a while, and then the blonde taps the brunette on the shoulder and says: "Hold on, there's a cop car behind us." "Shit!" says the brunette. "Are their lights on?" The blonde has to think for a moment, then says, "Er... Yes. No. Yes. No. Yes. No..."

↠ A blonde finds herself, inexplicably, in a university and meets a professor of psychology. Not wanting to appear as if she didn't belong here, she asks him: "Tell me, Professor, is it true there's a way to detect mental deficiency in people that appear completely normal?" "Oh, yes," the professor answers. "All you have to do is ask them a very simple question which anybody can answer, and then monitor their replies." "Really? Have you got an example?" the blonde asks, vaguely planning on fooling the professor next time she meets him. "Take this one: Captain Cook did three trips to the Pole and died during one of them. Which one was it?" The blonde laughs nervously and said, "Can you give me another example? I'm not very good at history."

↠ A blonde girl has a baby, and the family all come round to visit. They ask to see the baby, but she says, "Not yet, it's asleep." They wait a while and then they ask again. "Not yet, it's asleep," comes the answer. Finally it's getting late and they have to leave, so they ask once more to see the baby. "Not yet, it's asleep. You have to wait till it cries," comes the answer. "Why do we have to wait till it cries?" they ask. "Because I forgot where I put it down."

↠ A blonde goes to the electrical appliance sale and finds a bargain. She stops a salesman and says: "I'd like to buy this TV, please." "Sorry, we don't sell to blondes," the salesman replies. She storms out of the shop and hurries home, where she dyes her hair. She comes back to the same shop and again tells the salesman: "I'd like to buy this TV, please." "Sorry, we don't sell to blondes," he replies again. "How did he recognize me?" she wonders. Mortified, she rushes back home again and goes for the complete disguise this time – haircut, new colour, new outfit, big sunglasses – then waits a full day before returning to the shop. "I'd like to buy this TV, please," she says to the same man. "Sorry, we don't sell to blondes," he replies. Frustrated, she exclaims, "But how do you know I'm a blonde?" "Because that's not a TV, it's a microwave," he replies.

↔ A blonde has been asked on a date and is being treated to a seafood restaurant. On her way to her table, they pass an aquarium full of live lobsters. At the end of the meal, taking pity on the lobsters, she manages to get near the aquarium while her date is settling the bill and hides a couple of them in her bag. "Neat," she thinks triumphantly. "I'll ask Bill to stop by the woods and I'll free the poor creatures."

↔ A blonde has been in a taxi for some time when she realizes she doesn't have any money. "I'm sorry," she says to the driver, "you'll have to go back, I forgot my purse and it's already £10." The driver glances at her and says: "It's OK, I'll just stop in a dark alley and you can take off your bra." "I can't do that! You'd be cheating yourself," the blonde replies. "Cheating myself? How so?" "This bra only cost me a fiver."

↔ A blonde heard that 90% of accidents occur around the home, so she moved.

➻ A blonde is arrested at the airport check-in for having a bomb in her bag and is being grilled by the customs officer: "How come you have a bomb in your bag?" he barks. "It's just because I'm afraid of flying," the blonde wails. "You are afraid of flying, therefore you carry a bomb with you?" "Oh, I'm just afraid someone will bring a bomb on the plane." The customs officer shakes his head to try and clear his thoughts and asks again, in an incredulous tone, "If you're afraid of someone carrying a bomb with them on a plane, why do you carry one?" "It's simple," replies the blonde. "I figured the odds against two people carrying a bomb with them would be much higher, so the plane would be far safer."

➻ A blonde is complaining to her friend about her boyfriend and men in general. "I've had enough with men. They're cheap, they cheat on you, they don't respect you... Next time I want sex, I'll use my trusty plastic companion instead." "Yeah, but what will you do when the batteries run out?" her friend asks. "I'll fake an orgasm as usual."

I did a movie with Miss Bankhead in England. One day, she wandered into my dressing room completely nude. I couldn't help staring, and she said "What's the matter, dahling? Haven't you ever seen a blonde before?"

Donald Sutherland, 1934 – , on Tallulah Bankhead

➻ A blonde is crossing the road when a car hits her. The driver rushes over to see if she's OK. "My eyes, my eyes," she shouts, "Everything's gone all blurry! I'm going blind!" The driver's worried that he might have really injured her, so he says, "How many fingers have I got up?" "Oh no!" she cries, "Don't say I'm paralysed from the waist down as well!"

I'm blonde. What's your excuse?

Anonymous

↠ A blonde is flying on a four-engined plane. Suddenly there's a loud bang, the pilot comes on the radio and says, "I'm sorry, but we seem to have lost an engine. We'll probably be delayed by 45 minutes." A few minutes later, there's another bang. Once again, the radio comes on: "I'm sorry, but we seem to have lost another engine. We'll probably be delayed by two hours." A little while later, the third engine shuts off. This time, the pilot tells the passengers that they will be delayed by around three hours. The blonde turns to the guy sitting beside her and says, "Man, if they lose the fourth engine, we'll be up here all day."

↠ A blonde is looking at a bulletin board at her workplace and sees an ad which says, "Luxury Ocean Cruise Only £5." She copies the details, goes to the address and hands the ad and a fiver to the secretary. The secretary points to a burly guy sitting in a battered sofa, reading a newspaper. The guy stands up and knocks the blonde unconscious. When she wakes up, she's tied to a log and floating down the river. She starts to think maybe this wasn't such a good idea after all. Then she sees one of her colleagues (who is also blonde) floating right next to her. Sighing, she says, "So do you think they're going to serve us some food on this trip?" "They didn't last year," the other blonde replies.

❥ A blonde is sitting at the counter in a bar with a glass of vodka with an olive in it. She tries to pick the olive up with the toothpick but it always eludes her, skidding to the other end of the glass. This futile exercise has been going on for half an hour when the man next to her, exasperated, snatches the toothpick from her hand and adroitly skewers the olive in one stroke. "This is how you do it," he says to the blonde. "Big deal," the blonde mutters darkly. "I already had him so tired out, he couldn't get away."

❥ A blonde walks into a clothing store. She looks around for a while and finally picks out a scarf and brings it to the counter to pay for it. As she seems very pleased with her purchase, the cashier is surprised to see her again an hour or so later, holding the scarf out for a refund. "But this colour goes so well with your hair," the shop assistant remarks. "Why do you want to return it?" "Because it's too tight!" the blonde replies.

❥ A blonde walks into a library and says to the librarian at the counter, "Can I have a burger and fries, please?" "This is a library," the librarian answers reprovingly. "Oh, I'm so sorry," the blond says, and drops her voice to a whisper. "Can I have a burger and fries, please?"

❥ A blonde walks up to the counter of the local library and complains to the librarian: "Here's your book back. It's the most boring book I have ever read. There's no plot whatsoever, and far too many characters." "Oh, thank you," the librarian replies. "You must be the person who borrowed our phone book."

➻ A blonde wanted to buy a personalized license plate for her new car but she couldn't afford it. So, instead, she decided to change her name to KV08GML.

➻ A blonde was having a great time at a party and was soon spotted by a guy who swiftly led her upstairs. He started to undress her, then, surprised, saw that she was wearing shower caps on her tits. "Hey, what's with the shower caps?" the guy asked her. "What shower caps?" she answered, "These are booby condoms!"

➻ A blonde was strolling down the avenue when she saw a student wearing a sandwich board saying "Free Big Mac." She went up to him and asked: "Why? What did he do?"

➻ A blonde was trying to put together a jigsaw puzzle. She got very frustrated, so she decided to ask her husband for help. "It's supposed to be a tiger!" she cried. "Honey," said her husband, "put the Frosties back in the box!"

➻ A blonde went to the hospital emergency room with the tip of her left index finger blown off. "How did this happen?" the doctor asked. "Well you see, I was trying to commit suicide," the blonde replied. "By shooting your finger?" the doctor asked, baffled. "No, silly! First I put the gun to my chest and I thought, 'I just paid $6,000 for these boobs: no way I am blowing them off.' Then I put the gun in my mouth but I thought, 'I just paid $2,000 to get my teeth fixed: the teeth are staying!' So I put the gun in my ear and I thought, 'This is going to make a loud noise,' so I put my finger in my other ear before I pulled the trigger."

➼ A blonde, a brunette and a redhead are on a walk in the mountains when they find a bridge over a deep ridge. They are halfway across when a fairy appears out of nowhere. "Welcome to the fairy bridge," she says. "If you want to pass, you need to jump over and shout the name of an animal, then you will be transformed into this animal and land harmlessly." The brunette goes first and, as she jumps over the edge of the bridge, she shouts "Lion!" and, sure enough, whoosh! she gets transformed into a great lion which gently descends to the ground and disappears into the trees. When it is her turn, the redhead swings her legs over the edge of the bridge and shouts "Eagle!" and whoosh! she is transformed into a magnificent eagle which soars to the heavens. The blonde finds this pretty neat but, just as she jumps over the bridge, she realizes she hasn't thought about what animal she wanted to be. "Crap," she says.

➼ A blonde, a brunette and a redhead are running away from the cops when they stumble by chance upon an old barn to hide in. They find three big sacks on the floor of the barn and promptly jump in them. About a minute later, a police car comes to a screaming halt by the barn door and a policeman steps out. He enters the barn and spots the suspicious-looking sacks. He kicks the first one. "Meow," says the redhead. "It must be a cat," says the policeman, and he kicks the second sack. "Woof," says the brunette. "Must be a dog," mutters the policeman, and he kicks the third sack. "Potatoes," says the blonde.

➼ A blonde, a brunette and a redhead get into a lift, and notice a white sticky patch on the wall. "That's funny," says the brunette, "that looks like spunk." The redhead sniffs the air and says, "Yep, and

---

it smells like spunk." The blonde puts her finger in the sticky patch, licks her finger and says, "Well, it's nobody from our office."

➤ A blonde, a brunette and a redhead go out sailing, but a storm damages their craft and they end up being blown onto a beautiful but uninhabited island. After a couple of days, they reach the conclusion that their absence has not been noticed. The redhead says, "Listen girls, we're trapped on this island; we have enough food for about two more days, but it can't be more than six or seven kilometres to the mainland and I'm sure I can swim there." With that she dives into the water. She is quite a strong swimmer and she thinks she is making good headway. Sadly, the wind is blowing off the mainland and she has actually gone less than halfway when she begins to get very tired. She tries to go on, but exhaustion takes over and she drowns. A day later, when nothing has been heard on the island, the brunette says, "Do you think our friend has forgotten us? I'm a very good swimmer and I'm sure I can make it to the mainland. As soon I get ashore I promise I'll get help for you." Off goes the brunette. She is a stronger swimmer, but she is also unlucky, because the wind is in the wrong direction. She gets three-quarters of the way across before exhaustion gets the better of her and she too drowns. The blonde waits a couple of days for help to arrive, but of course, no one appears. Faced with the prospect of dying of starvation, alone on the island, or trying to swim for it, she decides to try to swim. Her luck is in because the wind has turned around and she quickly gets to within a half-kilometre of the shore. At this point she remembers that she left the fire burning on the island, so she turns back to put it out.

63

➥ A blonde, a brunette and a redhead are having a breaststroke swimming competition across the English Channel. The brunette finishes first, then the redhead second, but the blonde never finished. When the lifeboat found her, way behind, she said, "I don't want to be a telltale or anything, but the other two – you know? They used their arms."

➥ A blonde, a brunette and a redhead go trekking one day and stumble upon a cave, in which there is an old magical mirror. The dusty book next to it says that this mirror will grant a wish only if you tell the truth – if you lie, you disappear in a puff of smoke. They find this pretty neat, so the brunette goes first. "I think I'm the smartest woman on earth." "Poof!" She disappears. The redhead goes up to try. "I think I'm the prettiest woman on earth." "Poof!" She disappears. The blonde goes up, decided to tell the truth and nothing but the truth. "I think..." "Poof!"

➥ A blonde, a brunette and a redhead have been stuck on a deserted island for a long, long time when one day a magic lamp is washed ashore. The redhead rubs it hard and out pops a genie. "Thank you for letting me out of this bottle," he says. "As a reward, I can give a wish to each of you." The redhead goes first: "I hate it here. It is too hot and boring. I want to go home!" "All right," replied the genie, and the redhead disappears in a puff of smoke. Then it's the brunette's turn. "I miss my family, my friends and relatives. I want to go home, too!" "No sweat," the genie says and off she goes. Then the blonde starts crying and says, "I'm lonely: I wish my two friends were back here with me!"

➥ A blonde, a redhead and a brunette were looking at a dictionary for the hardest words they knew. The brunette's word was 'bereavement'. The redhead's word was 'deoxyribonucleic'. The blonde's word was 'dick'.

I remember Tallulah telling of going into a public ladies' room and discovering there was no toilet tissue. She looked underneath the booth and said to the lady in the next stall, "I beg your pardon, do you happen to have any toilet tissue in there?" The lady said no. So Tallulah said, "Well then, dahling, do you have two fives for a ten?"

Ethel Merman, 1904 – 1984, on Tallulah Bankhead

➥ A little boy is playing with his blonde friend when another, older boy comes in. "I found a condom on the veranda," he smirks. The blonde looks up and asks innocently: "What's a veranda?"

➥ A nervous blonde goes to the dentist. To calm her down, the dentist decides to tell her a short story. He thinks for a while, while putting his latex gloves on, then he has it. "Do you know how they make these gloves?" he asks genially to his patient. "There's a factory in Wales where there's a big vat of latex. They employ people of all ages, with various hand sizes, to dip their hands in the vat. They walk for a while until the latex solidifies a bit; then they take the gloves off." This story seems to have done the trick, because the blonde is smiling, a dreamy expression on her face. "I wonder where they make condoms," she breathes.

➥ A young blonde was on vacation in the depths of Louisiana. She had always wanted a pair of genuine alligator shoes and thought it was the perfect place to get some. She was disappointed, however, for the local shoe shops were still too expensive for her. Very frustrated, she decided to catch her own alligator so that she could get a pair of shoes at a reasonable price. Later in the day a man was driving home after a day of fly-fishing when he spotted the blonde standing waist-deep in the water, shotgun in hand. Just then, horrified, he saw a huge nine-foot alligator swimming quickly toward her. The blonde took aim, squeezed the trigger and killed the beast. She waded to the body and dragged it to the bank, where there were already half a dozen dead alligators lying in the mud. With an angry shout, the blonde flipped the alligator on its back, stared at it for a few seconds and howled out, "Damn it! This one isn't wearing any shoes either!"

➥ A young man stops at an ice cream van and asks the blonde serving girl, "What flavours do you have?" "Vanilla, chocolate, strawberry..." then she sneezes violently and her throat makes a rasping noise. "Have you got laryngitis?" he enquires in a sympathetic voice. "No, only vanilla, chocolate and strawberry."

➥ A young ventriloquist is touring the clubs and one night does a show in a pub in Shropshire. With his puppet on his knee, he's going through his usual dumb blonde routine when a blonde woman stands on her chair and starts shouting angrily: "I've heard enough of your stupid blonde jokes. What makes you think you can stereotype women that way? What does the colour of a person's hair have to do with her worth as a human being? It's guys like you who keep women like me from being respected at work and in the community and from reaching our full potential, because you and your kind continue to perpetuate discrimination against not only blondes, but women in general!" The ventriloquist, embarrassed, begins to apologize, but the blonde yells, "You stay out of this, buster! I'm talking to that little jerk on your knee!"

↪ After watching a program about Egyptians on TV, a blonde decides to treat herself to a milk bath. She leaves a note to the milkman which reads, "30 litres of milk tomorrow, please." On finding the note in the morning, the milkman is a bit confused and knocks on the door. "You mean three litres, right?" "No, you read right, 30 litres, please," the blonde smiles back. "Er...OK. Pasteurized?" "No: just up to my tits."

↪ It is winter and a blonde decides to go ice-fishing. After having spent some time getting all the right tools, she drives toward the nearest frozen lake and starts cutting a circular hole in the ice. Then from the heavens a voice boomed, "There are no fish under the ice." Startled, the blonde moves a bit further down the ice, pours herself a mug of coffee from a thermos and starts cutting another hole in the ice. Out of nowhere, the voice booms, "There are no fish under the ice." This time the blonde is pretty scared, so she moves to the far end of the frozen lake. Just as she starts cutting another hole, the very loud voice says, "There are no fish under the ice." The awed, and very scared, blonde slowly raises her head and says, in a small, contrite voice: "Is that you, Lord?" The voice answers, "No. It is the manager of the ice rink!"

↦ NASA sends a space shuttle up with two pigs and a blonde on board. While the shuttle is taking off, the NASA command centre calls the first pig and asks, "Pig One, do you know your mission?" The pig replies, "Oink oink. Get the shuttle into orbit and launch the trillion-dollar satellite. Oink oink." Then Mission Control asks the second pig, "Pig Two, do you know your mission?" The second pig replies, "Oink oink. Once Pig One has completed the trillion-dollar satellite launch, close hatch and land shuttle. Oink oink." Then NASA asks the blonde, "Blonde woman, do you know your mission?" The blonde woman replies, "Don't tell me, don't tell me... Oh yeah, I remember now. Feed the pigs, and don't touch a goddamned thing!"

I was in Hitchcock's "Lifeboat". So was Tallulah Bankhead, who didn't wear panties, and each morning when we climbed into a lifeboat – up on a mechanical rocker – she gave the cast and crew a hell of a view, hiking up her skirt! Eventually someone complained to Hitch, who didn't want to get involved. He explained that it was an interdepartmental matter – involving wardrobe, costume, and possibly hairdressing...

Hume Cronyn, on Tallulah Bankhead

↦ Three blondes go to a funfair and buy a raffle ticket. As it is for charity, everyone wins a small prize. The first blonde wins a case of spaghetti sauce. The second wins a small Stilton cheese. The third wins a toilet brush. The following day, they meet at the first blonde's place and she says: "Wasn't that great? I love spaghetti!" "And I adore cheese," comments the second blonde, then asks the third: "How's the toilet brush?" "Not so good , I'm afraid," she answers. "In fact, I think I'll go back to paper."

➥ Three blondes witness a violent crime. Two days later, they are summoned by the police to identify a suspect. In order to check they are reliable witnesses, the inspector says he will show them a mug-shot for 30 seconds, then ask each one for a description. He shows the mug-shot to the first blonde for 30 seconds, then covers it and asks her if she thinks she would recognize the face. "Yes, easy," she replies. "The guy in the picture has only one eye." The inspector blinks in confusion, then says, "He's got only one eye because it's a profile shot!" Shaking his head, he repeats the procedure for the second blonde and again asks if she would recognize him. "Easy! He only has one ear," she answers. "Come on, what's the matter with you two? It's a profile shot! You're seeing this man from the side!" shouts the inspector. Expecting the worst, he repeats the procedure with the third blonde, then says, "Would you recognize the suspect from this picture if you saw him in real life? And think before you give me a stupid answer." The third blonde looks hard at the photo, and remains silent for a minute, then says, "Yeah, it's easy, he's wearing contact lenses." This takes the inspector by surprise. He picks up the photo and looks really hard at it, but can't tell if the suspect wears contact lenses or not. With a suspicious look at the third blonde, he checks the full report on the suspect. Sure enough, when the mug-shot was taken, he was wearing contact lenses! Baffled, the inspector goes back to the third blonde and asks her, "How could you tell he was wearing contact lenses?" "Well," she says, "he can't wear regular glasses with only one eye and one ear, now, can he?"

➻ One day, a blonde went to see the doctor with a carrot in one ear, a cucumber in the other and two peas up her nose, complaining she wasn't feeling well. The doctor told her it was because she wasn't eating properly.

➻ The groom lay in bed on the first night of their honeymoon, while his blonde wife stood at the bedroom window, gazing at the stars. "Come to bed, darling," he whispered seductively after some time had passed. "Not likely," replied the bride, "my mother told me that this would be the best night of my life, and I'm not going to miss a minute of it."

➻ Two blondes are planning a bank robbery. One of them stays in the car with the engine running and the other one pulls on a balaclava. "Now," says the getaway driver, "You've got the gun?" "Yes." "You've got the rope?" "Yes." "And you've got the dynamite." "Yes." "Go for it!" So the blonde runs into the bank. She's been gone a long time and no explosion. Then she's been gone a very long time and still no explosion. The getaway driver is about to give up and drive off when the blonde runs out of the bank; no money, balaclava half off, pursued by a security guard with his trousers round his ankles, and jumps in the car. As they speed off, the getaway driver says, "I tell you every time – you're meant to tie up the guard and blow the safe."

➻ Two blondes are waiting at the bus stop. A bus pulls up and the doors open. The first blonde steps in and asks the driver "Will this bus take me to New Street?" "Sorry, it won't. You're at the wrong stop," the driver replies. The second blonde steps inside, throws her chest out, smiles devilishly and says "Will it take ME?"

➤ Two blondes take a stroll in the forest. Suddenly, one blonde stops and looks down. "Look at those deer tracks," she says to her friend. Her friend looks down and replies: "These aren't deer tracks: they're wolf tracks." "No way. They're deer tracks." "You're completely wrong. These are wolf tracks!" They kept on arguing for half an hour, at which point the train runs them over.

➤ To a blonde, what is long and hard? Primary school.

➤ Two blonde girls walk into a building. You'd have thought one of them would have seen it.

BLUDGERS

➤ Jesus walked into a bar in Balham. He approached three sad-faced gentlemen at a table, and greeted the first one: "What's troubling you, brother?" he said. "My eyes. I keep getting stronger and stronger glasses, and I still can't see." Jesus touched the man, who ran outside to tell the world about his, now, 20-20 vision. The next gentleman couldn't hear Jesus' questions, so the Lord just touched his ears, restoring his hearing to perfection. This man, too, ran out the door, praising God. The third man leapt from his chair and backed up against the wall, even before Jesus could greet him. "Don't you come near me, man. Don't touch me!" he screamed. "I'm on disability benefit!"

False of heart, light of ear, bloody of hand; hog in sloth, fox in stealth, wolf in greediness, dog in madness, lion in prey.

William Shakespeare, King Lear

BOATS

➥ There were twin brothers by the name of Joey and John Jones. They had lived in the same fishing village all their lives. John was married and Joey had always been single. Joey owned a knackered old boat. One day, Joey's boat sank on exactly the same day that John's wife passed away. A couple of days later a kindly old lady met Joey in the queue for the Post Office and she thought he was John. She said to him, "So sorry for your loss, you must be feeling awful and I'm not surprised." Joey, not at all worried about his crappy old boat, replied, "Well, I couldn't care less. She was a pile of crap right from the very beginning. Her bottom was all lumpy and she always stank of old fish. The first time I got in her she leaked faster than anything I'd ever seen before in my life. She had a crack and a huge hole in front that kept getting bigger and bigger every time that I used her. I could handle her fine, but when someone else was using her she leaked like a bastard and that's what finished her off, I reckon. Three or four blokes from out of town came over looking for a good time. I told them that she was useless and much too creaky for all of them, but they really thought she looked all right. Anyway, all of them tried to get into her at the same time. It was just too much and she cracked right up the middle!" The little old lady fainted!

Ocean racing is like standing under a cold, salty shower tearing up £5 notes.

Edward Heath on Sailing

BODY ISSUES

➺ A man and woman were lying in bed one night and the woman said to the man: "I really wish I had bigger tits." The man responded by saying she should rub toilet paper all over them. The woman looked at him and asked: "Toilet paper? What will that do?" The man said, "I don't know, but look what it's done for your arse."

➺ Did you hear about the two blood corpuscles named Romeo and Juliet? They loved in vein.

She was always wearing a loose bathrobe that covered up a body that would have won first prize in a beauty contest for cement blocks.

Richard Brautigan, Dreaming of Babylon

➺ If the effort that went into research on the female bosom had gone into the space program, we would now be running hot-dog stands on the moon.

➺ Three honeymoon couples find themselves in adjacent rooms in a hotel. As they are getting undressed, the first man says to his wife: "What huge buttocks!" Much offended, she throws him into the corridor. The second man, also undressing, says to his wife: "Christ! What huge tits!" She is also greatly offended and throws him out into the corridor. Several minutes later, the third newlywed husband arrives in the corridor as well. The other two ask: "What happened? Did you put your foot in it?" "No, but I could have," the third man replied.

BOOKS

Jane Austen's books, too, are absent from this library. Just that omission alone would make a fairly good library out of a library that hadn't a book in it.

Mark Twain on Jane Austen

↦ A pair of chickens walk up to the withdrawals desk at a public library and say, "Buk Buk BUK." Deciding that the chickens want three books, the librarian hands some over and the chickens cluck in thanks and leave. Around midday, the chickens come back to the desk and say, "Buk Buk BuKKOOK!" The librarian passes over another three books and the chickens leave as before. The chickens then return to the library in the early afternoon, approach the librarian and, looking very annoyed, cluck, "Buk Buk Buk Buk Bukkooook!" The librarian is by now a bit suspicious of these chickens, so she gives them a further five books, and decides to follow them. Trailing at a safe distance, she follows them out of the library, out through the town centre and to a park. Hiding behind a tree, she peeks out at the birds, who head down to the pond. When they get to the water's edge, she's horrified to see them throw all the books into the water. Suddenly, they come flying back out again and this frog sticks its head up and, in a smug tone of voice, says "Rrredit Rrredit Rrredit Rrredit Rrredit..."

BOOZE

↦ A bloke stumbles home completely plastered. He spends an hour trying to get the key into the lock, with no success, when a

74

policeman happens to pass by. "Is everything alright, sir?" asks the policeman. "I can't get the damn key in the lock, officer," slurs the man. The policeman helps him out with the key and starts to go on his way. "Wait, wait," shouts the drunk, "I really appreciate it. Let me show you my house!" "No, thank you, sir, I'll just be on my way," says the policeman. "I insist," presses the drunk, "It'll only take a second, and I really want to show you!" So the policeman agrees, to keep the peace, and they go inside. They enter the living room. "There's my TV, my stereo, and all that," says the man. "That's nice," the policeman replies. They go through to the kitchen. "There's my microwave, the new refrigerator...pretty nice, eh?" says the man. "Lovely," replies the policeman. Into the kids' bedroom: "Those are my two baby boys." "Yes, they look cute." Finally they get through to the man's bedroom. "And that's my wife, and that's me next to her."

The metallic flavour of this particular claret gives it a slight prison flavour.

John Mortimer

↦ A bloke walked into the pub and said, "Give me three shots, one each for my best friends and one for me." All through the following month, the bloke drank there in the same way – each time he had three shots, one each for his best friends and one for him. One day he went in and only ordered two shots. The landlord looked sympathetic and said, "What's up, did one of your friends pass away?" "Oh, no," the man replied, "the doctor made me give up drinking."

➤ A dark-haired woman was sitting in a pub, wearing a tube top. She never shaved her armpits so, as a result, she had a thick black bush under each arm. Every 20 minutes, she raised her arm to signal the landlord to pour her another drink. This went on all evening. Towards the end of the night, a drunk at the end of the bar pointed at her and said to the landlord, "Hey, I'd like to buy the ballerina a drink. What's she drinking?" The landlord replied, "She's no ballerina." The drunk said, "Come off it. Any girl that can lift her leg that high has to be a ballerina!"

➤ A drunken bum has too much to drink one night in his local. He can hardly stand up, but he knows that he absolutely has to take a piss. He staggers over to the toilets, getting his cock out as he does so. He crashes through the door, penis in hand, only to bump into two women because he's stumbled into the ladies instead. One of the women screams and shouts, "This is for ladies, my good man!" and the bum replies, as he fumbles to put away his thing, "So is this, lady!"

➤ A drunk bloke staggers into a pub, bumping into customers and spilling drinks as he makes his way to the bar. "Get out of here!" shouts the landlord when the drunk bloke finally makes it over. "I've gotta use the bog," slurs the drunk. "Sod off right this instant or I'll throw you out myself," yells the landlord. "I gotta use the bog," says the drunk bloke again and starts to unbutton his trousers. "For God's sake! Hold on, hold on," says the landlord. "Alright, you can go to the toilet, but afterwards you piss off!" The drunk agrees and stumbles off to the toilet. After about five minutes a loud scream rips through the crowded bar, and everyone goes absolutely silent. Suddenly there's another loud scream. The landlord and a couple of regulars sprint to the bathroom to find out what's going on. When they get there, they find the drunk sitting down in the corner. "What the hell is going on?" asks the landlord. "Look, 's your bog. I've had a pony, and every time I try to flush it crushes my balls!" says the drunk. "You stupid sod!" screams the landlord, "You've crapped in my mop bucket!"

→ A drunken bum has collapsed on the corner of the street. A policeman comes up to him and asks him what he's up to. "Well," the bum says, "apparently the world rotates on a 24-hour cycle, so I'm waiting for my house to come by. I don't think it'll be long, though, because I saw my neighbour not so long ago!"

→ A man walks into a bar and sits down for a beer. Now, this guy likes his beer, so when he sees a sign behind the bar that claims, "A lifetime's free beer for he or she who can pass the test," he starts thinking this could be his lucky day. When the owner of the bar comes in, the man says to him, "So what's this about some test, then?" The owner says, "Well, I'll tell you this much: many have tried and many have failed my test and to this day none has passed! It consists of three parts. The first part is simple: just drink one whole gallon of pure jalapeño-laden tequila in one go, without shuddering or uttering a noise. The second part is a little more difficult: there's a vicious croc outside – a pet of mine – and he's got a sore tooth. You have to wrestle him unconscious and get that tooth out using only your bare hands! The third part is tough, too: there's a woman upstairs who hasn't had an orgasm in her 70 years on this earth, and you have to make her come! Complete the three and you will drink free beer in this bar to the end of your days!" Now the man thinks that maybe it's going to be too tall an order, and he settles down for a decent evening's drinking. After a couple of hours the beer brain takes over and he starts to think, "You know, I reckon I could chin that 'Kila, take out that 'croc and I could do that bird – hell, yes!" So he shouts for the owner to come out and watch him pass the test: "Gizza go on that tequila, why don'tcha?" The owner puts the gallon jar of tequila on the bar and the man picks it up. He drains the whole huge bottle without saying a word and the tears stream from his eyes. Then he walks outside and for the next 20 minutes the sound of beating, ripping and screaming come from the backyard. Then, the door is kicked open and the man is standing there with his shirt ripped to shreds, covered in mud and sweat and panting for breath. And he says, "Now, where the hell's that woman with the bad tooth?"

➜ A man's disembodied head floats into a pub and orders a pint of beer. When it is served he uses his long tongue to lap up all the beer. No sooner has he finished than his torso appears. He orders another drink, laps it up, and suddenly he has legs, too. "This is great," he says to the landlord, "Give me another drink and we'll see if I can get my arms back, so that I can reach into my trousers, fetch my wallet and pay you." The landlord pours him another one and he laps that one up too. Next thing the landlord knows he's completely vanished. A bloke at the end of the bar turns to the landlord and says, "He should have quit while he was a head."

➜ A policeman broke up a scuffle outside a pub. "He started it!" said one man, infuriated. "It's not my fault!" replied the other. "Perhaps you could tell me what happened, Gents," said the policeman. "He kicked me in the bollocks!" accused the first man. "I didn't mean to," replied the second. "How was I supposed to know you were about to turn round?"

↔ A worrying new study has linked women's alcohol consumption with breast cancer, suggesting that women who get drunk regularly are more likely to suffer from the disease. The effects of this may be counterbalanced, however, by the fact that drunk women are likely to get their tits felt by a wide variety of blokes, and some of them could be doctors.

God, what on earth was I drinking last night? My head feels like there's a Frenchman living in it.

Ben Elton and Tony Curtis, Blackadder II

↔ After a major beer festival, the biggest brewery presidents decided to go out for a beer together. They picked a well-stocked pub and went in. The guy from Corona goes up to the bar and says, "Hey, señor, I would like the world's best beer, a Corona." The landlord takes a bottle from the shelf and hands it to him. The bloke from Budweiser says, "Give me the King Of Beers, a Budweiser." The landlord passes him one. The chap from Coors says, "I'd like the only beer made with Rocky Mountain spring water; give me a Coors." He gets it. The bloke from Guinness sits down and says, "Oh, give me a Coke." The landlord is a little surprised, but gives him what he ordered. The other presidents look over at him and ask, "What's up, why aren't you drinking Guinness?" The Guinness guy shrugs and replies, "Well, I decided if you lot weren't going to drink beer, neither would I."

➻ An English bloke, an Irish bloke and a Scots bloke went into a pub for a beer. When the pints rolled up, each one had a fly floating in the top. "Bloody hell!" said the English bloke, disgusted, "That's a bit much. Pour me another one, landlord." The Irish bloke shrugged, said, "Ah, stop making such a fuss, you big lemon," to the English bloke, "Sure now and it's only a little fly," and took a hearty swig. The Scots bloke was horrified. He snatched the fly out of his pint, shook it really hard and yelled, "Spit that oot, ye wee bastard! G'wan, spit it oot or ye'll be sorry!"

➻ An old soak is looking for a whorehouse and stumbles into a chiropodist's office. He walks up to the front desk and is directed to one of the inspection rooms. Without looking up, the receptionist waves him over to the inspection table and without looking up says, "Stick it through the curtain." Thinking, "How cool is this?", the drunk pulls his plonker out and sticks it through the middle of the curtain. "That's not a foot!" screams the nurse on the other side. "Well, lah-di-dah," says the drunk, "I didn't know there was a minimum!"

➻ Irritated wife: "What do you mean by coming home half-drunk?" Hubby: "It's not my fault...I ran out of money."

➻ It's a beautiful day in County Kerry and people all over the county are sitting outside the pubs enjoying stout by the pint. In a cosy pub one man turns to his friend and says, "You see that man over there?" His friend nods. "Have you noticed that he's the spitting image of me? It's bloody uncanny, that's what it is, to be sure. I'm going to go over there and ask him a few questions: after all, 'tis not every day that you get to meet someone who could be your exact double, now is it?" And off he goes to see the man he is talking about. He taps him on the shoulder and says, "Excuse me, I couldn't help noticing from over there that you look almost exactly the same as me. I was thinking what an incredible coincidence that was!" "Me too, me too," replies the man, "I noticed you earlier and I was just about to come over and talk when I saw you coming over anyway. 'Tis an incredible thing to be sure. So whereabouts are you from?" he asks. "Well, I'm from Galway, originally," says the first man. "No, that's incredible!" says the second, "Me too! It's just unbelievable. What street did you live in?" "Why, I lived in Moher Street for 20 years, so I did," comes the reply from the first man. "No! I can't believe it – I did, too," says the second. "And what number in that street was it?" he asks. "Why, I lived in number 20." "Unbelievable," comes the reply, "that's the number I lived in. And what were your parents' names?" "Ruari and Siobhan," comes the reply. "This really is uncanny," the first man says, "those are the exact names of my parents, too!" At this point, as the two men continue talking the new bar staff turn up for their shift. The new guy asks, "Anything happening?" and the guy about to go replies, "No, not really; just the Rix twins drunk again!"

➤ Once upon a time there was a very keen policeman who liked to hang around outside bars and nab people as they left to drive home with too much alcohol inside them. One night he's waiting outside his regular haunt and he sees someone come staggering out. The guy walks up to first one car and tries his key in the lock, then the next and then the next. None of them opens for him, and it isn't until he gets to the fifth car in the car park that he gets in and, after five minutes' fumbling, starts the engine. He backs the car up, narrowly missing most of the others in the car park, and he wheelspins across the road and away. The keen policeman follows him quickly with his lights already flashing and his siren screaming. He pulls the guy over only just round the corner from the bar and takes it easy as he warns him and gives him the breathalyzer test. To the by-now-smug cop's surprise, the guy does not seem to have a drop of alcohol in his system. "What's that all about, then?" asks the amazed young policeman, to which the man replies, "I'm tonight's designated decoy, officer!"

↠ Three blokes are driving around, necking beers and having a laugh when the driver looks in the mirror and sees the flashing lights of a police car telling him to pull over. The other two are really worried. "What are we going to do with our beers? We're in trouble!" "No," the driver says, "it's OK, just pull the label off of your bottle like this and stick it on your forehead. Let me do the talking." So they all pull the labels off their bottles and stick them to their foreheads, and the bloke pulls over. The policeman then walks up and says, "You lads were swerving all around the road back there. Have you been drinking?" "Oh, no, officer," says the driver, pointing to his forehead, "We're trying to give up, so we're on the patch."

↠ Trailertrash Cletus was enjoying his normal Saturday afternoon activities (watching TV and drinking beer) when his wife came storming into the trailer. "Cletus, some man's been real rude to me and I want you to go and kick his ass!" she screamed. "Why, sure thing, Maylene," said Cletus, getting to his feet, "you jus' tell me what he done did to you." "Well," said Maylene, "I was at the supermarket and

I dropped something. When I bent over to pick it up this man looked up my dress." Cletus started stamping his feet. "And then, when I got back up, he said, 'I'd like to fill you up with beer and drink the lot from down there!'" Cletus sat down straight away. Maylene asked, "Ain't you goin' do nothin', Cletus?" Cletus said, "You must be kidding, Maylene – I ain't gonna mess with someone who can drink that much beer!"

Spanish wine, my God, it is foul – catpiss is champagne, compared – this is the sulphurous urination of some aged horse.

DH Lawrence

➡ Two drunkards were sitting at the bar. One was crying. The other asked him what was wrong. "I've puked all over myself again, and my wife is going to leave me this time; she warned me about it." The other drunk said "Do what I do, pal. Explain to your wife that some other guy puked on you. Put a tenner in your shirt pocket, and tell her that he was sorry and gave you the cash to get your clothes cleaned." "Sounds like a great idea," said the first drunk. When he got home, his wife was furious and started shouting at him about his clothes, how disgusting he was and that she'd had enough; she was off. The drunk started telling his lie, saying: "Look for yourself; there's the money in my shirt pocket." His wife looked in the pocket and found twenty quid. "Hang on a minute," she said suspiciously, "I thought you said the bloke gave you ten pounds for puking on you, not 20." The drunk nods, "Yeah, he did, but he crapped in my pants too."

➥ What's the difference between an Irish woman and an Irish goddess? About five pints.

Bosses

➥ A fellow had just been hired as the new managing director of a large high-tech corporation. The managing director who was stepping down, met him privately and presented him with three numbered envelopes. "Open these if you run up against a problem you don't think you can solve," he said. Well, things went along pretty smoothly, but six months later sales took a downturn and the new MD was really catching a lot of heat. About at his wits' end, he remembered the envelopes. He went to his drawer and took out the first envelope. The message read, "Blame your predecessor." The new MD called a press conference and tactfully laid the blame at the feet of the previous MD. Satisfied with his comments, the press – and the City responded positively, sales began to pick up and the problem was soon behind him. About a year later, the company was again experiencing a slight dip in sales, combined with serious product problems. Having learned from his previous experience, the MD quickly opened the second envelope. The message read, "Reorganize." This he did, and the company quickly rebounded. After several consecutive profitable quarters, the company once again fell on difficult times. The MD went to his office, closed the door and opened the third envelope. The message said: "Prepare three envelopes."

➥ All play and no work will qualify you for life as a director.

➤ Secretary: "I would like to inform you that I have found a new position." Boss: "Great, what are we waiting for? Let's try it."

➤ A man goes to an office and sees a crying secretary. "Excuse me, but what is the matter with you?" "My boss told me that I'm not pretty enough to make so many typing errors..."

➤ As productivity has not increased since the implementation of the seven-day working week, the stoppage of all company health and retirement plans, the 20% pay cut, the ten-year pay freeze, the installation of video cameras in company restrooms, the hiring of the corporate truant officers to check up on all employees calling in sick, and the random drug and dirty underwear screenings, management has decided that the beatings and mandatory self-flagellations will continue until morale improves.

He does the work of three men:
Larry, Curly and Moe.
Anonymous

➤ The boss returned from lunch in a good mood and called the whole staff in to listen to a couple of jokes he had picked up. Everybody but one girl laughed uproariously. "What's the matter?" grumbled the boss. "Haven't you got a sense of humour?" "I don't have to laugh," she said, "I'm leaving on Friday."

➤ The morning after throwing a party for his boss, Nigel was nursing a king-size hangover and, finding his memory a bit sketchy, asked his wife, "What the hell happened last night?" She shuddered. "As usual, you made a complete idiot of yourself in front of your boss," replied the wife. "Piss on him," answered Nigel. "You did," said his wife. "He fired you." Nigel grunted, "Well, fuck him then." "I did," she replied, "and he gave you your job back."

> **He doesn't know the meaning of the word 'fear'**
> **– but then again he doesn't know the meaning**
> **of most words.**
>
> *Anonymous*

➤ The president of a large corporation opened his directors' meeting by announcing: "All those who are opposed to the plan I am about to propose will reply by saying, 'I resign'."

➤ When the Lord made man, all the parts of the body argued over who would be boss. The brain explained that since he controlled all the parts of the body, he should be boss. The legs argued that since they took the man wherever he wanted to go, they should be boss. The stomach suggested that since he digested all the food, he should be boss. The eyes said that without them man would be helpless, so they should be boss. And so it went on. The hands, heart, ears and lungs each demanded that they be made boss. Then the arsehole applied for the job, but the other parts just laughed, so the arsehole became mad and closed up. After a few days, the brain went foggy, the legs got wobbly, the stomach got ill and the eyes got crossed and unable to see. They all conceded and made the arsehole boss. This proves that you don't have to be a brain to be a boss, just an arsehole.

BOYFRIENDS

➤ "My boyfriend can dial my telephone number with his tongue."
"That's nothing, mine uses his Dictaphone."

➤ A hippie with no job kept begging his girlfriend to marry him. She declined for months, saying he needed to get a job first. He always told her, "We can live on love, baby." Finally she relented, and they got married. The morning after their honeymoon, she got up, turned the cooker on to a low setting, and sat on the ring. "What are you doing, baby?" asked the hippie. "I'm heating your breakfast," she replied.

➤ A man was on a blind date. He had spent the whole evening with this woman he just couldn't stand. She was everything he didn't like in a woman, and he was really bored to death. Luckily he had prepared for just this eventuality and had asked one of his mates to call the restaurant he was eating at, just in case he needed a getaway plan. So when the call came, he rushed over to the phone and feigned surprise and shock. When he returned to the table, his date looked up and asked, "Is everything all right?" He replied, "Not really. I'm afraid I'm going to have to go. My grandfather just died." "Thank God for that," the woman said. "If yours hadn't, mine would have had to!"

Love is not really blind – the bandage is never so tight but that it can peep.

Elbert Hubbard, 1856 – 1915

➠ John says to his girlfriend, "Why don't you shout my name out when you come?" she answers, "Yeah – like you're ever there when I come!"

➠ My boyfriend said that his doctor needed a urine sample, some faeces and a semen specimen. I told him, "Just hand them your boxers."

➠ My ex-boyfriend was a poor communicator. It's hard to drink beer and talk at the same time.

➠ One day in a jewellery shop a man is in the process of buying a really expensive necklace with a lovely silver locket on it. The jeweller asks him, "Would you like her name engraved on it?" The man has a think and then replies, "No, just put 'To my one and only love.' That way, if we split up and she throws it back in anger, I'll be able to recycle!"

➠ This guy had been dating this girl for some time when she invited him over to her parents' house for dinner to meet them. When they got there, the guy realized he was so tense that he was starting to get really bad gas. They sat down for dinner but he just couldn't hold it in any longer. A fart slipped out. The mother yelled "Spot!" The guy realized the family dog was under his chair, and was relieved that the dog had got the blame. A few minutes later he let another one go and the mother again yelled "Spot!" Again, the boyfriend was relieved that the dog had been told off, so he decided he might as well get it all out, and let this huge fart go. "Spot!" the mother yelled. "Get out from under there before he shits on you!"

➻ This mushroom girl was gushing to one of her pals about a new boyfriend. "Oh, Lucy," she said, "He's such a fun guy..."

Women are well aware that what is commonly called sublime and poetical love depends not upon moral qualities, but on frequent meetings, the style in which the hair is done up, and on the colour and cut of the dress.

Leo Tolstoy

➻ Two women had met for coffee. One noticed that her friend seemed troubled, and asked, "Is something wrong? You look stressed." Her friend sighed. "Well, my boyfriend just lost all his money and life savings in a nasty stock market crash. He's totally bankrupt," she explained. "Oh, that's dreadful," the other girl sympathised. "You must feel really worried about him." "Yeah, I am," replied her friend, "I don't know what he's going to do without me."

➻ What do you do if your bank account stops working? Ditch him.

BRUNETTES

➻ Are brunettes sexually active? Nope, they just lie there.

➻ How can two brunettes become invisible in a crowd of three? When they're with a blonde.

↢ The good thing about dwarf brunettes is that they're only half as ugly.

↢ What did the blonde mother say to her daughter on Saturday night? "If you're not in bed by 12, come home."

You see an awful lot of smart guys with dumb women, but you hardly ever see a smart woman with a dumb guy.

Erica Jong

↢ What do brunettes miss most about a great party? The invitation.

↢ What do you call a brunette in a waterbed? The dead sea.

↢ What do you call a brunette whose phone rings on Saturday night? Shocked.

↢ What do you call a brunette with large breasts? A mutant.

↢ What do you call a good-looking man with a brunette? A hostage.

↢ What is it called when a brunette dyes her hair blonde? Self-improvement.

↢ Why are brunettes flat-chested? It makes it easier to read their T-shirts.

↢ Why do brunettes take the pill? Wishful thinking.

➽ Why did they stop producing brunette Barbie dolls? Parents were scared that the dandruff might be contagious.

➽ Why do brunettes have to pay extra for breast implants? Because the plastic surgeon has to start from scratch.

BUGS

➽ "No!" said the lady millipede, crossing her legs, "no, a thousand times no!"

➽ A centipede is an inchworm gone metric.

➽ A fly goes into a pub and orders a drink. The customer on the next stool glances at him and says to the landlord, "What's with him?" The landlord says, "Oh, he works in the restaurant down the street." The man says to the fly, "That's fascinating. What kind of work do you do?" The fly sighs, "They put me in bowls of soup. It's tough on my health."

➽ A team of elephants had agreed to play a game of football against a team of ants. Things were going well for the ants – more agile and more nimble than the elephants – when the referee whistled loudly. Everybody from both teams gathered around the remains of an unfortunate ant, now completely squashed to bits on the pitch. "There you are," an ant complained bitterly. "You just can't trust the big people to play fair!" "I didn't want this to happen," the elephant said guiltily. "I just wanted to trip him over."

✦ How do you spot a gay termite? He'll only eat woodpeckers.

✦ In proportion to its body size, the drone (male) bee has one of the largest penises of any animal on earth. The size of its tackle is thought to be a direct cause of the drone's post-coital fate – death. Its genitals are contained in its abdomen, and presumably getting them out for a bit of slap-and-tickle places such a huge strain on the bee that it dies in the process. The most immediate cause of the drone's death, however, is that its privates are ripped off during the mating. Despite its status as the bee stud, the drone is not itself produced as a result of sex. On the contrary, it develops from an unfertilised egg: fertilised eggs become either workers or queens. The queen bee is capable of reproducing on its own, and drone bees have no father, only a grandfather. You may think your family has problems, but the chances are your grandpa ain't your daddy, and you don't have a four-foot cock buried in your stomach which gets torn off when you shag.

✦ On the most recent flight of the space shuttle, astronauts conducted an important scientific experiment with fruit flies and gleaned a valuable insight. Zero gravity makes the little buggers far easier to swat.

✦ The Washington Post reported in September 1993 that at the Third Annual Slugfest in Fairfax County, Va., 'Slippery' beat 49 other slugs in the Tour de Slug race. Also featured at the festival: slug face-painting, the slime toss, and the official drink – green 'slimeade'. A 12-year-old boy demonstrated his skill at flicking his tongue in and out of his mouth with his slug, Mickey, attached. He said that despite washing Mickey several times with soap beforehand, "the slime still sticks between your teeth. I've still got some slime from yesterday."

➤ This termite walks into a pub and says "Is the bar tender here?"

➤ Two boy silkworms pursued a luscious girl silkworm. They ended up in a tie.

It's a fine day. Let's go out and kill something creepy.

Anonymous

➤ What's the last thing that goes through a bee's mind when it hits a car windscreen at 70mph? Its arse.

➤ When a San Francisco insecticide manufacturer ran a contest in August, 1994, looking for the most cockroach-infested house in the country to demonstrate its pest control prowess, Rosemary Mitchell of Tulsa, Oklahoma, really wanted to win, and she did. The prize: a house call from a roach expert, entomologist Austin Frishman, aka television's 'Dr Cockroach', who began work on the home after estimating that her one-story house harboured between 60,000 and 100,000 roaches. Mitchell said, "I keep a pretty clean house," but admitted that she had to check the bed thoroughly every night and shake the shower curtains off every morning. Frishman said that he had seen a lot worse and rated Mitchell's house only a three on a scale of one to five.

➼ Two cockroaches were munching on garbage in an alley. "I was in that new restaurant across the street," said one. "It's so clean! The kitchen is spotless, the floors are gleaming white. It's so sanitary the whole place shines." "Please," said the other cockroach, frowning, "not while I'm eating!"

➼ What does the female part of a snail say during sex? Faster, faster, faster!

BULLS and COWS

➼ A farmer down the road has a fairly large herd of cows and three bulls. Each bull keeps a strict eye on his portion of the cows. A rumour comes around that the farmer is going to get another bull and the three bulls are standing in the field discussing this. The first bull says, "Well, there's no way he's going to get any of my cows." The second bull agrees, "Yeah, I'm not giving up any. He can wait till next year and get some of the new ones." The third bull, who was a bit smaller, says, "I don't have as many as you guys, so I'm not giving any up." Finally, the new bull arrives. The first three gather at the edge of the field to watch him being unloaded from the trailer. To their consternation, the biggest, meanest Aberdeen Angus bull they have ever seen, with hooves like flint anvils, comes strolling down the ramp and glares at them. He's at least three times bigger than any of them. The first bull looks around nervously and says, "Well, now, I suppose it would be a neighbourly thing to give this guy some cows. I think I'll give him 20 of mine." The second bull says, "Yeah, I guess so; I'll give him 30 of mine." They look over at the small bull. He's busy pawing the grass, snorting, and shaking his head. They go over and ask him what he's doing, and suggest that he should give up some cows too. "Yes, I know," he says, "I'm just making sure he knows I'm a bull!"

➻ A New York family bought a ranch out in the West, where they intended to raise cattle. When some stockbroker friends came out for a visit, they asked if the ranch had a name. "Well," said the new cattleman, "I wanted to name it the Bar-J, my wife favoured Suzy-Q, one son liked the Flying-W and the other wanted the Lazy-Y. We argued about it for a bit and then we decided to compromise, so we're calling it the Bar-J-Suzy-Q-Flying-W-Lazy-Y." "But where are all your cattle?" a friend asked. The rancher sighed. "Actually, none survived being branded."

Animals generally return the love you lavish on them by a swift bite in passing.

Gerald Durrell

➻ A non-too-bright zebra escaped from a zoo and ended up in a field full of cows. He walked up to one and said: "Hi there! What do you do around here then?" "I eat grass all day and get milked morning and night," replied the cow. "Oh," the zebra said. He walked idly about and met another cow. "Hi there! Say, what do you do around here then?" he asked again. "I eat grass all day and get milked morning and night," replied the cow. The zebra nodded, pleased by the quietness and the sense of purpose of the cows' lives, then walked over to a bull. "Hello," he said. "What do you do around here?" The bull looked him up and down and said: "Get those pyjamas off and I'll show you."

➻ A Norwich University professor has been studying cow flatulence for 20 years, and has determined that the average cow emits 200 to 400 litres of methane gas PER DAY, resulting in a total annual world cow methane output of 50 million metric TONS! This is why you should never allow a cow inside your sleeping bag!!

➻ A tourist went into a restaurant in Spain and ordered the speciality of the house. When his dinner arrived, he asked the waiter what it was. "These, señor," replied the waiter in broken English, "are the cojones – how you say, the testicles – of the bull that was killed in the ring today." The tourist swallowed hard but tasted the dish and, lo and behold, it was delicious. So he went back the next evening and ordered the same item. When it arrived, he had a look and said to the waiter, "These cojones, or whatever you call them...they're much smaller than the ones I had last night." "Si, señor," replied the waiter, "You see, the bull...he does not always lose."

➻ There was a herd of cattle all standing on a hill when an earthquake struck. All of the cows fell down, but the bull remained standing. The farmer, noticing this, went out and asked the bull, "Why didn't you fall down like the rest of the herd?" The bull replied: "We bulls wobble, but we never fall down."

➻ Two cows were chatting to each other over the fence between their fields. The first cow said, "I'm telling you, this mad cow disease really scares me. They say it's spreading fast – I heard it hit some cows down on old Patterson's farm." The other cow replied, "Oh, I'm not worried. It doesn't affect us ducks."

➡ Two cows were standing in a field. One cow says to the other, "Moooooo." The other says, "I was just going to say that."

I do not like animals, of any sort. I don't even like the idea of animals. Animals are no friend of mine. They are not welcome in my house. However, I like them just fine in the form of nice, crisp spare-ribs and Bass Weejun penny-loafers.

Fran Lebowitz

➡ What do bulls do to stay warm on cold days? Go into the barn and slip into a nice warm Jersey.

➡ What do you call a cow that has had an abortion? Decalfinated.

➡ Why do cows have bells? Because their horns don't work.

CANNIBALS

➡ Two cannibals walked into a pub and sat down beside a clown. Suddenly the first cannibal whipped out his hunting knife, stabbed the clown through the heart and proceeded to butcher him on the spot. He then cut off a couple of big chunks, handed one to his mate and they both started eating. Suddenly the second cannibal looks up at his friend and says, "Wait a moment. Do you taste something funny?"

➤ An ambassador from an African country was visiting Russia. The Russian ambassador to his country was entertaining him, and despite the obvious cultural differences, the two of them got on really well. The African gentleman was impressed by the hospitality that he was shown and on the final day of the visit the Russian offered to show him the traditional game of the country – Russian Roulette. The African man had not heard of this game, so the Russian explained the rules. "You pick up a revolver. You empty the cylinder. You replace one bullet. You spin the cylinder. You turn the gun to yourself and pull the trigger once." The African ambassador found this a bit scary, but coming from a proud warrior people he thought it would be exciting. The Russian man produced two revolvers and when both guns were loaded, both men turned them on themselves and pulled the triggers at the same time. There were two loud clicks and both breathed a huge sigh of relief. The African ambassador was very impressed with the game and thought about it all the way home. One year later, the Russian ambassador visited the Africa country to finalize a deal between the two countries. His hospitality was returned, much to his pleasure, and he and the African ambassador got on as well as before. On his last night, the African man said he would show him his country's traditional game. The Russian was impressed, and eager to see what the African had to offer him. The African ambassador led him to a plush room, deep in the state building. Standing before them were six beautiful women, all completely naked. The African said, "These are the most beautiful women from each of the six tribes of the country. Any one of them will give you the best blowjob of your life – just choose one." The Russian was impressed, but he couldn't help feeling there was something missing from this game. He said to the African ambassador, "That's great and everything, but compared to the national game from my country there is something missing – where's the danger, the excitement, the chance?" The African ambassador, with a wide grin on his face, answers, "One of these women is a cannibal!"

If there had been any formidable body of cannibals in the country he would have promised to provide them with free missionaries, fattened at the taxpayer's expense.

H L Mencken, on Harry Truman's 1948 presidential campaign

❧ Two explorers are walking through a rainforest when they are captured by a tribe of tiny, but highly aggressive, cannibals. Minutes later they find themselves tied up tight, sitting in a huge pot full of water and vegetables with an enormous fire burning underneath it. After a couple of minutes one of them starts to laugh. The other one is shocked and assumes the man has lost his mind. "What the heck is up with you?" he asks, "We're going to die in here and be eaten by a bunch of horrible cannibals. What on earth do you find funny about that?" The other replies, "I just peed in the pot!"

cars

❧ A car company is planning to build a new model made from all its previous engineering errors. The new model will be called Total Recall.

**To buy a Volvo 540 because it is better than the
Volvo 400 is like having someone to dinner because
they are better company than Myra Hindley.**

*Jeremy Clarkson, not quite comparing a Volvo
to a noted mass-murderess*

↦ A recent campaign calling for car safety awareness
was launched with a national Child Car Safety Week. A
spokesman said, "Over the course of this week we hope to
make everyone think about the safety of children in cars. All
children should wear a seatbelt. Then, next week, everyone
can go back to slinging their kids through windscreens as
normal."

↦ Where in the Bible does it describe the most people in one
automobile? In The Acts of the Apostles it says that 100 people
went to Jerusalem "in one Accord."

**What's the average man's life but a succession
of cars? When he dies, we should carve on his
tombstone simply the makes and years.**

Richard Needham

CATS

↦ A bloke is in his back garden one lazy Sunday afternoon when
he hears some crunching next door. Being nosy, he looks over
the fence and sees his neighbour digging a hole in his garden.
Naturally, he asks what the hole is for. "My canary died and I'm

burying it," said the neighbour. "Oh, I'm sorry about that," says the bloke insincerely. "That's a pretty big hole for a canary, isn't it?" he added. "Well, yes," replies the neighbour, "but it's inside your fucking cat!"

**Cat, n: A soft, indestructible automaton
provided by nature to be kicked when things
go wrong in the domestic circle.**

Ambrose Bierce, The Devil's Dictionary

↠ Cats are intended to teach us that not everything in nature has a function.

↠ Cats took many thousands of years to domesticate humans.

↠ Dogs come when called. Cats take a message and get back to you.

↠ How do you know when your cat's finished cleaning itself? He smokes a cigarette.

↠ How do you make a cat go woof? Douse it in petrol and throw a match at it.

↠ How do you spoil a cat? Leave it out in the sun.

↠ In ancient Rome, the cat was considered a symbol of liberty. Anyone who watches a cat can see that he always does exactly as he pleases.

➻ Janet went to a bridge club every Thursday night, and after a peaceful game or two with the ladies she would return home to fix her husband dinner when he got home from the pub. One Thursday she was playing a great game, and had an incredible hand, when she noticed the time. "Oh, no! I have to go fix my husband his dinner! He's going to be so angry if it's not ready on time." She dashed out of her friend's house, her great hand forgotten on the table. When she got home, she realised she had very little food in the cupboard and not enough time to go to the grocery store. All she had was a wilted lettuce leaf, an egg and a can of cat food. In a panic, she opened the can of cat food, stirred in the egg and garnished it with the lettuce leaf just as her husband was pulling up. While she watched in horror he sat down to his dinner – and then she realised he was really enjoying it! "Mmmm, darling, this is the best dinner you've made for me in 40 years of marriage. You can cook this for me whenever you want!" That night they had sex for the first time in months, and it was incredible! Needless to say, every Thursday from then on she made the cat food dinner for her husband. She told her bridge friends about it and they were horrified. "You're going to kill him," one said. "He's just winding you up," accused another. Janet continued to make him his cat food dinner on a Thursday, and then afterwards they would shag like fiends. Two months later, Janet's husband died. On the Thursday after the funeral, the bridge ladies attacked her for being so callous. "You killed him!" one said. "We told you that feeding him that cat food every week would do him in! How can you just sit there so calmly and play bridge knowing you murdered your husband?" Janet calmly replied, "Ahh, come off it. I didn't kill him. He smashed his skull falling off the mantelpiece while licking his arse."

↔ Radioactive cats have 18 half-lives.

The cat Percy, for all his sleek exterior, was mean and bitter. He had no music in his soul, and was fit for treasons, strategies and spoils. One could picture him stealing milk from a sick tabby.

PG Wodehouse, Cats Will Be Cats

↔ Some feline definitions:

Human being: An automatic door opener for cats.
Purranoia: The fear that your cat is up to something.
Purring: The sound of a cat making cuteness.
Purrpetual motion: A kitten at play.
Purrverse: Poem about a kinky cat.
Pussy Whip: The dessert topping for cats.

↔ The cat agenda: variety is the spice of life. One day, ignore people; the next day, annoy them. Only play with them when they're busy.

↔ What do you do with four dead cats and a sheet of glass? Make a coffee table.

↔ What goes plink, plink, fizz? Kittens in an acid bath.

↔ What is worse than a dead cat in a dustbin? Ten dead cats in a dustbin.

↔ What's more fun than nailing a cat to a fence? Ripping it back off.

➼ What's pink and spits? A cat in a frying pan.

➼ What's the difference between a cat and a bagel? You can put a bagel in the toaster, but you have to put the cat in the oven.

➼ What's worse than finding a dead cat on your pillow in the morning? Realizing you were drunk and made love to it the night before.

God save all here, barring the cat.

Irish saying

➼ Which is easier to unload, a truck full of dead cats or a truck full of bowling balls? Dead cats, because you can use a pitchfork.

CATERING STUDENTS

➼ How many catering students does it take to eat a hedgehog? Three: one to do the eating, and two to watch for cars.

➼ How many catering students does it take to make chocolate chip cookies? Three: one to mix the batter and two to squeeze the rabbit.

➼ A catering student decides to raise chickens, so he goes to the pet shop and buys some baby chicks. He takes the chicks home, and plants them with their heads sticking up. He waters them, but they die. He goes back to the shop and tells the proprietor that he bought defective chicks, and gets another set. This time he plants them with their heads sticking down. He waters them, but they die. Finally he sends a letter to his old college, describing the problem and asking for advice. They send a letter back asking for a soil sample.

The average cooking in the average hotel for the average Englishman explains to a large extent the English bleakness and taciturnity. Nobody can beam and warble while chewing pressed beef smeared with diabolical mustard. Nobody can exult aloud while ungluing from his teeth a quivering tapioca pudding.

Karel Capek, 1890 – 1938

→ Did you hear about the catering student who was tap-dancing? He broke his ankle when he fell into the sink.

→ Did you hear about the skeleton they just found in an old building at the Catering College? It was the 1938 hide and seek champion.

→ Did you hear that they outlawed 'the wave' at Catering College? Two poor students drowned at a game last year.

→ How can you tell which person is the catering student on a drilling rig? He's the one throwing bread to the helicopters.

→ Ice is no longer available in the drinks at the cafeterias at the Catering College. The student who knew the recipe graduated.

➻ Three college friends, one each from the universities of Oxford, Cambridge, and Loughborough, decided to pool their funds and go to the Olympics in Barcelona. The airfare and hotel rates ate up most of their money so they didn't have enough to get into the stadium to see the events. So they stood around the gate watching all the other people get in and then noticed that some people didn't have to pay. Whenever an athlete passed the guard with his (or her) equipment, the guard would simply nod and let them through. So the three visitors quickly trotted off to a nearby hardware shop and came back to try to get in. The Oxford student walked up to the guard and gestured at the long pole he carried. "Pole vaulting," he said, and the guard waved him through. The Cambridge student, having rigged up a ball to a length of chain, approached the guard next and showed off his wares. "Hammer throwing," he said, and the guard shrugged and waved him through. The catering student from Loughborough came last, with a roll of chain-link on his shoulder. "Fencing."

➻ Two ex-catering students decide to have a reunion. One decides to visit the other one, living in a big town. The visiting student gets lost and calls his friend: "Hey buddy, I am coming over but I am lost and have no idea where I am." His friend replies: "It's okay, just look at the street intersection, there will be two signs, read them to me." The lost one looks over and then says: "Okay, okay, I see them, one says Walk, the other one says Do not walk." "Oh good, you are right down the street. I'll be over to pick you up."

➻ Why don't catering students eat barbecue beans? Because they keep falling through the holes in the grill.

CHEATING AND INFIDELITY

➤ "I wanted sex with a fitter, more attractive man, so I signed my husband up for a slimming group." "Is it working?" "Oh yes – he goes to the meetings every week – and while he's there his hot younger brother comes round and fucks me."

> **I can understand companionship. I can understand bought sex in the afternoon. I cannot understand the love affair.**
>
> *Gore Vidal*

➤ A couple were sitting in the living room watching TV. The phone rang, so the husband picked it up. He listened for a moment, and then said, in a sarcastic tone of voice, "I have no idea. Why don't you call the weather centre?" and hung up. "What was that all about?" asked his wife. "Oh, I don't know," replied the husband. "Some idiot wanted to know if the coast was clear."

➤ A guy is having a quiet breakfast when he is suddenly interrupted by his wife, who starts yelling at him: "I found this piece of paper in your pocket! Who is Marylou?" "Oh, that's nothing dear," the bloke says. "It's a horse. I bet on this horse last week you see." His wife smiles contritely, realizes she's made a fool of herself and lets it go at that. The bloke goes to work and when he comes back home, he finds his wife on the porch, her face like a thundercloud, having made a mess of his stereo and his collection of CDs on the front lawn. "What is the matter, honey?" he asks. "You got a call from the horse."

➤ A doctor and his wife were having a big argument over breakfast. "Well, you're no bloody good in bed either!" he yelled, and stomped off to work. By midday, he had relented, and decided he'd better apologise. He called home, and after a great many rings, his wife picked up the phone. "What took you so long to answer?" he asked. "I was in bed," came the reply. "What were you doing in bed this late?" There was a moment's silence; then she said archly, "Getting a second opinion."

➤ A doctor rushed out of his study. "Quick, grab my bag, darling!" he said to his lovely young wife. "Why?" she asked, alarmed. "What's the matter?" "Some bloke just called and said he can't live without me," he gasped, reaching for his hat. His wife sighed. "Um, wait up a moment, will you," she said, gently. "I think that call was for me."

➤ A guy walks into a gun shop. "I'd like to buy a laser sight for a rifle, please." The salesman fetches one and encourages him to try it out. The man is looking around the neighbourhood when he sees, through a window, a man and a woman on the job. "Whoa! Check this out!" he says to the salesman, who has a look for himself. His eyes nearly jump out of his head as he sees that it is his wife with another man. No decent shot himself, he makes the guy the following offer: "If you can shoot him in the dick and her in the head I'll give you the laser sight and the rifle of your choice." "Sure thing," says the guy, and he takes aim and looses off a shot. "What luck – two for one, job done," he says.

↠ A little boy starts to notice the loud, heavy bouncing noises of his parents having sex at night. Curious, he asks his mother what the noises are. She doesn't really want to go into it, so just explains that she bounces on top of his father to help him to stay thin and to make his stomach smaller. "I don't think it's going to work," says the boy. "Why ever not?" asks the mother. "Because every morning after you go to work, Elsie from next door comes over and blows Daddy back up again!"

↠ A man and a woman were eating in a swanky restaurant. Their waitress, taking another order at a table a few feet away, noticed the man slowly sliding down his chair and under the table. The woman dining across from him appeared calm and unruffled, apparently unaware that her companion had disappeared. Wanting to make sure that no monkey business was going on the waitress finished taking her order, crossed over to the table and said to the woman, "Pardon me, madam, but I believe your husband just slid under the table." The woman calmly looked up, shook her head and replied, "No, he didn't. As a matter of fact he just walked in, and is heading in this direction..."

↠ A man and woman have been married for what seems like for ever. They have eight grown-up children and countless grandchildren. On their 60th wedding anniversary they have a very candid conversation. The wife says to her husband, "Honey, since we are so old now and we've been together for so long, I'm going to be totally honest with you. Is there anything you'd like to know about me and our relationship over the past six decades that you'd like to ask me about? If there is, I promise that I will answer you with total honesty." The husband pauses for a while, and then says,

"Dear, this isn't easy for me to say, but there is actually something that has been eating away at me for quite a few years now. It's just that of all our kids, there's one who looks decidedly different from the others. You know the one I mean, I'm sure, and I'm sure it's nothing but, as I say, I've wondered about this for years and I would like to know if he had a different father from the rest of the kids." The wife looks down at her feet and sighs loudly. "Well, dear, I'm sorry to say it, but you're right. I cannot tell a lie, that child did indeed have a different father from all the others." The husband looks miserable, but he's still curious. "And who would that be?" he asks. "Well, dear..." begins the wife slowly, "...you."

➥ A man came home one afternoon and discovered his wife busily trying to cover up the obvious signs of wild sex. "Was it my friend Steve?" he yelled, furiously. "No," she said. "Well, was it my friend Rael?" he then asked. "Look," she shouted back, irritated, "don't you think I have any friends of my own?"

➥ A man goes away on a business trip and, as it's a very swanky hotel, his wife comes to join him for the weekend. They have a nice dinner in the restaurant, a drink in the bar, and then they can't wait to go up to their room. In fact, they can't even wait that long – as soon as they get into the lift they're all over each other. The man is pulling her panties down and in less than a minute they're at it. Unfortunately, the doors open at the next floor and the chambermaid gets in. "Well, really!" says the chambermaid. "I'm sorry," says the woman, "we just had a couple of drinks and got a bit carried away. I don't normally behave this way." "I'm sure you don't," says the chambermaid, "but this is the fourth time this week I've caught him at it."

➤ A man had a beautiful but very demanding wife. She always wanted the latest fashion clothes and beautiful jewellery, but he didn't really make enough money to get her all that she wanted. One day she comes home showing off a brand-new diamond necklace. "Wow," he says to her, "where did you get that?" "Oh, I won it at bingo, darling," she says, rather unconvincingly. The next day the wife comes home wearing a brand-new mink coat. "Wow," he says to her, "where did you get that?" "Oh, I won it at bingo, darling – I've had a lucky week, you know." The next day the wife comes home in a brand-new Porsche. "Wow," he says, "where did you get that?" "Oh, stop asking me all those awkward questions, please. Leave me alone and do something useful. Go upstairs and run me a bath, there's a dear." The wife comes upstairs and into the bathroom. There's only a tiny amount of water in the bottom of the bath. The wife says, "What's up with the depth of that bath? That's not even going to reach my pussy!" And the husband replies, "Didn't want to get your bingo card wet, dear!"

➤ A woman is lying in bed with her lover when she hears her husband coming in. "Quick!" she says to her lover, "There's no time to get dressed. Stand in the corner and I'll cover you with talcum powder." In comes the husband and he immediately asks, "Is that a new statue?" "That's right," replies the wife, "The Smiths had one in their bedroom and I liked it so much I got one, too." The husband says nothing else, but gets into bed, leaving the 'statue' standing as still as he can in the corner. Around four in the morning, the husband gets up and comes back with a cup of tea and a plate of biscuits, which he puts down beside the 'statue'. "There," he says, "have a biscuit. I was stuck in the Smiths' bedroom for three days, and nobody offered me so much as a drink of water."

There is only one way to be happy by means of the heart – to have none.

Paul Bourget

➡ An old lighthouse keeper lives alone with his wife on a remote rock, until a young assistant is sent to join them. On the first day, the young assistant offers to take the first watch at the top of the lighthouse, so the keeper and his wife can have some time together. "But no shagging," he says. "I'm here without a wife or girlfriend, so it wouldn't be fair." The keeper and his wife stroll along the beach hand-in-hand, and the assistant shouts down, "Hey! No shagging!" "We're not shagging," calls the keeper, "we're just holding hands." They go and sit outside the keeper's cottage and do a crossword together, but the assistant shouts down, "Hey! I said no shagging! It's not fair!" "We're not shagging!" answers the keeper. After lunch, the wife offers to show the assistant around the island, and the keeper goes to the top of the lighthouse. "Well, I never!" he says to himself. "From up here, it does look exactly like they're shagging!"

➡ Mr Matthews sat in his attorney's office. "Do you want the bad news first or the terrible news?" the lawyer said. "Give me the bad news first." "Your wife found a picture worth a half-million dollars." "That's the bad news?" asked Matthews incredulously. "I can't wait to hear the terrible news." "The terrible news is that it's of you and your secretary."

➡ One day, a sweet little girl goes home to find that her dog has died. He is lying on the lawn on his back with his poor little legs sticking straight up in the air. She quickly runs to her father and asks him why her dog is lying down with his poor little legs in the air. "Well," her father explains, "that's because Jesus will be coming down to help poor doggy up to Heaven, and if his legs are up in the air like that it'll be a whole lot easier for him to go." The very next day when the father comes home, the sweet little girl runs up to him in a dreadful state. "Daddy! Daddy! Mummy almost died today – I'm sure of it!" "Oh, my!" says the father. "How do you know – is she OK?" "Yes, Daddy," the girl says, "she's OK now, but earlier on Mummy's legs were up in the air and she was shouting 'Oh Jesus, I'm coming, I'm coming,' and if the postman hadn't been there to hold her down I think she'd be in Heaven now!"

➳ This guy took his nymphomaniac wife to the sex therapist for treatment. "This is one hot potato of a lady, doctor," he said, "maybe you can do something for her. She goes for any man, any age, any time, anywhere...and it is just driving me crazy with jealousy." "We'll see," the therapist said. He directed the wife into his examining room, closed the door behind her, and told her to get undressed. Then he told her to get up on to the examining table on her stomach. The moment he touched her buttocks, she began to squirm and moan. It was too much for him to resist, so he climbed up on top of her and began screwing her. The husband heard the moans and groans coming from the examination room and, very suspicious, burst into the room. He was confronted by the sight of the doctor astride his wife and banging away. "Doctor, what are you doing?" he asked. Flustered, the therapist replied, "Oh, it's you. I'm only taking your wife's temperature." The husband pulled out a large pocket knife and began to hone it deliberately on his boot. "Well, doctor," he said, "when you take that thing out, it had better have numbers on it."

➼ Two blokes go into a pub to check out the local talent. The first one looks around, and says "Wow, look at the blonde over there in the crop-top. I bet she's really wild in the sack." He goes over to her and starts to make small-talk. Before long, the two of them are heading off out back to her place for a quick shag. The two blokes meet up again the next night in the same bar, and sure enough the blonde is there again. "She's really up for it," says the first one, "Why don't you go give it a shot?" Well, the second bloke goes over and pinches her ass; they start chatting, and five minutes later they're out the back of the pub. When he gets back after 20 minutes or so, he goes over to compare notes with his mate. "So, what do you think? I reckon my wife is better," says the first bloke. "Yeah," says the second bloke, "your wife is better."

That gentlemen prefer blondes is due to the fact that, apparently, pale hair, delicate skin and an infantile expression represent the very apex of a frailty which every man longs to violate.

Alexander King

➼ Two guys are trying to get in a quick 18 holes, but there are two terrible lady golfers in front of them hitting the ball everywhere but where it's supposed to go. The first guy says, "Why don't you go over and ask if we can play through?" The second guy gets about halfway there, stops and comes back. The first guy says, "What's wrong?" His friend says: "One of these two women is my wife and the other one is my mistress. There is no way I could be seen with both of them! You'll have to go." The first guy laughs. "Yes, I can see that could be a problem! You're right, I'll go over." He gets about halfway there and comes back. The second guy says, "What's wrong?" "Small world," the first guy says with an apologetic grin.

➼ What do men and women have in common? They both distrust men.

CHEMISTS

➼ A chap walks into a local pharmacy and walks up to the counter where a lady pharmacist is filling prescriptions. When she finally gets around to helping him he says, "I'd like 99 condoms, please." With a surprised look on her face the pharmacist says, "You want 99 condoms! Fuck me!" To which the guy replies, "Make it 100."

➼ A man goes into a chemist's shop and asks to speak to a male chemist, as he has an embarrassing problem. "I'm sorry," says the female chemist, "My sister and I run this shop, you'll have to speak to one of us about it." Well, the man's very embarrassed, but he tells her that he's had a permanent hard-on for the last year and whatever he does, he can't get rid of it for more than ten minutes. "Can you give me anything for it?" The chemist says she needs to consult her sister, and two minutes later comes back and says, "The best we can manage is £30,000 a year and a third share of the shop."

➼ A woman walks into a chemist and asks if they sell extra-large condoms. "Yes, we do – how many do you want?" "I don't want to buy any – but if anybody else does, can you give them my phone number?"

A perfectly good second-class chemist, a Beta chemist, she wasn't an interesting person, except as a Conservative. I would never, if I had amusing, interesting people staying, have thought of asking Margaret Thatcher.

Dame Janet Vaughn (Thatcher's university tutor)

↦ A woman wanted to get her pet dog in a smooth-haired dog contest and decided to help her dog a little by going to the chemist for some hair-removal lotion. The assistant hands her a bottle of special shampoo and says: "Remember to keep your arms in the air for at least three minutes." "Er, it's not for my armpits," the woman replies, blushing slightly, "it's for my Chihuahua." "In that case, don't ride a bike for three days," the assistant says.

CHICKENS

↦ A farmer decides it's time to get a new cock to look after his hens. The old one is a bit of a ragbag and, despite doing a reasonable job, the farmer figures he hasn't got all that long to go, so he may as well replace him sooner rather than later. He buys a new cock and lets him out in the barnyard to mix it up with the hens and sort it out with the old rooster. Now, the old rooster is pretty wise, and not the sort to take anything lying down, so he thinks to himself, "I'll have the last laugh here: I'm not ready to become lunch and dinner quite yet." So he walks up to the new cock and says, "So you think you're good enough to take over, then, do you? Well, I'll tell you what: instead of fighting and all that stuff, if you can beat me in a simple running race – just ten times around that old hen-house – I'll just leave quietly and not cause any fuss at all. I'll leave all the hens to you." "Old man, you've got yourself a deal," says the young rooster, puffing himself up and checking himself out in a mirror. "I'll even tell you what," continues the youngster with growing confidence, "you can have a half-lap head start – I know I'm going to win, after all!" So the race starts with the old rooster a good half-lap in front of the younger one. The old one has still got some strength left so he keeps a good pace for the first lap – he's not lost any distance. By the end of the second lap he is flagging just a little and by the end of the third the young rooster is noticeably gaining on him. By the time the fourth lap is over the old cock's lead has slipped seriously and at the end of the fifth the younger rooster can reach out and touch the older one. Still they run. At this point the farmer hears some noise from the chicken run. He walks out of the house, does a double-take, runs back in again and comes out with his shotgun. He stands and looks at the two roosters running for all they are worth around the hen-house, takes aim and BANG! blows the young rooster away. As he turns and walks away he mutters to himself, "Unbelievable: that's the third gay rooster I've bought in as many weeks!"

Physically, there is nothing to distinguish human society from the farm-yard except that children are more troublesome and costly than chickens and women are not so completely enslaved as farm stock.

George Bernard Shaw, Getting Married

➡ A farmer has a prize cock which has sired hundreds of young. It used to take care of every single one of the farmer's 200 chickens. But one day the old cock dies and the farmer is forced to get himself a replacement. The farmer looks at all the ads in Farmers' Weekly and orders a mail-order rooster named Randy. A couple of days later the new cock arrives. It is a very impressive and fit-looking bird. Before the farmer lets the rooster loose to work on his chickens, he gives it a bit of a pep talk. "Now, look here, Randy," the farmer says, "I need you as a long-term investment. I don't need a new rooster for just the next couple of days, I need one for a very long time. So take it easy and pace yourself when you get in there, OK?" Randy nods and the farmer puts him into the coop. But no sooner have Randy's claws hit the ground than he is off at the first brace of hens. The farmer looks on amazed as he sees the rooster making his way through the entire flock, doing all of the hens first once and then twice! The rooster doesn't even pause for breath. When he's done, he looks around and sees a load of ducks out by the pond. He sprints over and does them too – twice each. The farmer, while obviously impressed, is worried that his superb new rooster won't even make it through the night if he's that horny already. The farmer's worst fears are confirmed the next morning when he leaves the house after breakfast. Randy is lying a hundred yards from the hen-coop with buzzards circling around him. The farmer, shaking his head, walks slowly up to the chicken and looks down at him. "What the hell did I tell you, Randy?" he begins, "I knew you wouldn't make it if you didn't pace yourself!" Randy opens one eye and looks up at the farmer, then up at the buzzards. "Sshhhh," he says. "They're getting closer!"

↪ A farmer with lots of chickens posted the following sign: "Free Chickens. Our Coop Runneth Over."

↪ A guy approaches the window of the ticket office of a cinema carrying a chicken in his arms. "Hi: could I get two tickets, please? Oh – does my pet chicken have to pay full price?" "What do you mean, your pet chicken? Chickens aren't allowed into the cinema," the girl tells him. Outraged, he storms off, but after a few minutes, as he really wants to see this film, he decides to hide his chicken in his pants and try again. He returns to the booth and this time, to his delight, he is allowed to get a ticket. During the film, however, he can feel the chicken getting restless so he pulls his zip down and lets its head out for some fresh air. As it happens, he's sitting next to two blondes. One of them, turning to check what he's doing wiggling in his seat, turns to her friend and says: "Sally, the guy sitting next to me just unzipped his flies!" "It's OK; when you've seen one, you've seen them all," the other replies. "Yes, but this one is eating my popcorn!"

Son, in politics you've got to learn that overnight chicken shit can turn into chicken salad.
Lyndon Baines Johnson, 1908 – 1973, when asked why he was pleasant to Richard Nixon

↪ How do you make your cock look bigger? Buy smaller hens.

↪ Is it polite to eat fried chicken with your fingers? No. You should always eat your fingers separately.

↣ Which side of a chicken has the most feathers? The outside.

↣ Why did the chicken cross the road again? Because it was a double-crosser.

↣ Why did the chicken cross the road? To get away from Colonel Sanders.

↣ Why did the chicken cross the road? To see his friend Gregory Peck.

↣ Why did the chicken cross the road? To show the hedgehog it was possible.

↣ Why did the graduate student cross the road? He was writing a dissertation on chickens.

↣ Why did the Iraqi chicken cross the road? To take over the other side.

↣ Why did the rabbit cross the road? Because the chicken retired and moved to Florida.

↣ Why did the second chicken cross the road? He was stapled to the first chicken.

↣ Why do hens lay eggs? If they dropped them, they'd break.

CHURCH

➥ A Catholic priest felt despondent about being posted to a very rural parish in the middle of a forest. He wrote letters to his bishop constantly, requesting that he be posted somewhere more hospitable. No reply to his letters ever came, and soon the letters stopped. Some time later, when the archbishop was making the rounds of the rural churches, he dropped in to see how the unhappy priest was doing. He found a pleasant man, in an air-conditioned church. There were no parishioners, since the closest neighbours were many miles away. The archbishop admitted to some confusion, since the priest did not look like the desperate writer of so many letters. He asked the priest how he liked it out in the woods. "At first I was unhappy. But thanks to two things I have grown to love it out here." "And they are?" the archbishop inquired. "The first is my rosary. Without my rosary I wouldn't make it a day out here." "And the second?" At this the priest looked askance. "Well, to be honest, I have developed a taste for Martinis in the afternoon. They help to alleviate the boredom during the worst part of the day." He looked sheepish at this admission, but the archbishop just smiled. "Martinis, eh? Well, that's not so bad. In fact, I'd be glad to share one with you right now, if you don't mind that is." "Not at all!" the priest exulted. "Let me get one for you right away." Turning to the back of the church, the priest shouted, "Oh, Marti? Come meet the archbishop, sweetie."

➥ A little boy is sitting with his mother at a service when the sermon is about to start. He turns to her and says, "Mummy, I don't feel well. I think I am going to be sick." The mother is rather embarrassed, but it appears the rest of the congregation hadn't heard him. "You can't be sick here," she tells him. "I tell you what, go out now, before the sermon starts, and if you have to be sick, then at least you won't disrupt the priest or the service." The boy disappears and when the sermon ends, he makes his way back and sits down next to his mother. "Well, were you sick?" she asks felicitously. "Yes, Mummy, I was and I feel much better now." "Good, I am pleased you were so quiet. But, tell me, where were you sick?" she asks, thinking about the mess she would have to clear up. "I knew exactly where to go," he said proudly. "There was a big box at the back of the church with 'For the sick' written on it."

Parasitism is the only practice of the church, with its ideal of anaemia, its 'holiness', draining all blood, all love, all hope for life; the beyond as the will to negate every reality; the cross as the mark of recognition for the most subterranean conspiracy that ever existed – against health, beauty, whatever has turned out well, courage, spirit, graciousness of the soul, against life itself. I call Christianity the one great curse, the one great innermost corruption, the one great instinct of revenge, for which no means is poisonous, stealthy, subterranean, small enough – I call it the one immortal blemish of mankind.

Friedrich Nietzsche, 1844 – 1900, The Antichrist

•• One sunny Sunday in spring, Father Fitzpatrick noticed that there was a smaller gathering than usual for the noon service. So as soon as the final hymn was sung, he slipped out the back way and went along the street to see who was out and about instead of coming to church. The first person he saw was old Mrs O'Neill, sitting on a park bench with her cane beside her. The good cleric sat down next to her and said, "Good afternoon, Mrs O'Neill, why weren't you in church today?" Mrs O'Neill replied: "Well, Father, it was just such a lovely day today I didn't want to be cooped up in that stuffy old church." The priest was a bit taken aback by this blunt answer, so he thought for a minute, then asked, "But Mrs O'Neill, don't you want to go to heaven?" To his surprise, the elderly lady shook her head vehemently and said, "No, Father." At that, the priest got to his feet indignantly and said firmly, "Then I am ashamed for you." Now it was Mrs O'Neill's turn to be surprised. She looked up at him and said, "Oh, Father, I thought you meant right now."

➻ The pastor of a small congregation was trying to find a contractor to paint his church. Because the church fund was low and he couldn't pay very much, he selected the lowest bidder. The contractor decided to make the job pay better by skimping on materials. He thinned the paint with solvent and then only applied one coat. Within months, the poor paint job began to flake away and the church looked worse than it had before the work was done. The pastor sent a note to the contractor that said: "Repaint, repaint – thin no more!"

CLASS

The schoolteacher is certainly underpaid as a child-minder, but ludicrously overpaid as an educator.

John Osborne

✦ A young secondary school teacher is informed that, due to cutbacks, she will have to give her class their sex education lessons herself. Not wanting to have to explain much or draw pictures, she decides to use a mathematical approach and gets some flashcards for the following day's lessons. At the start of the lesson she holds up the first card, a picture of a breast, and says to the class, "Does anyone know what this is?" Susan puts up her hand and says, "I know; I know. It's a breast, and my Mummy has two of them." "That's very good, Susan," says the teacher and holds up the next card. It's of a penis. "Does anyone know what this is?" she asks. Tom puts his hand up and says, "I know; I know. It's a penis, and my Daddy has two of them." "Well, that's very good, Tom, it is a penis, but your Daddy can't have two of them." Tom replies, "He does, miss. He's got a little one he pees with and a great big one he brushes Mummy's teeth with!"

✦ At primary school one day, the teacher was reading the Three Little Pigs to her youngest class. When she got to the part about the pig building his house from straw she read, "And the little pig went to the farmer and said, 'Please mister farmer can I have some straw to build my house with?'" And then the teacher asked the whole class, "And what do you think the farmer said?" Little Johnny in the corner put up his hand and said, "I know, miss. He said, 'Screw me – a talking pig!'"

✦ It was the last day of nursery school and all the children had bought presents for their teacher, whom they'd never see again. Because it was the last day, the teacher decided to make a game of guessing what the presents were. First of all the sweetshop owner's daughter comes up with a box. It is quite heavy so the teacher shakes it and says, "Is this full of sweets?" "Yes, miss, it is," replies the little girl. Then the flowershop owner's son comes up with a box. It is very light, so the teacher shakes it and says, "Are these flowers?" "Yes, miss, they are," replies the little boy. Then the wine merchant's son comes up with a box. It is very heavy, so the teacher shakes it a little and notices that it is leaking a bit. She touches a drop of the liquid with her finger and tastes it. "Is this full of wine?" she says. "No, miss," comes the reply. So the teacher tries another drop and then says, "Is this full of champagne?" "No, miss," comes the reply. "In that case I give up," says the teacher, "What's in the box?" "A puppy," the boy says.

I am inclined to think that one's education has been in vain if one fails to learn that most schoolmasters are idiots.

Hesketh Pearson

↦ Little Billy was famous for his rectal prowess, but it was starting to disrupt classes, so the teacher called him back after school to discuss the problem with him. She began by asking him why he kept breaking wind all the time when he knew it offended many people. "Well, miss, it's because I'm the best and I'm really proud of myself. I want to share my gift with the world." "So, in that case," said his teacher, "if I can do it better than you, will you stop doing it in the classroom?" Little Billy said he surely would, mainly because he didn't think she would be able to do it better than him. So the teacher set up the test: she placed two pieces of paper covered in chalk dust on the floor, the idea being to blow as much dust as possible from the paper. Little Billy steps forward first, drops his trousers and pants and crouches down over the paper. He rips out his best effort and it clears most of the chalk dust from the page. At the teacher's turn, she hitches up her skirt, drops her knickers and squats over her piece of paper. She lets fly a huge blast that completely clears the chalk dust and also blows the paper across the room. Little Billy is impressed and asks the teacher if she can repeat what she's just done. She is flattered, so agrees to do it just one more time. As she crouches down, Little Billy takes a quick peek up her skirt. "Hey, that's not fair," he says. "No wonder you won, miss. Yours is double-barrelled!"

↦ Never let your schooling interfere with your education.

↦ Striking teachers today rejected the government's latest pay offer saying that it was blatantly copied from a previous offer, contained too many erasures and misspellings and was handed in late.

Everybody who is incapable of learning has taken to teaching.

Oscar Wilde

↦ While visiting a country school, the chairman of the Board of Education became provoked at the noise the unruly students were making in the next room. Angrily, he opened the door and grabbed one of the taller boys who seemed to be doing most of the talking. He dragged the boy into the next room and stood him in the corner. A few minutes later, a small boy stuck his head in the room and pleaded, "Please, sir, may we have our teacher back?"

COMPUTERS

↔ A computer once beat me at chess, but it was no match for me at kick-boxing.

   ↔ A collection of 'Ass' smileys

(_!_)	A regular "nice" ass.
(__!__)	A large ass.
(!)	A tight ass.
(_._)	A flat ass.
(_^_)	A bubbly ass.
(_*_)	A sore ass.
(_!__)	A lop-sided ass.
{_!_}	A squishy ass.
(_o_)	An ass that's been around.
(_O_)	And more...
(_x_)	Kiss my ass.
(_X_)	Get off my ass.
(_zzz_)	A tired ass.
(_o^o_)	A wise ass.
(_13_)	An unlucky ass.
(_E=mc2_)	A smart ass.
(_$_)	Money coming out of his ass.

↔ A woman had been married three times and protested that she was still a virgin. Somebody asked her how that could be possible. "Well," she said. "The first time I married an octogenarian and he died before we could consummate the marriage. The second time I married a naval officer and war broke out on our wedding day. The third time I married a Windows Vista sales guy, and he just sat on the edge of the bed and kept telling me how good it was going to be."

➻ A computer programmer was out walking one day when a frog called out to him and said: "If you kiss me, I'll turn into a beautiful princess." Delighted with his find, he bent over, picked up the frog and put it in his pocket. The frog spoke up again and said: "If you kiss me and turn me back into a beautiful princess, I will stay with you for one week." The computer programmer took the frog out of his pocket, smiled at it and returned it again. The frog then cried out: "Look, okay, if you kiss me and turn me back into a princess, I'll stay with you for one month and do absolutely anything you want." Again the computer programmer took the frog out, smiled at it and put it back into his pocket. Finally, the frog asked: "What's the matter with you? I've told you I'm a beautiful princess, that I'll stay with you for a month, and do anything you want. Why won't you kiss me?" The computer programmer said: "Look, I'm a computer programmer. I don't have time for a woman in my life: but a talking frog – now that's cool."

If the human race wants to go to hell in a basket, technology can help it get there by jet. It won't change the desire or the direction, but it can greatly speed the passage.

Charles Allen

➻ A trucker is driving a trailer loaded with computer equipment on the highway near Silicon Valley when he decides to stop for a bite to eat. He slows down and pulls over at a roadside café which has a sign outside saying: "Non-computer geeks only. If you are a computer geek, enter at your own risk." Finding this a bit strange, the trucker goes in and sits at the bar, where a suspicious barman looks him up and down and says: "You're sure you're not a computer geek?" "Hell no. I'm a truck driver." The barman leans over the bar and sniffs him unceremoniously. "You smell like one," the barman accuses. "Well, my trailer's full of computer equipment, that would be why," the trucker replies quickly, starting to feel a tad freaked out. The barman stares at him in the eye for a few seconds and then apparently decides the trucker is telling the truth and serves him lunch. While the trucker is having his lunch, a guy wearing an Apple hat, a calculator-wristwatch and carrying a laptop enters the bar, obviously preoccupied with some difficult programming problem. The barman silently picks up a shotgun from behind the bar, walks around and coldly shoots the geek down. While a couple of waitresses are grumpily disposing of the body, the barman explains that these things happen all the time round these parts. "Oh yeah," he says to the trucker. "Disposing of computer geeks is a state law here. There's just too many of them in Silicon Valley: we need to control the population, you know?" Puzzled, the trucker pays for his food and heads off. Unfortunately, his lunch makes him drowsy and soon he finds himself with his trailer in the ditch, doors open, computer gear on the tarmac. There are a lot of people wearing suits and glasses hurriedly grabbing computers, monitors and keyboards. Remembering the barman's words, he reaches for his shotgun and starts shooting computer geeks, too. He's starting to have fun when a patrol car stops and a couple of policemen restrain him. "What's the matter?" the trucker asks. "I thought it was a state law to get rid of computer geeks." "Oh, it is," one of the policemen says, "but you're not allowed to bait them."

↪ Beware of computer programmers who carry screwdrivers.

↞ A doctor, an engineer and a computer scientist were sitting around late one evening, discussing which was the oldest profession. The doctor pointed out that according to the Bible, God created Eve from Adam's rib. This obviously required surgery to obtain the rib, so his was the oldest profession in the world. The engineer countered with an earlier passage in the Bible that stated that God created order from the chaos. That was most certainly the biggest and best engineering project ever, so her profession was the oldest profession. The computer scientist leaned back in her chair, smiled, and responded, "Yes, but who do you think created the chaos?"

↞ A man walks into a Silicon Valley pet store looking to buy a monkey. The owner points towards three identical-looking monkeys in politically-correct, animal-friendly, natural mini-habitats. "The one on the left costs $500," says the owner. "Why so much?" asks the customer. "Because it can program in C," answers the owner. The customer inquires about the next monkey and is told, "That one costs $1,500, because it knows Visual C and Object-Relational technology." The startled man then asks about the third monkey. "That one costs $3,000," answers the store owner. "$3,000!!" exclaims the man. "What can that one do?" The owner replies, "To be honest, I've never seen it do a single thing, but it calls itself a consultant."

His computers take twice the gestation period of an elephant to warm up.

The Guardian newspaper on Alan Sugar, chairman of Amstrad

↦ A young man comes into the computer store: "I'm looking for a mystery adventure game with lots of graphics: you know – something really challenging." "Well," replied the clerk, "have you tried Windows Vista?"

↦ Alpha. Software undergoes alpha testing as a first step in getting user feedback. Alpha is Latin for "Doesn't work". Beta. Software undergoes beta testing shortly before it's released. Beta is Latin for "Still doesn't work".

↦ Alternative Windows slogans:

Double your drive space: Delete Windows!
Windows Vista and a PC: A turtle and its shell.
A computer without Windows Vista is like a fish without a
   hook through its lip.
Bang on the left side of your computer to restart Windows.
I still miss Windows, but my aim's getting better.
I'll never forget the first time I ran Windows Vista, but I'm trying.
Out of disk space. Delete Windows? [Y]es, [H]ell Yes!
Windows XP: The best solitaire game you can buy.
Windows Vista: Insert wallet into DVD Drive and press any
   key to empty.

↦ How do you tell an experienced hacker from a novice? The latter thinks there are 1,000 bytes in a kilobyte, while the former is sure there are 1,024 metres in a kilometre.

↦ How many Microsoft engineers does it take to screw in a light bulb? None. They just redefine the status of darkness.

➻ How many Internet mail list subscribers does it take to change a light bulb? 947:

1 – to change the light bulb and to post to the mail list that the light bulb has been changed.

14 – to share similar experiences of changing light bulbs and how the light bulb could have been changed differently.

7 – to caution about the dangers of changing light bulbs.

27 – to point out spelling/grammar errors in posts about changing light bulbs.

53 – to flame the spell-checkers.

156 – to write to the list administrator complaining about the light bulb discussion and its inappropriateness to this mail list.

41 – to correct spelling in the spelling/grammar flames.

109 – to post that this list is not about light bulbs and to please take this discussion.

111 – to defend the posting to this list saying that we all use light bulbs and therefore the posts *are* relevant to this mail list.

306 – to debate which method of changing light bulbs is superior, where to buy the best light bulbs, what brands of light bulb work best for this technique and what brands are faulty.

27 – to post URLs where one can see examples of different light bulbs.

14 – to post that the URLs were posted incorrectly, and to post corrected URLs.

3 – to post about links they found from the URLs that are relevant to this list which makes light bulbs relevant to this list.

33 – to concatenate all posts to date, then quote them including all headers and footers, and then add "Me Too."

12 – to post to the list that they are unsubscribing because they cannot handle the light bulb controversy.

19 – to quote the "Me Too's" to say, "Me Three."

4 – to suggest that posters request the light bulb FAQ.

❧ How many Pentium designers does it take to screw in a light bulb? Approximately 1,999,042,740,172.23554177896 – but that's close enough for non-technical people.

❧ If only women came with pull-down menus and online help...

❧ If software companies made toasters: Every time you bought a fresh loaf of bread, you would have to buy a toaster, or at least renew your licence for it. The new Vista Toaster would weigh 15,000 pounds (hence requiring a steel-reinforced worktop), draw enough electricity to power Birmingham, take up 95% of the space in your kitchen and would claim to be the first toaster which lets you control how light or dark you want your toast to be. This toaster would secretly interrogate your other appliances to find out who made them and send the details back to the parent company. It would have a protection device that will not let you toast bread. If you try to, it will use the internet to instruct the parent company's team of ninja lawyers to sue you to death. It will give you advice you don't need, such as: "Don't put your hand in the boiling water, only pasta," and would monitor your behaviour in the kitchen to record your bread-related habits to serve you better. It would have a reset button, the only place worn out on an otherwise shiny toaster. Everyone would hate toasters, but nonetheless would buy them since most of the good bread only worked with their toasters.

➼ In a vital boost for the Internet recently, several countries have agreed not to tax it, in order to help increase the prominence of electronic and to foster the growth of a truly world-wide communications network. Consumer groups have hailed the move as a great breakthrough, saying, "An Internet tax could have been disastrous. Most 11-year-olds are already strapped for cash, and would have real difficulty coping with any further rises in their weekly hardcore pornography bills."

To err is human. To really foul things up requires a computer.
Philip Howard

➼ Information age proverbs:

Home is where you hang your @.
The e-mail of the species is more deadly than the mail.
A journey of a thousand sites begins with a single click.
You can't teach a new mouse old clicks.
Great groups from little icons grow.
Speak softly and carry a cellular phone.
C:\ is the root of all directories.
Don't put all your hypes in one home page.
Pentium wise; pen and paper foolish.
The modem is the message.
Too many clicks spoil the browse.
The geek shall inherit the earth.
A chat has nine lives.
Don't byte off more than you can view.
Fax is stranger than fiction.

↦ Macronought today announced the release of JoeBlogs Operating System™, especially targeted at British thirtysomething yobboes, yuppies and club-goers. The operating system, commercialized with the motto "An OS for the lads", doesn't have a spreadsheet, a database program or even a word processor, but it can keep track of the football season, lists the best pubs between Inverness and Dover, and can even order curry and beer at the click of a mouse.

↦ New PC software error messages:
Smash forehead on keyboard to continue.
File not found. Should I fake it? (Y/N)
Runtime Error 6D at 417A:32CF: Incompetent User.
Enter any 11-digit prime number to continue.
Press any key to continue or any other key to quit.
Press any key except... no, no, no, not that one!
Press Ctrl-Alt-Del now for IQ test.
Close your eyes and press Escape three times.
Bad command or file name! Go stand in the corner.
This will end your current session. Do you want to play
    another game?
CONGRESS.SYS Corrupted: Re-boot Washington DC. (Y/N)?
Windows message: "Error saving file! Format drive now?
    (Y/Y)"
BREAKFAST.SYS halted... Cereal port not responding.

↦ Programming today is a race between software engineers striving to build bigger and better idiot-proof programs, and the Universe trying to produce bigger and better idiots. So far, the Universe is winning.

➻ One of Jim Portal's marketing assistants approached an applicant in a market research panel and said, "Excuse me. If a company made a version of a PC OS which only crashed once a year, would you buy it?" The customer's eyes glistened and he seemed to be making the sign of the cross: "Oh, yes!" The marketing assistant carried on: "... and if they made a version which crashed every five minutes?" The customer glared at him and said, "And what kind of customer do you think I am?" "We've already established that," the guy said. "We're just haggling over the frequency."

➻ One of the main host computers of a very busy internal network went down, bringing down with it half the intranet of the building which depended on it. The network in-house engineer soon gave up and told his boss to call for a specialist. The specialist arrived, had a talk with the engineer, then took one look at the computer and nodded thoughtfully. He then opened his briefcase, produced a small rubber hammer and, his ear stuck to the computer case, hit a spot softly, after which the system made a kind of "Wooosh" noise and restarted straight away. Two days later the office manager received a bill from the consultant for $2,000. Immediately he called the engineer's agency and exclaimed, "Two thousand dollars for fixing that computer? You were only here five minutes! I want the bill itemized!" The next day the new bill arrived. It read, "Tapping computer with hammer: $1. Knowing where to tap: $1,999."

➻ Sex Instructions for Tech Nerds
   1. Be user-friendly.
   2. Take bytes.
   3. Fondle joystick.

4. Spread sheet.
5. Fix surge protector.
6. Activate hardware.
7. Insert disk... all the way.
8. Do it until megabytes.
9. Back it up.
10. Eject floppy.

➻ Software magnate Jim Portal has finally died and Satan greets him. "Welcome, Mr Portal, we've been waiting for you," he purrs. "You've been a naughty boy, flooding the world with version after version of software that didn't work and not permitting any other software to exist. You are now in Hell and this will be your home for all eternity." Satan eyes Jim Portal and resumes his welcome speech: "But you're lucky, because I am in a good mood today and I will present to you three Hells for you to choose to be locked up in." Satan takes Jim to a huge lake of fire in which millions of poor souls are tormented and tortured. He then takes him to a massive amphitheatre where thousands of people are chased about and devoured by starving, nightmarish creatures. Finally, he takes Jim to a tiny room in which, to Jim's delight, there is a PC and, next to it, a cup of coffee. Without hesitation, Jim says: "I'll take this option." "Fine," says Satan, locking up Jim in the room. Outside, his second-in-command is waiting for him to process the next unfortunate soul. "So he chose this room, master, as you predicted," the aide says. "But I don't understand. You gave him quite a nice room, and with a PC, too..." "Ah, but you see, this is no ordinary PC," Satan sniggers. "The Control, Alt and Delete keys are missing and it's running Windows 95!"

↔ Sure signs that your co-worker is a hacker: You told him off once and your next phone bill was for £20,000. He's won the Reader's Digest sweepstakes three years running. When asked for his phone number, he gives it in hex. Seems strangely calm whenever the office LAN goes down. Somehow manages to get Sky Sports on his PC at work. Massive £40,000 contribution to the ritual Christmas booze trip to Calais made in one penny increments. His video dating profile lists "public-key decryption" among turn-ons. When his computer starts up, you hear, "Good morning, Mr President." You hear him murmur, "Let's see you use that credit card now, bitch!"

↔ Tech Support: "Tell me, in the bottom left-hand side of the screen, can you see the 'OK' button displayed?" Caller: "Wow. How can you see my screen from there?"

↔ Tech Support: "What does the screen say now?" Caller: "It says, 'Hit ENTER when ready'." Tech Support: "Well?" Caller: "How do I know when it's ready?"

↔ The Ultimate Computer had finally been built and, after making sure that the intensive indoor tests all proved 100% positive, the Ultimate Computer was presented to the CEO. The engineer stepped forward to give his prepared demo. "This," he said, "is the Ultimate Computer. It will give an intelligent answer to any question you may care to ask it." The CEO, amused, asked: "Where is my father?" After an infinitesimal pause, the super computer answer comes through the laser printer: "Your father is fishing off the coast of Florida." The COE's face falls. "Actually, my father is dead. He died five years ago," he says, in a tone suggesting he is not amused any more. The engineer gulps and mutters: "You should re-phrase the question – make it more precise. That might produce a correct answer this time." The CEO frowns and says: "All right. Where is my mother's husband?" There is a small pause again and the printer spits out the answer to the second question: "Your mother's husband is dead. However, your father is still fishing off the coast of Florida."

Computer software will never replace greyware.

Anonymous

→ Three software engineers were in the toilet, standing at the urinals. The first engineer finished and walked over to wash his hands. He then proceeded to dry them very carefully, using paper towel after paper towel and ensuring that his hands were completely dry. Turning to the other two engineers, he explained, "At Hughie Pickering, we are trained to be extremely thorough." He then began to check the fit of his suit. The second engineer finished his task at the urinal and, in his turn, proceeded to wash his hands. He used a single paper towel and made sure that he dried his hands using every available portion of it. He turned and said, "At Adomo, not only are we trained to be extremely thorough, but also extremely efficient." He then started grooming his hair in the mirror. The third engineer, rather peeved, finished his business and walked straight for the door, shouting over his shoulder: "At Affel, we don't piss on our hands."

→ The perfect computer has been developed. You just feed in your problems and they never come out again.

➼ Viruses are the bane of modern technology. Here is a list of dangerous new viruses you don't want to see spreading:

AIRLINE VIRUS
You're in London, but your data is in Inverness.

TONY BLAIR VIRUS
It doubles the files on your hard drive while stating it is decreasing the number of files; increases the cost of your computer; taxes its CPU to maximum capacity and then uses Quicken to access your bank accounts and deplete your balances.

BILL GATES VIRUS
This dominant strain searches for desirable features in all other viruses via the Internet. It then either engulfs the competing viruses or removes their access to computers until they die out.

DIET VIRUS
Allows your hard drive to lose weight by eliminating the FAT table.

DISNEY VIRUS
Everything in the computer goes goofy.

ELVIS VIRUS
Your computer gets fat, slow and lazy and then self-destructs, only to resurface at shopping malls and service stations across rural America.

FREUDIAN VIRUS
Your computer becomes obsessed with its own motherboard, or it becomes very jealous of the size of your friend's hard disk.

LORENA BOBBITT VIRUS
It turns your hard disk into a 3.5-inch floppy.

MISSING VIRUS
Virus '08 is promised for initial Beta release by the second quarter of this year, but recent court actions by the Federal government have cast doubt on the parent company's ability to incorporate this virus into the main OS in a seamless manner.

POLITICALLY CORRECT VIRUS
Never calls itself a virus, but instead refers to itself as an electronic micro-organism.

STAR TREK VIRUS
Invades your system in places where no virus has gone before.

TEENAGER VIRUS
Your PC stops every few seconds to ask for money.

X-FILES VIRUS
All your icons start turning alien.

TOBACCO INDUSTRY VIRUS
It contends that there is no reliable scientific evidence that viruses can harm your computer or that it targets adolescent computer users.

↦ Why do computer scientists make such lousy lovers? Because they always want to do the job faster than before. And when they do, they say the performance has improved.

↦ What does a baby computer call his father? Data.

➥ The librarian noticed a young man sitting in front of a computer, staring at the screen, his arms across his chest. After 15 minutes, he realized that the young man hadn't changed his position and was still there, doing nothing, staring blankly at the screen. Puzzled, he went to him and asked: "May I help you?" "It's about time!" he answered, "I pressed the Help button over 20 minutes ago!"

➥ Two programmers were walking across their company's campus when one of their colleagues appeared on a brand-new bicycle. "Where did you get such a great bike?" asks the first programmer. "Well, I was walking along yesterday minding my own business when a beautiful woman rode up on this bike. She threw the bike to the ground, took off all her clothes and said, 'Take what you want.'" The second IT guy nodded approvingly. "Good choice; the clothes probably wouldn't have fitted."

➥ WARNING: There is a new virus called Viagra! It turns your 3.5-inch floppy into a hard drive!

➥ What happened when the computer fell on the floor? It slipped a disk.

➥ What is a computer's first sign of old age? Loss of memory.

➥ Windows versions:

Windows 1.0: The joke's on you.
Windows 2.0: Still funny!
Windows 3.0: It's finally worth buying. Just
Windows 3.1: It's finally worth using. Just

Windows 95: Going boldly where Mac has been for years.

Windows 98: More usable! Less stable!

Windows 98SE: More stable! Less usable!

Windows CE/ME/NT: Turning computers into the building material their names suggest.

Windows 2K: Works almost as well as Windows 98! Honest!

Windows XP: It works. WOW!

Windows Vista: It works too, but it works for the music companies, and spends all its time spying on you to see if you're trying to do something that they can sue you for.

⇢ Your computer is lying to you.

It says: "Press Any Key." It means: "Press any key you like, but I'm not moving."

It says: "Fatal Error. Please contact technical support quoting error no. 1A4-2546512430E." It means: "... where you will be kept on hold for ten minutes, only to be told some crap that will hide the fact they can't understand a word I say either."

It says: "Installing program to C:\..." It means: ".... and I'll also be writing 200 megabytes of files into various directories and you'll NEVER find them."

It says: "Please insert disk 11." It means: "Because I know darn well there are only ten disks."

It says: "Please Wait..." It means: "... Indefinitely."

It says: "Directory does not exist..." It means: "... any more. Whoops."

It says: "The application caused an error. Choose Ignore or Close." It means: "... Makes no difference to me, you're still not getting your work back."

➻ Who was the first computer operator in the Bible? Eve; she had an Apple in one hand and a Wang in the other.

➻ Why are computers like women? Nobody, however long they work with one, understands their internal logic. Even your smallest mistakes are immediately, permanently committed to memory for future reference. The native language used to communicate with other computers is incomprehensible to everyone else. The message "Bad command or file name" is about as informative as, "If you don't know why I'm mad at you, then I'm certainly not going to tell you." As soon as you make a commitment to one, you find yourself spending half your pay cheque on accessories for it.

cornwall

➻ A Cornishman is visiting his cousin's farm, and the farmer shows him round the chicken sheds, the pig pens, the paddocks and so on. Finally he points to a tree about 30 feet away and tells the first guy: "Under that tree is where I first had sex." Then he points to another tree and says: "... and that's where her mother stood and watched us." The first guy gasps and asks: "What did she say?" His cousin grins, and replies: "Baaa."

➻ In Truro recently three armed men robbed a jeweller and decided to use his car for a getaway vehicle. Exiting the shop, they all piled into the car, only to discover that it had a manual gearstick. They were last seen fleeing on foot.

➳ Did you hear about the Cornishman who passed away and left his entire estate in trust for his widow? She can't touch it 'til she's 14...

➳ How does a Cornishman know when his girlfriend is having an orgasm? He doesn't care.

The older the Cornishman, the more a madman.

English saying

➳ Mr Trevarrick: "Roger, where was yer son-in-law when y' first saw'n?" Mr Toms: "Right smack in t' middle of my sights."

➳ Mr Trevarrick: "What'm yer son goin' t' be when he graduates, m'dear?" Mr Toms: "An old man, I fancy."

➳ There was a Cornish girl who finally found a good job in the city. One night, shortly after arriving in the city, she was invited to a very exclusive party. She didn't know anyone, so she was trying to find someone to talk to when she saw an elegantly-dressed lady standing alone. She approached the lady and said, "Where'm you from?" The lady gave an indignant look and said, "Well! Where I am from, we DON'T end our sentences with a preposition. The young girl thought about it and replied, "Oh, well, where'm you from, slag?"

➳ What are the three biggest lies a Cornishman tells? 1) Yes, I do really have an O-level. 2) No, she's not my cousin. 3) Honest officer, I was only trying to help the sheep over the fence.

↠ Two Cornishmen were standing around on a sheep farm, during the coldest winter they'd had in years. Bill turned to Roger and confessed that he really couldn't wait until it was time to shear the flocks. The other nodded, rubbing his hands together in anticipation. "We'm be having a top time selling t' wool, and spending t' money on beer and women, eh?" "No, that bain't it," said Bill, "I'm just carn't wait t' see'm naked."

↠ What do you call the layer of sweat between two Cornish folk having sex? Relative humidity.

↠ What's the difference between a good old boy and a Cornishman? The good old boy raises sheep. The Cornishman gets emotionally involved.

↠ What's the most popular pick-up line in Truro? "Nice tooth, m'dear."

↠ Where do Cornishmen meet girls? At family barbecues.

↠ Down in Cornwall, they say that customs have changed very little over the centuries. Many a man still sleeps with a battle-axe by his side.

↠ In Cornwall in the good old days, men were 'real' men, women were 'real' women, and small furry animals were 'real' small furry animals. You knew where you stood. If you didn't, you planted a flag in the ground and claimed the place for King and Country, and everyone else knew where you stood. Nowadays, Cornishmen wear long hair and Cornishwomen wear trousers. People have sex with other people regardless of gender or species. Men are 'real' women, women are 'real' men, and small furry animals are real afraid.

COUNTRYSIDE

**From every Englishman emanates a kind of gas,
the deadly choke-damp of boredom.**

Heinrich Heine

↦ Two country doctors out in the Yorkshire Dales were discussing the population explosion in the world. One physician said: "Why, at t'current rate o' population growth, there'll soon be no'but standing room on t'whole planet." After a thoughtful pause, the other doctor replied, "Aye, but that'll slow t'buggers down a bit."

COURTROOMS

↦ Prosecutor: "Did you kill the victim?" Defendant: "No, I did not." Prosecutor: "Do you know what the penalties are for perjury?" Defendant: "Yes, I do. And they're a hell of a lot better than the penalty for murder."

↦ The defendant who pleads his own case may have a fool for a client, but at least he knows that his lawyer won't be ripping him off.

➻ A circuit judge in a small-town court was hearing a drunk-driving case and the defendant, who had both a record and a reputation for driving under the influence, demanded a jury trial. It was nearly 4pm. And getting a jury would take time, so the judge called a recess and went out in the hall looking to empanel anyone available for jury duty. He found a dozen lawyers in the main lobby and told them that they were a jury. The lawyers thought this would be a novel experience and so followed the judge back to the courtroom. The trial was over in about ten minutes and it was very clear that the defendant was guilty. The jury went into the jury room, the judge started getting ready to go home and everyone waited. After nearly three hours, the judge was totally out of patience and sent the usher into the jury room to see what was holding up the verdict. When the usher returned, the judge said: "Well, have they got a verdict yet?" The usher shook his head and said: "Verdict? No, M'lud, they're still doing nominating speeches for the foreman's position."

Freedom of speech in England is little else than the right to write or say anything which a jury of twelve shopkeepers think it expedient should be said or written.

A Dicey, 1835 – 1922

➻ A man on trial at the Old Bailey had previously pleaded not guilty. However, once the jury, – eight women and four men – had been seated and the trial was under way, the defendant switched his plea. "Why the change?" asked the judge. "Were you persuaded to plead guilty?" "No Sir," the man replied, "when I pleaded not guilty, I didn't know women would be on the jury. I can't fool one woman, so I know I can't fool eight of them."

➥ A witness was called to the stand to testify about a head-on car crash. "Whose fault was this accident?" one lawyer asked. "As near as I could tell," replied the witness, "they hit each other at about the same time."

➥ In a courtroom, a mugger was on trial. The victim, asked if she recognised the defendant, said, "Yes, that's him. I saw him clear as day. I'd remember his face anywhere." Unable to contain himself, the defendant burst out with, "She's lying! I was wearing a mask!"

➥ In a terrible accident at a railroad crossing, a train smashed into a car and pushed it nearly 400 yards down the track. Though no one was killed, the driver took the train company to court. At the trial, the engineer insisted that he had given the driver ample warning by waving his lantern back and forth for nearly a minute. He even stood and convincingly demonstrated how he'd done it. The court believed his story and the suit was dismissed. "Congratulations," the lawyer said to the engineer when it was over, "you did superbly under cross-examination." "Thanks," he said, "but he sure had me worried." "How's that?" the lawyer asked. "I was afraid he was going to ask if the lantern was lit."

➥ When you go to court, just remember that you are trusting your fate to 12 people who weren't clever enough to get out of jury duty!

CRICKET

➻ One night, while a woman and her husband were making love, she suddenly noticed something sticking in his ear. When she asked him what it was, he replied: "Are you mad, woman? I'm listening to the cricket."

To the spectators, cricket is more a therapy than a sport. It is like watching fish dart about a pool.

Michael Wale, on Cricket

➻ Two alien scientists visited Earth to examine local customs. When they met to pool their knowledge the first alien told of a peculiar religious ceremony it had seen, of impressive magical power. "I went to a large green arena shaped like a meteorite crater. Several thousand worshippers were gathered around the outside. Two priests walked to the centre of the field, where a rectangular area was marked, and hammered six spears into the ground, three at each end, then linked the spears in each set of three with small tubes. Then 11 more priests came out, clad in white robes. Finally, two high priests wielding clubs walked to the centre area. One of the white-robed priests produced a red orb and hurled it at the ones with the clubs." "Wow," replied the other alien, "what happened next?" The first alien said, "Every time they performed the ceremony, at this point it began to rain!"

CRITTERS

➡ A baby rabbit was orphaned. Fortunately, though, a family of squirrels took it in and raised it as if it were one of their own. This adoption led to some peculiar behaviours on the part of the rabbit, including a tendency for it to eschew jumping but rather to embrace running around like its step-siblings. As the rabbit passed through puberty, however, it soon faced an identity crisis. It went to its foster-parents to discuss the problem. It explained how it felt different from its brothers and sisters, was unsure of its place in the universe and was generally forlorn. The father squirrel just sat back and cracked another nut, saying: "Don't scurry, be hoppy."

> **The tortoise is the animal equivalent**
> **of a Tonka toy.**
>
> *Nick Hancock*

➡ A blonde is walking down the street with a pig under her arm. She passes a man who, puzzled, asks "Where did you get that?" "I won her in a raffle!" the pig replies.

➡ A panda spent the night in bed with a prostitute. The following morning as he is about ready to leave, the prostitute yells after him: "Hey, aren't you going to pay me?" The panda appears confused so she throws a dictionary at him and tells him to look up 'prostitute'. The definition reads: "A woman who engages in promiscuous sexual activity for pay." The panda throws the dictionary back at the prostitute and tells her to look up 'panda'. The definition reads: "An animal that eats bamboo, shoots, and leaves."

➻ A mother and baby camel were talking one day when the baby camel asked, "Mum, why have I got these huge three-toed feet?" "Well, son, when we trek across the desert your toes will help you to stay on top of the soft sand," the mother replied, "OK," said the son. A few minutes later, the son asked, "Mum, why have I got these great long eyelashes?" "They are there to keep the sand out of your eyes on the trips through the desert." "Thanks, Mum," replied the son, and went off to think on his own. After a short while, the son returned and asked, "Mum, why have I got these great big humps on my back?" The mother, now a little impatient with the boy, replied, "They're to help us store water for our long treks across the desert, so we can go without drinking for long periods." "That's great, Mum: so we have huge feet to stop us sinking, and long eyelashes to keep the sand from our eyes and these humps to store water. But Mum..." "Yes, son?" "Why the heck are we in London Zoo?"

➻ A polar bear was out driving one day when he suddenly started having engine trouble. He pulled into the next service station and asked the walrus there to take a look at it. The walrus drove the car into the workshop and put it up on the hoist. After looking at it for a bit he returned and said to the polar bear, "You've blown a seal," to which the bear replied, "No, honestly! That's just mayonnaise from lunch."

➻ An ant and an elephant share a night of romance. Next morning the ant wakes up and the elephant is dead. "Damn," says the ant. "One night of passion and I spend the rest of my life digging a grave!"

↝ A snail got mugged by two tortoises. When he went to the police, they questioned him as to what happened. He said: "I don't know; it all happened so quickly!"

↝ A snake slithers into a pub and up to the bar. The landlord says, "I'm sorry, but I can't serve you." "What? Why not?" asks the snake. "Because," says the landlord, "you can't hold your booze."

A camel looks like a horse that was planned by a committee.

Anonymous

↝ Deep in the forest, a tortoise was slowly padding towards a tall tree. Ever so slowly she started climbing the tree. After a few days of this, she managed to climb high enough to reach the lowest branch, but it was apparently not high enough, as she carried on upwards. It took her a week to reach a suitable branch and then another three days to arrive at the end of the branch. Once there, she took a deep breath and hurled herself forward, instantly falling like a brick all the way down, finishing her trip with a thud in the dirt below. A couple of birds had been watching the whole process for a week and the male bird turned to his mate and chirped, "Dear, I know how much this will upset you, but we'll have to tell her she's adopted."

↝ How do porcupines make love? Veerry carefully!

↝ How do you keep a skunk from smelling? Hold his nose.

➥ So this mouse walks in the jungle with his elephant friend, looks back and says: "Wow, look how much dust we leave behind!"

➥ Some veterinarians are prescribing Prozac for dogs. Animal rights activists are thrilled. Things have finally come full circle. Finally, a drug for animals that has been tested on humans first.

➥ The Chicago Tribune reported in June 1994 on a local sex therapist, Robert Herd, who works exclusively helping animals to mate. He says a surprising number of dogs and horses exhibit sexual dysfunction.

➥ Three rats are sitting at the bar talking. The first says: "I'm so hard, once I ate a whole bag full of rat poison!" The second says, "Well I'm well hard; once I was caught in a rat trap and I gnawed it apart!" Then the third rat gets up and says, "'Bye, chaps, I'm off home to screw the cat..."

➥ Two rabbits escape from the laboratory and see grass for the first time. They're bouncing through the grass when they meet an older rabbit. "Hello," says the older rabbit. "Would you like to come and stay at my warren?" "What's a warren?" ask the two rabbits. "Don't worry," replies the older rabbit. "Come and see." So off they go. They like the tunnels and chambers of the older rabbit's warren, and decide to stay. In the morning, the two rabbits are awakened by the thumping of the older rabbit. "Come on out for the cabbages," calls the older rabbit. "What's a cabbage?" ask the two rabbits. "Don't worry," replies the older rabbit. "Come and see." So off they go, and they enjoy a day in the fields, eating cabbages. They return very satisfied, with their tummies full of cabbage, and agree a good day was had by all. The following day it's, "Come on out for the cabbages" again, and the same for the day after that. At the end of the third day Rabbit 23 says to Rabbit 17, "These cabbages are good but there must be more to life. Let's go and find it." Rabbit 17 agrees, so off they go, across the grass. They meet a younger rabbit. "Hello," says the younger rabbit. "Come and live in my warren. I've got lots of young girly rabbits staying, and I could use some help." "Girly rabbits?" they ask. "Don't worry," replies the younger rabbit. "Come and see." So they agree, and for three days it's thump-thump-thump. At the end of the third day Rabbit 23 says to Rabbit 17, "It's no good: I've got to get out of here." "Why?" asks Rabbit 17. "This is the best time of our lives!" he exclaims. "Yes," agrees Rabbit 23, "but it's been a week and I'm dying for a cigarette."

➥ Two vampire bats wake up in the middle of the night, thirsty for blood. One says: "Let's fly out of the cave and get some blood." "We're new here," says the second one. "It's dark out, and we don't know where to look. We'd better wait until the other bats go with us." The first bat replies: "Who needs them? I can find some blood somewhere." He flies out of the cave. When he returns, he is covered with blood. The second bat says excitedly: "Where did you get the blood?" The first bat takes his friend to the mouth of the cave. Pointing into the night, he asks: "See that black building over there?" "Yes," the other bat answers. "Well," says the first bat, "I didn't."

➥ What's another name for an adolescent rabbit? A pubic hare.

➻ Two whales, a male and a female, are swimming happily through the ocean. On seeing a boat, the male says to his friend: "Hey, I've got a great idea! Let's swim up under that boat and blow out really hard through our blowholes!" The female says, "Uh... I don't know..." "Come on, it'll be fun: just this once!" The female agrees and they swim up under the boat and blow out, capsizing the boat and sending the hapless sailors into the water. As they are swimming away, the male says, "Wow! That was fun, wasn't it? Hey! I've got another idea! Let's swim back there and eat all the sailors!" The female, exasperated, replies, "Look, I agreed to the blow job, but I'm not swallowing any seamen."

➻ What do you get when you cross a chick with an alley cat? A peeping tom.

If dolphins are so intelligent, how come they ain't got Walkmans?

John Lydon

➻ What do you get when you cross an onion with a donkey? A piece of ass that'll bring tears to your eyes.

➻ What's the difference between a toad and a horny toad? One goes "Gribbit"; the other goes "Grabbit".

➻ Which meat is cheapest in the USA? Deer balls – you'll find them under a buck.

➻ Which pine has the longest needles? A porcupine.

➥ Why did the koala fall out of the tree? Because it was dead.

➥ Why did the turtle cross the road? To get to the Shell garage.

➥ Why do bunny rabbits have soft sex? Because they have cotton balls!

➥ Why do seagulls live near the sea? Because if they lived near the bay, they would be called bagels.

➥ Why do walruses go to Tupperware parties? They love a tight seal.

CROCODILES

➥ A bloke walks into a pub with a yellow, long-nosed, short-legged dog under his arm. "That's one ugly dog," says another patron, petting his Doberman. "Heh," says the bloke, "that he is, but he's a mean little bastard." "Is that so?" asks the other patron, "I'll bet you £50 my dog will kick his arse in less than two minutes." The bloke agrees, so they put their dogs face to face and each gives the command to attack. In the twinkling of an eye, the little yellow dog has bitten the Doberman clean in half. "Christ!" shouts the Doberman's devastated owner, "He killed Fang! What kind of damn dog is this?" "Well," says the bloke, "before I cut off his tail and painted him yellow he was a crocodile."

➤ A man walked into a bar with his crocodile and asked the bartender: "Do you serve lawyers here?" "Certainly," replied the bartender. "Good," said the man. "Give me a beer, and I'll have a lawyer for my croc."

An appeaser is one who feeds a crocodile hoping it will eat him last.

Winston Churchill, on Neville Chamberlain

➤ An old man walks into a bar using a cane and carrying a crocodile. The barman says, "Sorry, mate, no animals allowed in here – especially dangerous ones like that." The man says, "Oh, go on: my croc can do a fantastic trick and it'll have people coming from miles around to see it. Let me show you." "Well, OK then," says the barman, "but if I think it's crap I'm going to chuck the pair of you out." So the old man says something to the croc, who gets up on his hind legs and opens his mouth. The man then drops his trousers and puts his pecker into the croc's mouth. The croc shuts its mouth tight around his pecker. The crowd in the bar all gasp out loud, but then the man picks up his cane and raps the croc's head with it three times – tap, tap, tap! The croc opens its mouth and the man's pecker is there – still attached – without even a scratch on it. Everyone in the bar starts clapping and cheering the old man. "Now," says the man looking around the bar, "Does anybody else think they're up to this fantastic trick? Would anyone else like a go?" There is silence and all the men look to the floor. Suddenly an old lady pipes up, "I'll have a try, but you only need to hit me on the head once!"

➤ What did the one crocodile say to the other crocodile? "What's with the long face?"

➤ One upon a time a long way away there was a kingdom with a king who had a daughter. He wanted her to marry a brave man who would desire her and make her happy. So he devised a test: if any man could swim across his huge lake of crocodiles they could have the choice of a castle, untold riches or his daughter's hand in marriage. People gathered from miles around and many volunteered to try. "I can do it," a man cried, jumped into the water and was instantly swallowed up by the crocodiles. "I can do better than that," said another, who jumped in and was instantly swallowed up by the crocodiles. Next, there was a loud splash and a man began to swim. He made it all the way and was greeted by the king. "Would you like the castle, the cash or the fair princess, brave sir?" he asked. "None of them," the man replied, "I want the dirtbag who pushed me into the lake in the first place!"

CULTURE CLASH

➤ An Indian walks into a saloon dressed like a cowboy. He goes up to the bar, looks at the landlord and says, " Me wantum beer." So the landlord gives him a beer. He drinks it. He then goes into the bathroom, pulls out his rifle, shoots the toilet, walks back out, grabs his bag, opens it, pulls out a mangy-looking cat and takes a big bite out of it. The landlord looks at him and says, "Son, what the Sam Hill are you doing?" The Indian replies, "Me being like the white man. Me drink beer, shoot shit and eat pussy."

000

Frustrate a Frenchman, and he will drink himself to death; an Irishman, and he will die of angry hypertension; a Dane, and he will shoot himself; an American, and he will get drunk, shoot you, then establish a million-dollar aid programme for your relatives. Then he will die of an ulcer.

S Rudin, 1938 – 1994

➻ A man walks into a Chinese restaurant but is told that there will be at least a 20 minute wait and he is asked if he would like to wait in the bar. He goes into the bar and the bartender says, "What'll it be?" The man replies, "Give me a Stoli with a twist." The bartender squints at him for a few seconds, then smiles and says: "Once upon time there were four little pigs..."

DeaTH

➻ A lawyer named Strange was shopping for a gravestone. After he had made his selection, the stonemason asked him what inscription he would like on it. "Here lies an honest man and a lawyer," responded the lawyer. "Sorry, but I can't do that. In this country, it's against the law to bury two people in the same grave. However, I could put 'Here lies an honest lawyer'." "But that won't let people know who it is," protested the lawyer. "Certainly will," retorted the stonecutter. "People will read it and exclaim, 'That's strange'."

➻ A woman went into a hardware shop to buy an axe. "It's for my husband," she told the assistant. "Did he tell you what poundage he was after?" asked the guy. "Are you joking?" she said. "He doesn't even know I'm going to kill him!"

Radio is death in the afternoon, and well on into the night.

Arthur Miller

↝ A Sloaney Londoner is getting old so she decides to make her will and to include her final requests. She is talking to her priest and she tells him that when she has been cremated she would like to have her remains scattered in Harvey Nicks, dear. "But why's that?" asks the priest. The woman replies, "I want to be sure that my daughters will visit me at least once a week!"

↝ An old man had died. The funeral was in progress, and the vicar was talking at some length about the good life of the dearly departed, what an honest man he had been, what a loving husband and kind father, and how his poor family would miss him. Finally, unable to cope any longer, the widow whispered to her elder son, "Just pop on up there a moment and have a look in the coffin, will you? I want to be sure he's talking about your father."

I had rather be set quick i' th' earth and bowl'd to death with turnips.

William Shakespeare, the Merry Wives of Windsor

↝ What's the difference between an Irish wedding and an Irish funeral? There's one fewer drunk at the funeral.

➻ At the funeral of a lady were her doctor, a friend and her lawyer. Each had promised her that at her funeral they would toss £1,000 into her grave. The doctor and friend each tossed in their £1,000 cash, after which the lawyer removed the cash and placed a cheque for £3,000.

➻ Janine had been married to Tom for 75 years. When he passed on she just couldn't envisage life without him, so she decided to end it all by herself. Remembering that Tom had an old army pistol and some live ammunition, Janine did some research. She found out on the Internet that a shot to the heart would be the best way to get it over with quickly. She read a page that said her heart would be a couple of inches below the left breast. She said her last rites, turned off the gas, cancelled the milk and pulled the trigger. Later that night Janine was admitted to the local hospital with a bullet wound to the left thigh.

➻ The doctor looked at the worried wife and said, "I'm going to be frank. I'm afraid your husband is at death's door." The wife said, "Isn't there any way you can open it and push him through?"

➻ The former president of the Swiss National Bank, Markus Lusser, died recently at the age of 67. His family have announced their plans to bury him in a secret grave somewhere in Zurich, marked only by a long string of coded numbers.

DENTISTS

A dentist is a prestidigitator who, putting metal in your mouth, pulls coins out of your pocket.

Ambrose Bierce

↦ A dentist is treating a Buddhist monk for a nasty cavity and is quite surprised to hear the patient say 'No' to painkillers. "But why?" the dentist asks. "It is just an anaesthetic." "I want to transcend dental medication," the monk replies.

↦ A dentist told his female patient she needed a root canal operation. "I'd rather have a baby," replied the woman in disgust. The dentist said, "Well, you'd better make your mind up before I finish adjusting this chair."

↦ A woman goes to the dentist. As he leans over to begin working on her, she grabs his balls. The dentist says: "Madam, I believe you've got hold of my privates." The woman replies, "Yes. We're going to be careful not to hurt each other, aren't we?"

↦ At a medical convention, a respected specialist gave a speech detailing a miraculous new antibiotic he had discovered. "What will it cure?" asked someone in the audience. "Oh, nothing that seven or eight other antibiotics won't fix more quickly," he replied. "What's so miraculous about that?" asked the questioner, surprised. "It has a major side-effect of short-term memory loss," explained the specialist. "Several of my patients have paid their bill three, four, even five times..."

➜ A friend of mine went to the dentist recently. He commented that it must be tough spending all day with your hands in someone's mouth. He said, "I just think of it as having my hands in their wallet."

I never worked with him, but I had a brief crush on Gable. One day, I happened to mention it to my dentist, in his office. I was fairly new to Los Angeles, but a few dentists serviced most of the stars. This one was also Gable's dentist, and he asked what I particularly liked about Gable. I said, "His bright smile." He said, "Would you like to see that bright smile today?" My heart was pounding. I thought Gable must be the next patient, after me. I could hardly wait for the session to end, and then the dentist led me to an adjoining room and there, under glass, was a pair of Gable's very white dentures...

Bette Davis on Clark Gable

➜ Dentist: "Could you help me? Could you give me a few of your loudest, most agonised screams?" Patient: "Why? It isn't that bad." Dentist: "Well, there are loads of people in the waiting room, and I'm playing golf at four."

➜ One day, a man walked into the dentist's office for some dental work. The dentist said: "Sir, you have a tooth I must pull, what type of painkiller would you like?" The man looked at the dentist and said, "None, thanks, I have experienced the second greatest pain in my life." The dentist said, "Sir, pulling this tooth will be painful, I suggest a painkiller." The man looked back at the dentist and said, "I have experienced the second greatest pain in my life. Nothing else will ever compare." The dentist said, "Sir, I'm telling you, use a painkiller." The man again said to the dentist, "I have experienced the second greatest pain in my life, I do not need painkillers, now pull the tooth." The dentist then said, "Okay, you asked for it, but first, tell me what was the second greatest pain in your life?" The man said, "Yes, I remember it well. I was hunting in some woods north of here one snowy day. Walking through the woods, the urge came upon me and I headed over to a tree. Well, I started to do my thing, and when the first part dropped, it set off a large bear trap that was hidden in the snow that closed on my balls. That was the second greatest pain in my life." The dentist then said, "Ouch! But then what was the first greatest pain in your life?" The man replied, "When I reached the end of the chain."

➻ Patient: "How much to have this tooth pulled?" Dentist: "£90." Patient: "£90 for just a few minutes' work?" Dentist: "I can extract it very slowly if you like."

DISABILITY

➻ A blind man with a guide dog at his side walks into a department store. The man walks to the middle of the shop, picks up the dog by the tail and starts swinging it around in circles over his head. The manager, who has seen all this, thinks it a little odd, so he approaches the blind man and says: "Pardon me. May I help you with something?" The blind man says: "No thanks, I'm just looking around."

➤ An Irishman's been at a pub all night, drinking. The landlord finally says that the bar is closed, so he stands up to leave and falls flat on his face. He decides to crawl outside and get some fresh air, in the hope that it will sober him up. Once outside, he tries to stand up again and falls flat on his face again. So the Irishman crawls home. At the door he tries to stand up yet again, only to fall flat on his face once more, so he crawls through the door and up the stairs. When he reaches his bedroom, he tries one final time to stand up. This time he collapses right on to the bed and, exhausted, falls fast asleep. When he wakes up the next morning, his wife is standing over him yelling, "You've been out drinking again!" "How did you know?" he asks. "The pub called, you stupid eejit. You left your wheelchair there again."

Before World War I, Turkey was known as the sick man of Europe. Now it is almost terminal.

Richard Nixon, 1909 – 1983

➤ Two friends were deaf-mutes and had grown up together, attending the same schools and everything. After university they had lost touch but one day, ten years later, they met up again in the street, quite by chance. They got around to talking via sign language and they chatted for ages. It turned out that one of them was no longer mute but had learned to talk. The other guy was amazed and was also really curious to know exactly how his friend had learned to talk after all this time. The guy who could now talk explained to his friend that he'd visited an extraordinary doctor who had performed revolutionary new surgery on him, but that it was rather expensive. He gave his friend the doctor's address and bade him good day. The deaf-mute hopped straight into a cab and shot over to the address. He was given an interview with the doctor straight away, and the doctor explained that he would have to come in every day for 26 days and that the course would cost him exactly one million euro. The man thought this very expensive but agreed, having seen the result on his friend earlier that day. He paid the money and begged the doctor to start on him right away. The doctor agreed and asked the man to strip naked and to lie on the examination table. The doctor walked over to the cupboard in the room and took out a broom handle with a doorknob on the end and a huge jar of Vaseline. The doctor dipped the doorknob in Vaseline and, taking a running leap, proceeded to shove the whole thing up the deaf-mute's behind. "Aaaaaaaaaaaaaa!" screamed the deaf-mute. "Very good," replied the doctor, "and tomorrow we'll work on 'B'."

DIVORCE

**My husband and I had our best sex during our divorce.
It was like cheating on our lawyers.**

Priscilla Lopez, Cheaper to Keep Her

→ A man was complaining to a friend: "I had it all – money, a beautiful house, a big car, the love of a beautiful woman; then, pow! it was all gone." "What happened?" asked the friend. "My wife found out..."

→ How do you know when your divorce is getting ugly? When your lawyer doesn't seem like the evil bloodsucking leech anymore.

➻ An elderly man and his wife decided to separate. Before being allowed to do so legally, the Family Court insisted that they undergo some counselling from the marriage guidance mob, to see if their union could be saved. The counsellor did her best, but to no avail. The old folk were absolutely determined to go through with separation, leading to divorce. Finally, in some desperation, the counsellor said: "But you're 95 and your wife is 93. You've been married for 72 years. Why do you want to separate now?" The wife replied, "We haven't been able to stand each other for the last 46 years, but we thought we should wait until all the children died before we split up."

DOCTORS

➻ "Congratulations, Mr Brown, you're in great shape for a man of 60. Pity you're only 40."

➻ "The doctor said he would have me on my feet in two weeks." "And did he?" "Yes, I had to sell the car to pay the bill."

➻ A man swallowed a mouse while sleeping on the couch one day. His wife quickly called the doctor and said: "Doc, Doc, please come quickly. My husband just swallowed a mouse and he's gagging and thrashing about." "I'll be right over," the doctor said. "In the meantime, keep waving a piece of cheese over his mouth to try to attract the mouse up and out of there." When the doctor arrived, he saw the wife waving a piece of smoked herring over her husband's mouth. "Er, I told you to use cheese, not herring, to lure the mouse." "I know, doctor," she replied, "but first I've got to get the bloody cat out of him."

↤ Bill: "Doc, Doc. my wife beats me." Doctor: "Oh dear. How often?" Bill: "Every time we play Scrabble."

↤ Patient: "Doc, Doc, I think I need glasses." Teller: "You certainly do. This is a bank."

↤ Patient: "Doc, Doc, should I file my nails?" Doctor: "No, throw them away like everybody else."

↤ Patient: "Tell me, doctor. Is it serious?" Doctor: "Well, I wouldn't advise you to start reading any thick books."

First doctors try to get on, then they honour, then they get honest.

Humphrey Rolleston

↤ The patient shook his doctor's hand in gratitude and said: "Since we are the best of friends, I would not want to insult you by offering payment. But I would like you to know that I have mentioned you in my will." "That is very kind of you," said the doctor emotionally, and then added, "Can I see that prescription I just gave you? I'd like to make a little change..."

↤ "Doctor, my tongue tingles when I touch it to a cracked walnut wrapped in used toaster-oven aluminium foil, what's wrong with me?" "You have far too much free time."

↦ "Doctor, what fish did you say I had?" "You don't have a fish, you idiot! You've got cancer!"

↦ "What kind of job do you do?" a woman asked the bloke next to her on the train. "Actually, I'm a naval surgeon," he replied. "Goodness!" said the woman, "You doctors do specialise in some arcane fields!"

↦ "Doctor, I'm not feeling so well," says the patient. "Would it be possible to run some tests?" "Sure thing," says the doctor. "Stop by the surgery some time today and ask the nurse. Bring a urine sample, too. We'll talk about the results over the phone." The patient does as instructed and waits for the results. One day passes: nothing. The following day he gets a phone call from his doctor who says: "Well, I have good news and bad news." "What is the good news?" the patient asks. "You have 24 hours left to live." "WHAT? What's the bad news, then?" "I forgot to call you yesterday."

↦ A lady wanted bigger breasts, so she went to her doctor to refer her to a plastic surgeon. "I can do that," said her doctor, "but I would like you to try a simple exercise before surgery or drugs." He stood up to demonstrate, holding his arms straight out to the side, rotating them counter-clockwise, and singing, "Ashes to ashes, dust to dust, if I do this enough, I'll have a big bust." "Do that as often as you can and come back in a week." One week later, she's back at the doctor, and tells him that it didn't work. "How often have you done the exercise?" the doctor asks her. "Three to four times a day," she says. "Bah! Not nearly half enough!" the doctor scoffs. "Do it at least 30 to 40 times a day and come back in a week." She tries this, performing the exercise whenever she can, which means that she does it on her local Tesco parking lot, before getting into her car. "Ashes to ashes, dust to dust, if I do this enough, I'll have a big bust." The driver of the car parked next to hers turns around, looks at her with round eyes and asks: "Do you see Dr. Johnson?" "Well, yes, as a matter of fact. How did you know?" she queries. The man faces her, places both hands on his hips, moves his hips in a circular motion, and says, "Hickory dickory dock..."

➻ A man comes to a doctor because of a sore throat. The doctor tells him to pull down his pants and to swing his genitals out of the window. "What does this have to do with my throat?" "Nothing, I just hate the neighbours."

I do not love thee, Doctor Fell,
The reason why I cannot tell;
But this I know, and know full well,
I do not love thee, Doctor Fell.

Martial, 40-102AD, as translated by Thomas Brown (1663 – 1704)

➻ A man goes to see a doctor and tells him he hasn't been feeling very well lately. The doctor examines him for a few minutes and then takes three jars of big, coloured pills from a medicine cabinet. "Here is your treatment: you are going to take this green pill in the morning, with a big glass of water, then the yellow pill after lunch, with a big glass of water and finally this red pill, again with a big glass of water. As you can see, these pills are pretty big, you might actually need two glasses of water at night." The patient stares at the huge pills, horrified. "Jeez, doc, that's a lot of pills. Er, what exactly is my problem?" "You're not drinking enough water," the doctor replied.

➼ "Doctor, what does the X-ray of my skull show?" "Absolutely nothing."

➼ A handsome doctor was so vain that whenever he took a woman's pulse he adjusted the results downwards by 10 over 2 to compensate for the fact that he had touched her.

➼ A man goes to the doctor with a strange problem. "Doctor, whenever I break wind there is no smell at all. It's really strange, and no matter what I eat, I get the same result – no smell whatsoever!" The doctor has a cursory investigation and then asks the man if he can possibly break wind there and then. The man drops his trousers and pants and farts extremely loudly. The doctor sniffs at the air a couple of times and immediately says, "Oh yes, this is a common one. I know exactly what the problem is," and he walks out of the room. He comes straight back with a six-foot pole with a large brass hook on the end. "Jesus Christ, doctor; what the hell are you going to do with that pole?" asks the man. "I'm going to open the bloody window," says the doctor, "You've got a blocked nose!"

➼ A man goes to the doctor with a terrible problem with bad breath. "I've tried everything, doctor," he says, nearly in tears. "I changed toothpaste ten times, tried mints, mouthwash – you name it. I can't get rid of this terrible odour." The doctor nods and asks the guy to get undressed. After a thorough examination, he allows him to put his clothes back on. "You seem to have a rash around your anus. We will have to treat this first. In the meantime, try not to chew your fingernails."

↔ A man goes to the doctor's office one day. The attractive nurse says: "The doctor is over at the hospital right now. He won't be back for about an hour. Could you tell me your symptoms, please?" He tells her. She looks at him appraisingly and decides he's just tense. She offers: "Well, um, for £50, I've got just the thing for you." He agrees, and she takes him into an examining room and screws the daylights out of him. About a week later, he returns, only to find that the doctor is there. The doctor listens to the man's symptoms, examines him and decides the man is just tense. The doctor writes out a prescription for a sedative and says, "That'll be £150 for this visit." The man says, "If it's all the same to you, doctor, I'd rather have the £50 cure."

↔ A man has been suffering from a tenacious cold for the past week. He goes to his doctor, who prescribes him some tablets. A week later, the same guy comes back, every bit as ill as before. Frowning, the doctor prescribes him a stronger version of the drugs and sends him home. It doesn't work, though, and the man comes back a week later just as miserable as before. The medicine obviously doesn't work and the doctor reckons it is a case of 'intractable cold of an unknown nature'. "All right," says the doctor. "What I want you to do is to open your bedroom window tonight and spend an hour naked in front of it." "What?" exclaims the patient. "I'll catch pneumonia!" "Pneumonia is fine," the doctor replies. "I can treat pneumonia."

↔ A patient with a sore throat goes to see his doctor. After examining him, the doctor says, "I'm afraid your tonsils will have to be removed." "I want a second opinion," says the man, unhappily. "OK," replies the doctor, "You're damn ugly, too."

➠ A man, looking like a mechanic in stained overalls, comes into the reception of the posh local surgery, full of mothers and their children, well-to-do professionals and retired people looking at him with disdain. He approaches the receptionist and says, in a voice that is altogether too loud for this sort of place: "There's something wrong with my dick." "We don't use this kind of language here," says the nurse reprovingly. "Please try again and be more polite this time: say you have a problem with your ear or something." The man seems about to explode but, with visible effort, decides just to let it go. He takes a deep breath and says: "There is a problem with my ear." "Is there, my dear?" the receptionist says smugly. "What kind of problem?" The man gives her an evil grin and says: "I can't piss out of it."

➠ A pipe burst in a doctor's house. He called a plumber. The plumber arrived, unpacked his tools, did mysterious plumber-type things for a while and handed the doctor a bill for £600. The doctor exclaimed: "This is ridiculous. I don't even make that much as a doctor." The plumber waited for him to finish and quietly said: "Neither did I when I was a doctor."

➠ A woman went to her new doctor for a check-up. He turned out to be absolutely gorgeous. He told her he was going to put his hand on her back and he wanted her to say "Eighty-eight." "Eighty-eight," she purred. "Good. Now I'm going to put my hand on your throat and I want you to again say 'Eighty-eight.'" "Eighhty... eighhhhtttt." "Fine. Now I'm going to put my hand on your chest and I want you one more time to say 'Eighty-eight.'" "One, two, three, four, five..."

❤ A psychiatrist and a proctologist became good friends and agreed to share offices to cut down on expenses. To economize even further, they had just one sign printed:

Dr John Wayland, Psychiatrist
Dr Stan Smith, Proctologist
SPECIALIZING IN ODDS AND ENDS

❤ A woman went to her doctor for a follow-up visit after the doctor had prescribed testosterone (a male hormone) to her. She was a little worried about some of the side-effects she was experiencing. "Doctor, the hormones you've been giving me have really helped. I feel much better, but I'm wondering if you got the dosage right. I've started growing hair in places that I've never grown hair before." The doctor reassured her. "A little hair growth is a perfectly normal side-effect of testosterone. Just where has this hair appeared?" "On my balls."

He wrote with a doctor's hand – the hand which from the beginning of time has been so disastrous to the pharmacist and so profitable to the undertaker.

Mark Twain on doctors

❤ An attractive young woman goes for her annual check-up and is asked by the new doctor to get undressed, for he must take her temperature rectally to be sure. She agrees, but a few minutes later says indignantly, "Doctor, that's not my rectum!" "Madam," says the doctor, "that's not my thermometer."

➻ A young lady entered the doctor's office carrying an infant. "Doctor," she explained, "the baby seems to be ailing. Instead of gaining weight, he lost three ounces this week." The doctor examined the child and then started to squeeze the lady's breasts. Too stunned to react, she lets him unbutton her blouse, deftly removing the bra and stroking her right nipple, emitting a thoughtful Hmm. "Young lady," he announced, "No wonder the baby is losing weight, you haven't got any milk!" "Of course not!" she shrieked. "It's not my child, it's my sister's!"

➻ A young woman was going to marry one of those elderly, wealthy eccentrics who want a virgin bride. Since she wasn't, she went to a doctor to reconstruct her hymen. The doctor told her that would cost around £500 to do it surgically, but that there was another way that would cost only £50 and could be done straight away in his office. The woman agreed to try the cheap way, paid the money and lay down on the consultation bed, feet in the stirrups. The doctor worked on her for several minutes, then congratulated her on her forthcoming marriage and showed her the door. After the honeymoon, the woman came back to the doctor and told him that it was perfect: the pain, the blood, everything was there. "How did you do it?" she asked. "Very simple," he replied. "I tied your pubic hair together."

➻ After the baby was born, the panicked Japanese father went to see the obstetrician. "Doctor," he said, "I'm a little upset. You see, my baby daughter has red hair. She can't possibly be mine." "Don't worry," the doctor said genially. "Even though you and your wife both have black hair, one of your ancestors might have contributed red hair to the gene pool." "This is impossible," the man insisted.

"We're pure Oriental. There have never been redheads in any of our families." "Well," said the doctor, "let me ask you this. How often do you have sex?" The man seemed ashamed. "I've been working very hard for the past year. We only made love once or twice a month." "There you have it!" the doctor said confidently. "It's just rust."

↦ American doctors have the letters "MD" after their names to warn you that they are Mentally Deficient!

Americans are people who laugh at African witch doctors and then spend $100 million dollars on fake reducing systems.

LL Levinson

↦ An extremely old man visits his doctor and tells him, "I need my sex drive lowered." The doctor, incredulous, says, "What? You want your sex drive lowered?" To which the old man replies: "It's all in my head. I need it LOWERED."

↦ As the doctor completed an examination of the patient, he said: "I can't find a cause for your complaint. Frankly, I think it's due to drinking." "In that case," said the patient, "I'll come back when you're sober."

↦ Doctor: "Did you take the patient's temperature?" Nurse: "No. Is it missing?"

↦ Doctor: "Did you take those pills I gave you to improve your memory?" Patient: "Pills?"

↦ Doctor: "Does it hurt when you do this?" Patient: "Yes." Doctor: "Well, don't do it, then."

↦ Doctor: "Have you ever had this before?" Patient: "Yes." Doctor: "Well, you've got it again."

↦ Doctor: "What seems to be the trouble? " Patient: "Doctor, I keep getting the feeling that nobody can hear what I say." Doctor: "What seems to be the trouble?"

↦ Doctor: "You're in good health. You'll live to be 80." Patient: "But, doctor, I am 80 right now." Doctor: "See, what did I tell you?"

↦ I was 12 years old before I realized I could cough without having a doctor holding my bollocks.

↦ Mrs Smith: "Help me, doctor! Little Tommy's swallowed the can-opener." Doctor: "Don't panic. He'll be alright." Mrs Smith: "But how do I open the frigging beans? The toast's getting cold."

↦ Patient: "Doc, Doc what should I do if my temperature goes up a point or more?" Doctor: "Sell!"

↦ Patient: "Doc, Doc, I have yellow teeth. What do I do?" Dentist: "Wear a brown tie..."

↦ Patient: "Doc, Doc, I think I swallowed a pillow." Doctor: "How do you feel?" Patient: "A little down in the mouth."

↦ Patient: "Doc, Doc, I've got five penises." Doctor: "Well, how do your pants fit?" Patient: "Like a glove."

↦ Patient: "Doc, Doc, if I give up wine, women, and song, will I live longer?" Doctor: "Not really. It will just seem that way."

↦ Patient: "Doc, Doc, you've got to help me. Every night I get the uncontrollable urge to go downstairs and stick my dick into the biscuit tin. Do you know what's wrong with me?" Doctor: "Yes... You're fucking crackers."

↦ Patient: "Doc, Doc, you've got to help me. I eat apples, apples later come out into the toilet. I eat bananas, bananas come out." Doctor: "That's easy. Eat shit."

↦ Patient: "Doctor, doctor. My hair keeps falling out. What can you give me to keep it in?" Doctor: "A shoebox."

↦ Patient: "I am having a hard time hearing. I can't even hear myself cough." Doctor: "Here is a prescription, take the medicine for seven days, then return for a check-up." Seven days later – Patient: "Thanks a million, doctor. At least, I can hear myself cough now. So what did you do to make me hear better?" Doctor: "Nothing. I gave you an expectorant to increase your cough."

↦ Patient: "What's good for excessive wind, doctor?" Doctor: "A kite."

↦ Patient: "Will it hurt, doctor?" Doctor: "Only when you get my bill."

➻ The doctor entered the waiting room. "I have some good news for you, Mrs Douglas." "Pardon me," she interrupted coldly, "but it's Miss." The doctor corrected himself and said, "I have some bad news for you, Miss Douglas."

➻ Three doctors are in a duck blind and a bird flies overhead. The GP looks at it and says: "Looks like a duck, flies like a duck... it's probably a duck," and shoots at it, but he misses and the bird flies away. The next bird flies overhead and the pathologist looks at it, then looks through the pages of a bird manual, and says: "Hmmmm...green wings, yellow bill, quacking sound... might be a duck." He raises his gun to shoot it, but the bird is long gone. A third bird flies over. The surgeon raises his gun and shoots almost without looking, brings the bird down, turns to the pathologist and says: "Go and see if that was a duck, would you, old chap?"

➻ What does it mean when the doctor says you have six months to live? You have five months to pay.

➻ You can always tell when a death certificate has been completed by a Russian doctor. He signs in the 'Cause of death' box...

DOGS

➻ A butcher is leaning on the counter towards the close of day when a wee dog with a basket in its jaws comes pushing through the door. "An' wot's this then?" he asks. The dog knocks the basket sharply into the butcher's shins. "You little bugger." As he reaches down to smack the dog, he notices a note and a tenner in the basket. The scribble on the note asks for three pounds of his best mince. The butcher reckons this is too easy. He goes to the window and reaches for the dried up stuff that's been sitting out all day. The dog growls at him. The butcher turns around and, glaring at the mutt, gets the best mince from the fridge. Weighing out about 2 1/2 pounds, he drops it on the scale with his thumb. "Hmm, a bit shy. Who'll know?" Again, the dog growls menacingly. "Alright, alright," he says, as he throws on a generous half pound. He wraps it up, drops it in the basket, and drops in change from a fiver. The dog threatens to chew him off at the ankles. Another fiver goes in the basket. The butcher is quite impressed and decides to follow the little dog home. The dog quickly enters a high-rise building, pushes the lift button, enters the lift, and then pushes the button for the twelfth floor. The dog walks down the corridor and smartly bangs the basket on the door. The door opens, the dog's owner screams abuse at the dog and then tries to kick the dog inside. "Hey, what are you doing?" says the butcher. "That's a really smart dog you've got there." "That's the third time this week the stupid mutt has forgotten his key."

↦ A dog is a dog, except when he is facing you. Then, he is Mr. Dog.

↦ A dog went into a telegram office, took out a blank form and wrote, "Woof. woof. woof. woof. woof. woof. woof. woof. woof." The clerk examined the paper and told the dog: "There are only nine words here," he said. "You could send another 'woof' for the same price." "Yes," the dog replied, "but that would be silly."

➻ A doctor, an engineer and a lawyer go out hunting in the woods one day. Each of them brings along his hunting dog, and they spend most of the morning arguing about which of the dogs is the smartest. Early in the afternoon, they discover a clearing in the forest. In the middle of the clearing is a large pile of animal bones. Seeing the bones, the doctor turns to the others and says: "I'm going to prove to you two that my dog is the smartest. Watch this." He then calls his dog over and says: "Bones. See the bones? Go get 'em." The dog rushes over to the pile, rummages around for a bit and then proceeds to build a replica of the human skeleton, perfect down to the last detail. The doctor grins smugly; after all, his dog has just built a human skeleton from animal bones. The engineer, however, is totally unimpressed. "That's nothing," he says. "Watch this." He calls his dog over, and points out the pile. "Bones. Get the bones." The dog rushes over, tears down the skeleton and in its place builds a perfect replica of the Eiffel Tower. It even has a little French flag waving at the top. The doctor is forced to agree that the engineer's dog is, in fact, smarter than his own. The lawyer, however, is still not impressed. "My dog is smarter," he says. "Watch." He then calls his dog over, points to the pile, and says simply "Bones." The dog rushes over to the pile, tears down the tower, eats half the bones, buries the other half, screws the other two dogs and takes the rest of the afternoon off.

It's the one species I wouldn't mind seeing vanish from the face of the earth. I wish they were like the White Rhino – six of them left in the Serengeti National Park, and all males.

Alan Bennett on dogs

➤ A Labrador, a Rottweiler and a Chihuahua spot a nice-looking female poodle. They rush to meet her and the poodle, aware of her charms, pouts coquettishly and tells them: "I will go out with the one of you who can use the words 'liver' and 'cheese' in a proper sentence." The Labrador goes first, racks his brains and blurts out: "I like liver and cheese." "What imagination!" giggles the poodle. The Rottweiler growls and prances, then says lamely: "I hate liver and I hate cheese." "That's even worse than the Labrador!" howls the poodle in glee. Then the Chihuahua winks at her and says, "Liver alone. Cheese mine."

➤ A local business was looking to employ someone to help in the office. The manager put a sign in the window saying: "Help wanted. Must be able to type, good with a computer and bilingual. We are an Equal Opportunities Employer." Soon afterwards a dog trotted up to the window, saw the sign and went inside. He looked at the receptionist and wagged his tail, then walked over to the sign, looked at it and barked sharply. Getting the idea, the receptionist fetched the office manager, who looked at the dog with surprise. However, the dog looked determined, so he led him into his office. Inside, the dog jumped up on a chair and stared at the manager. The manager said, in as friendly a tone as possible, "I can't hire you. The sign says you have to be able to type." The dog jumped down, went to the typewriter and proceeded to type out a perfect letter. He took out the page in his mouth and gave it to the manager, then jumped back onto the chair. The manager was stunned, but then told the dog, "The sign says you have to be good with a computer." The dog jumped down again and went to the computer. The dog proceeded to demonstrate his expertise with various programs. After a few minutes he produced a sample spreadsheet and database and presented them to the manager. By this time the manager was totally dumbfounded. He looked at the dog and said, "I realize that you are a very intelligent dog and have some interesting abilities. However, I still can't give you the job." The dog jumped down and went to a copy of the sign and put his paw on the part about being an Equal Opportunities Employer. The manager said, "Yes, I know, but the sign also says that you have to be bilingual." The dog looked at him straight in the face, and said: "Miaow."

➻ A man and his dog walk into a bar. The man says: "I'll bet you a round of drinks that my dog can talk." Bartender: "Yeah! Sure... go ahead." Man asks the dog: "What covers a house?" Dog says: "Roof!" Man asks the dog: "How does sandpaper feel?" Dog says: "Rough!" Man asks the dog: "Who was the greatest baseball player of all time?" Dog says: "Ruth!" Man says to the bartender: "Pay up. I told you he could talk." Bartender throws both of them out the door. Sitting on the sidewalk, the dog looks at the man and says: "Should I have said Gehrig, then?"

➻ A man decided he wanted to become a hunter, so he set about getting himself all the equipment. Last on his list was a dog, so he went off to see the local dog breeder. The dog breeder took him out to the woods with his best dog so the man could see what a top hunting dog it was. The dog breeder snapped his fingers at the dog and shouted, "Go!" The dog ran off at top speed and they could hear much crashing in the undergrowth. The dog came running back, out of breath, and barked once. "What does that mean?" said the man. "One bark means that the dog saw one rabbit in the woods," said the dog breeder. The man thought this was cool, but that he'd better see it again in case it was a scam. Again, the dog merchant snapped his fingers and shouted, "Go!" The dog ran off at top speed and they could hear more crashing of undergrowth. The dog came running back, out of breath, and barked twice. "What does that mean?" said the man. "Two barks mean that the dog saw two rabbits in the woods," said the dog breeder. The man asked to see it one more time, and the dog breeder snapped his fingers at the dog and shouted, "Go!" The dog disappeared again, but this time he came back carrying a stick and began to hump the dog breeder's leg. "What the hell does that mean?" asked the man, astonished. "Well, that means he just saw more effing rabbits than you can shake a stick at!"

For many of us, particularly myself, a dog is a set of sharp teeth mounted on four legs.
Robert Morley

➤ A man goes to a dog-breeder to buy a guard dog, only to be presented with a scruffy terrier mongrel. "What use is that?" he asks. "Ah, but he's a trained killer, this one," promises the breeder. "Watch: Guard Dog? That chair!" In a blur of little snappy teeth and yapping, the chair is reduced to splinters. "Amazing!" says the man. "Can I have a go? Guard Dog? That box!" In seconds the box is shredded to mere fluff. Delighted, he buys the mutt and rushes home to show his lady wife. "Look at our new guard dog," he says. "He's a trained killer!" "What, that thing?" she replies. "Guard dog, my arse!"

➡ A man was out walking his pit bull and decided to stop in the local tavern for a quick beer. Some time later, a second man entered the establishment and asked: "Who owns the pit bull outside?" The first man answers: "I do. Why?" The second man says: "Well, my pet Chihuahua's out there killing it." "What rubbish! I don't believe it!" the first man says. "Suit yourself, but he's choking to death on it."

➡ A man went to visit a friend and was amazed to find him playing chess with his dog. He watched the game in astonishment for a while. "I can hardly believe my eyes!" he exclaimed. "That's the smartest dog I've ever seen." His friend shook his head, "Nah, he's not that bright. I beat him three games in five."

➡ A talent scout is walking down the street and comes across a man and his dog. The little dog is singing. He has a lovely voice and the talent scout says, "Come to my office. I want to sign you and this marvellous dog to a contract. This dog can make us both rich." The man brings his little dog to the talent scout's office. The little dog is just about to finish singing 'La Donna E' Mobile', when a large dog runs into the room and grabs him by the scruff of the neck. She (it's a bitch) runs away with him in her mouth. The talent scout yells, "Stop her! She's taking away our fortune!" The man replies, sadly, "It's no use. That's his mother. She doesn't want him to be on stage. She wants him to be a doctor."

➡ An old man had a dog he just loved but this dog had the nasty habit of attacking anything that moved, including people. His friends told him if he had the dog "fixed", he would lose his aggression and quit this behaviour. Thinking it might be a good idea, the old man had his dog fixed. A few days later he was in his front room when the postman came up the steps. The dog jumped up, went right through the door and attacked the postman. The old man ran out, pulled his dog away and began apologizing. "I am so sorry," he said. "I don't know what to do or say. My friends told me he would quit attacking people if I had him fixed, but it didn't work. I just don't know what to do." The postman picked himself up and said, "You should have had his teeth pulled. I already knew when he came through the door that he didn't want to screw me."

➡ Did you hear about the new breed of dog? They crossed a pit bull with a collie, and came up with a long-haired mutt that bites your leg off and then goes for help.

➡ I put contact lenses in my dog's eyes. They had little pictures of cats on them. Then I took one out and he ran around in circles.

Don't make the mistake of treating your dogs like humans, or they'll treat you like dogs.

Martha Scott

➡ The life sentence of Taro the dog was commuted in February 1994, permitting his release from the Bergen County Jail and his deportation from New Jersey. Taro had been sentenced to die under the state's 'vicious dog' law, but appeals had continued until Taro had spent more than 1,000 days behind bars in his climate-controlled kennel and had cost American taxpayers more than $100,000 in expenses.

➺ I turned on my lawn sprinkler as my dog was crossing the yard. He thought it was the lamp-post getting even with him.

➺ I went to the cinema the other day and in the front row was an old man and with him was his dog. It was a sad, funny kind of film. You know the type. In the sad part, the dog cried his eyes out, and in the funny part, the dog laughed its head off. This happened all the way through the film. After the film had ended, I decided to go and speak to the man. "That's the most amazing thing I've seen," I said. "That dog really seemed to enjoy the film. It's remarkable!" "Yeah, it is," said the man. "He hated the book."

➺ In a two-day period in New York City recently, a homeless man, a train maintenance worker, and a dog were killed on the subway tracks. Ninety people telephoned the Transit Authority to express concern about the dog, but only three called about the worker, and no-one phoned in about the homeless man.

➺ The more people I meet, the more I like my dog.

➺ What do you do with a dog with no legs? You take it out for a drag.

➺ Wife: "We've got such a clever dog. He brings in the daily newspapers every morning." Husband: "Well, lots of dogs can do that." Wife: "But we've never subscribed to any papers."

➺ Would a pun about a Mexican long-haired Chihuahua puppy qualify as a short shaggy dog story?

DRUGS

➼ The Colombian navy recently discovered a ship transporting more than a ton of cocaine out of the country in direct violation of Colombian law. Under current directives, no vessel is allowed to leave Colombia carrying less than three tons of coke.

DUMB

➼ A pig farmer is worried because none of his pigs is getting pregnant. His pigs are his livelihood, so he calls the vet and asks him what on earth he can do to make them procreate. The vet says that if the pigs really won't do the business he should try artificial insemination. The farmer doesn't have a clue what artificial insemination is, but he reckons it must mean he has to get the pigs pregnant by himself. So he loads them all into his truck, drives them to the woods and shags them all. The next day he calls the vet again and asks him how he will be able to tell if his pigs are pregnant. The vet tells him that the pigs will be lying down rolling in mud. The farmer looks out of the window and sees that all his pigs are really clean and all standing up in their field. So he herds them into his truck, drives them to the woods and shags them all again. The next morning the farmer gets up and looks at the pig field. All the pigs are still clean and all standing. So the farmer herds them yet again into his truck, drives them to the woods and shags them all. Early the next morning the farmer is exhausted so he asks his wife to have a look at the pigs to see if they are rolling in mud. His wife gets up, looks out at the pig field and says, "That's very odd: the pigs are all in your truck. Two of them are waving over here and one's tooting the horn!"

➳ "So, Cletus; how did your first day of upper school go?" said Cletus' father. "It was great, Daddy," said Cletus. "Teacher asked each one of us to count to one hundred. Some of the kids couldn't get past the number 30, but I counted all the way to one hundred without making a single mistake. It was great." "That's great, son," said the father, "it's because you're from Arkansas." The next day the father asked, "So how was school today, Cletus?" Cletus said, "It was fine: we had to say the alphabet in class today, Daddy. Some of the kids couldn't get past the letter Q, but I got all the way from A to Z without any mistakes. It was great." "That's great, son," said the father, "it's because you're from Arkansas." After the third day, Cletus came back with a worried look on his face. "What's the matter, son? No good news from school today?" asked Daddy. "Well, Daddy," said Cletus, "we had PE today, and after the lesson, in the shower, I noticed that I had the biggest wee-wee of anyone in the class. It must have been ten times longer and hairier than anyone else's. Is it because I'm from Arkansas?" "Not quite, son," said Daddy. "It's because you're 18 years old."

There is not a more mean, stupid, dastardly, pitiful, selfish, envious, ungrateful animal than the public. It is the greatest of cowards, for it is afraid of itself.

William Hazlitt

➳ A bloke went into a pizza parlour with a friend. Naturally they could not decide what type of pizza to get, so to save hours of pointless wrangling they decided to go half and half. "I'd like a large ham and mushroom pizza, please, but with extra pepperoni on one half." The dumb-looking guy behind the counter looked at him and asked, seriously, "Which half do you want the pepperoni put on?" Quick as a flash the bloke said, "Put it on the left-hand half." The guy at the desk duly wrote down, "Ham and mushroom, pepperoni on the left," and handed the order to the chef, who grinned and got on with making the pizza. About half an hour later, the guy at the desk called the bloke over to give him his pizza. When he got there, he noticed that the pepperoni half was facing him so, unable to resist, he said, "Hey, I wanted that pepperoni on the left, not on the bottom!" The desk guy looked upset, grabbed the pizza and with one swift motion threw it into the rubbish bin. "I'm really sorry, sir," he apologised. "I'll get the chef to make you another one..."

➟ A primary school teacher explains to her class that she is a Manchester United fan. She asks the little ones to raise their hands if they are Manchester United fans, too. Not knowing what a Manchester United fan is, but wanting to be liked by their teacher, their hands fly into the air. There is, however, one exception. A little boy named Johnny has not gone along with the crowd. The teacher asks him why he has decided to be different. "Because I'm not a Manchester United fan," he retorts. "Then," asks the teacher, "What are you?" "I'm a proud Arsenal fan!" boasts the little boy. The teacher is a little perturbed now, her face slightly red. She asks Johnny why he is a Gunners fan. "Well, my Dad and Mom are Arsenal fans, so I'm a Arsenal fan, too," he responds. The teacher is now angry. "That's no reason," she says loudly. "What if your Mom was a moron, and your dad was an idiot. What would you be then?" Johnny smiles and says, "Then I'd be a Manchester United fan."

➻ A General to a Major: "Do you have a couple of smart Captains?" "Yes, I do." "Send them to me. I need to move my furniture around."

➻ A man goes to see his doctor. He pokes himself in the arm, leg, and torso, complaining that it hurts when he does this. The doctor asks him if he is Irish. The man replies that he is, to which the doctor replies that the man's finger is broken.

The majority never has right on its side. Never, I say! That is one of the social lies that a free, thinking man is bound to rebel against. Who makes up the majority in any given country? Is it the wise men or the fools? I think we must agree that the fools are in a terrible overwhelming majority, all the wide world over. But, damn it, it can surely never be right that the stupid should rule over the clever!

Henrik Ibsen, 1828 – 1906, An Enemy of the People

➻ A soldier, not noted as being very bright, was sitting at the table, looking at a mug upside-down. A Sergeant came to sit next to him with his lunch and the soldier told him: "I can't drink from this mug. It has no opening." The Sergeant examined the mug and says: "You're right. And besides, it has no bottom either."

➻ A woman starts dating a doctor. Before too long, she becomes pregnant and they don't know what to do. About nine months later, just about the time she is going to give birth, an Irish priest goes into the hospital for a prostate gland infection. The doctor says to the woman: "I know what we'll do. After I've operated on the priest, I'll give the baby to him and tell him it was a miracle." "Do you think it will work?" she asks the doctor. "It's worth a try," he says. So the doctor delivers the baby and then operates on the priest. After the operation he goes in to the priest and says, "Father, you're not going to believe this." "What?" says the priest. "What happened?" "You gave birth to a child." "But that's impossible." "I just did the operation," insists the doctor. "It's a miracle! Here's your baby." About 15 years go by, and the priest realizes that he must tell his son the truth. One day he sits the boy down and says, "Son, I have something to tell you. I'm not your father." The son says, "What do you mean, you're not my father?" The priest replies, "I'm your mother. The archbishop is your father."

↦ A young man, freshly promoted to the rank of Second Lieutenant, takes possession of his new office. He lovingly arranges a set of plaques and medals in prominent view on his desk, puts up a full-length mirror, spends some time looking in it and wonders whether his shoulder buttons need another polish. Then a young soldier comes in. Wishing to pass for a hotshot, the Second Lieutenant picks up the phone, waves the soldier to stand at attention and wait. He then starts throwing in the names of a few Generals, hints at a golfing date, whispers the name of, and describes, the amorous behaviour of a fictitious young lady and various other rubbish. This comedy lasts for ten minutes, after which he hangs up and turns his attention to the soldier. "Can I help you, soldier?" "Yes, Sir. I'm here to activate your phone line."

➤ Albert Einstein arrives at a party and introduces himself to the first person he sees and asks, "What is your IQ?" to which the man answers: "241." "That is wonderful!" cries Albert in delight. "We shall talk about the Grand Unification Theory and the mystery of the missing mass." The next person Albert introduces himself to is a woman and he asks her: "What is your IQ?" To which the lady answers, "144." "That is great!" responds Albert, very pleased with this party indeed. "We can discuss politics and current affairs. We will have much to discuss!" Albert goes to another person and asks, "What is your IQ?" to which the man answers, "51." Albert responds, "Spurs are doing well this season aren't they?"

➤ An Irish bloke walked into a café and ordered a big mug of tea. When it arrived he carefully spooned ten teaspoons of sugar slowly into the tea and then started sipping it gently, leaving all the sugar on the bottom. Puzzled, the waitress asked him, "I know it's none of my business, sir, but why didn't you stir your tea?" The bloke looked at her, smiled, and replied, "Well now my lass, I don't like sweet tea."

➤ This bloke walks into a pub and orders a beer. The barman looks at the bloke and says, "Have you seen Eileen?" The bloke is rather confused and asks, "Eileen who?" The landlord replies, "How about I lean over and you kiss my hairy arse?" The man is fairly offended by this, and walks out of the door and into the bar across the street, where he sits down and orders a beer. While he is drinking his beer, he tells the landlord what the other barman said to him. The landlord says, "You know, what you should do is go back over there and ask him if he has seen Ben, and when he says 'Ben who?' you say 'How about I bend over and you kiss my hairy arse?'" So the bloke goes back across the street, and asks the barman if he has seen Ben. The barman immediately replies, "Yep, he just went out the door with Eileen." The bloke looks puzzled for a moment, then asks "Eileen who...?"

↦ Two Irish blokes were out hunting ducks. Despite a whole day of vigorous hunting, though, they completely failed to harm even one duck. Finally, one turned to the other and said, "Maybe we'd do better if we threw that dog a bit higher."

↦ Two Irish builders were working on a house. One was on a ladder, nailing planks. He repeatedly reached into his nail pouch, pulled out a nail, looked at it, and either tossed it over his shoulder or proceeded to nail it into the wood. The other one looked up at him, perplexed, and called out, "Why are you throwing some of the nails away?" The first bloke explained, "When I pull the nail out of my bag, it's either pointed towards me or pointed towards the house. I can only use the ones that are pointed towards the house. You can't hammer a nail in flat end first. Do you think I'm stupid?" His mate shook his head, and called back, "Sure and y'are stupid! You shouldn't throw away those nails that are pointed towards you! They're for the other side of the house!"

↦ Two morons are standing on a cliff with their arms outstretched. One has some budgies lined up on his arms, and the other has parrots tied to his. After a couple of minutes they leap off the cliff and splat! Lying next to each other in intensive care at the hospital, the first moron says to the second one, "I don't think much of this budgie jumping." The other moron replies, "Yeah, I'm not too keen on this parrotgliding either."

➻ Three convicts were on their way to prison. Each had been allowed to take one item with them to help them occupy their time while behind bars. On the bus, one turned to another and said, "So, what did you bring?" The second convict pulled out a box of water paints. "I am going to learn painting. I will produce masterpieces and get filthy rich," he says. Then he asked the first fellow, "What did you bring?" The first convict pulled out a deck of cards and grinned and said, "I brought cards. I can play poker, solitaire and gin, and any number of games. I'll get filthy rich in jail." They both turned to the last convict, quietly sitting by himself, grinning insanely. "Why are you so smug?" the others asked. "What did you bring?" The guy pulled out a box of tampons and said, "I brought these." The other two were – understandably – puzzled. "What can you do with those?" The guy winked and said, pointing to the box "Well according to this, I can go horse riding, swimming, roller-skating..."

➻ When Willie retired from the railway after 50 years' service, the company presented him with an old coach to keep in his garden as a memento. One wet day, his friends found him sitting on the step of the coach, smoking his pipe with an old sack over his shoulders to keep out the rain. "Hullo, Willie," said his pals, "why are ye no' inside on a day like this?" "Can ye no' see?" replied Willie, with a nod toward the coach. "They sent me a non-smoker."

eLePHants

➻ A guide at the zoo: "Now, ladies and gentlemen, this is the elephant, the largest living animal to roam the earth today. Every day, the elephant eats three dozen bunches of bananas, six tons of hay, and 2,000 pounds of assorted fruits. Madam, please don't stand there...Excuse me, madam, please don't stand near the elephant's backside...Madam, yes, you in the...Madam...Oh, fuck, too late. George, get digging."

↠ An elephant is walking through the jungle when she gets a thorn in her foot. She is in absolute agony when she sees an ant strolling by. The elephant asks the ant for help but the ant refuses, unless the elephants is prepared to let the ant have his wicked way with her. "Anything! Anything!" replies the elephant. So out comes the thorn and up gets the ant and proceeds to enjoy himself. Meanwhile, in a tree directly above them, a monkey, who witnessed the whole episode, was in fits of laughter. He laughed so much he fell out of the tree on top of the elephant. "Ouch!" says the elephant. "Yeah," says the ant, "take some more, bitch!"

↠ An elephant was down by a watering hole having a drink when he saw a turtle out of the corner of his eye. Reacting with immediate swiftness he ran down to the water's edge, jumped up into the air and landed on the turtle, turning it into a revolting pulp. A giraffe standing nearby noticed this and, faintly sickened, asked the elephant why he'd squished the turtle. The elephant calmly replied by saying that particular turtle had bitten him nastily on the trunk some 50 years earlier, with no provocation, and he had now got his revenge. "Wow," said the giraffe, "you must have an incredible memory." The elephant nodded proudly, "Yes, it's turtle recall!"

↠ Have you heard about Hannibal crossing the Alps with elephants? None of the offspring survived.

→ The United Nations held a competition to discover which nation could produce the best book on elephants. The British submitted a dry historical account, "The Elephant and the British Empire." The French entered a text "The Sensuality of the Elephant – A Personal Account." The Germans submitted an extensive 47-volume work entitled, "An Elementary Introduction to the Foundation of the Science of the Elephant's Trunk." The Americans submitted an article from Money magazine entitled, "Elephants – the Perfect Tax Shelter for the '00s." Sweden commissioned Greenpeace to write a counter-entry "Elephants: They're Better Than People." The Russians put in a terse, melancholy manuscript entitled "The Superiority of the Soviet Elephant," and the Polish submitted a poem, "The Joy and Freedom Brought Forth by the Soviet Elephant." The Greeks sent in a short recipe for clay-baked elephant in a garlic yoghurt sauce, scribbled on the back of a beer-mat. The prize, however, went to the Japanese, for their promotional flyer: "We Have No Elephants, but Wouldn't You Just Love to Buy a Honda Instead?"

essex girls

→ A painting contractor was speaking with a woman about the job. In the first room she said she would like a pale blue. The contractor wrote this down and went to the window, opened it, and yelled out, "GREEN SIDE UP!" In the second room she told the painter she would like it painted in a soft yellow. He wrote this on his pad, walked to the window, opened it, and yelled, "GREEN SIDE UP!" The lady was somewhat curious but she said nothing. In the third room she said she would like it painted a warm rose colour. The painter wrote this down, walked to the window, opened it and yelled, "GREEN SIDE UP!" The lady then asked him, "Why do you keep yelling 'Green side up'?" "I'm sorry," came the reply. "but I have a crew of Essex girls laying turf across the street."

How you dress has a huge effect on how people perceive you. Your clothing can emphasise or obscure aspects of your anatomy – although never as much as you'd like – and it makes comments about you as a person. Sometimes, those comments are rather insulting.

Anonymous

➻ A young Essex woman is asked out on a date and accepts. The boy picks her up and they go to a nearby carnival in town. They ride a few rides, play a few games, and seem to be generally hitting it off well. During a sort of romantic lull, however, the boy says, "What do you want to do now?" "I want a weigh," she says. Well, okay, thinks the boy. They walk over to the fortune scales, and weigh her. They play a few more games and stop for food. "What do you want to do now?" asks the boy again. "I want a weigh," she says. "Hmmm, a little odd but I'll put up with it", thinks the boy. Again they get her weight and fortune. After yet another few games and an exquisite fireworks show, the boy repeats, "What do you want to do now?" "I want a weigh," she says. "Damn, thinks the boy,", she's just too weird for me. They get her weight and fortune, and the boy drives her home. As she walks into the house, her sister asks, "How'd your date go?" "Wousy," says the girl.

↦ An Essex girl and a brunette were discussing their boyfriends. Brunette: "Last night I had three orgasms in a row." Essex girl: "That's nothing; last night I had over a hundred." Brunette: "My god! I had no idea he was that good." Essex girl: (looking shocked) "Oh, you mean with one guy."

↦ An Essex girl and her boyfriend were sharing a bath. The Essex girl said to her boyfriend: "Is it true that if you pull your finger out, I'll sink?"

↦ It was this Essex bloke's first morning as a married man, and he'd had a wild night of mad sex with his new wife. Absent-mindedly forgetting where he was, he got up silently, dressed quickly, left fifty quid on the dresser and headed for the door. On the way out, he realised his mistake and sheepishly went back into the honeymoon suite. His new wife was there, tucking the cash into her bra...

↦ Maggie's first pregnancy had produced triplets. With considerable pride, she was telling her Essex girlfriend how this happened once in every 200,000 times. The Essex girl's eyes widened: "How did you ever find time to do any housework?"

Families

↦ A doctor and his wife are sitting in front of the TV one evening and the good doctor is relaxing by throwing peanuts in the air and catching them in his mouth and eating them. It goes on for a while until the end of the program, when a comment his wife makes distracts him and the peanut lands in his ear. He tries to shake it out, to no avail. Trying to take it out with his little finger, he just manages to get the damn thing even deeper. "Come on," says his worried wife. "Let's go to the hospital and get this out." The doctor agrees, sighs heavily and puts his coat on, just as their daughter comes back from the cinema with her boyfriend. He explains what has happened while his wife is looking for the car keys. On hearing the story, the boyfriend comes forward and says he can help. He asks the good doctor to sit down again, unceremoniously sticks two fingers up his nose and tells him to blow as hard as he can. Sure enough, the peanut pops out of the doctor's ear and goes "Ping!" against the mirror on the mantelpiece. As the daughter and her boyfriend go through to the kitchen to get drinks, the doctor and his wife sit down to discuss their luck. "So," the wife says, "What do you think he'll become after he finishes school? A GP or a surgeon?" "Well," replies the doctor, rubbing his nose, "by the smell of his fingers, I think he's likely to be our son-in-law."

➼ A Manchester couple discovered the wife was pregnant, but the family simply couldn't afford any more children. They looked around and found an excellent Hispanic family to adopt the child. Then...they found out she was going to have twins. Fortunately, a family of Arab immigrants agreed to adopt the other child. Twin healthy boys were born and passed on to the families, who named them Juan and Amal. The biological parents kept in close touch with the adoptive parents in a very amicable relationship. One day, Juan's family sent a picture of the youth in his cricket uniform. The biological mother was so proud of her son. She said to her husband: "He is so handsome. I wish we had a picture like this of our other son, too." He replied, "Dear, they are twins. When you've seen Juan, you've seen Amal."

**Ever since I saw you in your family tree,
I've wanted to cut it down.**

Anonymous

➻ After a long time procrastinating, a man finally agrees to see a doctor about a lump on his belly, but only if his grown-up son goes with him. On the appointed day, they receive the terrible news that he is suffering from cancer and that he doesn't have long to live. They are both shocked and the son decides to take his dad to his local for a pick-me-up. In the pub they find all his father's friends and his dad tells them in hushed tones that he is going to die of AIDS. The son is rather surprised and, when they find a table to sit at for a chat, he asks his dad: "Tell me, why did you tell your friends you're dying of AIDS? You don't have AIDS." "I know," the father replies, "but I don't want them screwing your mother after I'm gone!"

FaRM anD COUNTRY

➻ A city bloke went out to spend a holiday on a small farm, out in the country. While he was there, he saw the farmer feeding his pigs in a most extraordinary manner. The farmer would lift a pig up to a nearby apple tree and let the pig eat the apples off the tree directly. He moved the pig from one apple to another until the pig was satisfied, then he would start again with another pig. The city man watched this activity for some time with great astonishment. Finally, he could not resist sharing his time management expertise with the farmer, and said, "Forgive me, but that is the most inefficient method of feeding pigs that I can imagine. Just think of the time that would be saved if you simply shook the apples off the tree and let the pigs eat them from the ground!" The farmer looked puzzled, and replied, "What's time to a pig?"

↪ A farmer was sitting in his farmyard eating a sandwich when a hen zoomed by, with a cockerel in hot pursuit and closing fast. Suddenly the cockerel slammed on the anchors, screeched to a halt and began pecking at the crumbs from the sandwich. "Damn," muttered the farmer, "I hope I never get that hungry!"

↪ A guy gets a new sports car and takes his girlfriend out for a spin. She keeps telling him to go faster and faster, but at around 100 miles an hour he gets a bit scared. "If I take off my top, will you do 120?" He says yes, so she takes off her top and he does 120. "If I take off all my clothes, will you do 150?" she says. He says yes, so she takes off all her clothes, and he does 150. "If I give you a blow job, will you do 200?" she says. He says yes, so she starts giving him a blow job and he puts his foot down. Before they know it, they've run off the road, she's been thrown clear and he's trapped under the car with only one foot sticking out. She tries to pull him out, but his shoe just comes off. "Go and get help!" he shouts. "I can't, I'm naked and all my clothes are trapped under the car," she says. But there's nothing else to be done, so she covers her privates with his shoe, runs to the nearest house and bangs on the door. An old farmer opens the door and she starts shouting, "Please, you've got to help me, my boyfriend's stuck. Can you help me pull him out?" The old farmer looks slowly down at the shoe and says, "Nope, I reckon he's too far in for that."

➡ One morning the farmer's son got up early to go and play on the farm, but his mother told him he would have to do chores because now he was old enough to be helping out. The boy didn't like the thought of this much, but didn't have a lot of choice. He started in the barn, where he milked the cow. When he'd finished he booted the cow up the arse. Then he went to feed the pig. When he'd finished, he booted the pig up the arse. Then he went to feed the chickens. When he'd finished, he booted the chickens up the arse. Now his chores were done, he went back to the house for breakfast. His mother gave him a bowl of dry cornflakes. "What about milk and my fried breakfast?" asked the boy. "Well, you don't get any milk because you kicked the cow up the arse," said his mother. "And you don't get any bacon because you kicked the pig up the arse," she continued, "and you don't get any eggs because you kicked the chickens up the arse." At that moment, the farmer walks in as the cat walks past the door. In a bad mood, the farmer launches a kick at the cat and gets it up the arse. The boy is silent for a while, then looks at his mother and says, "Do you want to give him the bad news or shall I?"

**I heard you were born on a farm.
Any more in the litter?**

Anonymous

➡ There was a farmer with three daughters. One Saturday night they each had a date. One by one the dates arrived and the farmer answered the door each time. The first fellow knocked on the door. The farmer answered and the fellow said, "Hello, Mr Farmer. My name is Joe, I'm here to take your daughter Flo out for some dough." "That's just fine," said the farmer, and off went Joe with the eldest daughter. The second fellow knocked on the door. The farmer answered and the fellow said, "Hello, Mr Farmer. My name is Freddy, I'm here to take your daughter Betty out for some spaghetti." "That's just fine," said the farmer and off went Freddy with the middle daughter. The third fellow knocked on the door. The farmer answered and the fellow said, "Hello, Mr Farmer. My name is Chuck – " "Get the hell out of my house," yelled the farmer.

➻ There were these three catering students driving along an old country road one day when they saw a farm. So they pulled in, and knocked on the farmer's door. The farmer answered the door and the three students introduced themselves and said: "We were just passing by and saw your field of buttercups and were wondering if we could go and get a bucket full of butter" The old farmer scratched his head and said: "You boys ain't gonna get no butter from buttercups but you're more than welcome to try." About an hour later, the three came back, thanked the farmer, and drove off with their bucket full of butter. The farmer once again scratched and shook his head, mumbled under his breath and went on about his business. About three months later, the same three students came up to the farm, knocked on the door, and asked the farmer if he remembered them. He chuckled and asked what he could do for them this time. One of them said: "We were just driving by and happened to see you now have a field of milkweed and we were wondering if we could go out and get a bucket of milk?" Once again, the old farmer chuckled, shook his head, scratched it and sarcastically said: "You boys go on out there and get your milk from my milkweeds." Once again, about an hour later, the three came back with their bucket overflowing with fresh milk and drove off. This time, the farmer was really confused, but just a little less sceptical. It was about three or four months later when the three agricultural students came back and again knocked on the farmer's door, saying that they were driving by and saw the field full of pussywillows. This time the farmer went with them.

FaTIGUE

↦ A soldier arrives in a small town a bit late: in fact, just after a whole infantry platoon. He cannot find a free hotel room until a manager takes pity on his tired state and tells him: "Well, I may have something. There is this guy who comes here every time his company stops by and he always sleeps in the same room. He's snoring so much we have to put him apart from the other tenants, but there's a spare bed in his room." "That's fine, I'll take it," says the soldier, relieved. "But what about the snoring? Let me tell you, this man snores very loudly!" "I'll deal with the snoring, trust me." The manager leads the soldier to the room. Indeed, the guy's snores can be heard two corridors away. The soldier thanks the manager and enters the room. The following morning, he goes to pay the bill. "So, did you have a good night's sleep after all?" the manager sneers. "Never better, you run a very good hotel," the soldier replies. "How did you manage to sleep through the snoring?" the manager asks, baffled. "The guy didn't snore!" "How come?" "It's quite simple," the soldier explained. "Just before going to bed I woke him up, kissed him on the cheek and said, 'Goodnight, beautiful.' He spent the whole night awake watching me."

When the Frenchman sleeps,
the devil rocks him.

French saying

➜ A woman had been driving 16 hours straight when she decided she'd had enough: she was still at least six hours away from her destination, it was almost seven o'clock in the morning and she had dozed off and nearly crashed into a telegraph pole. She decided to pull on to a side road and rest for a bit before carrying on. She turned off the car and closed her eyes... drifting off to sleep, precious sleep... All of a sudden an old man in a bright blue jogging suit knocked on her window, scaring her half to death. "Sorry to wake you," he huffed, jogging in place. "But can you tell me what time it is?" The woman glanced at her watch. "7:15," she said through the glass. "Thank you," the jogger said, and left. "Just my luck," the woman muttered angrily. "I'm parked on someone's jogging route." She considered driving off and parking somewhere else, but she was too tired, so she settled back into the seat, trying to re-capture the beautiful dream she was having... Suddenly another jogger knocked on her window. "Hi, do you have the time?" he said. The woman sighed and looked at her watch. "7:19," she said. "Thanks," the jogger said, then trotted off. She looked down the road and saw more joggers coming her way. Irritated, she retrieved a pen from the glove box and scrawled "I DO NOT KNOW THE TIME" on the back of a magazine. She jammed the hastily-constructed sign in the window with her shoulder and settled back to sleep. A jogger knocked on the window just as she started dozing off. The woman pointed at the sign and shouted, "Can't you read?" "Sure I can, ma'am. I just wanted to let you know: it's 7:27."

Finance

Show me a capitalist, and I'll show you a bloodsucker.

Malcolm X

❧ "We have a terrible time making ends meet on Bob's income," his wife told her best friend. "How do you two manage? And you even have kids." "We get along okay," her friend said. "You see, we work on our budget every evening. That saves us lots of money." "Really? How can that be?" "Well, by the time we get it all balanced, it's too damn late to go anywhere and do anything."

❧ A man who scraped through the Black Monday stock-market crash with just a fraction of his fortunes left called his stockbroker the next day and asked, "May I speak to Mr Spencer, please?" The operator replied, "I'm sorry. Mr Spencer is deceased. Can anyone else help you?" The man said "No," and hung up. Ten minutes later, he called again and asked for Mr Spencer, his broker. The operator said, "You just called a few minutes ago, didn't you? Mr Spencer has died. I'm not making this up." The man again hung up. Fifteen minutes later he called a third time and asked for Mr Spencer. The operator was getting offended by this time. "I've told you twice already, Mr Spencer is dead. Why do you keep asking for him when I say he's dead?" The man replied: "It's just so good to hear."

❧ "Get my broker, Miss White." "Certainly, sir. Stock or Pawn?"

➤ A man, 92 years old, is told by his doctor that he has tested positive for HIV. Distraught and befuddled, he retires as usual to spend the afternoon at the park bench with other senior citizens. He tells his friend: "Can you believe it? I have HIV, at 92." His friend replies, "You think you have troubles? I have IBM at 80."

➤ A Scotsman and a Jew were arguing over who could make 20p go further. They decided to give it a try and meet up later to compare notes. When they got back together again, the Jew said, "Well, I used my 20p to buy two cigarettes off a tramp. The first day I smoked one and saved the ashes. The second day I smoked the other and saved the ashes. On the third day I ate the cigarette-butts and used the ashes I'd saved to fertilise my plants." "Ah, you were robbed," replied the Scot smugly. "I used my 20p to buy a black pudding from the butcher. The first day I slit open the casing, scooped out half of the pudding and ate it. The second day I scooped out the other half and ate that. The third day I crapped into the empty black pudding skin. I then took it back to the butcher and said, 'This black pudding smells like shit!' He agreed, and gave me my 20p back!"

Don't get me wrong. I have nothing against businessmen. They are a necessary life form, like earthworms and dung beetles and the E. coli bacteria which inhabit the human gut. Without them we would have no shopping malls, junk mail, leisure complexes, direct insurance sales lines, dial-a-pizza services or countless other benefits of modern civilization.

John Naughton

➨ All I ask is the chance to prove that money cannot make me happy.

➨ Bankers are excellent lovers, because they have an excellent knowledge of the penalties for early withdrawal.

➨ In these up-and-down market periods there is one sure-fire way to secure the attention of your broker. Snap your fingers in the air and call, "Waiter! Waiter!"

FISH

What strange fish hath made his meal on thee?

William Shakespeare, The Tempest

➨ A fish staggers into a bar. "What can I get you?" asks the landlord. The fish croaks "Water..."

➨ A fisherman accidentally left his day's catch under the seat of a bus. The next evening's newspaper carried an ad: "If the person who left a bucket of fish on the number 47 bus would care to come to the garage, he can have the bus."

➨ Men and women have been calling to fish, pleading with them and swearing at them without response since the beginning of time. Scientists have set out to translate fish language. They are not far along yet, but have made some headway. Various clicks and whistles have been recorded that indicate that one fish has a way to communicate what is on his mind to another fish. If the research continues as planned, it should be only a matter of time until man will be able to reproduce fish noises and communicate what is on his mind to bass, perch and catfish. All right-minded fishermen agree that fish-talk research projects should be cancelled and the scientists on them forced to seek other employment. The reasoning behind this point of view is simple and sound. If the research continues to its logical conclusion, fishing will cease to be the pleasant and relaxing sport that it now is. Fishing will become a business of bellowing speeches in fish language designed to convince fish that they would be better off on the bank or in the boat than they are in the water. In such circumstances, any fool knows who the men who'll catch all the fish will be...they'll be politicians.

↦ Why was the bluefish blue? Because the blowfish wouldn't.

FISHING

The depressing thing about an Englishman's traditional love of animals is the dishonesty thereof – get a barbed hook into the upper lip of a salmon, drag him endlessly around the water until he loses his strength, pull him to the bank, hit him on the head with a stone, and you may well become fisherman of the year. Shoot the salmon and you'll never be asked again.

Clement Freud

↦ "I didn't see you in church last Sunday, Nigel. I hear you were out playing football instead." "That's not true, vicar. And I've got the fish to prove it."

➦ A priest was walking along the cliffs at Dover when he came upon two locals pulling another man ashore on the end of a rope. "That's what I like to see," said the priest, "a man helping his fellow man." As he was walking away, one local remarked to the other: "Well, he doesn't know the first thing about shark-fishing."

➦ Fishermen are proud of their rods.

➦ Fishermen do it for reel.

➦ Most Japanese do not know that the English have their own word for sushi. We call it 'bait'.

Dried fish is a staple food in Iceland – it varies in toughness. The tougher kind tastes like toe-nails, and the softer kind like the skin off the soles of one's feet.

WH Auden

➦ The Game Warden, fresh out of school, spots a man walking on the bank of the lake carrying two fish in a bucket. "Can I see your fishing licence, sir," he asks. "I did not catch these fish," the fisherman says. "They are my pets. Every day I come down to the water and whistle and these fish jump out and I take them around to see the sights only to return them at the end of the day." "I do not believe it... You know it is illegal to fish without a licence." "If you don't believe me, then watch," the guy says as he throws the fish back into the water. "Now whistle to your fish and show me that they will come out of the water," the warden says in an ironic tone, to which the man replies, "Fish? What fish?"

↝ The real reason men like to go fishing is that it's the only time anyone will ever say to them, "Oh my God, that's a big one!"

↝ Two blokes were out fishing. One of them was making a cast when a stunningly beautiful young woman ran past, stark naked, laughing. Well, it put him off his cast, but he let the matter slip. As he was about to cast again two men in white coats pounded past, neck and neck, grinning. They were less of a distraction, and he was almost ready to cast again when a third bloke ran past, panting desperately, carrying a heavy bucket of sand in each hand. Unable to bear it any longer, the fisherman called to the bloke in the next bay: "Sorry, mate, but do you have any idea what was going on there?" The guy nodded. "There's a nut-house just through those woods. Once a week, regular as clockwork, that woman escapes, rips off all her clothes and runs around the lake. Those three blokes in the white coats are care nurses. They have a race to see which of them can catch her first. The winner intercepts her, and carries her back to the mental home. Occasionally, she insists on having wild sex with her captor before she'll go back." "What about the buckets of sand?" asked the first bloke. "Well," replied his informant, "that's the one who caught her last week. The buckets of sand are his handicap."

↝ There's a fine line between fishing and standing on the shore looking like an idiot.

→ To catch the fish, it's not how you throw the bait, but how you wiggle your worm.

→ This bloke was a passionate fisherman, and spent all weekend at the waterside regardless of the weather. One Sunday he headed off to the riverside as usual. However, it was freezing cold and pouring with rain and, uncharacteristically, he decided to go home. When he got back, he noticed that his wife was still in bed, so he made a cup of coffee for the two of them, went up to the bedroom and said, "Hello, darling. I've made some coffee. It's really dreadful out there, freezing cold and lashing with rain." "Yeah," she said sleepily, "and that stupid bloody husband of mine went fishing anyway!"

FOOD

→ A couple of lads had a go at using pickles for a ping-pong game. They found themselves in The Volley of the Dills...

→ A family of three tomatoes are walking downtown one day when the little baby tomato starts lagging behind. The big father tomato walks back to the baby tomato, stomps on her, squashing her into a red paste, and says, "Ketchup!"

→ A guy goes to visit his aunt in the nursing home. It turns out she's napping so he just sits down in a chair in her room, flips through a few magazines, and munches on some peanuts sitting in a bowl on the table. Eventually, the aunt wakes up, and her nephew realizes he's absentmindedly finished the entire bowl.

"I'm so sorry, auntie, I've eaten all of your peanuts!" "That's okay, dearie," the aunt replied. "After I've sucked the chocolate off, I don't care for them anyway."

**Tofu. Girls, have you ever had a yeast infection?
It's not two hundred miles away from what
Tofu looks like.**
Ruby Wax

➤ A new experimental car was designed that ran on used chip fat. It did 400 miles to the gallon and let off very few fumes, but you had to stop every 20 miles to change the vinegar.

➤ A woman stopped to admire her neighbour's tomatoes. "How do you get them so red?" she asks. "I must admit," he says, "I'm a bit of an exhibitionist and I like to flash in my garden. I think the tomatoes blush every time I do it, that's why they're so red." "Thank you, I might try that myself," she says. A few weeks later the same man sees the woman digging her own garden, but her tomatoes are still green. "So you didn't try my technique?" he asks her. "Oh yes," she says. "My tomatoes stayed the same – but my cucumbers are huge."

➤ Being overweight is something that just sort of snacks up on you...

➤ Clearly it is not the lovelorn sufferer who seeks solace in chocolate, but rather the chocolate-deprived individual, who, desperate, seeks in mere love a pale approximation of bittersweet euphoria.

➻ How do you know when you're using food as a substitute for sex? You can't even get into your own pants.

➻ There was a bloke who was absolutely devoted to baked beans. He ate them at every chance he got. He adored them. He even found himself dreaming about them. Unfortunately, they were not as fond of him as he was of them, and they always had a vicious reaction, making him fart like an elephant. One day he met a girl, and they fell in love. As their relationship deepened, he came to understand that they would be married, and he thought to himself, "She's a sweet and gentle girl. She'd never understand me farting all the time like a platoon of troopers," and realising how much it would embarrass and humiliate her he decided to do the only thing he could – he gave up the baked beans. Shortly afterwards they were married. Some months later his car broke down, and, working in a village not that far from his home, he decided to walk home, there not being any taxis. He called his wife and explained that he'd be an hour or two later for dinner because of the breakdown. As he left his office, he thought, "I'll just pop in and grab a quick snack at the café round the corner, to fortify myself for the journey." But when he got inside, the scent of baked beans overwhelmed him. He thought about it, and decided that he'd be able to walk the effects off on the way home, and he'd been so good for so long, and so he'd treat himself, just this once. Next thing he knew, he'd eaten four platefuls of beans. Even as he was leaving the café he could feel the effects; he barely made it out of the door before letting off a fart that rattled the window-panes. He farted constantly all the way home. Two hours later, he was feeling fairly confident that he'd farted his last. He knocked on the door and his wife rushed out, hugged him impulsively and said, "Oh, I'm so glad to see you, darling. I have the most wonderful surprise for you for dinner tonight." He smiled, kissed her, and then she blindfolded him, led him by the hand to the table and sat him down. She was about to remove the blindfold when the phone rang. "I'll just be a moment, love," she told him. "Now wait there, and don't you dare touch that blindfold!" She dashed into the hall and closed the door. As she did so, a terrible spasm rippled through his intestines – the beans' final message to his bottom. Thanking God that his wife was in the hall, he eased his weight onto one buttock and farted. It was a legendary thing; a fart from the pages of history itself. It started off slow and squeaky, then rapidly grew in volume as it dropped in pitch, becoming so thunderous that the table rattled. It went on and on and on, for over 30 seconds. It stank like the very Pit itself, too; thick and sulphurous, with the sickly-sweet odour of rotting fruit. It was enough to make him gag silently, and he'd been used to his own wind for a long time. Grinning in amazement, he grabbed his napkin from the table, and started fanning the air to disperse this astonishing last stand before his wife got back. The last vestiges of the stench were just fading five minutes later when she came back from the hall, and apologised for taking so long. "Did you peek, darling?" she asked him. He smiled, and assured her that he had not moved a muscle. She went round behind him, hugged him and whipped off the blindfold. "You're going to be a father," she gushed, "and everyone's come round to celebrate." His parents, his wife's parents, the vicar and his wife, the local GP, her husband and his boss and her husband all stared back at him, reproachfully.

➡ The other day, I dropped a piece of bread and it fell butter-side up. I was dreadfully shocked, until I realised what had happened – like an idiot, I'd buttered the wrong side.

⟶ I know about stressed...it's desserts spelled backwards.

⟶ In a particularly callous and heartless move, the owners of a large mail order diet pill business with tens of thousands of clients sold their mailing list to the boss of a quality chocolate company which was preparing a mailing. The chocolate company's sales rose immediately by 400%; a few weeks later, so did the diet pill company's sales.

⟶ It's OK to use food in sex, but be safe – always use a condiment.

⟶ Scientists have discovered that we actually live on only about a third of what we eat. Health farms, gymnasiums and diet pill manufacturers live on the other two-thirds.

Foods that are said to do one good generally taste of sawdust and burnt rubber.

RH Howarth

⟶ There was a sign in the baker's window that read, "Cakes 66p. Upside-down cakes 99p"!

⟶ This bloke had a nasty accident in a fish-and-chip shop, and tipped some vinegar into his ear hole. He now has a bad case of pickled hearing!

⟶ This bloke picked up a tin of sweetcorn in a supermarket and looked at the label. "Contains no artificial additives or preservatives," it read. Then, a few inches below, was another message saying, "Contains reclaimed aluminium." The bloke showed the label to his wife and said, "Frankly, I'd rather have the additives..."

➻ This bloke walks into a pub and sees this cute doughnut babe drinking a beer. So he walks up to her and asks, "Hey, baby, what's your sign?" The doughnut looks at him with disgust and says "I'm a torus, you moron..."

➻ What is the most common speech impediment? Chewing gum.

➻ What's another name for pickled bread? Dill-dough.

GAY AND LESBIAN

➻ A bloke went into the pub and spotted two gorgeous women sitting by the bar. "Great," he thought, "I'll have a shot at these two." So he walked over, introduced himself and asked if he could buy them some drinks. They accepted, so fancying his luck he bought them some more and stayed and chatted with them. After a few rounds the women just stood up and walked off, without saying anything. "Fuck," thought the bloke, "I guess I blew it." About half an hour later, though, one of the women walked back in and said, "Thanks for the drinks, by the way." The bloke nodded glumly, and said "Sure." She then said, "Y'know, my girlfriend's out in the car right now with her legs spread. She wants to know if you'd like to smell her pussy." Suddenly excited again, the bloke said, "God, yes, absolutely." The woman smiled sexily, took a big, deep breath, exhaled in his face, and said: "Smells good, eh?"

➻ A robber escapes from prison and breaks into a house occupied by a young couple. He ties them up and leaves them alone in the bedroom for a while. As soon as they are alone, the husband turns to his young wife, skimpily dressed in her black nightie, and says, "Now listen, dear. This man probably hasn't had sex with a woman for years. If he wants to have sex, just go along with it and pretend that you're enjoying it. It will probably mean the difference between living and dying for us." "I'm so glad you feel that way, my darling," said the wife, "because he just told me he loves your smooth skin and firm arse!"

Izzard: I'm a lesbian trapped in a man's body.
Skinner: A bit like Martina Navratilova.

Eddie Izzard and Frank Skinner, on tennis player Martina Navratilova

➻ Did you hear about the two gay men who argued in the bar? They went outside to exchange blows.

➻ Did you hear about the new gay sitcom? It's called Leave It, It's Beaver.

➻ Did you hear about the new lesbian leather shoes? They're called Dikes, have an extra-long tongue and you can get them off with only one finger!

➻ Did you hear there's a new PC word for lesbian? Vagitarian.

➻ Did you know that 70% of the gay population were born that way? The other 30% were sucked into it.

↦ Four retired friends decide to go golfing. One of them pays the fees, while the other three go up to tee off. They are all bragging about their sons. The first man says, "Well, my son's in construction, and he's so successful that he gave one of his friends a brand-new house for free." The second man says, "Well, my son's a car salesman, and he's so successful that he gave one of his friends a Porsche for free." The third man says, "Well, my son's a stockbroker, and he's so successful that he gave one of his friends a share portfolio for free." At this point the fourth man arrives on the scene and they tell him, "We were just discussing how our sons were doing. Is yours successful?" The man says, "Well, my son is gay, and he's an erotic dancer in a gay bar." There is silence as the others look embarrassed for the man. "I'm not really thrilled about the dancing, but still," the man continues, "he does pretty well anyway. His last three boyfriends gave him a share portfolio, a Porsche and a brand-new house for free!"

I heard that my "Darling Lily" taskmasters, Blake Edwards and Julie Andrews, were implying to the press that I'm gay. I could hardly believe it! Talk about the kettle calling the pot black!

Rock Hudson on Julie Andrews and Blake Edwards

↦ What did the lesbian frogs say to each other? We do taste like chicken!

↦ What do homosexuals and ambulances have in common? They both load from the back and go whoo-whoo!

➠ How can you tell a hardcore lesbian bar? Even the pool table has no balls.

➠ Right-wing politicians have recently defended tobacco advertising, saying that kids don't start smoking because of posters, but because of stars like Leonardo DiCaprio smoking in high-impact films such as Titanic. There is of course no proof of this, but since the release of the film there has been a marked increase in the numbers of gay American teenagers shagging fat English girls as part of an attempt to prove that they're heterosexual.

McCarthy says he had no idea that Monty Clift was homosexual and was absolutely amazed. Why, he said, it never even crossed his mind. Well, it had crossed the mind of every single trolley-car conductor in Hollywood, so it was very difficult to believe it hadn't crossed the mind of his best friend for seven and a half years. I mean, how far can hypocrisy go?

Truman Capote on Monty Clift and Kevin McCarthy

➠ This rural bloke goes into his local one afternoon and to his amazement spots a pair of absolutely stunning babes sitting in one corner of the pub. He goes up to the bar, calls the landlord over and nodding at the girls says, "Keith boy, you'd best tell me what it is they're drinking, 'cos I'm going to get them another one." The landlord gives him a funny look, and says, "Well, I don't know if that's such a good idea, Tom. They're lesbians, see." Tom looks blank. "Lesbians? What's that, then?" The landlord shakes his head and says, "Tell you what, why don't you go ask them?" So

Tom shrugs, strolls over to the girls and says, "Well now, forgive my ignorance, but old Keith over at the bar tells me you two are lesbians. What does that mean?" They both smile, and one says, in a slow, sexy drawl, "Well, it means that we like to fuck girls. We like to kiss and stroke each other, and all sorts of other things." Tom nods, smiling broadly, and calls to the landlord, "Keith lad, three drinks over here for us lesbians!"

↔ What do you call a lesbian dinosaur? Lickalottapus.

↔ What do you call a lesbian from Canada? A Klondyke!

↔ What do you call a lesbian from India? Minjeeta.

↔ What do you call a lesbian with fat fingers? Well-hung.

↔ What do you call three lesbians in bed together? Ménage à twat.

↔ What do you call two lesbians in a canoe? Fur traders.

↔ What's the biggest crime committed by transvestites? Male fraud.

↔ What's the difference between a cream cracker and a lesbian? One's a snack cracker...

↔ What's the difference between a gay prince and a book-lover? A book-lover uses a bookmark – a gay prince likes his pages bent over.

↦ What's the difference between a lesbian carpenter and a straight carpenter? One uses tongue and groove, and the other just screws.

↦ Where do homosexuals park? In the rear.

↦ Which two words clear out a men's changing room quickest? "Nice cock!"

↦ Why were glow-in-the-dark condoms invented? To enable gay people to play Star Wars.

GIRaFFes

↦ A guy walks into his local with a giraffe and a monkey. All three of them get utterly blotto. The man and the monkey manage to prop each other up and make it to the door, but the giraffe is too big for them to help and he collapses on the floor. As the man opens the door the barman shouts across the bar, "Oi, mate, you can't leave that lyin' there!" and the man shouts back, "That's no lion – it's a giraffe and I can't move him!"

↦ When do giraffes have eight legs? When there are two of them.

↦ Why didn't they invite the giraffe to the party? He was a pain in the neck to talk to.

↦ Two mice walk into a bar for a few ales when a giraffe walks in. "Look at that. She's a beauty," says one mouse. "Well, why not try your luck?" his friend suggests. So the mouse goes over to the giraffe and starts talking to her, and within five minutes they're out the door and gone into the night. Next day, the second mouse is in the bar drinking away, when his friend staggers in. The mouse is absolutely shattered, worn out, ruined. The mouse helps his pal up on to a stool, pours a drink down his throat and asks "What the hell happened to you? I saw you leave with the giraffe. What happened after that? Was she all right?" The first mouse says, "Yeah, she was really something else. We went out to dinner, had a couple of glasses of wine and she invited me back to her place to spend the night. And oh, man! I've never had a night like it!" "But how come you're in such bad shape?" "Well," says the mouse, "between the kissing and the screwing, I must have run a thousand miles!"

Having met you, I now know why some animals eat their own children.

Anonymous

↦ What's worse than a giraffe with a sore throat? A centipede with athlete's foot.

GOLF

➻ A golfer was practising at the driving range after work one evening. He got a large bucket of balls from the kiosk and worked his way through them, but couldn't correct the slice he was trying to iron out. He didn't have the cash for a second bucket of balls, and as he was alone at the range he decided to go and scavenge some, so he walked up the edge of the range collecting balls from bushes and weeds, trying to be inconspicuous. To be able to carry more, he loaded the big, deep pockets of his baggy trousers. Walking back to the tee, he noticed a pretty young woman who had started practising. When he got closer, he saw that she was staring at the strange-shaped bulges in his groin. A bit embarrassed, he explained to her: "Um... they're just golf balls." She looked at him with a mix of sympathy and awe, and said, "That's like tennis elbow, yeah?"

➻ A keen golfer was sometimes accompanied by his wife. On one particular afternoon he was having a disastrous time. Teeing off on the 14th he pulled his shot so badly it spun off towards a groundsman's hut. Unfortunately, the hut was obstructing the line. However, his wife, who was along that day, noticed that the hut had two doors, and it was possible that if both doors were opened he would be able to play through. Of course, he asked his wife to go round the back and open the far door. When she did, sure enough, there was a clear path through to the green, although the ball needed to keep flat. He pulled out a wood, lined up and took the shot. As the ball cracked off his wife, curious, looked round the doorway. Tragically, the ball hit her in the centre of the forehead, killing her stone dead. Well, a few weeks later the widower was playing the same course with a friend. Again, he pulled his shot at the 14th, and ended up in front of the hut. "Hey, you might be able to play through if we opened both doors," observed the friend. The bloke shuddered and went pale. "No way. Very bad memories. Last time I did that, I ended up with a seven."

➻ A man books into a new and fancy resort which advertises an all-inclusive, do-all-you-can kind of holiday. Looking through the hotel's book, he finds there are tennis courts on the premises, so he calls the desk to find out how to go about playing a set or two. "Just meet the pro at the tennis shop, he will lend you all that you need and will find you someone to play with." "How much is that going to cost me?" the man asks. "Nothing, this is on the room," answers a very polite clerk. So the man plays tennis all afternoon. The next day he decides to try horseback riding and again finds it doesn't cost him a penny more than the price of the room. After a week at the hotel he has done just about everything that's available except golf. On his last day, he decides to play a round so he goes to the clubhouse, gets what he needs and starts his game. At the end of his round the pro asks him how the game went. "Not so good," the man answers, "in fact I lost five balls." "Well," says the pro, "that will be £5,000 sir." "What do you mean £5,000, for five damn golf balls? You have to be kidding. I played an afternoon of tennis, went horse riding, scuba diving, deep-sea fishing and more, and was never charged a penny. Now that I have lost five golf balls, you charge me £5,000?" "Yeah," says the pro, "This place really gets you by the balls."

➻ "I have a confession, love," a bloke said to his new wife. "I'm a golf-player. Much as I love you, you're not going to see me at weekends during the golfing season, I'm afraid." "That's OK," she replied, "I have a confession too. I'm a hooker." "No problem," replied the bloke. "Just keep your head down and straighten your left arm."

➻ A man has been on a desert island for five years. One day, while he was knee deep in the sea spearing a fish, he notices a strange movement in the water. A few minutes later, a few feet away from him, a gorgeous woman in a tight wet suit stands up. Dumbfounded, he simply watches her approaching, dripping with water, teeth flashing, hips swaying. "How long has it been since you last had a cigarette?" she asked in a throaty voice. "Man, it's been ages," the guy answers in a shaky voice. The woman diver opens the zip of her breast pocket and fishes out a packet of cigarettes and a lighter. She places a cigarette in his mouth and lights it. She lets the guy take a drag and then asks: "How long has it been since you last had a nice Scotch?" "A long, long time," the guy replies, holding his breath. The woman pulls down the front zip of her wet suit, just enough to reach down and bring out a bottle of bourbon. She places her hands around the neck and gently twists the cap open. She takes a swig, licks the liquid on her lips and passes the bottle to the guy and then asks, her finger toying suggestively with her front zip, "Tell me, how long has it been since you last played around?" "Oh my God," breathes the guy. "Don't tell me you have golf clubs in there, too..."

➻ A minister is out playing a round of golf one day with three of his friends, who are also ministers, when on one of the par fives he reaches the edge of the green in three, leaving himself with about a 40 foot birdie putt. He lines the putt up so that he feels pretty comfortable with it and strikes what looks to be a perfect putt, headed straight for the hole. Just as the ball gets to the hole, it stops, hanging right on the rim of the hole. Being a preacher and a man of God, he looks up to the sky and says to God, "How about a little help?" Just as he says this, a moth flies onto the green, briefly buzzes around their heads and then decides to rest right on his ball, but the ball still doesn't move. So he says: "You didn't send a big enough moth." Just as he says this, the moth starts crawling around the ball, and eventually crawls to the hole side of the ball, causing the ball to drop straight into the hole. The minister simply looks up to the sky and says: "Amen!"

Golf is a game where white men can dress like black pimps and get away with it.

Robin Williams, on Golf

↔ A poor golfer spent the day at an expensive country golf club courtesy of a rich friend, playing badly and enjoying the luxury of a caddy. By the time he got to the 18th he was 88 over par. Seeing a pond over past the green, he said to the caddy, "I've played so badly today that I'm tempted to go and drown myself in that lake." The caddy looked back at him and said, "To be frank, I find it difficult to believe that Sir could keep his head down long enough."

➻ A policeman called a bloke in to question him about his wife's death. "Could you tell me what happened?" he asked. "Well," said the bloke, "I didn't realise my wife was at the red tee getting ready to swing. I drove off, and the ball struck her in the head." The policeman nodded, and said, "That agrees with the coroner's report, but I have another question. Why did she also have a golf ball up her arse?" The bloke shrugged. "Oh, that was my mulligan."

➻ A Scot and a Yank were talking about golf. "In most parts of the United States we can't play in winter. We have to wait until the spring," said the American. "Och, ye big softies," replied the Scot. "Surely ye can play if ye put a will to it? We dinnae let the snow and cold fess us." The Yank looked doubtful. "Well, what do you do, paint your balls black?" he asked. "No," replied the surprised Scot. "We'll just put on a thick pair of thermal troosers."

➻ A top executive lawyer decides that he needs some holiday and to improve his golf, so combines the two with a week's-worth of golf at his local course. On the first round of the first day, he is playing behind a woman whom the lawyer notices is very attractive – and not bad at golf, either. He makes the effort and catches up with her quite quickly. He suggests to her that they play together and she agrees. They begin to play and it soon turns out that they are very evenly matched. Eventually the woman wins with the last stroke on the last hole. They have got on really well, so the man offers his congratulations and offers the woman a lift home. As they are driving, the woman tells the man how much fun she's had, and that she is surprised at how well they got on and how close the competition was. They stop at her place, and she says, "I'd like to show you just how much I appreciated the game and your company," she says, and proceeds to give the lawyer a blowjob. The next morning the lawyer sees the woman teeing off at the first and again suggests a partnership. She agrees, and they play another round of close, competitive golf. The man is pretty disappointed that he didn't manage to win the previous day's game so he really puts everything into it, but it is to no avail. The lady wins once more, again by just one stroke. Again, he gives her a lift home and she gives him a blowjob. This pattern carries on all week, with the woman winning the golf every day. The man is pretty sick about this, but he's getting to spend a lot of time with a beautiful woman who performs sexual favours for him, too, so he's not really complaining. On the Friday night as he is driving her home, he announces that in honour of spending such a great time with her, he's booked them a table for a candlelit dinner at the most exclusive restaurant in town, and then a penthouse apartment at the best hotel. Upon hearing this, the woman bursts into tears, sobbing, "I can't, I can't." The lawyer asks her what on earth is wrong. She sobs out that she just can't go with him, not because she doesn't want to, but because she isn't really a woman – she is, in fact, a transvestite. The guy is gobsmacked and says nothing. "I'm so sorry," she cries. "You total bastard!" he screams suddenly, all red in the face, "You bloody cheat. You've been playing off women's tees all week!"

➥ Do you know why they called it golf? Well, all the other four-letter words were taken...

➡ A woman has just started to play golf when she gets stung on the arm by a bee. She rushes back to the clubhouse, hoping to find a doctor. She asks: "Is anyone here a doctor?" One fairly drunk guy stands up and says: "I'm a doctor, what can I help you with?" "I've been stung by a bee." "Oh really, where?" "Between the first and second holes" "Well, clearly your stance is too wide."

➡ An accountant has been working for a billionaire client for 25 years. To celebrate the event, the billionaire says he'd like to get the accountant a present, so the accountant asks for a set of golf clubs. "How many are in a set?" asks the billionaire. "Basically 14," replies the accountant. "Should be able to do that," says the rich man. A month passes, and the accountant is starting to wonder if perhaps he should have been more modest and asked for a watch, when the billionaire calls again. "I've got you some golf clubs," says the billionaire. "Thank you!" says the accountant, "It's really very generous and..." "Hell," says the billionaire, cutting him off, "it's nothing. I wasn't even able to get you a full set, just the ten. It's worse than that, too. Only six of them have hotels within the grounds."

➡ Golf is a game that needlessly prolongs the lives of some of our most useless citizens.

➡ Golfers have it down to a tee.

➡ In Africa, some of the native tribes have a custom of beating the ground with clubs and uttering spine-chilling cries. Anthropologists call this a form of primitive self-expression. In Britain we call it golf.

↪ Moses and Jesus were part of a threesome playing golf one day. Moses stepped up to the tee and hit a long drive. The ball landed on the fairway, but rolled directly towards a water hazard. Quickly Moses raised his club, the water parted and the ball rolled to the other side, safe and sound. Next, Jesus strolled up to the tee and hit a nice long drive directly towards the same water hazard. It landed right in the centre of the pond and kind of hovered over the water. Jesus casually walked out on the pond and chipped the ball right up onto the green. The third guy got up and sort of randomly whacked the ball. It headed out over the fence and into oncoming traffic on a nearby street. It bounced off a truck and hit a tree. From there, it bounced onto the roof of a shack close by and rolled down into the gutter, down the drainpipe, out onto the fairway and straight towards the pond. On the way to the pond, the ball hit a little stone and bounced out over the water and onto a lily pad, where it rested quietly. Suddenly, a very large bullfrog jumped up on a lily pad and snatched the ball into his mouth. Just then, an eagle swooped down and grabbed the frog and flew away. As they passed over the green, the frog squealed with fright and dropped the ball, which bounced right into the hole for a beautiful hole in one. Moses turned to Jesus and said: "I hate playing with your Dad."

↪ Taffy gets his first golf lesson. His instructor tells him: "You see that little flagpole over there? Just hit the ball and try to get it as close to it as you can." So Taffy gives it a good whack and upon approaching the hole they see that he has ended up 5cm from the hole. "Very good," the instructor says, amazed. "Now, you have to hit it into the hole." "What!" exclaims Taffy. "Why didn't you say so in the first place?"

↔ Three blokes assembled for a round of golf on Mothering Sunday. All were quite surprised at having been able to escape from the family for the day, and so they compared notes on how they managed it. The first bloke said, "I bought my wife a dozen red roses, and she was so surprised and touched that she let me go." The second guy said, "Yeah. I bought my wife a diamond ring, and she was so thrilled that she let me go." The third guy shook his head, and said, "I woke up this morning, farted thunderously, scratched my arse, then turned to my wife, belched and said, 'Golf course or intercourse?' She blinked and replied, 'I'll put your clubs in the car.'"

After animals, somehow the business community seems to follow on naturally. That's why senior managers take such great pains to make sure they never actually have to do anything, and go and play golf together instead. It's the modern version of the men forcing the womenfolk to walk miles to the watering hole with big jugs on their heads.

Anonymous

↔ Three friends were getting ready to play golf when a bloke walked down the path to the first hole and asked if he could join them. They agreed, and began golfing. The new guy played left-handed, and shot a wonderful round. After they finished, the fourth golfer was invited back the following week. "I'd love to, thanks," he said, "But I might be a little late." The next week, he turned up on time and again shot a great round, but to everyone else's surprise, he was playing right-handed. Again he was invited back, and again he said. "I'd love to, thanks, but I might be a little late." The following week he again turned up on time and played left-handed. He played another good round, and when he was asked back another time, replied, "I'd love to, thanks, but I might be a little late." Well, he was on time again, played left-handed again, and got another good round in. When he was invited back to his now-regular slot, he again warned the others that he might be a little late. Unable to bear it any longer, one of the three friends asked him: "We've seen you play superbly both left- and right-handed, which I think is fantastic, and you always tell us you might be late. Why is that?" The golfer responded, "Well, like many players, I'm superstitious. When I wake up to go golfing, I look at my wife. If she's sleeping on her left side, I golf left-handed. If she's sleeping on her right side, I golf right-handed. If she's on her back, well, I'm going to be a little late..."

➻ Tiger Woods was having a quiet holiday far away from the sport paparazzi, driving around North Wales in his Volvo. One evening, noticing that he is almost out of petrol, he stopped at a station to fill up. An old man came out from behind an antiquated counter and approached the car. "Fill her up," Tiger Woods said, getting out of the car to stretch his legs. As he did so, a tee fell from his pocket and landed at the feet of the old timer. The petrol attendant picked it up, turned it around in his hands, obviously puzzled, for a full minute. Then, defeated, not able to figure out what it was, he turned to Tiger Woods and asked: "Say, what is this, young man?" "Oh, this is called a tee," the champion golfer answered. Seeing the lack of comprehension in the old timer's eyes, he elaborated: "It's to rest my balls on when I am taking long drives." The man looked him up, then at his car and said admiringly: "They really think of everything at Volvo."

→ Two blokes are out at the sixth, teeing off. The first makes a reasonable drive but the second gives it a tremendous wallop. Ahead, on the fairway, a groundsman wanders out and into the path of the ball. It hits him square on the temple, and he collapses. The two golfers rush up, but find the guy dead, with the ball lodged in the side of his skull. There's blood everywhere. "Oh, Christ, no!" yells the second guy, "what am I going to do?" The first guy looks at him. "Come on, it's not that bad. A pitching wedge has the loft to get that free."

→ Two blokes were out playing golf. "Did you hear about William Rogers?" asked one. "No," said the other curiously, "what about him?" "Well," said the first one, "he went mad last Saturday and beat his wife to death with a golf club." The other one shuddered. "God, that's awful." They paused for a moment's reflection, and then the other asked, "How many strokes?"

→ There's only one thing you'll hear on a golf course that you'll never hear in a brothel – "Bite, you cocksucker, bite!"

→ Two Scotsmen, Jim and Freddie, were out playing golf, and they decided to put some competition into the game by putting money on the round – 50p. Well, with such a sum at stake both men were concentrating fiercely, and they were perfectly matched for the first nine holes. On the tenth, though, Jim drove into the rough and couldn't find his ball. He called Freddie over to help and the pair searched around. Finally, desperate to avoid the four-stroke penalty for a lost ball, Jim popped a new ball out of his pocket when Freddie wasn't looking. "Freddie lad, I've found the ball," said Jim. "You filthy, cheating swine!" exploded Freddie. "I never thought that any friend of mine would stoop so low as to cheat in a game that had money on it!" "I'm not cheating!" protested Jim, "I've found my ball, and I'll play it where it lies." "That's not your ball," sneered Freddie. "I've been standing on your ball for the last five minutes!"

➥ A poor golfer was having a bad round. He was 30 over par after four holes, had lost 14 balls in the same piece of water and had practically ploughed the rough trying to get a ball out. Then, on the green of the fifth, his caddy coughed just as he took a ten-inch putt, and he sliced it. The golfer went wild. "By God! You've got to be the worst damn caddy in the whole wide world!" The caddy looked at him sourly, and replied, "I doubt it. That would be too much of a coincidence."

➥ A vicar walloped his ball deep into a bunker. His face twisted in irritation, but mindful of his vocation, he didn't swear. When he got up to have a look, he saw that it was lodged up under the lip of the bunker, and was going to take shots and shots to extract. Scowling like thunder, he still stayed silent, lips pressed together. Finally, after four strokes, the ball popped out of the sand, only to land in a small stream nearby. Incensed, he grabbed his club and snapped it over his knee, jumped up and down on his golf bag and threw all his balls as far into the rough as he could. Finally in control again, he muttered, "It's no good. I'm going to have to give it up." His caddy looked sympathetic, and asked: "Won't you miss the game?" The vicar shook his head. "You misunderstand, my son. As of this moment, I am giving up the fucking bloody Church!"

⤞ When another foursome is on the green, "Fore!" is not an excuse, "So what?" is not an apology and "Up yours!" is not an explanation.

⤞ Two golfers were playing near the edge of the course. One of them looked over the fence in amazement and said, "Look! Those idiots over there are out skating on the pond in this blizzard!"

GOVERNMENT

**Since a politician never believes what he says,
he is quite surprised to be taken at his word.**

Charles de Gaulle, 1890 – 1970

⤞ There's a bar where all the regulars are really into body-building. The owner is a body-builder and he only employs body-builders as bar staff. The walls are covered in body-builder photos and they are always having body-builder competitions. On the wall behind the bar is a sign that says, "Win £1,000: Beat The Bartender." Written below it are the rules to the competition: "The bartenders are so strong that, after any one of them has squeezed a lemon with his bare hands, nobody can ever squeeze anything else out of it: anyone who can will win the prize." The space around the bar is filled with photos of people who have tried to win the competition but failed. One day a skinny little man walks into the bar and announces that he'd like to try for the prize. It is a Saturday night, the bar is packed and everybody starts to laugh. The guy's head is about the size of the bartender's hand and nobody believes he has a chance. The bartender picks up a lemon and starts to squeeze it. The juice gushes out quickly, but after a few seconds it stops as the man squeezes everything out: juice, pips, pith and even squashed rind. The bartender then hands the lemon to the tiny old man. The man puts his hand around the wizened, almost unrecognizable lemon and starts to squeeze. To the astonishment of everyone present, juice begins to drip from the fruit and before long seven, eight, nine, and then ten full drops have been squeezed! Everyone starts to cheer and the bartender coughs up the money. "That's amazing – really amazing," says the bartender. "Are you a secret body-builder? Are you a martial arts expert? How did you do it?" "Easy enough," says the man, "I work for the Inland Revenue."

A good politician is quite as unthinkable as an honest burglar.

H.L. Mencken, 1880 – 1956, Minority Report

➻ A bloke was sitting in his garden one afternoon when a lorry pulled up in front of his house. The driver got out of the lorry, walked to the grassy area by to the road, dug a hole, then got back into the truck. A few minutes later, a different chap got out of the passenger seat, walked to the hole, proceeded to fill it back in, and then returned to the lorry. The driver then moved the lorry 50 feet up the road, and the process repeated itself. This went on all up the road. The bloke, who was already a bit upset about the poor quality of the road, couldn't believe his eyes. He stormed down to the lorry, pounded on the window, and demanded to know what was going on. The driver replied, "We're part of a road improvement project. The bloke who plants the trees called in sick."

➡ Government studies show that a 7% unemployment level is acceptable to 93% of the population.

**A gentleman will blithely do in politics what
he would kick a man downstairs for doing
in ordinary life.**
Earl Rosebery, 1847 – 1929

➡ The Inland Revenue have been trying to cheer people up regarding their self-assessment taxation by using snappy slogans and jolly catch-phrases. They're currently considering, "We've got what it takes to take what you've got!"

➡ What is orange and sleeps five? A council road-repair van.

GUITARS

➡ At a convention of biological scientists, one researcher remarks to another: "Did you know that in our lab we have switched from mice to guitar players for our experiments?" "Really?" the other replies, "Why did you switch?" "Well, for several reasons. We found that guitar players are far more plentiful; the lab assistants don't get so attached to them; the animal rights activists leave us alone; and there are some things even a rat won't do...However, sometimes it is very hard to extrapolate our test results to human beings."

➡ Did you hear that they've isolated the gene for guitar playing? It's the first step to a cure!

❧ Don't tell my mum I'm a guitar player. She thinks I'm a pornographer.

She takes every ballad and turns it into a three-act opera. She simply cannot leave a song alone!

Truman Capote on Barbra Streisand

❧ I recently had surgery on my hand, and asked the doctor if, after surgery, I would be able to play the guitar. He said, "I'm doing surgery on your hand, not giving you a lobotomy."

❧ I used to play guitar on TV but my Mum told me to get off before I broke it.

GYNAECOLOGISTS

❧ A famous artist started to lose her eyesight at the height of her career. Understandably concerned, she went to the best eye surgeon in the world, and after two months of painstaking treatment and delicate, intricate surgery, her eyes were repaired. She was extremely grateful, so in addition to paying his bill, she painted him a gigantic water-colour of a vivid eye, and had it hung in his office one weekend. The press were fascinated, so she and the doctor held an unveiling of the new masterpiece, followed by a press conference. "Tell me, Doctor Schwartz," said one journalist, "what were your first thoughts on seeing this exquisite new work of art?" The doctor shrugged, and replied, "I thought 'Thank Christ I'm not a gynaecologist!'"

➻ A woman walks into the dentist's, takes off her knickers and sits in the chair with a leg over each arm. "Madam, I think there's some mistake," says the dentist, "the gynaecologist's surgery is on the next floor." "No mistake," replies the woman, "yesterday you put in my husband's new dentures. Today I want you to take them out."

I wish I loved the human race;

I wish I loved it's silly face;

I wish I liked the way it walks;

I wish I liked the way it talks;

And when I'm introduced to one

I wish I thought "what jolly fun."

Sir Walter Raleigh

➻ After much soul-searching and having determined the husband was infertile, the childless couple decided to try artificial insemination. When the woman showed up at the clinic, she was told to undress from the waist down, get on the table and place her feet in the stirrups. She was feeling rather awkward about the entire procedure when the doctor came in. Her anxiety was not diminished by the sight of him pulling down his pants. "Wait a minute. what the hell is going on here?" yelled the woman, pulling herself into a sitting position. "Don't you want to get pregnant?" asked the doctor. "Well, yes, I do," answered the woman. "Then lie back and spread 'em," replied the doctor.

"We're all out of the bottled stuff. You'll just have to settle for what's on tap."

→ Gynaecologists have a power that makes some men envious. They can go into a room where a woman is waiting for them and say, "Get undressed. I'll be with you in a minute."

→ Patient: "Doc, Doc, when I wasn't married I had six abortions, and now I've got married and can't get pregnant." Doctor: "Evidently you don't breed in captivity."

→ The brash young gynaecologist, fresh out of medical school, took one look at his voluptuous new patient and abandoned his professional ethics entirely. As he stroked the supple skin of her naked body, he asked: "Do you understand what I am doing?" "Yes," the patient answered. "You're checking for dermatological abrasions." "Correct," the doctor lied. Next, he fondled her breasts long and lovingly. Again, he inquired, "Do you understand what I am doing?" "You're feeling for cancerous lumps," she ventured. "Very astute," the doctor complimented, getting more excited. He placed the woman's feet in stirrups, dropped his pants, and slipped his member inside her. "And do you know what I am doing now?" "Yes, you're catching herpes."

→ What do a gynaecologist and a pizza man have in common? They can both smell it, but they can't eat it.

→ What do puppies and near-sighted gynaecologists have in common? They both have wet noses.

➻ What do you call a gynaecologist who specializes in geriatric care? A spreader of old wives' tails.

➻ Woman: "Doc, Doc, my husband tells me my pussy's too big. So I'd like you to tell me if you find it unusual." Doctor: "Please, take off your clothes and I'll examine you. [shouting] What a giant pussy. What a giant pussy." Woman [angry]: "Did you have to say it twice?" Doctor: "I didn't."

HARPS

➻ A Celtic harpist spends half her time tuning her harp, and the other half playing it out of tune.

➻ A harp is a nude piano.

Thou art like the harpy, which, to betray, dost with thine angel's face, seize with thine eagle's talons.

William Shakespeare, Pericles

➻ One evening, after a symphony rehearsal, some of the players went out to Sam's Discotheque to unwind. After several relaxing drinks, they all went their separate ways home. The next night, the harpist showed up at the concert hall and realized that he didn't have his instrument. "Oh no," he cried, "I left my harp in Sam's damn disco..."

Heaven

➡ A busload of priests have an accident and all of them are killed instantly. On arriving at the Pearly Gates, they find there's a terrible queue. St Peter is there looking at a big book, jotting down notes, mumbling occasionally. There is a person standing in front of his desk being processed. After some time St Peter says, "Next", and another person steps up. The wait seems to take for ever and there are an enormous number of people waiting, but St Peter doesn't seem to be hurrying. People are arriving all the time, some in mangled states, some famished and some looking 'normal'. Then a dishevelled man comes in, cigarette butt hanging from his lips like it has taken root. The stubble on his chin looks as though it could sand diamonds. He stands at the back of the queue like everyone else. St Peter, however, spies him and hurries over to him. "Oh come in, come in. Welcome! No need to queue, we have you already processed. Your residence is in order. There's special treatment for you." The priests have something to say about that. "Hey," says their spokesman, "how come he gets the special treatment? We are, after all, men of God." "That man," says St Peter, "was a taxi driver. He has scared far more people into praying than any of you lot ever did."

> **Mencken, with his filthy verbal haemorrhages, is so low down in the moral scale, so damnable dirty, so vile and degenerate, that when his time comes to die, it will take a special dispensation from Heaven to get him into the bottommost pit of Hell.**
>
> *Letter to the Jackson News newspaper, on HL Mencken*

↤ A Catholic, a Jew, and an Episcopalian reach the Pearly Gates. The Catholic asks to get in and St Peter says, "No, sorry." "Why not?" says the Catholic, "I've been good." "Well, you ate meat on a Friday in Lent, so I can't let you in." The Jew walks up and again St Peter says no. The Jew wants an explanation so St Peter replies, "There was that time you ate pork...sorry, you have to go to the other place." Then the Episcopalian goes up and asks to be let in and St Peter again says no. "Why not?" asks the Episcopalian, "What did I do wrong?" "Well," says St Peter, thinking quickly, "you once ate your entrée with the salad fork."

↤ A devout, good couple were about to get married, but a tragic car accident ended their lives. When they got to heaven, they asked St Peter if he could arrange for them to be married, saying that it was what they had hoped for in life, and they still desired wedded union. He thought about it and agreed, but said they would have to wait. It was almost one hundred years later when St Peter sent for them. They were married in a simple ceremony. So things went on for thirty years or so, but they determined, in this time, that eternity was best not spent together. They went back to St Peter, and said, "We thought we would be happy for ever, but now we believe that we have irreconcilable differences. Is there any way we can get divorced?" "Are you kidding?" said St Peter. "It took me a hundred years to get a priest up here to marry you. I'll never get a lawyer."

↤ A group of new arrivals were sitting in the foyer in heaven, waiting for their turn to see St Peter. On the walls of the reception room were hundreds of clocks all ticking away. Every once in a while, however, a clock would suddenly move ahead several minutes in one jump. Curious, one fellow who was waiting turned to the receptionist and said: "Excuse me, but why do some of those clocks jump ahead now and then?" The receptionist answered: "Oh, those are the clocks that keep track of the days that people still have to live on Earth. Each person has a clock. Every time they do something sneaky or bad, they lose some of their allotted time on Earth and their clock jumps ahead a few minutes." Interested, the man asked, "Can I see my little daughter's clock?" "Sure, said the receptionist," and showed him a clock that ticked calmly and steadily along. "Now, can I see my wife's clock, please?" asked the man. "Why not?" said the receptionist and showed him a clock that for the most part ran smoothly, once in a while jumping ahead two or three minutes at once. The man said, "You know, I was a Democrat back there on Earth, can I see Bill Clinton's clock?" "I'm afraid not," said the receptionist. "It's down in the accounting department. Their air conditioning broke this morning and they're using it for an electric fan."

➻ A man dies, and finds himself in heaven. St Peter offers to give him the tour. They walk around a little, and the man sees Samoans worshipping God in a Samoan way, and Zoroastrians worshipping in a Zoroastrian way, and Eskimos worshipping in an Eskimo way, and so on...on and on, till at one point they come to an enormous fortress made of stone, completely sealed off, with no windows or doors. Dimly, from within, they can hear the sound of wild partying. "Shhh," says St Peter. "Be very quiet." The two tiptoe past the fortress in utter silence, and when they have left it a way behind, the man turns to St Peter and says, "Why did we have to be so quiet back there? Who's in the fortress?" St Peter answers, "Oh, those are the Jehovah's Witnesses. They don't know anyone else is here."

➥ A man who is an avid golfer finally gets a once-in-a-lifetime chance for an audience with the Pope. After standing in line for hours, he gets to the Pope and says, "Holiness, I have a question that only you can answer. You see, I love golf, and I feel a real need to know if there is a golf course in heaven. Can you tell me if there is?" The Pope considers for a moment, and says, "I do not know the answer to your question, my son, but I will talk to God and get back to you." The next day, the man is called for another audience with the Pope to receive the answer to his question. He stands before the Pope, who says, "My son, I have some good news and some bad news in relation to your question. The good news is that heaven has the most fabulous golf course that you could imagine and is in eternally perfect shape. It puts all courses on Earth to shame. The bad news is that you tee-off tomorrow morning."

➥ A rabbi went to heaven and met God for the first time. A thought hit him and he asked God about what souls eat when they go to hell. God told him to look at what was being served. So the rabbi peeked down below the clouds and, behold, it was mealtime in hell. The souls there were being offered a seven-course meal with steak, mashed potatoes, tossed salad and a blue cheese sauce, and a bottle of wine was being passed round. Meanwhile God informed the rabbi that it was time for his meal – a peanut butter sandwich. The rabbi asked God why the guys down there were getting the royal treatment while he had to eat sandwiches. God replied: "It simply does not pay to cook for two."

➥ An elderly couple died in a car accident and found themselves being given a guided tour of heaven by Saint

Peter himself. He took them to the area they would be living in, saying, "Over there is your beachside villa – the tennis courts and swimming pools are round the back; the community centre is down the road a bit, there's a pair of golf courses just past that hill, and if you feel hungry or thirsty, just drop by one of the pubs or restaurants. Everything is free, of course, and you'll find that you have plenty of energy if you do want to exercise. I know you'll be happy; everybody is." Then he smiled and flew off. The bloke turned to his wife and muttered, "Honestly, Alice. If you hadn't insisted on all that damn bran and low-fat milk, we could have been here 15 years ago!"

If I could not go to Heaven but with a party, I would not go there at all.

Thomas Jefferson, private correspondence, on political affiliations

↦ Four nuns die and go to Heaven. At the Pearly Gates, Saint Peter stops them. "Before you enter Heaven, you must be completely pure," he says. "Sister Mary, have you ever had the slightest contact with a man's penis?" "I must confess that I have," says Sister Mary, "I once saw a man's penis." "Wash your eyes out with this holy water and pass into Heaven," says Saint Peter. "Now, Sister Martha, have you ever had the slightest contact with a man's penis?" "I must confess that I have," says Sister Martha, "I once stroked a man's penis with my hand." "Wash your hand in this Holy Water and pass into Heaven" says Saint Peter. But before he can get any further, the other two nuns have started pushing and shoving. "Sisters!" says Saint Peter sternly, "There is room for all in the Kingdom of God – what is the meaning of this unseemly scuffling?" "If I'm going to have to gargle with that Holy Water," says the fourth nun, "I want to get to it before Sister Catherine sticks her fat arse in it."

In our English popular religion the common conception of a future state of bliss is that of a kind of perfected middle-class home, with labour ended, the table spread, goodness all around, the lost ones restored – hymnody incessant.

Matthew Arnold, 1822 – 1888, on the English view of heaven

➻ St Peter was at his post at the Pearly Gates and in rather a bad mood. That day, only couples were on line to get in. "Next," he called out, in a bored fashion. Up stepped a couple. "Name?" asked St Peter. "Smith," replied the husband. St Peter slowly looked up from his desk, looked them over for a moment, and finally asked with a bit of a sneer: "Says here that you were a banker in your time, Smith." St Peter then leaned forward, pointed his finger at them, and said: "You know, I don't like bankers. You're cheap. Always grubbing for money...cheating people...I don't know if I want to let you two in here today. So what's your wife's name?" "Penny," replied Mr Smith. "PENNY!" exclaimed St Peter. "Look at that, you even married a woman named after money. Get out of here, try again some other time. Next," he called out, still agitated. Up stepped the next couple. "Name?" asked St Peter. "Jones", replied the husband. Again St Peter slowly looked up from his desk, looked them over for a moment, and asked with a sneer: "Jones the Publican?" "Why, yes," said Mr Jones. St Peter again leaned forward, pointing his finger at them, and said: "You know, I don't like publicans. You drink too much. Always getting drunk on your own stock and throwing up all over the streets... beating up your wives and kids during drunken rages...I don't know if I want to let you two in here today. So what's your wife's name?" "Sherri" replied Mr Jones. "SHERRI!" exclaimed St Peter. "Look at that, you even married a woman named after a drink. Get out of here, try again some other time." Meanwhile, several couples back, a man overhearing all of this turns to his wife and says: "Let's get out of here, Fanny."

⇢ The man died. Having not lived an all-that-honest life he found himself at the gates of Hell. "Welcome to Hell" announced the Devil greeting him warmly. "Glad you could join us. As your last taste of free will, you are allowed to choose which of three possible places in which you will spend the rest of eternity." There were three doors behind the Devil. He opened the first door. Flames shot into the room and the man could see thousands of people in the fire. "No," said the man, "not this one." The Devil opened the second door. The man could see thousands of people slaving away at a large rock pile. They were all being whipped as they hammered the large boulders into smaller boulders. "No," said the man again. Finally, the Devil opened up that last door which showed thousands of people in an incredibly large lake with vomit up to their chins. All of them were chanting: "Don't make waves, don't make waves..." "That's awful!" commented the man in revulsion. "You think that's bad?" asked the Devil. "You should see it when the angels spend the weekend here water-skiing."

➤ In Heaven, the lovers are French, the comedians are English and the engineers are German. In Hell, the comedians are German, the engineers are French and the lovers are English.

HOOKERS

➤ A man is drinking in his local watering-hole in New York when he spots a bit of top totty hanging out with a really cheap, loser type. He's amazed that a dullard like that can pull such top crumpet, so he goes up to the bartender and asks him about it. He discovers that the woman is a prostitute, so he keeps an eye on her and, sure enough, a while later, she leaves on the man's arm and comes back later with someone else. The next night the man is in the same bar and in comes the prostitute. He still thinks she looks magnificent, so he goes up to her and asks her what her rates are. She is totally unfazed, and says, "Well, my rates start at $100 for a handjob and go up from there." "A hundred dollars," the guy interrupts, "for a handjob? You must be joking!" "Listen, buddy," says the woman, pointing out of the window at a huge Mercedes outside, "I bought that car for cash with the money I made from giving handjobs! Trust me: it'll be worth it." The man is certainly impressed, and thinks for a few seconds before deciding to get himself a handjob from the woman. They leave together and the man gets what he thinks is probably the finest sexual experience that he's ever had with anyone. The next night he is back in the bar, eagerly awaiting the woman. When she shows up, he walks straight up to her, saying, "Last night really was incredible." "Of course it was: I told you, didn't I?" the prostitute replies, "but just you wait until you try one of my blowjobs." The man is tempted, but he asks, "and how much would that be?" The woman replies, "$1,000." "One thousand dollars?" the guy almost shouts, before the woman says, "Listen, buddy: I bought myself a ten-storey downtown condominium for cash with the money I made from giving blowjobs. Trust me: it'll be worth it." The man is impressed again and, based on the evidence of the previous evening, decides to get himself a blowjob from the woman. They leave together and the man gets what he knows is far and away the greatest single experience of his life – he nearly faints! The next night he is back in the bar, waiting again. He is so excited he can hardly sit in a chair. When the prostitute does eventually show up, he runs up to her and says, "You're the best: you're the best: just tell me what it'll cost for some pussy!" The woman grabs his hand and pulls him outside the bar into the street. Away in the distance he can see Manhattan. She says, "You see that island?" To which the guy replies, "Come on – you can't be serious!" The prostitute nods her head and says, "Yup: if I had a pussy, I'd own Manhattan!"

I am persuaded that Satan has not a more speedy way and fitter school to work and teach his desire, to bring men and women into his share filthy lusts of wicked whoredom than those plays and theatres.

John Northbrooke, 1542 – 1608

↔ What do you get by crossing a prostitute with an elephant? A whore who'll fuck you for peanuts and won't forget you afterwards.

➻ One day, after striking a rich seam of gold in Alaska, a miner came down from the mountains and walked into the nearest saloon in the nearest town. "Ah'm a-lookin' for the meanest, roughest, toughest whore in the Yukon!" he said to the barman. "Well, we got her!" replied the barkeep. "She's upstairs, second room on the right." The miner handed the landlord a gold nugget to pay for two beers and the whore. He grabbed the bottles, stomped up the stairs, kicked open the second door on the right and yelled, "Ah'm a lookin' for the meanest, roughest, toughest whore in the Yukon!" The woman inside the room looked at the miner and said, "Honey, you just found her!" Then she stripped naked, turned her back on the guy, bent over and grabbed her ankles. "Hey, hold on a minute!" said the miner, "I should get to say how we screw." "Relax, sugar, you will," replied the whore, "but I thought you might like to open those beers first."

> **Paris is like a whore. From a distance she
> seems ravishing, you can't wait until you have
> her in your arms. Five minutes later you feel empty,
> disgusted with yourself. You feel tricked.**
>
> *Henry Miller, 1891 – 1980, on Paris, France*

➻ Two village idiots go to a brothel and hammer on the door. "What the hell do you want?" shouts the madam. "We've come for women," say the idiots. "How much money do you have on you?" shouts the madam again. The idiots scrabble through their pockets and see. "We've got a tenner!" they shout. "For that much you can go screw yourselves," laughs the madam. Just five minutes later, the idiots return and bang on the door again: "We've screwed ourselves: now we've come to give you the tenner!" they shout.

↪ What do bungee-jumping and prostitutes have in common? They both cost too much for an afternoon, and if the rubber breaks, you're fucked!

↪ What do you call kids born in whorehouses? Brothel sprouts.

↪ Why can a prostitute make more money than a drug dealer? Because she can wash and re-sell her crack.

HORSES

↪ A man went into a small Yorkshire pub and ordered a beer. The landlord served him, and then turned to the news on the TV. Tony Blair was busy giving yet another speech. "God, not that horse's arse again!" said the man. The landlord immediately leaped over the bar and punched the man so hard he knocked him clean off the bar stool. "Look, sorry," said the man, "I didn't know I was in Blair country." The landlord said, "Watch it, lad. You're not in Blair country... You're in horse country."

↪ Why did the woman get thrown out of the riding stable? She wanted to mount the horse her way.

↪ What do you call an Amish man with his hand up a horse's arse? A mechanic.

➦ A horse and a chicken are friends. They are playing around together one day when the horse tumbles into a pit and begins to sink. He begs the chicken to fetch the farmer to get him to pull him to safety. The chicken runs off but he cannot find the farmer. Ever resourceful, the chicken jumps into the farmer's Porsche (obviously a French farmer, full of EU subsidies) and roars off to the hole where the horse is rapidly sinking. He takes a tow-rope from the boot, ties it around the bumper and throws the other end to the horse. The horse manages to grip the rope in his teeth and the chicken pulls forward in the Porsche, thus pulling the horse from danger and saving his life. A couple of days later the horse and the chicken are playing the same game in the same place. This time, the chicken falls into the same hole and begins to sink. The chicken screams for help and the horse, even more resourceful than the chicken, straddles himself over the hole, positioning his penis over where the chicken is sinking. "Quick, chicken," he says. "Grab hold of this and pull yourself out!" The chicken follows his instructions and only a few seconds later, both animals are safely on solid ground. The moral of the story? If you're hung like a horse, you don't need a Porsche to pull the birds!

Dangerous at both ends, and uncomfortable in the middle.

Ian Fleming, on horses

➦ This bloke walks into a pub and there's a horse behind the bar serving the drinks. The bloke stares at the horse in amazement, so the horse says, "Look, what are you staring at, mate? Haven't you ever seen a horse serving drinks before?" The bloke says, "No, it's not that...it's just that I never dreamed that the parrot would sell the place."

↔ Why couldn't the pony talk? Because he was a little hoarse.

HUNTING

↔ It was Frank's first time at bear-hunting. After some time in the mountains, he spotted a small brown bear and shot it. Just then there was a tap on his shoulder. He turned around to see a big black bear. The bear said "That was cruel. You've got two choices. I either maul you to death or we have sex." Frank decided to bend over. Even though he felt sore for two weeks, Frank soon recovered and vowed revenge. He headed out on another trip where he found the black bear and shot it. There was another tap on his shoulder. This time a huge grizzly bear stood right next to him. The grizzly said "What a huge mistake, Frank. You've got two choices. Either I maul you to death or we have rough sex." Again, Frank thought it was better to comply. Although he survived, it took several months before Frank finally recovered. Outraged, he headed back to the mountains, managed to track down the grizzly and shot it. He felt sweet revenge, but then there was a tap on his shoulder. He turned round to find a giant polar bear standing there. The polar bear said "Admit it, Frank. You don't come here for the hunting, do you?"

↔ Old hunters never die, they just stay loaded.

↦ An Indian scout was checking the area on behalf of some buffalo hunters, searching for the herds. He put his ear to the ground. "Ugg", he said, "Deer come!" The hunters looked at him with awe. "How the heck can you tell that?" asked one. The scout answered, "Simple. Ear sticky."

**Boxing is as cruel a blood sport as hunting,
although the victims aren't dumb animals
but poor blacks.**

Michael Arditti

↦ Two blokes were on an African safari when they came across some lion tracks. Suddenly nervous, one said to the other, "You follow these forward and find out where the lion's got to. I'll follow them backward, and find out where it's been..."

↦ Hunters do it with a bang.

INSTRUMENTS

↦ A bloke decided to take a holiday and travel somewhere exotic, so he booked a trip to a small, relatively unspoiled Pacific island where the native culture was still intact. He flew into Thailand and set sail from Jakarta on a specially chartered boat to the island paradise. As the boat was approaching the island, he noticed the sound of drums. "How quaint," he thought, "the natives are performing an ancient drum ritual." He arrived at the island, and got something to eat in a charming local bar. He finished his meal, but the drums were still throbbing away. After a few hours, he began to wonder when they were going to stop. Curious, he asked a native why the drums were going on so long. Rather than reply though, the native ran away screaming with a terrified look on his face. Thinking he had probably broken some taboo by asking an intrusive question, the bloke decided to just forget about the drums and enjoy his holiday. After two days of continuous drumming, broken sleep, mild headaches and so on though, the drums were really starting to get to him. On the beach, he crossed over to a local, a man with his wife and kids, and asked, "When are the drums going to stop?" The native looked at him in horror. All of a sudden, the whole family was backing away, then they turned and fled. The bloke decided to leave it another night, ears stuffed with cotton wool. The next morning though, they were still pounding away in the hills. He went outside, found an old native man, then pounced on him and grabbed him in a vicious headlock. "Listen to me, old man," said the bloke, "You will tell me when the drums stop, or I'll snap your damn neck." The old man looked up at him, shuddering, and said, "I would rather die than be the one who stops the drums." The bloke, perplexed, asked him why. Slowly, reluctantly, the old man said, "You are a foolish young man. When the drums are over, the harmonica solo starts!"

↦ A trumpet is an instrument – when it is not an elephant sound.

↦ An accordion is a bagpipe with pleats.

↦ How do you get five oboists in tune? Shoot four of them.

↠ A Russian pianist, a Cuban guitarist, a Scottish piper and an English drummer were sharing a compartment on a train. The Russian, in an attempt to impress the other passengers, said, "In Russia we have so much vodka that we can afford to throw it away." He then pulled out a bottle of fine Russian vodka and, to the dismay of the Scot, threw it out the window. In a spirit of one-upmanship, the Cuban replied, "In Cuba, we have so many cigars that we can simply throw them away," and proceeded to dump a box of the finest Cuban cigars onto the track. Everyone looked at the Scot, who glowered back. He said, "Well, in Britain..." and then grabbed the English drummer and threw him out of the window.

These people have no ear, either for rhythm or music, and their unnatural passion for pianoforte playing and singing is thus all the more repulsive. There is nothing on earth more terrible than English music, except English painting.

Heinrich Heine

↠ It is easy to teach anyone to play the maracas. Just grip the neck and shake him in rhythm.

↠ Seems that the censors banned the transmission of a TV show that claimed to introduce young people to the worlds of jazz and classical music. Their reasoning? Too much sax and violins.

↠ What is another name for a bassoon? A farting bedpost.

↠ What is the difference between a bull and an orchestra? The bull has the horns in front and the arsehole in the back.

➻ What is the difference between a saxophone and a chainsaw? It's all in the grip.

➻ What is the range of a tuba? Twenty yards, if you've got a good arm.

➻ While at a concert being performed by a very bad orchestra, George Bernard Shaw was asked what he'd like them to play next. "Dominoes," he replied.

➻ Why do bagpipers walk when they play? To get away from the noise.

JEWISH

➻ A Jew and a Chinese guy were sitting at a bar drinking. All of a sudden the Jew turned and punched the Chinese guy in the face, knocking him off his stool. Stunned, the Chinese guy got up and said, "What the hell was that for?" The Jew replied, "That was for Pearl Harbour." The Chinese guy said, "That was the Japanese. I'm Chinese." The Jew says, "Well, you have black hair, slitty eyes and buck teeth. It's all the same to me." The Chinese guy says "Okay," sits on his stool and continues drinking. About a minute later the Chinese guy turns round and punches the Jew in the face, knocking him off his stool. The Jew gets up and says, "That had better not be for me hitting you before." The Chinese guy says, "No, that was for the Titanic." The Jew replies, "The Titanic? That was an iceberg." The Chinese guy looks coolly at the Jew and says, "Iceberg, Goldberg, it's all the same to me..."

➻ A Jewish couple have a son who is a bit troublesome. At the age of five he starts in school, and pretty soon, his parents get to hear that things aren't going well. After a couple of months, they are asked to take him out of school, since he is not setting a good example to the other Jewish children. Things go from bad to worse: after only a month in reform school he's thrown out again, and even the state correction centre can't deal with him. Eventually, in desperation, the parents take him to the only place left: a local Catholic school. They don't hear anything concerning his performance, no reports of trouble, but their curiosity is really aroused when he comes home at the end of the term with a report card showing three Bs and the rest As. Things continue in the same vein, and at the end of the second term, he's running straight As. By the end of the school year, his performance has been so good that he is top of the class. His mother takes him aside and asks, "What's going on? We send you to your own people, and they throw you out. The reform school can't deal with you, and even the state correction centre wasn't enough. But now, with these Catholics, you're getting the best grades ever." "Well Mum," says the boy "I wasn't too bothered by those other places, but the first thing I see when I go into that Catholic school is a Jewish kid nailed to a couple of planks. I know when to back down."

➻ Sam Cohen, father of three and faithful husband for over 40 years, unexpectedly drops dead one day. His lawyer informs his widow that Jacob Schwartz, Sam's best friend since childhood, is to be executor of the will. The day comes to divide Sam's earthly possessions – over a million pounds' worth. In front of Sam's family,

Jacob reads the will: "Jacob, if you're reading this, then I must be dead. You were such a good friend for so long, how can I ignore you in this will? On the other hand, there are my beloved Rachel and my children to be looked after. Jacob, I know you can make sure my family is taken care of properly. So, Jacob, give what you want to her and take the rest for yourself." Jacob then looks at the survivors and tells them that, in accordance with Sam's instructions, he will give fifty thousand pounds to Sam's widow. The rest he is retaining for himself. The family is beside itself. "This is impossible. Forty years of marriage and then this? It can't be." So the family sues. Their day in court arrives, and after testimony from both sides, the judge gives his verdict: "To Jacob Schwartz, I award fifty thousand pounds of the contested money. The remainder shall go to Rachel Cohen, widow of the deceased." Needless to say, the family is elated, but Jacob is dumbfound. "Your Honour, how can you do this? The will made Sam's wishes quite clear: 'Give what you want to her and take the rest for yourself.' I wanted the lion's share. What gives?" The judge answered back, "Mr Schwartz, Sam Cohen knew you his whole life. He wanted to give you something in gratitude. He also wanted to see his family taken care of. So he drew up his will accordingly. But you misread his instructions. You see, Sam knew just what kind of a person you are, so with his family's interest in mind, he didn't say, 'Give what you want to her and keep the rest for yourself.' No. What Sam said was, 'Give what YOU want to HER, and keep the rest for yourself.'"

Jews generally give great value. In my experience, the men who want something for nothing are invariably Christians.

George Bernard Shaw, St. Joan

↝ A man is confused about sex and the Sabbath day. He just cannot work out whether having sex on the Sabbath is a sin or not because he doesn't know whether it is work or play. He goes to see his local priest and asks him what his opinion is on this question. The priest gets his Bible down and flicks through it, reading a passage here and a passage there. Eventually he tells the man, "Well my son, after consulting the Good Book I have decided that sex is closest to work and that therefore you should not practise it on the Sabbath." The man thanks the priest but, as that wasn't really the answer he was looking for, he decides to go and see the local minister, who is married and may see things a bit more his way. He asks the minister the question and, to his disappointment, the minister gives him the same answer as the priest, "No sex on the Sabbath." The man decides to go and see another type of holy man – the local Rabbi. The Rabbi is asked the question and he ponders it over. Eventually he says, "Well my son, I have come to the conclusion that sex is definitely play so therefore you can have sex on the Sabbath." The man says, "That's great Rabbi, but how do you come to that conclusion when so many others disagree?" The Rabbi thinks a little and then says quietly, "If sex were work, my wife would get the maid to do it!"

Jews, Scotsmen and counterfeits will be encountered throughout the world.

German saying

➤ There was an elderly Alabama widow who lived in a large mansion. She was feeling generous when it came to Thanksgiving, so she called up the local military base, and asked to speak with the lieutenant. "Please send up four nice young men to eat dinner here on Thanksgiving, but please, don't send any Jews. Please, no Jews." The lieutenant replied, "No problem ma'am, and I am sure I speak for the army when I say we all appreciate your kindness." Well, Thanksgiving rolled around, and the widow went to answer the door when the bell rang. She was surprised to see four of the blackest boys that anyone had ever seen, especially in the south. "But, but, there must be some mistake," she stammered. One of them replied: "No ma'am Lieutenant Goldstein doesn't make mistakes."

➤ Three rabbis were playing golf one day. Another fellow, who had no golfing partner, asked if he could join in to make up a foursome. The rabbis were more than willing and they all had a jolly good round of golf. At the end of the game the man had lost miserably, and his score was a good 30 shots higher than all the rabbis. He found this confusing, because he's quite a keen weekend golfer, and the rabbis were men of the cloth. So he asks, "How come you guys are all such good golfers?" One of the rabbis replies, "Well son, when you lead a good, religious and pure life as part of a temple, your rewards are many. Being good at golf is just one of our rewards." So the man goes home and has a think, and decides, what the hey, I don't have much going on in my life anyway, I may as well go for it and try to improve my golf. So he finds a temple near where he lives, he joins it and attends classes three times a week. One year later the four of them all play golf again, but it is the same story: the man loses miserably again. "So what's that all about?" he asks the rabbis again. "I joined a temple, I go three times a week and I lead a good, pure life." One of the rabbis replies, "Which temple did you join?" and the man says, "Shalom Shalom on 4th Avenue." The rabbi says, "Oh no! That one's for tennis!"

KIDS

The thing that impresses me most about America is the way parents obey their children.
The Duke of Windsor, 1894 – 1972

➤ A 13-year-old boy goes into a pub and says to the barmaid, "Get me a double Scotch on the rocks." "What do you want to do," asks the barmaid, "get me in trouble?" "Maybe later," says the kid, "but I'll start with the Scotch."

➤ A couple had children who were very inquisitive, so were finding it hard to communicate about adult things like having sex. To avoid having to teach the children about the birds and the bees, they decide to use a code instead, using the word "typewriter" as a substitute for sex. A couple of days later the husband thinks it will be amusing to use the code for the first time, so he calls his five-year-old daughter over and says to her, "Go and tell your mother that Daddy would like her to come up and type a letter on the typewriter, please." The girl goes off and comes back a couple of minutes later. She says, "Mummy says that she can't type a letter for

Daddy today because she's got a red ribbon stuck in the typewriter." A few days later the daughter comes up to the father and says, "Mummy told me to tell you that she can type that letter now." The father says, "Well, you go and tell Mummy not to worry because Daddy couldn't wait for the typewriter, so he decided to write the letter by hand!"

➤ A husband and his wife advertised for a live-in maid to cook and do the housework. A likely-looking girl came in from the country, and they hired her. She worked out well, was a good cook, was polite, and kept the house neat. One day, after about six months, she came in and said she would have to quit. "But why?" asked the disappointed wife. She hummed and hahed and said she didn't want to say, but the wife was persistent, so finally she said: "Well, on my day off a couple of months ago I met this good-looking fellow from over in the next county, and – well, I'm pregnant." The wife said: "Look, we don't want to lose you. My husband and I don't have any children, and we'll adopt your baby if you will stay." She talked to her husband; he agreed, and the maid said she would stay. The baby came, they adopted it, and all went well. After several months, though, the maid came in again and said that she would have to quit. The wife questioned her, found out that she was pregnant again, talked to her husband and offered to adopt the baby if she would stay. She agreed, had the baby, they adopted it, and life went on as usual. In a few months, however, she again said she would have to leave. Same thing – she was pregnant. They made the same offer, she agreed, and they adopted the third baby. She worked for a week or two, but then said, "I am definitely leaving this time." "Don't tell me you're pregnant again?" asked the lady of the house. "No," she said, "there are just too many damn kids here to tidy up after."

➼ A woman is nearly caught with her lover when her husband comes home early. To hide the man she puts him in the closet, but the lover soon discovers that he is not alone. The breathing he hears belongs to the woman's young son. "Gosh, it's dark in here," says the boy. "Bloody hell, child, please shut up," replies the nervous man. "Well, mister, I think I'm going to scream." "Please, kid, don't scream." "Can I have some money?" asks the boy. "Well, here, – here's five quid, it's all I've got." The boy, sensing that the man is lying, presses on. "I really feel like screaming." "No, kid, look, here's 50 quid, just don't scream." "Well, I don't know." "Here's the last of my money, just don't scream." The boy, satisfied, agrees to be quiet. Later, he goes with his mother to a store where a brand new bike is on sale. When he tries to buy it with his new-found cash, his mother becomes suspicious of the source of this money. So, being a good Catholic, she takes him to see the local priest in confession. "Gosh," says the boy, not used to being in the confessional, "it's dark in here." "Don't start with that again," says the priest.

➼ A little boy and his younger brother were bored one day so decided to do interesting, grown-up stuff like swearing. The older boy says to his brother, "I know: next time we're downstairs with mum, I'll say 'Hell' and you can say 'Ass' – how's about that?" The younger boy nods his agreement and they troop off downstairs to have their breakfast. As they walk into the kitchen their mother says to the older child, "And what would you like for your breakfast, dear?" to which he replies, "Well, hell, mum, I'd like some cornflakes, please." Upon hearing such profanity, the mother whacks the child really hard around the back of the head.

The boy starts crying and runs off upstairs. The mother turns to the younger boy and looks him square in the face. "And what would you like for your breakfast, young man?" she says. "I don't really know, mum," he starts to say, "but you can bet your ass it won't be cornflakes!"

Three things are in trouble: birds in the hands of children, young girls in the hands of old men, and wine in the hands of Germans.

Italian saying

➡ A man was walking on the sidewalk and noticed up ahead that little Johnny was wearing a red fireman's hat and sitting in a red wagon. It appeared that the wagon was being pulled slowly by a large Labrador retriever. When he got closer to the lad, he noticed that Johnny had a rope tied around the dog's testicles, which probably accounted for why the dog was walking so gingerly. Smiling, he spoke to the little boy, "That's really a nice fire engine you have there, son, but I'll bet the dog would pull you faster if you tied that rope around his neck." "Yeah," little Johnny replied, "but then I wouldn't have a siren."

➡ A mother and her young daughter have just finished shopping for food and all the groceries are scattered over the kitchen floor in plastic bags. While the mum busies herself putting things away, the daughter picks up a box of animal crackers and empties its contents on the table, making quite a mess. "What are you doing?" her mum yells. "Well, it says on the box, 'Do not eat if seal is broken.' I'm looking for the seal."

➤ A little girl goes into Santa's grotto and he asks her what she wants for Christmas. "I want Barbie and Action Man," she says. "Oh," says Santa, "I thought Barbie came with Ken." "No," says the little girl, "Barbie comes with Action Man – she just fakes it with Ken."

➤ A young mother teaches her son to go to the bathroom by numbers. She teaches him the following lesson: "1. Unzip your flies. 2. Gently lift out your family jewels. 3. Pull back the foreskin. 4. Let nature take its course. 5. Slide the foreskin forward. 6. Replace the family jewels. 7. Zip back up." The mother would often check that he was following instructions by listening outside the door of the bathroom. She would hear, "One, two, three, four, five, six, seven. All done!" However, one day she was walking past the bathroom and was disturbed to hear, "Three–five, three–five, three–five, three–five..."

➤ After his first day at school, Tommy comes home full of questions for his parents. Unfortunately, some of them are not really what his parents hoped he'd be learning at school. So Tommy goes up to his mother and says, "Mummy, what's a pussy? Everyone says that word in the playground and I don't know what it means." Tommy's mother picks up an illustrated dictionary and flicks to the page with a cat on it. She shows him the picture. Then Tommy says, "Mummy, what's a bitch? Everyone says that word in the playground and I don't know what it means." Tommy's mother picks up the dictionary and flicks to the page with a dog on it, and shows Tommy the female. Tommy is still curious so he goes to find his father. He says, "Daddy, what's a pussy? Everyone says that word in the playground and I'm still not sure what it means." Tommy's dad figures it is time to teach the boy a thing or two, so he picks up a jazz mag, draws a circle around the pussy that's on the page and shows the picture to the boy. "That's a pussy," he says. Then Tommy says, "Daddy, what's a bitch? Everyone says that word in the playground and I'm still not sure what it means." Tommy's father replies, "Everything outside the circle!"

> **They fuck you up, your mum and dad**
> **They may not mean to, but they do.**
> **They give you all the faults they had.**
> **And add some extra, just for you.**
>
> *Philip Larkin, 1922 – 1986*

It now costs more to amuse a child than it once did to educate his father.

Little Johnny's maths teacher asks him to define 'average'. "It's a kind of bed, Miss," says little Johnny. "A bed?" "Yes, I overheard my mum saying she has three orgasms a week on an average."

Dad was happily typing away on his computer and didn't notice his six-year-old daughter sneaking up behind him. Then she turned and ran into the kitchen, squealing to the rest of the family, "I know Daddy's password! I know Daddy's password!" "What is it?" her sister asked eagerly. Proudly she replied, "Asterisk, asterisk, asterisk, asterisk, asterisk!"

➥ Did you hear about the child who thought Jesus was a giant teddy bear called Gladly, who had something wrong with his eyes, because every time she went to church they would sing ,"Gladly the cross I'd bear."

➥ Once upon a time there was a sweet little girl who always wore pretty little dresses to school. However, at lunchtime every day she would sit on the bench by the tuck-shop and cry. Nobody knew why, so one day one of her classmates, Tony, plucked up the courage to ask her why she always cried. She explained that she really loved chocolate but that she never had any money to buy some. So Tony says to her, "Tell you what: if you climb up that tree over there, I'll give you the money to buy some chocolate." "That's just great," the little girl says, and she runs off to climb the tree. As she does so, Tony and all the other boys in her class gather round and watch her climb. As she gets down, Tony gives her the money and thanks her. The next day the same thing happens and the sweet little girl climbs the tree again to get the chocolate. Again, all the boys watch her go up and down. This becomes a daily occurrence at school and eventually the girl's mother asks her where she gets her chocolate money from. "It's easy, mum," the sweet little girl explains. "The boys in my class all give me money to climb the tree every day." "Oh, dear, don't do that: those nasty boys just want to see your underwear as you climb." "OK, mum," the girl says; but the next day at lunchtime there is an even bigger crowd by the tree as the sweet little girl climbs it. When she gets home that evening her mother asks her where she got her chocolate that day. "Oh, mum: I got it from climbing the tree," she explains simply, but the mother says, "Honey, I told you not to do that. Those boys just want to see your underwear!" So the sweet little girl says, "Don't worry, mum: I didn't wear any underwear today!"

**Children begin by loving their parents.
After a time they judge them. Rarely, if ever,
do they forgive them.**

Oscar Wilde

↔ One day, Johnny asked: "Daddy, are caterpillars good to eat?" His father was irritated. "I've told you not to talk about things like that during meals." "Why did you want to know?" asked his mother. Johnny said: "It's because I saw one on daddy's lettuce, but now it's gone."

↔ Two brothers went to confession; the younger one went in first. The priest always liked to ask questions of the children before their confession, so the priest asked the little boy: "Do you know where God is?" The little boy ran out and told his brother, "Let's get the hell out of here, the priest has lost God and wants to blame it on me."

↔ What did the little girl say to her dad when she opened the box of Cheerios? "Look, daddy, doughnut seeds!"

Lawyers

➥ "You seem to be displaying an unusual level of intelligence for a man of your background," sneered a lawyer at the witness. "If I wasn't sworn under oath," replied the witness, "I'd return the compliment."

➥ "My husband and I have been trying anal sex recently," the woman says, somewhat red-cheeked, to her doctor. "I mean, is this OK?" "Do you enjoy it?" the doctor asks. "As a matter of fact, we do," she replies "Does it hurt you?" "No, it's fine," she replies. "Well, I don't see why you shouldn't carry on, as long as you're careful not to get pregnant." "Pregnant?" the woman says, astonished. "I can get pregnant this way?" "Well, of course. Where do you think lawyers come from?" the doctor replies.

➥ "You're a cheat," shouted the attorney to his opponent. "And you're a liar," bellowed the opposition. Banging his gavel sharply, his Honour interrupted: "All right; now that both barristers have been identified, let's get on with this case."

➥ A lawyer died and appeared before the pearly gates. When he arrived, a chorus of angels began to sing in his honour and St Peter himself came out to shake his hand. "Mr Morris," said St Peter, "it is a great honour to have you here at last. You are the first being to break Methuselah's record for longevity. You have lived 1,028 years." "What are you talking about?" said Morris. "I'm 56." "56? But aren't you John Morris?" "Yes." "A lawyer?" "Yes." "From

Knightsbridge?" "Yes." "Let me check the records," said St
Peter. He slapped his hand against his forehead. "Now I see
the mistake; we added up your billing hours."

↦ A gang of robbers broke into a lawyer's club by mistake. The
old legal lions gave them a fight for their lives, and the gang was
lucky to escape. "It ain't so bad," one crook noted when the gang
got back to their den. "We got out with £50." "I warned you to
stay clear of lawyers!" the boss screamed. "We had over £270
when we broke in!"

↦ A lawyer's dog, running about unattended, heads straight
for a butcher shop and runs off with a big joint of meat.
The butcher, recognising the dog, goes to the lawyer's office
and asks, "If a dog running unleashed steals a piece of meat
from my shop, do I have a right to demand payment for the
meat from the dog's owner?" The lawyer nods, and replies,
"Absolutely." The butcher smiles, and says "Then you owe
me £14.23. Your dog got loose, and stole a joint from me
earlier." The lawyer nods, and writes the butcher a cheque
for £14.23. The next morning, the butcher opened his post
and found a letter from the lawyer. Inside was an invoice –
£100 for consultation without appointment.

↦ A lawyer died in poverty and many barristers of the city
subscribed to a fund for his funeral. The Lord Chief Justice was
asked to donate a pound. "Only a pound?" said the Justice, "Only
a pound to bury a lawyer? Here's twenty quid; go and bury a few
more of them."

➤ A bloke was charged with stealing a car. After a long trial, he was acquitted by the jury. Later that day, the bloke came back to the judge who had presided at the hearing. "Your honour," he said, "I want that damn lawyer of mine arrested." "Why?" asked the judge, surprised. "He got you off. What do you want to have him arrested for?" "Well, your honour," replied the bloke, "I didn't have any money to pay his fee, so he went and took the car I stole."

➤ A man went into the Town Hall of a small town, obviously desperate. He asked the man at the counter, "Is there a criminal lawyer in town?" The man replied: "Yes, but we can't prove it yet."

The first thing we do, let's kill all the lawyers.

William Shakespeare, Henry VI pt II

➤ A primary school teacher was asking students what their parents did for a living. "John, you first," she said. "What does your mother do all day?" John stood up and said, "She's a doctor." "That's wonderful," said the teacher. "How about you, Amy?" Amy shyly stood up, scuffed her feet and said, "My father is a mailman." The teacher smiled, and said, "That's lovely. Thank you, Amy. What about your father, Billy?" Billy proudly stood up and announced, "My dad is a pimp at the local brothel." The teacher was horrified, and promptly changed the subject. Later that day, at lunchtime, she went round to Billy's house and rang the bell. His father answered the door. The teacher explained what his son had said and demanded an explanation. The man sighed, and said, "Actually, I'm a libel lawyer, but how do you explain a thing like that to a seven-year-old?"

➻ A small town that cannot support one lawyer can always support two.

➻ A zombie popped down to his local brains shop to get some brain for supper. The sign boasted about the quality of the professional brain sold there, so he asked the butcher, "How much is it for Doctor's brain?" "That's £3 an ounce." The zombie nodded, and asked, "How about Engineer's brain?" "£4 an ounce, sir." "What about lawyer's brain?" "Ah," replied the butcher, "that's £100 an ounce." The zombie was aghast. "Why is lawyer's brain so much more?" The butcher looked at him. "Do you have any idea how many lawyers you need to kill to get one ounce of brain?"

➻ An airliner was having engine trouble and the pilot instructed the cabin crew to have the passengers take their seats and prepare for an emergency landing. A few minutes later, the pilot asked the flight attendants if everyone was buckled in and ready. "All set back here, Captain," came the reply, "except one lawyer who is still passing out business cards."

➻ An old lady paid a solicitor for an appointment to sort out her will with a £50 note. As she was leaving, the solicitor realised that there was a second £50 note stuck to the back. He suddenly found himself wrestling with an urgent ethical problem. "Do I tell my accountant?"

➥ At a conference, four surgeons are discussing operating on people from different professions. The first surgeon says, "My favourite are accountants. I love to open up accountants: when you do, everything is numbered." The second surgeon says, "Not bad, but you should try electricians. I love to open up electricians: when you do, everything is colour-coded." The third surgeon says, "Not bad, but you should try filing clerks. I love to open up filing clerks: when you do, everything is in alphabetical order." The fourth surgeon says, "Not bad, not bad, but you're all wrong. The easiest to operate on are lawyers. I love to open up lawyers: when you do, there are no guts, no heart, no spine, and the head and arse are completely interchangeable!"

➥ At the turn of the century, a respectable western lawyer was filing some insurance papers when he came to a question which asked, "If your father is dead, state the cause." Unwilling to reveal that his father had been hanged for cattle rustling, the lawyer evaded the problem by answering, "He died taking part in a public ceremony; he was killed when the platform gave way."

➥ Between grand theft and a legal fee, there only stands a law degree.

➥ Have you heard about the lawyers' word processor? No matter what font or type size you select, everything comes out in fine print.

➻ Did you hear about the new sushi bar that caters exclusively to lawyers? It's called Sosumi.

Lawyers Can Seriously Damage Your Health

Michael Joseph

➻ Did you hear about the terrorist that hijacked an aeroplane full of lawyers? He threatened to release one every hour if his demands weren't met.

➻ Experts are people who know a great deal about very little and who go along learning more and more about less and less until they know practically everything about nothing. Lawyers, on the other hand, are people who know very little about many things and keep learning less and less about more and more until they know practically nothing about everything. Judges are people who start out knowing everything about everything but end up knowing nothing about anything because of their constant association with experts and lawyers.

➻ God decided to take the devil to court and settle their differences once and for all. When Lucifer heard the news, he laughed and said, "Where does the old fool think he's going to find a lawyer?"

➤ How many lawyers does it take to change a light bulb? Such number as may be deemed necessary to perform the stated task in a timely and efficient manner within the strictures of the following agreement: Whereas the party of the first part, also known as "Lawyer", and the party of the second part, also known as "Light Bulb", do hereby and forthwith agree to a transaction wherein the party of the second part (Light Bulb) shall be removed from the current position as a result of failure to perform previously agreed upon duties, i.e.: the lighting, elucidation, and otherwise illumination of the area ranging from the front (north) door, through the entryway, terminating at an area just inside the primary living area, demarcated by the beginning of the carpet, any spill over illumination being at the option of the party of the second part (Light Bulb) and not required by the aforementioned agreement between the parties. The aforementioned removal transaction shall include, but not be limited to, the following steps: 1) The party of the first part (Lawyer) shall, with or without elevation at his option, by means of a chair, stepstool, ladder or any other means of elevation, grasp the party of the second part (Light Bulb) and rotate the party of the second part (Light Bulb) in a counter-clockwise direction, this point being non-negotiable. 2) Upon reaching a point where the party of the second part (Light Bulb) becomes separated from the party of the third part (Receptacle), the party of the first part (Lawyer) shall have the option of disposing of the party of the second part (Light Bulb) in a manner consistent with all applicable European, local and Government statutes. 3) Once separation and disposal have been achieved, the party of the first part (Lawyer) shall have the option of beginning installation of the party of the fourth part (New Light Bulb). This installation shall occur in a manner consistent with the reverse of the procedures described in step one of this self-same document, being careful to note that the rotation should occur in a clockwise direction, this point also being non-negotiable. Note: The above described steps may be performed, at the option of the party of the first part (Lawyer), by any or all persons authorized by him, the objective being to produce the most possible revenue for the party of the fifth part, also known as "Partnership". Charge: £2,185.

Apart from cheese and tulips, the main product of Holland is advocaat, a drink made from lawyers.

Alan Coren

➻ The son of a Spanish lawyer graduated from college and was considering the future. He went to his father, who had a very large office, and asked if he might be given a desk in the corner where he could observe his father's activities. He could be introduced to his father's clients as a clerk. That way, he could decide on whether or not to become a lawyer. His father thought this a splendid idea and this arrangement was set up immediately. On his son's first day at work, the first client in the morning was a rough-hewn man with calloused hands, in workman's attire, who began the conversation by saying: "Mr Lawyer, I work for some people named Gonzales who have a ranch on the east side of town. For many years I have tended their crops and animals, including some cows. I have raised the cows, tended them, fed them, and it has always been my understanding and belief that I was the owner of the cows. Mr Gonzales died and his son has inherited the farm, and he believes that since the cows were raised on his ranch and fed on his hay, the cows are his. In short, we have a dispute as to the ownership of the cows." The lawyer said: "I have heard enough. I will take your case. DON'T WORRY ABOUT THE COWS." After the tenant farmer left, the next client came in, a young, well-dressed man, clearly a member of the landed class. "My name is Gonzales. I own a farm on the east side of the town," he said. "For many years, a tenant farmer has worked for my family tending the crops and animals, including some cows. The cows have been raised on my land and fed on my hay, and I believe that they belong to me, but the tenant farmer believes that since he raised them and cared for them, they are his. In short, we have a dispute over ownership of the cows." The lawyer said, "I have heard enough. I will take your case. DON'T WORRY ABOUT THE COWS." After the client left, the son came over to his father with a look of concern. "My father, I know nothing of the law, but it seems to me that we have a serious problem regarding these cows." "DON'T WORRY ABOUT THE COWS," said the lawyer. "The cows will be ours."

➨ There are two kinds of lawyers – those who know the law, and those who know the judge.

➨ There is a cartoon showing two people fighting over a cow. One is pulling the cow by the tail; the other is pulling on the horns. Underneath is a lawyer milking the cow.

➨ There is no better way to exercise your imagination and creativity than to study the law.

➳ There was a doctor who refused to pay the rent on his outdoor toilet. He didn't like the lawyer living in the cellar.

Lawyers and painters can soon turn white to black.

Danish saying

➳ This bloke happened upon a little antique shop, so he went in and took a look around. Way up on a high shelf he saw a little brass mouse figurine, and he really liked it. He asked the owner how much it was, and she replied, "It's £50 for the mouse, and £100 for the story that goes with it." The bloke thought about it, then handed over fifty quid and said, "I'll just take the statue, thanks." He walked out with the mouse. As he was walking home, he noticed the figurine was hollow, with two little holes. Holding it up to his mouth, it made a melodious whistle. No sooner had he started than he was being followed by three little mice. When he stopped, they stopped. When he turned left, they turned left. "That's strange," thought the bloke. As he continued walking, the mice were joined by more mice, until the bloke looked like the Pied Piper, leading a huge procession of mice. Spooked out, he ran over to the side of a nearby canal and flung the statue into the water. The mice leaped over the edge and down into the water, following the statue, and drowned. In a bit of a daze, the bloke went back to the antique shop. When he walked through the door, the owner gave him a smug smile and said, "So, you've come back to hear the story?" The bloke shook his head. "No. As a matter of fact, I was wondering if you had any little brass lawyers."

➼ What did the harassed lawyer say? "Get off my case."

➼ What do you call a lawyer with an IQ of 50? Your Honour.

➼ What do you call a person who assists a criminal in breaking the law before the criminal gets arrested? An accomplice. What do you call a person who assists a criminal in breaking the law after the criminal gets arrested? A lawyer.

LIMERICKS

We know what happens to people who stay in the middle of the road. They get run down.

Aneurin Bevan

➼ There once was a girl from Beroda
Who built an erotic pagoda.
The walls of its halls
Were festooned with the balls
and the tools of the fools who bestrode her.

➼ A popular girl is Miss Cholmondeley,
She's youthful, attractive and comely,
And never objects
To suggestions of sex,
But simply cooperates dumbly.

➻ A Scotsman who lived on the loch
Had holes down the length of his cock.
He could get an erection,
And play a selection
Of Johann Sebastian Bach.

➻ From deep 'neath the crypts of St Giles
Came a scream that resounded for miles.
Said the abbot, "Good Gracious!
Has Brother Ignatius
Forgotten the Bishop has piles?"

➻ The sea captain's tender young bride
Fell into the sea at low tide.
You could tell by her squeals
That one of the eels
Had found the best place to hide.

➻ There once was a juggler named Drops,
Who couldn't hang on to his props.
He tossed 'em and heaved 'em,
Then dropped and retrieved 'em,
Till the audience told him to stop.

➻ There once was a man from Cape Horn,
Who wished that he'd never been born.
He wouldn't have been
If his father had seen
That the end of his condom was torn.

➻ There once was a man from Nantucket
Whose dick was so long he could suck it.
He said with a grin,
As he wiped off his chin,
"If my ear was a cunt, I would fuck it."

➻ There was a young dentist called Sloan,
Who catered to women alone,
In a moment's depravity,
He filled the wrong cavity,
And said, "Look how business has grown!"

➻ There was a young lady from Kew
Who filled her vagina with glue.
She said with a grin,
"If they pay to get in,
They'll pay to get out of it too!"

**This is a fault common to all singers: that
among their friends they never are inclined to sing
when they are asked; unasked, they never desist.**

Horace, Satires Book 1, 65 – 8BC

➻ There was a young man from Bel Air
Who was screwing his girl on the stair.
But the banister broke,
So he doubled his stroke,
And he finished her off in mid-air.

➼ There was a young man from Belgrave
Who stashed a dead whore in a cave.
He said, "I admit
I'm a bit of a shit,
But think of the money I'll save!"

➼ There was a young man of St John's
Who wanted to bugger the swans.
But the loyal hall porter
Said, "Pray take my daughter,
Those birds are reserved for the dons."

One that hath wine as a chain about his wits, such a one lives no life at all.

Alcaeus, 611 – 580BC

➼ There was an old girl of Kilkenny,
Whose usual charge was a penny.
For half of that sum,
You could finger her bum;
T'was a source of amusement for many.

➼ There was an old man from Australia
Who painted his arse like a dahlia.
The colours were fine,
Likewise the design,
But the smell, alas, was a failure.

Lines and Icebreakers

↠ Are you free tonight, or is it going to cost me?

↠ Can I have your phone number? I don't seem to be able to find my own.

↠ Can I tickle your belly from the inside?

↠ Do you believe in love at first sight, or should I walk past again?

↠ Do you have a mirror in your pocket? Because I could see myself in your underwear.

↠ Do you know the difference between a hamburger and a blowjob? You don't? Wanna do lunch?

↠ Do you know what winks and fucks like a beast? [Then wink, you dozy sod!]

↠ Do you know why you should masturbate with these two fingers? Because they're mine.

↠ Do you like short love affairs? I hate them. I've got all weekend.

↠ Do you sleep on your stomach? Do you mind if I do?

↠ Do you want to go out for a coffee and sex? What, you don't like coffee?

➻ Excuse me, is that dress felt? Would you like it to be?

➻ Excuse me, ma'am, do you go down on strangers? No? Well, allow me to introduce myself.

➻ Excuse me: do you want to screw, or should I apologize?

➻ Forget that. Playing doctor is for kids. I prefer to play gynaecologist.

➻ Have you ever tried those prickly condoms?

➻ Hey baby, do you want to see something really swell?

➻ I definitely go down on the first date: how about you?

➻ I hope you know CPR, because you take my breath away!

➻ I may not be Fred Flintstone, but I bet I can make your bed rock.

➻ I was just thinking that your outfit would look great in a crumpled heap on my bedroom floor tomorrow morning.

➻ I wish you were a Postman Pat van outside Tesco's, because then I could ride you all day for a quid.

➻ I'd really love to screw your brains out, but it looks like someone beat me to it.

➻ I'll cook you dinner if you cook me breakfast.

➼ I'm a birdwatcher and you seem to have some of the characteristics of the Big-Breasted Bed Thrasher... I'd like to do more research.

➼ I'm a necrophiliac – how good are you at playing dead?

➼ I'm pretty sure I could fall madly in bed with you.

➼ If I could re-arrange the alphabet, I'd put U and I together.

➼ If I gave you sexy underwear, would there be anything in it for me?

➼ If you cut your arms off, you'd look just like Venus de Milo.

➼ If you think you might regret this in the morning, we can always sleep until the afternoon.

➼ If you were a car, I'd buff you up and ride you all over town.

➼ If you've lost your virginity, can I have the box it came in?

➼ If your left leg was Christmas and your right leg was New Year, could I spend some time between the holidays?

➼ Inheriting eighty million pounds doesn't mean a lot when you have a weak heart like mine.

➼ Is it hot in here or is it just you?

↤ Is that a Tic-Tac in your trousers or are you just pleased to see me?

↤ Let's go back to my place and get something straight between us.

↤ Let's go to my place and do all the things I'll tell everyone we did anyway.

↤ Look at you: all those curves and me with no brakes.

↤ Nice dress – can I talk you out of it?

↤ Nice shoes. Wanna fuck?

There is no greater bane to friendship than adulation, fawning and flattery.

Marcus Tullius Cicero, De Amicitia XVI, 106 – 43BC

↤ Oh, I'm sorry, I thought that was a Braille name-tag.

↤ Screw me if I'm wrong, but do you want to kiss me?

↤ That shirt is very becoming on you, but if I were on you, I'd be coming, too.

↤ The word of the day is 'legs'. Let's go back to my place and spread the word.

↤ There are 265 bones in the human body. How would you like another one?

➥ Want to play 'Down at the Fair'? That's where you sit on my face and I try to guess your weight.

➥ Why don't you sit on my lap and let us see what pops up?

➥ You know what would look really good on you? Me.

➥ You may not be the best-looking girl here, but beauty is only a light switch away.

➥ You must be from the Caribbean, because Jamaican me crazy.

➥ You must be jelly, because jam doesn't shake like that.

➥ You've got the whitest teeth I've ever come across.

Love

➥ A soldier serving in Hong Kong got quite upset when his girlfriend wrote to him, breaking off their engagement and asking for her photograph back. The soldier went out and collected all the unwanted photographs of women that he could find from his friends, bundled them all together and sent them back with a note saying, "Regret cannot remember which one is you. Please keep your photo and return the others."

➥ Love is the triumph of imagination over intelligence.

➻ A woman may very well form a friendship with a man, but for this to endure, it must be assisted by a little physical antipathy.

➻ Besides "I love you", what three words does a wife want to hear most? "I'll fix it."

**Some of the greatest love affairs I've known
have involved one actor, unassisted.**

Wilson Mizner, 1876 –1933

➻ If life were fair, the acquisition of a large bosom or a massive inheritance would have no bearing on your ability to attract the opposite sex.

➻ If you meet somebody who tells you that he loves you more than anybody in the whole wide world, don't trust him; it means he experiments.

**When one is in love, one begins by deceiving
oneself, and one ends by deceiving others.
This is what the world calls a romance.**

Oscar Wilde, A Woman of No Importance

➻ The bachelor who complained that the women he selected would not remain his friend for more than a few weeks was told: "Your problem is that you are looking for a particular kind of woman. You ought to be looking for the kind of woman who is not particular."

➠ Love is the delusion that one man or woman differs from another.

madness

➠ A group of psychiatrists go to tour an insane asylum that is known for its progressive rehabilitation methods. They begin by visiting some of the patients. The first patient they visit is a young woman. She is practising ballet. One of the psychiatrists asks: "What are you doing?" She replies, "I'm studying ballet so when I get out of here I can possibly join a troupe and be a productive member of society." "Wow, that's wonderful." The next person is a man reading a book with a pile of books next to him. The same question is asked of him, "What are you doing?" "I'm studying biology, chemistry, and physics, so I can enter medical school when I get out." Room after room, they witness the incredible success and attitudes of the patients, until they finally reach a room the asylum's director is reluctant to open. Finally, he is persuaded to open it. Inside is a man balancing a peanut on his penis. The psychiatrist exclaims, "My God what are you doing?" The man replied: "I'm fucking nuts and I'm never getting out of here."

➠ A man telephoned the mental hospital and enquired as to who was in Room 23. "That room is empty," replied the nurse. "Great!" said the bloke, "That means I must have escaped!"

➠ A patient goes to a psychiatrist. The psychiatrist gives him a Rorschach test; he shows a patient a circle with a dot inside it and asks, "What do you see?" The patient replies, "Two people are having sex in the middle of the circular room." The psychiatrist shows the patient another picture of a square with a dot inside it and asks, "What do you see?" Patient answers, "Two people are having sex in the square room." The psychiatrist shows the patient one more picture of a triangle with a dot outside it and asks: "What do you see now?" Patient replies, "What are you, some kind of pervert?"

↔ A psychiatrist visited a Norwich mental institution and asked a patient, "How did you get here? What was the nature of your illness?" He got this reply... "Well, it all started when I got married, and I reckon I should never have done it. I married a widow with a grown daughter who then became my stepdaughter. My dad came to visit us, fell in love with my lovely stepdaughter, then married her. And so my stepdaughter was now my stepmother. Soon, my wife had a son who was, of course, my daddy's brother-in-law, since he is the half-brother of my stepdaughter, who is now, of course, my daddy's wife. So, as I told you, when my stepdaughter married my daddy, she was at once my stepmother. Now, since my new son is brother to my stepmother, he also became my uncle. As you know, my wife is my step-grandmother since she is my stepmother's mother. Don't forget that my stepmother is my stepdaughter. Remember, too, that I am my wife's grandson. But hold on just a few minutes more. You see, since I'm married to my step-grandmother, I am not only the wife's grandson and her hubby, but I am also my own grandfather. Now can you understand how I got put in this place?"

↤ Have you heard Broadmoor's answering machine? It says: "Welcome to the Psychiatric Hotline. If you are obsessive-compulsive, please press 1 repeatedly. If you are co-dependent, please ask someone to press 2. If you have multiple personalities, please press 3, 4, 5 or 6. If you are schizophrenic, listen carefully and a little voice will tell you which number to press. If you have paranoia, we already know who you are and what you want, and we're already watching you, so just stay on the line. If you are depressed, it doesn't matter which number you press. No one will listen to your message."

There is no great genius without some touch of madness.

Seneca, Moral Essays, 8BC – 65AD

↤ The head doctors in a lunatic asylum have a meeting and decide that one of their patients is potentially well. So they decide to test him and take him to the movies. When they get to the movie theatre, there are 'Wet Paint' signs pointing to the benches. The doctors just sit down, but the patient puts a newspaper down first and then sits down. The doctors get all excited because they think he may be in touch with reality now. So they ask him: "Why did you put the newspaper down first?" He answers: "So I'd be higher and have a better view."

↤ There is a costume party at a mental hospital. The theme of the party is war. The first person comes up on to the stage and says, "I'm an atomic bomb." He gets his applause and steps down. The second person comes up and says, "I'm a hydrogen bomb." Again, there's applause and he steps down. And then a naked little man comes up to the stage and says, "I'm dynamite." Everybody runs away hysterically. When one of them is asked why, he says, "Didn't you see how small his fuse was?"

↬ One night in the pub, the landlord is lamenting the fact that business is so quiet on Mondays, Tuesdays and Wednesdays. As he moans to some of the regulars a stranger, dressed in a tweed jacket and wearing glasses, wanders over and says: "I'm sorry, but I couldn't help overhearing your conversation. I'm a doctor at the lunatic asylum up the road and I'm trying to integrate some of the more sane individuals into the community. Why don't I bring some of my patients along, say next Tuesday.? You'll have some customers and my patients will have a night out." Well, the publican isn't sure but the thought of more paying customers on a quiet night appeals, so he agrees. So, the following Tuesday the guy in the tweed jacket and glasses shows up with about ten lunatics. He says to the publican: "Give them whatever they want, let them practise paying with milk bottle tops, put it on a tab and I'll settle up at closing time." The publican has a great time selling loads of drinks and encouraging the loonies to eat crisps and peanuts. The loonies have a great time getting drunk but they behave themselves and hand over bottle-top money for their drinks. At closing time the publican adds up the bill and it comes to just over a hundred pounds. The guy with the glasses and the tweed jacket starts to organize the loonies ready to take them back to the asylum. Finally he comes over and asks for the bill. The publican, feeling that he's charged them rather a lot and he should do his bit to help these poor unfortunate people gives him a discount. "It's 80 quid," he says. The guy in the tweed jacket smiles and says: "That's fine. Have you got change for a dustbin lid?"

magical reality

➻ A man finds a genie in a bottle, and is offered three wishes. First he asks for a sports car and bouf! There's a shiny red car. Then he asks for a big luxurious house and bouf! There's a huge mansion. Finally he asks to be made irresistible to women. Bouf! He turns into a box of chocolates.

➻ A skeleton walks into a pub one night and plops down on a stool. The landlord asks "What can I get you?" The skeleton says, "I'll have a beer, thanks." The landlord passes him a beer and asks "Anything else?" The skeleton nods. "Yeah... a mop..."

➻ A wolf had been chasing a rabbit in the forest for an hour when they arrived near the Enchanted Oak, where the genie lived. They were making such a racket that they woke up the genie, who said (he was a bit of a hippy): "OK, OK: I see that there is no sleeping in peace in here until you two have resolved your differences. Therefore, I am going to grant you three wishes and you'll go on your way much happier." The wolf had the first go and he said: "I want all the wolves in this forest to be female." The genie sighed and said that it now was so. He turned to the rabbit and said: "What is your first wish, rabbit?" "I'd like a helmet," the rabbit says, a faint smile on his face. The genie finds it a bit odd, but a wish is a wish and the rabbit is fitted with a nice crash-helmet. "I want all the wolves in this country to be female," says the wolf for his second wish. The genie sighs again but complies and all the wolves in the country become female. "For my second wish, I want a motorcycle," the rabbit says. The genie says "OK" and grants the rabbit a nice, powerful motorbike which goes very well with the helmet. The rabbit's smile is getting bigger now. True to his character and showing remarkable consistency, the wolf says: "For my third wish, I want all the wolves in the whole world to be female!" Marvelling at the single-mindedness of the wolf's wishes, the genie complies and turns all the wolves in the world female. He then turns to the rabbit, who is grinning from ear to ear. "So what is your last wish, rabbit?" The rabbit straps the helmet on his head securely, climbs on the motorbike, revs up the engine and says: "I wish the wolf was gay!"

➼ An old woman saved a fairy's life. To repay this, the fairy promised to grant the old woman three wishes. For the first wish, the old lady asked to become young and beautiful. Poof! She became young and beautiful. For the second wish, the old lady asked to be the richest woman in the world. Poof! She was the richest woman in the world. For the last wish, she pointed at the cat she had kept for years. She asked that he be turned into the most handsome man on earth. After all, he had been her best friend for so many years. Poof! The fairy turned the cat into the most handsome man on earth. The old lady and the fairy said their goodbyes. After the fairy left, the handsome man strolled over to her and asked: "Now aren't you sorry you had me neutered?"

↔ How do you know when a hitch-hiker is a witch? When she strokes the driver's leg he turns into a lay-by.

↔ Marty was doing some river fishing. A big one bit, and when he fished it out he had a big surprise: it was a goldfish. "Oi, fisherman," said the fish, "if you set me free I'll give you whatever you want. I'm a magic fish and I'll grant you three wishes." "Sounds good to me," thought Marty, "I've got it made now." "OK, then," said Marty. "My first wish is to have a truck full of money." "At your command," said the goldfish. A top-of-the-range truck filled to the brim with cash appeared on the road next to the river; the key appeared in Marty's hand. "My second wish is to have a different top model to sleep with every night of every year." "At your command," said the goldfish, and a diary appeared in Marty's hand with a full schedule of women filled in. "My third wish is to have a cock that touches the floor," said Marty. "At your command," said the goldfish, and he cut Marty's legs off.

How now, you black and midnight hags?

William Shakespeare, Macbeth

↔ One afternoon, there was a good witch who was flying along when all of a sudden she heard this soft crying from down below. When she landed, she saw a yellow frog. Touched by his sadness, the witch asked why he was crying. "Sniff. None of the other frogs will let me join in all their frog games. Boo hoo." "Don't cry, little one," replied the witch, and with a wave of her magic wand, the frog turned green. All happy now, the frog was checking himself over when he noticed that his penis was still yellow. He asked an embarrassed witch about this, and she told him that there were some things that she just couldn't do, but that the wizard could fix things up for him. So happily, the little green frog hippity-hopped along his merry way. Feeling quite happy about herself, the witch once more took to the skies, and once again, she heard some crying, but this time of a thunderous sort. So down to the ground she flew, only to discover a pink elephant. The witch asked him why he was crying. "Sniff. None of the other elephants will let me join in all their elephant games. Boo hoo." Now, if you have ever seen an elephant cry, you know it to be a pathetic sight, but a pink elephant crying is just downright heart-breaking, and that is just how the witch felt. So once again, she waved her magic wand, and – poof – the elephant was all grey. All happy now, the elephant was checking himself all over when he noticed that his penis was still pink. He asked an embarrassed witch about this, and she told him that there were some things that she just couldn't do, but that the wizard would fix things up for him. At this point, the elephant started wailing again: "I don't know where the wizard is," he sobbed. "Oh, that's easy," said the witch, "Just follow the yellow- pricked toad."

↦ Two vampires walked into a bar and called for the landlord. "I'll have a glass of blood," said one. "I'll have a glass of plasma," said the other. "Okay," replied the landlord, "that'll be one blood and one blood lite."

↦ What did the alien say when he landed in the garden? "Take me to your weeder!"

↦ What is the noisiest thing in the world? Skeletons bonking on a tin roof.

↔ Why do ghouls and demons hang out together? Because demons are a ghoul's best friend!

↔ Why does the Easter bunny hide his eggs? He doesn't want anyone to know he's screwing a chicken!

> **This goat-footed bard, this half-human visitor to our age from the hag-ridden magic and enchanted woods of Celtic antiquity.**
> *John Maynard Keynes, Essays and Sketches in Biography, 1883 – 1946, on Lloyd George*

↔ Why don't skeletons fight each other? None of them has the guts!

↔ Why don't witches wear panties when flying on their broomsticks? Better traction.

maRRiaGe

↔ "Before I married my wife," this bloke complained, "everything was wine, women, and song. Now that I'm her husband it's all coffee, mother, and nagging."

↔ "If I died," asked Mike, "would you remarry?" His wife thought about it. "Well, I suppose so." "And would you and he sleep in our bed?" His wife thought again, and said, "I guess so. It makes sense." Mike pressed on, "Would you make love to him?" "Of course," replied his wife, "as he would be my husband then." "How about my golf clubs?" asked Mike, "Would you give those to him?" His wife shook her head. "There wouldn't be any point – he's left-handed."

↦ "My husband is an angel," a woman said to her friend. "You're lucky," replied the friend. "Mine is still alive."

O curse of marriage, that we can call these delicate creatures ours, and not their appetites!

William Shakespeare, Othello

↦ "You're claiming that several men proposed marriage to you," asked the incredulous husband. "Yes, several," his wife replied. "God! I wish you'd married the first idiot who proposed," he lamented. "I did," she sneered, "but the others proposed anyway."

↦ "I don't know what to get my wife for her birthday," says Bob, "She already has everything, and she earns more than I do, so she can afford to buy anything she wants." "Why don't you give her a voucher saying she can have 60 minutes of great sex, any way she wants?" asks his friend. "Well, I can't think of anything else," says Bob, "So I'll give it a try." The next day, Bob's back in the bar. "I gave her the voucher," he says. "Did she like it?" asks his friend. "Oh yes! She loved it. She kissed me, thanked me for the best present I'd ever given her, and then she ran out of the door shouting, 'I'll be back in an hour!'"

➤ "It's just too hot to wear clothes today," said Jack as he stepped out of the shower. "Honey, what do you think the neighbours would think if I mowed the lawn like this?" "That I married you for your money."

➤ "The guys down at the pub say the milkman has seduced every woman on our street except one," Bob told his blonde wife. She thought for a moment. "I'll bet it's that snooty Mrs. Jenkins."

➤ A bloke bounced into the pub grinning and said to the landlord, "The beers are on me! My wife just ran away with my best friend." The landlord smiled and said, "Well, that's a shame. How come you aren't sad?" "Sad?" replied the bloke, "They've saved me a fortune! They were both pregnant!"

➤ A bloke turned to his wife and suggested, "Let's go out and have some fun tonight." "Okay," replied the wife enthusiastically, "but if you get home before I do, leave the hallway light on."

➤ A couple have been married for years and years. On their 60th anniversary they decide to go on a second honeymoon. "Let's go to all the same places that we did just after our wedding," the wife says. "Sure," says the husband. "And let's do all the same things that we did just after our wedding," the wife says. "Sure," says the husband. "And we'll make love just like we did after our wedding," the wife says. "Sure," says the husband, "only this time it's me who gets to sit on the side of the bed crying, 'It's too big, it's too big!'"

↣ A couple move into a flat with very thin walls, and they're worried that the neighbours will hear them talking in bed. "I know," says the wife, "when you want sex, put your hand on my breast and squeeze once. If you don't want sex, squeeze it twice." "Ok," says the husband. "If you want sex, put your hand on my penis and pull it once. If you don't want sex, pull it 50 times."

↣ A funeral service is being held for a woman who has recently died. Right at the end of the service the bearers pick up the coffin and begin to carry it to where it will enter the cremation chamber. As they turn a corner in the chapel the coffin hits the wall and there is a loud, audible "OUCH!" from inside it. They drop the casket to the floor and it turns out that, wonder of all wonders, the woman is actually alive. The woman lives for two more years and then dies – presumably for real this time. Everyone goes through the same ceremony, but this time, as the bearers round the corner, the woman's husband shouts out, "Careful, you lot, don't hit the damn wall this time!"

↣ A guy hasn't been feeling well for a while, so he goes to the doctor for a check-up. After he sees the doctor, the doctor tells him he has a very serious condition and says that he would like to talk to the man's wife. So the man leaves and sends his wife in. The doctor tells the wife that her husband has a very serious condition and that he is going to die. However, the doctor tells her that there is one way she can save his life – she must cook him three meals a day and have sex with him every night for six months and then he'll be okay. When the wife leaves the office her husband asks her what the doctor said. She looks at her husband and tells him: "He said you're gonna die."

➝ A best man's speech should be like a mini-skirt – short enough to be interesting, but long enough to cover the bare essentials.

Tho' marriage makes man and wife one flesh, it leaves them still two fools.

William Congreve, The Double Dealer, 1670 – 1729

➝ A guy walks into a bar and orders a double whisky – straight. As he begins to drink he reaches into his wallet and pulls out a photograph. He takes a quick peek at it and then puts it back quickly in his wallet. He then finishes his whisky, calls the barman over and orders another. He begins to drink it and, as he does so, he reaches into his wallet and pulls out the photograph again, looks at it and then puts it quickly away. He continues doing this for about an hour. Eventually the barman asks him, "Hey, mate, what's with the photo? I'm not worried by the amount you're drinking, I'd just really like to have a look at the picture – what on earth is it?" The man replies, "It's a photograph of my wife. When she starts to look good, I know it's time to go home!"

➝ A lawyer was trying to console a weeping widow. Her husband had passed away without a will. "Did the deceased have any last words?" asked the lawyer. "You mean right before he died?" sobbed the widow. "Yes," replied the lawyer, "they might be helpful, if it's not too painful for you to recall." "Well," she began, "he said, 'Don't try to scare me. You couldn't hit the broad side of a barn with that gun.'"

➨ A man answered a knock on his front door to find an Encyclopaedia Britannica salesman standing there. "Sorry," he said to the salesman, "We don't need it. My wife always assures me she knows all about everything going on."

➨ A man is talking in his favourite bar with his favourite friends on a Sunday night. He says, "So, check this out – last night when I was down here with you lot, a bloody burglar broke into my house." "Well out of order," says his mate. "Did he get anything?" says another. "Yup," says the man, "a smack in the face, a kick up the arse, a plank in the nuts and a dinner-plate over his head – the missus thought it was me coming home pissed again!"

➨ A recent survey shows that the commonest form of marriage proposal these days consists of the words: "You're WHAT?"

➨ A wife was having coffee with a friend when she confided to her, "Our marriage has never been great, but this year has been an absolute nightmare. Bill shouts at me all the time, criticises me, puts me down, tells me I'm shit, never does anything at all around the house, and I know he's fucking that little tart of a secretary of his – I found her knickers in his briefcase. I can't eat, I can't sleep...in fact, I've lost eight pounds so far this month." "You should dump the bastard," her friend said, "then take him for everything he's got." The wife replied, "Oh, I'm going to, don't worry. First, though, I want to get down to eight stone."

➼ A woman arrives home after a shopping trip, and is horrified to find her husband in bed with a pretty, firm young woman. She is about to storm out of the house when her husband stops her by saying, "Honey, before you go, at least give me one chance to explain how on earth this happened!" The woman decides that she owes him this much at least, so stops to listen to his story. He begins, "Well, I was driving home in the pouring rain and I saw this poor thing at the bus stop, soaked. There's a bus strike on, so I offered her a lift and it turned out that she was really hungry. So I brought her home and gave her some of last night's leftovers. I noticed her clothes were shabby so I offered her that jumper you wore once and didn't like and those trousers that don't fit you any more. I noticed her shoes were full of holes, so I gave her a pair of your shoes that you never liked, too. Anyway, so just as she was about to leave she asked me, 'And is there anything else that your wife doesn't use any more?' So here we are!"

➼ A woman asked her friend, "Would it kill you if your husband ran off with another woman?" The friend thought about it a bit, then said, "Well, it might. They say that sudden, intense delight can cause heart attacks."

**All the marriages are happy – it's trying
to live together afterwards that
causes the problems.**

Shelly Winters

➼ A young couple were on their honeymoon. The husband was sitting in the bathroom on the edge of the bathtub saying to himself, "Now how can I tell my wife that I've got really smelly feet and that my socks absolutely stink? I've managed to keep it from her while we were dating, but she's bound to find out sooner or later that my feet stink. Now, how do I tell her?" Meanwhile, the wife was sitting in the bed saying to herself, "Now how do I tell my husband that I've got really bad breath? I've been very lucky to keep it from him while we were courting, but as soon as he's lived with me for a week, he's bound to find out. Now, how do I tell him gently?" The husband finally plucked up enough courage to tell his wife and so he walked into the bedroom. He walked over to the bed, climbed over to his wife, put his arm around her neck, moved his face very close to hers and said, "Darling, I've a confession to make." And she said, "So have I, love." To which he replied, "Don't tell me, you've eaten my socks."

➻ A young man enters the doctor's office complaining of being run-down. "Well, what can I say?" says the doctor. "Book a few days off and rest – take a vacation, even: spend the weekend at home and sleep." "I can't do that, doctor," the young man replies, shaking his head. "I work in the stock market; it's a very profitable line of work and I'll lose a lot of money if I take time off." "In that case, change your lifestyle, don't go clubbing and so on: cut down on sex, for instance." "What? I'm a young man, I'm in my prime, and you want me to give up sex?" "Well, you could get married," the doctor mused. "That way you could taper off gradually."

➻ At the marriage guidance bureau, a woman was complaining, "What's-his-name here says I don't give him enough attention."

➻ An Amish boy and his father decided to visit a shopping mall. They were amazed by everything they saw, but especially by two shiny, silver walls that moved magically forward and backwards together by themselves. The young boy said to his father, "Daddy, what is this for? What miracle is this?" and the father replied that he did not know. As the two watched, an 80-year-old lady walked in and the doors closed. Lights above the doors flashed upwards and then down again, before the doors opened again, silently, and a beautiful 25-year-old woman walked out. The father and son looked at each other before the father said to the boy, "Go and get your mother!"

➻ Bachelors know more about women than married men; if they didn't, they'd be married too.

➻ Bachelors should be heavily taxed. It is not fair that some men should be happier than others.

➻ Before you marry, a man will lie awake all night thinking about something you said. After you marry, he will fall asleep before you finish saying it.

➻ Brian was dying, and his family were standing around the bed. In a weak voice, he said to his wife, "Dear, when I'm dead, I want you to marry Pete White." His wife was shocked, and said, "What? No! I couldn't marry anyone after you, darling." "But I want you to," said Brian. "Why?" asked his wife. "Well," he wheezed, "I've hated that bastard for 30 years."

↣ Did you hear about the new girlie mag that caters for the married market? It's just like Playboy or Penthouse, but it's all the same model, month after month after month...

↣ Do you know what it means to come home to a man who'll give you a little love, a little affection and a little tenderness? It means you're in the wrong house.

↣ Don't keep him in the doghouse too often or he might give his bone to the woman next door.

↣ Don't marry for money; you can borrow it cheaper.

Men marry because they are tired, women because they are curious. Both are disappointed.

Oscar Wilde, A Woman of No Importance

↣ During the wedding ceremony, when the minister comes to the part about, "If anyone knows any reason why these two people should not marry, speak up now or for ever hold your peace," have a four-year-old boy run up the aisle yelling, "Daddy, Daddy..."

↣ Every mother generally hopes that her daughter will snag a better husband than she managed to do, but she's certain that her boy will never get as great a wife as his father did.

↣ How do you turn a fox into an elephant? Marry it.

↣ Husband: "Darling, will you love me when I'm old and feeble?" Wife: "Of course I do, honey."

↠ I don't worry about terrorism. I was married for two years.

↠ I told my wife that a husband is like a fine wine; he gets better with age. The next day, she locked me in the cellar.

↠ Ian and Polly had just got married and were driving to Blackpool for their honeymoon. Along the way Ian, who was at the wheel, reached over shyly and stroked Polly's knee. Polly smiled, and blushed, and said, "We're married now, love. You can go farther if you want." So they drove to Edinburgh instead.

↠ If you want to sacrifice the admiration of many for the criticism of one, go ahead, get married.

↠ In marriage, as in war, it is permitted to take every advantage of the enemy.

↠ In olden times, sacrifices were made at the altar, a custom which is still very much practised.

↠ Insurance is like marriage. You pay, pay, pay, and you never get anything back.

↠ It destroys one's nerves to be amiable every day to the same human being.

↠ It doesn't much signify who one marries, for one is sure to find out next morning it was someone else.

↠ It is better to have loved and lost than to have had to live with that bitch for the rest of my life.

✎ It's not true that married men live longer than single men. It only seems longer.

✎ It's sad that a married couple can be torn apart by something as simple as a pack of wild dogs.

The amount of women in London who flirt with their own husbands is perfectly scandalous. It looks so bad. It is simply washing one's clean linen in public.

Oscar Wilde on married couples

✎ Little Johnny's dad picks him up after school because Johnny has been trying out for a part in the school play. Johnny is all excited and his dad says, "So, son, it looks like you got a part – that's great!" Johnny says, "Yes, dad, I did: I get to play the part of a man who's been married for a quarter of a century." "That's great, son," says his father, "and if you keep trying harder and harder, one day you'll get a speaking part!"

✎ Love is an ideal thing, marriage is a real thing. A confusion of the real with the ideal never goes unpunished.

✎ Love: a temporary insanity often curable by marriage.

✎ Marriage is a ceremony that turns your dreamboat into a barge.

✎ Marriage is a rest period between romances.

➤ Marriage is a three-ring circus: engagement ring, wedding ring and suffering.

➤ Marriage is the high sea for which no compass has yet been invented.

➤ Marriage is the process of finding out what kind of person your spouse would have really preferred.

➤ Marriage: A ceremony in which rings are put on the finger of the lady and through the nose of the gentleman.

➤ My ex-wife is an excellent laxative...If the sight of her doesn't make you crap yourself, she'll irritate the shit out of you in a couple of hours.

➤ My husband bought a waterbed but then we started to drift apart.

➤ My opinions are my wife's, and she says I'm damn lucky to have them.

➤ My wife is really immature. It's pathetic. Every time I take a bath, she comes in and sinks all my little boats.

➤ Never try to guess your wife's size. Just buy her anything marked 'petite' and hold on to the receipt.

➤ One morning at breakfast, Chuck walks up behind his wife and pinches her arse. "You know, Daisy, if you firmed this up we'd be able to get rid of your girdle," he says. Now Daisy is most insulted by this, of course, but she decides to let it go – it's only breakfast time, after all. The next day, Chuck walks up behind his wife and pinches her breast. "You know, Daisy, if you firmed this up we'd be able to get rid of your bra," he says. Daisy can't bite her lip another time, so she turns around and grasps his cock firmly, saying, "You know, Chuck, if you firmed this up we'd be able to get rid of the postman, the gardener, the pool man and your brother!"

➻ One Sunday, a man is working in the garden as his wife gets up and bathes. He is clearing leaves and soon realizes that he cannot find his rake, the essential tool for the job. He can see his wife in their bedroom window, so he shouts up, "Where's my rake?" The wife doesn't understand him and mouths, "What?" Again the man shouts, "Where's my rake?" The wife still doesn't understand, so shrugs her shoulders to signify a lack of comprehension. The man, tiring of shouting, points to his eye, then his knee, and then makes a raking motion with both hands. The wife is still clueless, so shrugs again, to say, "What?" The man repeats the gestures, and mouths "eye, knee, the rake" as he does so. The wife understands finally, and signals her reply. She points to her eye, her left breast, her arse and finally her crotch. The man's eyes nearly pop out and it is obvious he hasn't got a clue what she is going on about. Giving up, he walks into the house and runs upstairs. "What the hell was that all about?" he says. The wife replies, "Eye, left tit, behind, the bush!"

➻ Sex is hereditary. If your parents never had it, chances are you won't either.

↔ Six months into a marriage, a man was asked by his best friend how everything was going. He replied: "Oh, just fine. We practically never have any arguments. In the morning, she does what she wants. In the afternoon, I do what she wants. And at night, we both do what she wants."

↔ Sometimes I wonder if men and women really suit each other. Perhaps they should live next door and just visit now and then.

↔ The days just before marriage are like a snappy introduction to a tedious book.

↔ The definition of a husband: A man who stands by his wife in troubles she'd never have been in if she hadn't married him.

↔ The Devil walks into a crowded bar. When the people see who it is, they all run out screaming except this one old man. So the Devil saunters up to him and asks, "Do you know who I am?" The old man sips his beer, looks at the Devil, and answers, "Yup, happen I do." The Devil says, "Well, aren't you afraid of me?" The old man looks him up and down and says, "I've been married to your sister for 47 years. Why the hell should I be scared of you?"

↔ The doctor came out of the operating room to talk with the man's wife. "I don't like the look of your husband," he said. "Neither do I," said the wife, "but he's not home much, and he's great with the kids."

↔ The only way to make a husband love you and nobody else is to become his secretary.

↦ This bloke was down the pub, chatting to his mates. "I called the local insane asylum this morning," he said, "to check on whether any inmates have escaped recently." One friend asks, "Oh? Why, feeling nervous?" "No," the bloke replied, "Somebody ran off with my wife last night!"

↦ This day of the year always brings back a lot of sad memories. It was two years ago to the day that I lost my wife and children. I'll never forget that poker game.

Marriage is like a cage; one sees the birds outside desperately trying to get in, and those inside equally desperate to get out.

Michel de Montaigne, 1533 – 1592

↦ This woman was so jealous that when her husband came home one night and she couldn't find any unfamiliar hair on his jacket, she screamed at him, "God! Only you would cheat on me with a bald woman!"

↦ Two bits of advice to the new bride: 1) tell your new husband that you have to have one night a week out with the girls, and 2) don't waste that night on the girls.

↦ Two men and a woman were sitting in a bar discussing their lives. The first man says, "You know, I'm a YUPpie – that's Young, Urban Professional." The second man says, "Well, me and my missus, we're DINKs – that's Double Income, No Kids." Then the first man asks the woman, "So what are you?" She replies, "I'm a WIFE – that's Wash, Iron, Fuck, Etcetera!"

→ Two men who hadn't seen each other in years met on the street. While they were talking and trying to catch up on all those intervening years, one asked the other if he had got married. "No," the other man replied. "I look this way because someone just spilled a cup of coffee on me."

→ Watching her mother as she tried on her new mink coat, the daughter protested, "Mum, do you realize some poor, dumb beast suffered so you could have that coat?" Her mother glared back at her and said, "Don't talk about your father that way."

→ What could men do to make their marriages last longer? Pay less attention to prenuptial agreements and more to postnuptial affection and sex.

→ What do you call a woman who knows where her husband is all the time? A widow.

**The pain of death is nothing compared
to the pain of sharing a coffee-pot with
a peevish woman.**

John Cheever, on married life

→ What food diminishes your sex drive by 75%? Wedding cake.

→ What is a wedding tragedy? To marry a man for love, and then find out he has no money.

↣ What term describes a woman paralyzed from the waist down? Married.

↣ What's a wife? An attachment you screw on the bed to get the housework done.

↣ What's the difference between a man buying a lottery ticket and a man arguing with his wife? The man buying the ticket at least has a one in 16 million chance of winning!

↣ What's the late-night difference between a bachelor and a married man? A bachelor comes home, sees what's in the refrigerator and goes to bed. A married man comes home, sees what's in the bed and goes to the refrigerator.

↣ When a woman gets married, she wants the three Ss: Sensitivity; Sincerity; and Sharing. What does she get? The three Bs: Belching; Body odour; and Bad breath.

↣ Whenever a husband and wife begin to discuss their marriage, they are giving evidence at an inquest.

↣ Why is sex with your wife like a late-night grocery? The goods are unattractively packaged, there's very little variety and there's a high price to pay, but there's just nothing else available at 2am.

↣ You know that the honeymoon is over when the husband takes his wife off the pedestal and puts her on a budget.

masTURBaTion

➻ A rickety woman walks into a sex shop. She is having trouble walking and half hobbles and half hops over to the counter. She eventually makes it and holds on for dear life. She says to the boy behind the counter, "D-d-d-d-ooo yo-yo-you s-s-s-sell d-d-d-d-d-dildos-s-s-?" The boy says, "Yes, ma'am, we sell dildos. In fact we sell all sorts, in all shapes and sizes." The woman says, "D-d-d-d-d-o yo-yo-you h-h-h-h-have w-w-w-ww-wun th-th-th-th-that is sm-sm-sm-sm-small and b-b-b-b-black, s-s-s-s-s-ix i-i-i-i-i-inches l-l-l-l-ong b-b-b-b-b-but three i-i-i-i-i-i-inches th-th-th-th-thick?" The boy says, "Why, yes we do: that's one of the most popular models." "W-w-w-w-w-w-ell, c-c-c-c-c-c-can you t-t-t-t-t-t-tell m-m-m-me-e-e- how-w-w-w-w to t-t-t-t-t-t-turn-n-n-n-nn the fu-fu-fu-fucking thing-g-g-g-g- off-f-f-f-f-f-f-f-f-f-f?"

I look on the sex with something like the admiration with which I regard the starry sky in a frosty December night. I admire the beauty of the Creator's workmanship; I am charmed with the wild but graceful eccentricity of the motions; and I wish both of them goodnight.

Robert Burns

➻ A woman goes into a shop and asks if they sell batteries. "Yes, we have some in the back room," says the assistant, "Come this way." "If I could come this way," says the woman, "I wouldn't need the batteries."

↔ How did Pinocchio discover he was made of wood? His hand caught alight!

↔ What did the banana say to the vibrator? What are you shaking for? It's me she's going to eat!

↔ What did the sign on the door of the brothel say? We're closed. Beat it.

↔ What's the definition of a 'Yankee'? It's like a 'quickie', but you do it alone!

↔ What's the ultimate in sexual rejection? Your hand falls asleep while you're masturbating!

↔ What's white, eight inches long, takes two batteries, gives complete satisfaction in three minutes and once you've tried it you'll never go back to the manual method? An electric toothbrush.

↔ Why is a dildo like a Soya bean? They're both a poor substitute for meat.

maths

↔ Hot dogs come in packs of ten, buns in packs of eight, beer in packs of six, ham comes in packs of 16 slices, condoms come in packs of three. Why can't they get it straight? Nowadays, a man needs a calculator just to have a weekend...

➼ A dull old maths teacher left a letter for his wife one Friday night: "Dear Janet, as you know, I am 56, and by the time you read this letter I will be settled in at the Luxor Hotel, tucking into my beautiful, sexy, 21-year-old teaching assistant." When the teacher arrived at the hotel, he found that a message had been left for him: "Dear John, as you know, I too am 56, and by the time you read this letter I will be settled in at the Excelsior Hotel, tucking into my handsome, virile, 21-year-old toy boy. You, being a maths teacher, will appreciate that 21 goes into 56 a lot more times than 56 goes into 21!"

➼ Did you hear the one about the constipated mathematician? He worked it out with a pencil.

> **Mathematics may be defined as that subject in which we never know what we are talking about, nor whether what we are saying is true.**
>
> *Bertrand Russell*

➼ What is the square root of 69? Ate something.

meDICaL maTTeRS

➼ A famous heart surgeon is having a friendly charity barbecue when he is approached by a loudmouth. "Hey, Doc," the guy says, "I'm the best mechanic in town. I can take an engine apart, take the valves out, clean them, tune them and after I put everything back together the baby will purr like a newborn kitten. We're basically doing the same job, so how come you get more money than me, hey?" "Try to do that with the engine running," the heart surgeon says softly.

➡ A man staggers into hospital with two black eyes and a golf club tightly wrapped round his throat. The doctor on duty asks him what happened. "Well, Doc, it was like this," the man says. "I was out for a quiet round of golf with the missus and she shanked her ball something terrible. It landed in a field full of cows, so we both went to look for it. I was having a good look round but couldn't find it. Anyway, I noticed a white thing in the arse of one of the cows so I walked over, lifted up its tail and there was my wife's golf ball, rammed right up there. That's when I made my only mistake." "And what was that, then?" asked the doc. "Well, I turned to get my wife's attention, lifted the cow's tail and shouted, 'Hey! This looks like yours!'"

➡ A man goes to hospital for a circumcision operation and he wakes up in the morning surrounded by hospital staff. He wonders what the hell is going on and then he feels an enormous piece of padding between his legs. The head surgeon says to him, "Look here, sir; we're all really, really sorry, but I'm afraid we made a mistake and got a bit carried away with the chopping. We've ended up giving you a complete sex change operation." The man screams and shouts and cries his eyes out. "Oh, my God," he says eventually. "There's so much I'll never be able to do again. I will never, ever be able to experience an erection." The surgeon strokes him on the head and says, "Of course you will, of course you will. It just won't be yours, that's all!"

➻ A few days before his proctological exam, a one-eyed man accidentally swallowed his glass eye. He was worried for a while and kind of expected to see it pop up at some point, but there were no ill effects, it didn't re-appear and so he forgot about it. The day for the appointment arrived and he was lying on his belly, after having changed into a surgical gown behind a screen. The doctor approached, lifted the gown up and came face to face with the glass eye stuck in his patient's anus staring right back at him. "You know," he says in a gentle, reproving tone, "you should learn to trust me better than that."

Those healths will make thee and thy state look ill.

William Shakespeare, Timon of Athens

➻ A man working at a lumberyard is pushing a tree through a band saw when he accidentally shears off all his fingers and thumbs. He rushes to the emergency entrance of a nearby hospital where the awaiting doctor takes a look and says. "Yuck! Well, give me the fingers and I'll see what I can do." "I haven't got the fingers." The doctor says, "What do you mean, you haven't got the fingers? This is the age of medical advances. We've got microsurgery and all sorts of incredible techniques. Why didn't you bring me the fingers?" "Well, heck, doctor, I tried, but I couldn't pick 'em up."

➻ A new clinic, with several different specialists, opened in a trendy part of the city. Wanting to be different and creative with the design, the administration decided that each doctor's office door would, in some way, be representative of his practice. So, when construction was complete, the eye doctor's door had a peep-hole, the orthopaedist's door had a broken hinge, the psychiatrist's door was painted all kinds of crazy colours. As for the gynaecologist's door, it was left open... just a crack.

→ A proctologist pulls out a thermometer from his shirt pocket. He looks at it and says: "Shit, some arsehole has my pen."

→ A woman had just given birth to her first baby. She was tired and haggard, but she noticed that the baby was nowhere to be seen. "Where's my baby?" she asks. "I want to see my baby." The doctor, apologizing, says "Er, well, you see, mmm... I know it will come as a shock, but there's a problem with your baby. She has no arms..." The mother is stunned. "Wh... What..? No arms?" Then she wails "I don't care, she's my baby – I want to see my baby! I hurt all this time to get her. I want to see her!" "Er..." says the doctor, eyes downcast, "you see, she has no legs either..." The mother is speechless for a few seconds, then erupts in tears and wails "I want to see my baby!" The doctor relents and nods to the nurse outside, who brings in a cot. The blonde mother peers inside and the smile dies on her face. Inside the cot is a big ear. "Is... is this my baby?" she whispers. "Speak louder," says the doctor, "she's deaf."

→ Doctor: "We need to get these people to a hospital." Nurse: "What is it?" Doctor: "It's a big building with a lot of doctors in it. Why do you ask?"

➠ A woman went to the surgery. She was seen by one of the new doctors, but after about four minutes in the examination room she burst out, screaming as she ran down the hall. An older doctor stopped and asked her what the problem was, and she explained, obviously in shock. The older doctor marched back to the first and demanded, "What's the matter with you? Mrs Johnston is 67 years old: she has four grown children and seven grandchildren, and you told her she was pregnant?" The new doctor smiled smugly as he continued to write on his clipboard. "Cured her hiccups, though, didn't I?"

➠ A young couple get married and they've never made love before. On their wedding night, the new bride is quite anxious to get things going, but the man seems to be having some difficulty. Finally, he starts to undress. When he takes off his trousers, she notices that his knees are deeply pockmarked and scarred. So his wife says, "What happened to you?" The man says, "When I was young, I had the kneesles." He then takes off his socks and his wife sees that his toes are all mangled and deformed. "Hmmm, well what happened to your feet?" inquires the wife. "When I was a young boy, I had tolio." So, finally, the man takes off his shorts and the woman says: "Don't tell me. Smallcox, right?"

➠ An old man of 87 went to the hospital to get a radical new surgical procedure done where they stretch the skin and pull all the wrinkles up on to the top of the scalp, making you appear years younger. On his way out of the hospital, he met an old friend who didn't recognize him at first. "Rob, is that really you?" said the friend. "You look years younger. I didn't know you had a dimple in your chin." "It's not a dimple, it's my belly button" said the old man and his friend laughed. "If you think that's funny, take a look at what I'm wearing for a tie."

Exercise is bunk. If you are healthy you don't need it, and if you are sick you shouldn't take it.

Henry Ford, 1863 – 1947

➡ Fun things to do with an ambulance:

Drive too fast over speed bumps.
Stop with the siren on at a petrol station to fill it up.
Get involved in an accident.
Stop several times to ask for directions.
Drive by a McDonald's to ask if they want to buy fresh meat.
Shoot at the dogs which always chase the ambulance.
Replace the siren with the music of an ice-cream van.
If there's not enough work, drive over people yourself.
Fill the air tanks with liquids.
Ask your boss for the new Lamborghini Diablo ambulance.
Put a twirling disco light in the back.
Drive around the graveyard.
Paint "Satan loves you" on the side.
Throw bloody lamb chops out of the back door.
Keep circling the same block with your head out of the window and your tongue hanging out.
Drive to a morgue and ask if they've got any live ones they want you to take.

↔ Have you heard about the new medication that is both an aphrodisiac and a laxative? It's called "Easy Come, Easy Go."

↔ It is said that the limbic system of the brain controls the four Fs: Feeding, Fighting, Fleeing and Reproduction.

Exercise is like a cold bath. You think it does you good because you feel better when you stop it.

Robert Quillen

↔ It is the ophthalmologist's 40th birthday and, in the middle of the party, he is blindfolded and taken by the hand to a table in the centre of the dining room. His loving wife takes the blindfold off with a flourish and he finds himself in front of a huge cake with 40 eyes made of marzipan around it. The specialist stares at the cake and then erupts in laughter. He laughs so much that a couple of his friends have to pick him up from the floor. After a few minutes, wiping a tear of mirth from his eye, he says: "I'm sorry, this is a great cake. It's just that I suddenly thought about my colleague Terry, who's a proctologist. It's his 50th birthday tomorrow."

↔ Mavis: "My daughter believes in preventative medicine, doctor." Doctor: "Oh, really?" Mavis: "Yes, she tries to prevent me from making her take it."

↔ My father always thought laughter was the best medicine. That's probably why half of us died from tuberculosis.

↣ Once I was sick and I had to go to an ear, nose, and throat specialist. There are ear doctors, nose doctors, throat doctors, gynaecologists, proctologists. Any place you have a hole, there's a guy who specializes in your hole. They make an entire career out of that hole. And if the ear doctor, nose doctor, throat doctor, gynaecologist, or proctologist can't help you, he sends you to a surgeon. Why? So he can make a new hole.

↣ Proctology is the rare profession in which the doctor starts out at the bottom and stays there.

↣ The worst thing you can hear as the anaesthetic starts to hit is, "Lord of This World, Father of Lies, Prince of Darkness, accept this, our Sacrifice..."

↣ Two friends are playing golf together, when the first woman swings a mighty shot...that goes up, and up, and down, smack amid a male foursome playing on the next hole. The women watch in horror as the ball actually hits one of the guys, apparently in a most delicate place. They are powerless as they witness the man yelping in pain, both his hands on his crotch and collapsing in a foetal position on the grass. The woman, guilty of the disastrous swing, rushes to meet the foursome and says to the guy in agony on the grass "Listen, I can help. I am a physiotherapist. I can ease your pain, trust me." "I am alright," the bloke says between clenched teeth. "Come on, I can really help." The man agrees and manages to stand up. The physiotherapist then gently unzips his trousers and reaches inside to massage him. "Now?...Are you feeling better now?" "Yeah," the man admits, "that's great, but my thumb still hurts like hell!"

↦ This bloke dropped out of medical school. It was tragic. He really wanted to be a doctor, but he just couldn't stand the sight of cash.

↦ What do you call a surgeon with eight arms? A doctopus!

↦ What's grey, sits by a bed and takes the piss? A dialysis machine.

↦ What's the worst bit about a lung transplant? The first time you cough, it's not your phlegm!

men

↦ "Did you see that guy?" a woman asked a friend. "He doesn't sweat!" The second woman replied, "Yes, I know. Snakes generally don't."

↦ "I don't know why you wear a bra," said the husband, "You've got nothing to put in it." "You wear boxers, don't you?" replied the wife coolly.

↦ 90% of men give the other 10% a bad name.

↦ A husband is living proof that a wife can take a joke.

↦ A man and woman are on their honeymoon after a long and very happy courtship. On their honeymoon, they decide to take their horses through the beautiful mountain passes of Europe. The horses are crossing a small stream when the woman's horse stumbles and jostles the man's wife. Once across the stream the man dismounts, walks over to the horse and stares into its eyes. Finally, he states: "That's one." The man remounts his horse and they continue their ride. A bit further down the path, the woman's horse stumbles when stepping over a fallen tree. The man dismounts, stares the horse in the eyes, and boldly states: "That's two!" He returns to his saddle and they move on. As the afternoon sun began to set, the woman's horse loses its footing on a mossy slope. The man dismounts, moves to the woman's horse and helps his wife out of the saddle. The man, moving to the front of the horse, stares it in the eyes and firmly says: "That's three." He removes a pistol from his coat, and shoots the horse dead. The woman, quite upset at seeing the beautiful horse killed, says to her husband, "That's terrible, why would you do such a thing." The man stares at his wife and firmly says: "That's one!"

➻ A man was sitting beneath a tree, thinking about how good his wife had been to him and how fortunate he was to be married to her. He asked God, "Why did you make her so kind-hearted, Lord?" The Almighty responded, "So you could love her, my son." The man nodded. "Why did you make her so good-looking, Lord?" "So you could love her, my son," replied God. "Why did you make her such a good cook, Lord?" he persisted. "So you could love her, my son," came the answer. The man thought about it. Then he said, "I don't mean to seem ungrateful or anything Lord, but why did you have to make her so stupid?" God sighed. "So she could love you, my son."

➻ A woman and a man are involved in a really nasty car accident. Both their cars are totally demolished, but neither of them are hurt. After they crawl out of their cars, the woman says, "So you're a man – that's interesting. I'm a woman. Wow, just look at our cars! There's nothing left, but we're unhurt. This must be a sign from God that we should meet, get acquainted and live together in peace for the rest of our days." The man feels great at having such good luck, so says, "Oh, yes, I agree with you completely! This must be a sign from the Lord!" The woman continues, "And look at this – another miracle. My car is demolished, but this bottle of wine didn't break. Surely God wants us to drink this wine and celebrate our good fortune." She hands the bottle to the man, who nods his head in agreement, opens the bottle and drinks half of it before handing it back to the woman. The woman takes the bottle and immediately puts the cap back on. The man asks, "Aren't you having any?" The woman replies, "No. I think I'll just wait for the police!" The moral of this story: Women are clever. Don't mess with them.

History teaches us that men and nations behave wisely once they have exhausted all other alternatives.

Abba Eban

➻ A woman was chatting with her next-door neighbour. "I feel really good today. I started out this morning with an act of unselfish generosity. I gave a fiver to a dosser." "You mean you gave a dosser five quid? That's a lot of money to give away like that. What did your husband say about it?" "He said 'Thanks'."

➻ According to a recent survey, men say the first thing that they notice about women are their eyes. Women say the first thing they notice about men is that they're a bunch of liars.

➻ According to women, pricks come in three sizes: Small, medium and ohmigod. According to men, there are also three sizes: large, average and size-doesn't-matter.

➻ At 35, a woman thinks about having children. At 35, a man thinks about dating children...

➻ Before money was invented, what did women find attractive about men?

➻ Behind every great man, there is a surprised woman.

➻ Being a woman is quite difficult, since it consists mainly of dealing with men.

➻ Boys will be boys but one day all girls will be women.

➻ Colonel Sanders was a typical man. The only three things he cared about were legs, breasts, and thighs.

➻ Diamonds are a girl's best friend, while dogs are a man's best friend. You tell me which sex is smarter...

➻ Ever notice how so many of women's problems can be traced to the male gender? MENstruation, MENopause, MENtal breakdown, GUYnaecology, HIMmorrhoids...

⊷ Every man has it in his power to make one woman happy... by remaining a bachelor.

⊷ Fred and Jane were relating their holiday experiences to a friend. "It sounds as if you had a great time in Cornwall," the friend observed, "but didn't you tell me you were going to Scotland?" "Yes, it's just ridiculous," said Jane, "Fred simply will not ask for directions."

⊷ How are men like noodles? They're always in hot water, they lack taste and they need dough.

⊷ How are men like UFOs? You don't know where they come from, what their mission is, or what time they're going to take off.

⊷ How can you tell if a bloke is aroused? He's breathing.

⊷ How can you tell the difference between a present your husband buys for the hell of it, and a present he buys because he's feeling guilty? The guilty present is nicer.

⊷ How can you tell when a man is well-hung? His face is blue and he's stopped struggling.

⊷ How do men exercise on the beach? They suck in their stomachs every time they see a bikini.

⊷ How do men sort their dirty clothes? 'Dirty' and 'dirty-but-wearable.'

➥ How do you get a man to always leave the toilet seat down? Cut off his penis.

➥ How do you get a man to really listen to what you say? Talk in your sleep.

➥ How do you know when you've found Mr Right? His first name is 'Always.'

➥ How do you ruin a man's ego? By asking, "Is it in yet?"

➥ How does a bloke make up his mind? He puts mascara on his bollocks.

➥ How does a man show he's planning for the future? He buys two cases of beer instead of one.

➥ How many honest, intelligent, caring, sensitive men does it take to do the dishes? Both of them.

➥ How many men does it take to tile a bathroom? Two – if you slice them thinly enough.

➥ How many times ever, in total, is a bachelor's bed made? One – when it was in the factory.

➥ If a bloke is better than you at something, he will tell you how important it is. If you are better than he is, he will claim it's nothing useful.

➻ If a man appears sexy, caring and clever, give him a day or two. He'll soon be back to his usual self.

➻ If a man hears what a woman says, she is not beautiful.

➻ If blokes are so clever, how come you always see signs reading "Danger! Men Working?"

➻ If he asks you if you're faking it, tell him, "No. I'm just practising."

➻ If one man can wash one stack of dishes in one hour, how many stacks of dishes can four men wash in four hours? None. They'll all sit down together and watch football on television.

Love is the victim's response to the rapist.

Ti-Grace Atkinson

➻ If you think he's listening to you, you're wrong. He's trying to find the childish innuendoes in what you just said.

➻ It would be wonderful if there was a potion that could give an average bloke the physique of Sylvester Stallone, the brains of Steven Hawking and the humour of Jo Brand. Of course, it could be horrendous. One little slip and you might end up with a bloke who had Jo Brand's body, Sylvester Stallone's brain, and the charm of Steven Hawking. Actually, thinking about it, who could tell?

↔ Jim and Nick are hanging out on the beach trying to pull. Nick has plenty of luck, but Jim's a bit short in the "front" so he says to Nick, "What's up, Nick? I'm just not having much luck with the ladies?" Nick replies, "It must be that you aren't appealing enough to the basic animal instincts. Try putting a nice big potato down your swimming trunks. The birds'll take one look and be all over you like a rash!" Now Jim knows that Nick pulls all over the place, so thinks he might as well give it a damn good go. The next day the two of them meet up again and Jim is in no better a mood. He says to Nick, "I tried it with that potato and you know, it did me no good at all. In fact, even more of the chicks are avoiding me than before. What's that all about?" Nick has a quick look and says, "Well, mate, I think it'd probably help a lot if you put the potato down the front!"

↔ Men are like animals. They're messy, insensitive and potentially violent, but occasionally they make great pets.

↔ Men are like blenders. You have this feeling that you need one, but you're really not sure why.

↔ Men are so reluctant to become fathers because they're still too busy being children.

↔ Men are those creatures with two legs and eight hands.

↔ Men call us birds; is that because of all the worms we pick up?

↔ Men can't get mad cow disease. They're all pigs.

→ Men say that women wear make up and perfume because they are ugly and smell bad. Why don't men wear make up and perfume, then? They're ugly and smell bad too, but they can't tell...

→ Men who say they can see through women are missing a lot.

→ Most husbands don't like to hear their wives struggling with housework – so they turn up the volume on the television.

→ Most men prefer looks to brains, because most men see better than they think.

→ Most women's idea of the perfect man is someone who is obedient, well-mannered, faithful, can empty the garbage and is great in bed. If only you could train dogs to screw in positions other than doggie-style, and bestiality was more socially accepted...

→ Never hit a man with glasses. Hit him with a baseball bat.

→ Nothing astonishes men so much as common sense and plain dealing.

→ Once upon a time, there was a beautiful, independent princess who was very self-assured. One day she was walking in the forest when she chanced upon a frog sitting on a rock in a stream. To her amazement, the frog begins to talk to her, "Fair princess, I am a handsome prince, trapped by a witch in the foul, slimy body of this poor frog. Won't you kiss me once to break the spell and we can live happily ever after in my castle with my mother and my father and my knights and you can bear my children and look after them and prepare my meals and clean my sheets and all will be well?" That night, as the beautiful, independent princess ate her frog's legs, she laughed out loud and thought to herself, "Not this time!"

↭ Only a man would buy a £300 car and put a £2,000 stereo in it.

↭ Pre-menstrual tension is something that makes women act once a month like blokes do every day.

↭ Sadly, all men are created equal.

↭ Short skirts remind blokes of their manners. Have you ever seen a bloke push on to a bus in front of a girl in a short skirt?

↭ Single women claim that all the good men are married, but married women complain that their husbands are appalling. This proves, for once and for all, that there is no such thing as a good man.

↭ So many men, so many reasons not to shag any of them.

↭ Take an interest in your husband's activities: hire a detective.

↭ The best way to get a bloke to do something is to suggest that he is far too old for it.

➻ The next-door neighbour of a middle-aged wife came over to inform her that her retired husband was chasing around after young prostitutes. The woman smiled. "So what?" The neighbour was surprised: "It doesn't bother you that he's running around with those women?" The woman replied, "I have a dog who chases cars and buses that he can't drive, too."

➻ The only real problem holding women back is men.

➻ The only time a woman values a man's company is when he owns it.

I know many married men, I even know a few happily married men, but I don't know one who wouldn't fall down the first open coal-hole running after the first pretty girl who gave him a wink.

George Jean Nathan

➻ The only treatment to save a patient is a brain transplant. His family is gathered in the doctor's office, taking in the bad news. "Er, doctor, how much is this going to cost?" "Well, it's about £600,000 for a male brain and £200,000 for a female brain," the specialist answers. The men in the room all sit up and start chuckling, a superior expression appearing on their faces. The youngest daughter casts her eyes towards the ceiling and asks the doctor: "And why is a female brain cheaper?" "Oh, it's standard practice, Miss," he replies. "The brain has to be marked down because it was used by its original owner."

➤ Things never to say to an excited, naked man:

I've smoked fatter joints than that.
Wow – and your feet are so big!
Why don't we skip right to the cigarette?
Is that an optical illusion?
Does it come with an air pump?
It's OK: we'll work around it!
Maybe it looks better in natural light.
Maybe if we water it, it'll grow.
But it still works, right?
How sweet: you brought incense.
Can I be honest with you?
Why, oh, why is God punishing me?
Oh no... a flash headache! (giggle and point)
Can I paint a 'smiley face' on it?
Why don't we just cuddle?
Only if you get me real drunk first.
This explains your car.
You know, they have surgery to fix that.
Ahhhh, isn't it cute!
Are you cold?
It looks so unused.
It's a good thing you have so many other talents.
Make it dance!
At least this won't take long.
I suppose this makes me the 'early bird.'
What is that?
Will it squeak if I squeeze it?
I never saw one like that before.
So this is why you're supposed to judge people on personality.

➺ The only way to hurt a man with your words is to hit him in the face with your dictionary.

➺ The trouble with some women is that they get all excited about nothing and then marry him.

➺ There are only two four-letter words that are offensive to men – "stop" and "don't".

➺ There is no reason for any wife to have an inferiority complex. All she has to do is to spend a week sick in bed and leave her husband to manage the household and the kids.

➺ They put one man on the moon. Why can't they put them all there?

➺ They say that men only think about sex. That's not exactly true. They also care a lot about power, world domination, money and beer.

➺ Three guys were out fishing when one caught a mermaid. She offers to grant each fisherman one wish, in exchange for her freedom. "Alright, double my IQ," said the first fisherman. "Done," said the mermaid, and the man – to his amazement – began to recite Shakespeare. The second fisherman was so staggered that he forgot all about making his dick larger, and said to the mermaid, "Triple my IQ!" "Done," said the mermaid, and he started deducing solutions to mathematical problems that he had never even realised existed. The third fisherman was beside himself. "Quintuple my IQ!" he screamed. The mermaid looked at him and said, "Normally I wouldn't try to change someone's minds about a wish, but I'd really like you to reconsider." The bloke shook his head stubbornly. "No, I want my IQ increased five times. If you don't do it, I won't set you free." "Please," said the mermaid, "it will alter your entire view of the universe." No matter what the mermaid said, the third fisherman insisted. So the mermaid sighed and said, "Done." With that, the third guy became a woman.

➜ What did God say after creating man? "Hmm. I can do better than that."

➜ What did the elephant say to the naked man? How do you breathe through something that small?

➜ What do a clitoris, an anniversary and a toilet have in common? Men will always miss them.

➜ What do blokes and atheists have in common? Neither believe in a second coming.

➜ What do husbands and lawnmowers have in common? They're hard to start in the morning, they belch out noxious odours and half the time they don't even work.

➜ What do most men think mutual orgasm is? An insurance company.

➜ What do you call a beautiful woman on the arm of an ugly man? A tattoo.

➜ What do you call a guy who never farts in public? A private tutor.

➻ What do you call a man who expects to have sex on the second date? Slow.

➻ What do you call an intelligent man in England? A tourist.

➻ What do you give to the man who has everything? A woman who can explain how to work it.

➻ What does it mean when a man is in your bed gasping for breath and calling your name? You didn't hold the pillow down long enough.

➻ What happens when a man tries to hide his baldness by combing his hair across his head? The truth comes shining through.

➻ What has eight arms and an IQ of 60? Four guys watching a football match.

➻ What is the difference between a golf ball and a G-spot? Men will spend hours searching for a golf ball.

➻ What is the difference between savings bonds and blokes? It takes a few years, but eventually bonds mature.

➻ What is the one thing that all men at singles bars have in common? They're married.

➻ What is the only time a man thinks about a candlelit dinner? When the power goes off.

↦ What is warm and soft when a man comes in drunk at night and hard and stiff when he wakes up in the morning? The pile of puke at the bottom of the stairs.

↦ What must be the lightest thing known to man? A penis – even a thought can raise it!

↦ What's a man's idea of helping with the housework? Lifting his legs so you can vacuum.

↦ What's the best way to have your husband remember your anniversary? Get married on his birthday.

The majority of husbands remind me of an orang-utan trying to play the violin.

Honoré de Balzac

↦ What's the definition of a slag? A woman with the sexual morals of a man.

↦ What's the definition of macho? Jogging home from your own vasectomy.

↦ What's the difference between "Oh!" and "Aaah!"? About two inches.

↦ What's the difference between a beer and a man? The beer comes in a can, not in your mouth.

↦ What's the difference between a man and a battery? A battery has a positive side.

↦ What's the difference between a man and a condom? Condoms aren't thick and insensitive these days.

↦ What's the difference between a man and a cup of coffee? A cup of coffee can keep you awake all night.

↦ What's the difference between a man and a holiday? Nothing – neither of them is ever long enough.

↦ What's the difference between a man and a Slinky? Nothing. They're both slightly amusing when they're falling down the stairs, but are otherwise useless.

↦ What's the difference between a man and ET? ET phoned home.

↦ What's the difference between a new husband and a new dog? The dog is still excited to see you a year later.

↦ What's the difference between a singles' bar and a circus? Clowns don't talk at the circus.

↦ What's the difference between a sweater and a jumper? With a sweater your sheets are always soaking – with a jumper you don't dare bend over to put them in the washing machine.

↦ What's the difference between a tampon and a cowboy hat? Cowboy hats are for arseholes.

➼ What's the last thing 'Tickle Me Elmo' receives before he leaves the factory? Two test tickles.

➼ What's the sex speed limit? 68, because at 69 you have to turn around.

➼ What's the word for a man who's watching a woman undress? Grateful.

➼ What's easier to build, a snowman or a snow woman? A snow woman is easier, because once you've made a snowman you have to scoop all the snow out of his head and use it to make his testicles.

➼ When a car skidded on a wet road and struck a telegraph pole, several bystanders ran over to help the driver. A woman was the first to get to the victim, but a bloke rushed in and shouldered her out of the way. "Step aside, love," he said, "I've got a certificate in first aid." The woman observed for a minute or so, then tapped the bloke on the shoulder. "I just thought you should know that when you get to the part about calling for a doctor, I'm right here."

➼ When a man puts his best foot forward, it usually ends up in his mouth.

➼ When a man says, "Darling, we don't need material objects to prove our love," he means, "Fuck! I forgot our anniversary again!"

➨ When a man says, "Good idea," he means, "It'll never work, and I can spend the rest of the day gloating about it."

➨ When a man says, "Have you lost weight?" he means, "I've just blown our last £50 on a power drill."

➨ When a man says, "I brought you a present," he means, "I won a free paperweight as a booby prize in the pub's meat raffle."

➨ When a man says, "I split up with her," he means, "She ditched me."

➨ When a man says, "I've read all the classics," he means, "I collect Playboy, and have done since 1972."

I feel sorry for men – they have more problems than women. In the first place, they have to compete with women as well as with each other.

Francoise Sagan

➨ When a man says, "She's one of those rabid feminists," he means, "She refused to make me a cup of tea."

➨ When a man says, "That's women's work," he means, "It's difficult, dirty and thankless."

➨ When a man says, "Will you marry me?" he means, "Both my flatmates have moved out, I can't find the washing machine and the bin is full of pizza boxes."

➻ When a man says, "You look terrific," he means, "Oh, please don't try on any more outfits. I'm starving."

➻ When do men insist that women are illogical? When a woman doesn't agree with them.

➻ When he asks you if he's your first, say, "I'm not sure. You might be. You do look slightly familiar."

➻ Where do you have to go to find a man who is truly into commitment? A mental hospital.

➻ While shopping, women get excited and happy when they buy that perfect item. Men experience the same feelings when they find a good parking space.

➻ Why are dogs better than men?

1. If a dog wants to go out, it will let you know.
2. A dog will express affection in public.
3. A dog will play ball without telling you how to throw overarm.
4. You can train a dog to understand what 'no' means.
5. If a dog wants its balls licked, it will do it for itself.
6. After six months, a dog will still look excited to see you.
7. Just because you've had some fun with a dog, it doesn't think it can sleep on your bed.
8. Dogs feel guilt.
9. Dogs are grateful when you stroke them.
10. When your dog gets old, you can just get a younger dog.

❖ Why are men and spray paint alike? One squeeze and they're all over you.

❖ Why are men endowed with half an ounce more brains than dogs? So they know not to embarrass themselves by humping women's knees at parties.

❖ Why are men like clothes shops? They're most interesting when their clothes are 50% off.

❖ Why are men like cowpats? The older they get, the easier they are to pick up.

❖ Why are men like paper cups? They're disposable.

❖ Why are men like popcorn? They satisfy you, but only for a little while.

❖ Why are men like tights? They never quite fit between the legs, and they usually run after one night out.

❖ Why are some men uncircumcised? The doctors were afraid of causing brain damage to the infant.

❖ Why are women so much more interesting to men than men are to women?

❖ Why can't women read maps? Because only the male mind can comprehend the concept of an inch equalling a mile.

✦ Why did God give woman nipples? To make suckers out of men.

✦ Why do bachelors like clever women? Opposites attract.

✦ Why do doctors slap babies' arses as soon as they're born? To knock the penises off the clever ones.

✦ Why do female black widow spiders kill their partners after mating? To stop the snoring before it starts.

✦ Why do men find it difficult to make eye contact? Tits don't have eyes.

✦ Why do men have holes in their penises? So their brains can get some oxygen occasionally.

✦ Why do men like big breasts and tight pussies? Because they've got big mouths and small pricks.

✦ Why do men like blonde girl jokes? Because they can understand them.

✦ Why do men like frozen microwave dinners so much? They love being able to satisfy urges in under five minutes.

✦ Why do men like masturbation? It's sex with the only person they love.

✦ Why do men like sleeping with virgins? They can't stand criticism.

➻ Why do men name their penises? Because they don't like the idea of having a stranger make 90% of their decisions.

➻ Why do men snore? When they fall asleep, their balls cover their arseholes and they get blow-back.

➻ Why do men whistle on the toilet? It helps them to remember which end to wipe.

➻ Why do only ten% of men make it to Heaven? Because if they all got there, it would be Hell.

I'd like to get to the point where I can be just as mediocre as a man.

Juanita Kreps

➻ Why do penises have a hole in the end? So men can be open-minded.

➻ Why do schools in Kentucky only have driving education classes two days a week? Because they need their cars for sex education classes for the other three days!

➻ Why do women get PMT and cellulite? God made Man first, and he just couldn't help making a few helpful suggestions.

➻ Why do women rub their eyes when they wake up in the morning? Because they don't have any balls to scratch.

↝ Why does a man eating oysters improve a woman's sex life? Because if he'll eat one of those, he'll eat anything!

↝ Why does a penis have a big head on the end? To stop the man's hand sliding off and hitting him in the eye.

↝ Why does it take one million sperm to fertilize one egg? None of them bother to stop for directions.

↝ Why don't little girls fart? Because they don't get arseholes until they're married.

↝ Why don't men give their penises female names? Because they don't want a woman running their life.

↝ Why don't men show their true feelings very often? Because they don't have true feelings.

↝ Why don't women blink during foreplay? They don't have enough time.

Once a woman is made man's equal, she becomes his superior.

Margaret Thatcher

↝ Why don't men get haemorrhoids? Because they are all perfect assholes.

↝ Why is a man like a dining table? They both have an extra bit that extends for entertaining.

➻ Why is a man like a Swiss Army Knife? He's meant to have a useful and versatile tool, but he spends most of his time just opening beer.

➻ Why is a woman like a TV remote control? Because a man will just sit there pushing buttons randomly till something happens.

➻ Why is food better than men? Because you don't have to wait an hour for seconds.

➻ Why is it dangerous to let a bloke's mind wander? It's too little to be allowed out on its own.

➻ Why is it so difficult to find men who are sensitive, caring and good-looking? They already have boyfriends.

➻ Why is psychoanalysis quicker for men than for women? When it's time for regression, men are already there.

➻ Why is sleeping with a man like a soap opera? Just when it's getting interesting, it's all over until next time.

➻ Women are indeed silly. They sleep with men who – if they were women – they wouldn't even have bothered to have lunch with.

➻ You can tell if a guy is playing around when he sends you love notes that have been photocopied, and begin with the phrase, "To whom it may concern..."

↦ Women sometimes make fools of men, but most guys are the DIY type.

↦ Women truly are better than men. Otherwise, they'd be intolerable.

↦ Women would be better off if men treated them like cars. They'd get lovingly rubbed all Sunday morning, filled to the brim twice a week, and a damn thorough servicing every six months or 50,000 miles, whichever comes first.

money

Genghis Cohn once interviewed me, with an eye towards hiring me. As you may know, I lost my right eye at the age of three, and he wouldn't come out and say it – he kept referring to my "deficiency." I thought he meant vitamins or something. Then he tells me I'm off-centre on my vision and it'll show on the screen. So I do a screen test to prove that it doesn't, and he calls me back into his office and explains "Thank you Mr. Falk, but for the same money I can get an actor with two eyes."

Peter Falk on Harry Cohn

↦ A Scotsman was in a restaurant. "How much do you charge for one single drop of whisky?" he asked the waitress. "That would be free, sir," she smiled. "Excellent," said the Scots bloke, "drip me a mugfull."

➤ The stock market may be bad, but I slept like a baby all through the Black Friday crash and its aftermath. Every hour, on the hour, I woke up crying.

➤ Why did the man put his money in the freezer? He wanted some cold, hard cash!

MOTHERS-IN-LAW

There are three classes of elderly woman – first, that dear old soul; second, that old woman; third, that old witch.

Samuel Taylor Coleridge, 1772 – 1834

➤ "Simon," his wife said, nose buried in the paper, "it says here that the government is going to trim down the navy. They're going to destroy six superannuated battleships." Simon looked up and said, "I'm sorry to hear that, dear. You'll miss your mother."

➤ A bloke was travelling down a country road when he saw a large group of people outside a house. He stopped and asked a farmer why such a large crowd was gathered. The farmer replied, "Joe's mule kicked his mother-in-law and she died." "I'm impressed," replied the man, "she must have had a lot of friends." "Nope," said the farmer, "We're all here to bid for the mule."

➤ A mother-in-law paid a visit to her daughter's husband. He opened the door and said, "Good afternoon, dear! I'm so glad to see you! It's been ages. Come in, please! How long are you staying?" The mother-in-law smiled and said, "Oh, until you get tired of me." The bloke looked at her and said, "Won't you at least have a cuppa?"

➤ A person receives a telegram informing him of his mother-in-law's death. It also enquires whether the lady should be buried or burnt. He replies: "Don't take chances. Burn the body and bury the ashes."

➤ Generally speaking, mothers-in-law are generally speaking.

➤ My mother-in-law broke up my marriage. My wife came home from work one day and found me in bed with her.

➤ Phil came home from work and found his wife crying. "Your mother really offended me today," she sobbed. "My mother?" he asked. "How? She's on holiday in Australia!" "I know," she wailed. "This morning a letter addressed to you arrived, and I opened it, because I was curious." "Hmm, OK, and?" "Well, it was from her. At the bottom, she'd written 'PS: Dear Catherine, when you've read this, don't forget to pass it on to Phil'."

➤ Steve was down the pub, nursing a beer in the corner. "Steve, mate, what's wrong?" asked the landlord. Steve sighed bitterly. "I had a quarrel with my mother-in-law. She swore to me she wouldn't talk to me for a month." The landlord looked puzzled. "What's so bad about that?" "You don't understand," sighed Steve. "That was four weeks ago, and today is the last day."

➻ The following sign was seen in a small restaurant: "Thanks for visiting. If you liked the food, send your friends. If not, send your mother-in-law."

She is a stern woman, who looks as if her idea of a good time would be knitting, preferably under the guillotine.

William McIlvanney, The Kiln

➻ The law prohibits a man from marrying his mother-in-law – a classic example of useless legislation.

➻ The newlywed wife said to her husband when he returned from work: "I have great news for you. Pretty soon, we're going to be three in this house instead of two." The husband glowed with happiness and kissed his wife until she added: "I'm glad that you feel this way, as tomorrow morning my mother moves in with us."

➻ A woman is tidying up around the house one day when she hears a strange humming noise coming from her daughter's bedroom. The mother knocks on the door but just opens it immediately. She walks in and finds her daughter lying naked on the bed, pleasuring herself with a vibrator. The mother is a little shocked, but retains her composure and says, "What on earth are you doing that for, dear?" The daughter replies, "Well, mother, I am nearly 40 years old and I live at home with my parents. I never date guys, so I figure this is the nearest thing I'll get to a husband!" That night her father can't sleep, so he wanders downstairs and hears a strange humming noise coming from the front room. He walks in and finds his daughter lying naked on the sofa, pleasuring herself with a vibrator. The father is a little shocked, but retains his composure and says, "What on earth are you doing that for, dear?" The daughter replies, "Well, father, I am nearly 40 years old and I live at home with my parents. I never date guys, so I figure this is the nearest thing I'll get to a husband!" The next day the mother is once more tidying up around the house when she hears that same humming noise coming from the front room. She walks in and, to her surprise, she sees her husband watching TV with the vibrator just placed on the sofa beside him. "What the hell are you doing?" she says to her husband, shocked. He replies, "Just watching the game with the son-in-law."

MOTHER'S WISDOM

➻ A closed mouth gathers no foot.

➻ A conclusion is the place where you got tired of thinking.

➻ A couple of months in the lab can often save a couple of hours in the library.

➻ A penny saved is virtually worthless.

➻ A short cut is the longest distance between two points.

➻ After things have gone from bad to worse, the process will repeat.

➠ Almost everything in life is easier to get into than to get out of.

➠ Anybody can win, unless there happens to be a second entry.

➠ Anyone can admit they were wrong; the true test is admitting it to someone else.

➠ Anything that doesn't eat you today is saving you for tomorrow.

➠ Artificial intelligence usually beats real stupidity.

➠ Assumption is the mother of all fuck-ups.

➠ Beware of altruism. It is based on self-deception, the root of all evil.

➠ Beware the fury of a patient man.

➠ Blessed are those who go around in circles, for they shall be known as wheels.

➠ Blessed is he who expects no gratitude, for he shall not be disappointed.

➠ Brains x Beauty x Availability = 1.

➠ By the time you can make ends meet, they've moved the ends.

↣ Change is inevitable, except from a vending machine.

↣ Choose a wife by your ear rather than by your eye.

↣ Common sense is not so common.

↣ Creativity is great, but plagiarism is faster.

↣ Diplomacy is the art of letting someone else have your way.

↣ Don't be so open minded that your brain falls out.

**A man said to the Universe, "Sir, I exist."
"However," replied the Universe, "the fact has not
created in me a sense of obligation."**

Stephen Crane, 1871 – 1900

↣ Don't lend people money...it gives them amnesia.

↣ Eat the rich. The poor are tough and stringy.

↣ Errors are human, but if you really want to screw things up, you need a computer.

↣ Even paranoids have enemies.

↣ Everything in moderation, including moderation.

↣ Everything tastes more or less like chicken.

↠ Experience is what causes a person to make new mistakes instead of old ones.

↠ Familiarity breeds children.

↠ Fidelity is a virtue peculiar to those who are about to be betrayed.

↠ For every action, there is a corresponding over-reaction.

↠ Friends come and go, but enemies accumulate.

↠ He who beats his sword into a ploughshare usually ends up ploughing for those who kept their swords.

↠ He who dies with the most toys is still dead.

↠ I worry all the time: I worry about worrying too much. I worry when I'm not worried that there's something I should be worried about. I worry when I'm worried whether I should worry about what I am currently worried about or whether I should worry about something else that worries me, even if I'm not worried about it, but should be worried about it, or at least worry about the fact that I'm worrying about not possibly having to worry at all, about worrying.

↠ If something just cannot go wrong, it will do anyway.

↠ If at first you do succeed, try to hide your astonishment.

↠ If everything seems to be going well, you have obviously overlooked something.

↔ If ignorance is bliss, most of us must be orgasmic.

↔ If only one price can be obtained for a quotation, the price will be unreasonable.

↔ If there is a possibility of several things going wrong, the one that will cause the most damage will be the one to go wrong.

↔ If you don't care where you are, then you aren't lost.

↔ If you perceive that there are four possible ways in which a procedure can go wrong and circumvent these, then a fifth way, unprepared-for, will promptly develop.

↔ Information travels more surely to those with a lesser need to know.

↔ It is impossible to make anything foolproof, because fools are so ingenious.

↔ It's always blackest before you step on the cat.

↔ It's always darkest just before it goes pitch-black.

↔ Left to themselves, things tend to go from bad to worse.

↔ Make your mark in the world, or at least spray in each corner.

↔ Money is better than poverty, if only for financial reasons.

➳ Never do anything you wouldn't be caught dead doing.

➳ Never volunteer for anything.

The world is like a cucumber. Today it's in your hands, tomorrow it's up your ass.
Arab saying

➳ No good deed goes unpunished.

➳ No matter how many times you've had it, if it's offered, take it, because it'll never be quite the same again.

➳ Old age and treachery shall overcome youth and talent.

➳ Sharks will only attack you if you're wet.

➳ Some come to the fountain of knowledge to drink, some prefer just to gargle.

➳ Sometimes too much drink is not enough.

➳ Take heart; the only person who always got his work done by Friday was Robinson Crusoe.

➳ The bigger they are, the harder they hit.

➳ The easiest way to find something lost around the office is to buy a replacement.

➸ The idea is to die young as late as possible.

➸ The race is not always to the swift nor the battle to the strong, but that's the way to bet.

➸ The sun goes down just when you need it the most.

➸ They say that a fool and his money are soon parted. What I'd like to know is how the fool and his money got together in the first place...

➸ Two heads are more numerous than one.

➸ When all else fails, read the instructions.

➸ When it's you against the world, bet on the world.

➸ When you go out into the world, always remember, being placed on a pedestal is a right, not a privilege.

➸ Why is it never the cold girl who gets given the fur coat?

➸ Winning isn't everything, but losing isn't anything.

➸ Work hard and save your money and when you are old you will be able to buy the things only the young can enjoy.

➸ One cardinal rule of marriage should never be forgotten: "Give little, give seldom, and above all, give grudgingly." Otherwise, what could have been a proper marriage could become a filthy orgy of sexual lust.

➻ You can fool some of the people and really piss them off.

➻ Once upon a time, there was a non-conforming sparrow who decided not to fly south for the winter. However, soon after the weather turned cold, the sparrow changed his mind and reluctantly started to fly south. After a short time, ice began to form on his wings and he fell to earth in a barnyard almost frozen. A cow passed by and crapped on this little bird and the sparrow thought it was the end, but the manure warmed him and defrosted his wings. Warm and happy, the little sparrow began to sing. Just then, a large tom cat came by and hearing the chirping investigated the sounds. As Old Tom cleared away the manure, he found the chirping bird and promptly ate him. There are three lesson to be learnt from this story: 1) Not everyone who shits on you is necessarily your enemy. 2) Not everyone who gets you out of the shit is necessarily your friend. 3) If you are warm and happy, keep your silly mouth shut.

The defect of equality is that we only desire it with our superiors.

Henri Bregne, 1837 – 1899

➻ Christopher invites his nosy mother over for dinner. She's been encouraging him to find a wife for years, and when she arrives she notices that the live-in housekeeper is a very attractive woman who gets on very well with her son. She can't help wondering if maybe there's something going on – they get on so well – but her son denies everything: "Mother, I assure you that my relationship with my housekeeper is strictly professional." A few days later, the housekeeper tells Christopher that ever since his mother came over for dinner she has been unable to find the silver tray that the brandy is always served on. A curious affair indeed, thinks Christopher: I wonder what my mother is up to now. So he writes his mother a letter:

Dear Mother,
Regarding my silver tray. I'm obviously not saying that you did take it, and I'm not saying that you did not take it, but the fact remains that I have been unable to find it since you came over for dinner.
Love, Christopher.

A couple of days later, Christopher receives a reply:

Dear Christopher,
Regarding your housekeeper. I'm obviously not saying that you do sleep with her, and I'm not saying that you do not sleep with her, but the fact remains that if she was sleeping in her own bed she would have found the silver tray by now!
Love, Mother.

mum, mum!

↠ "Mum, Mum! Dad just poisoned my kitten!" "Never mind, dear. Perhaps he had to do it." "No, he didn't; he promised me I could!"

➤ "Mum, Mum! Are you sure this is how to learn to swim?" "Shut up and get back in the sack."

➤ "Mum, Mum! Can I wear a bra now I'm 16?" "Shut up, Albert."

➤ "Mum, Mum! Dad's running down the street!" "Shut up and step on the accelerator!"

➤ "Mum, Mum! Grandpa's going out!" "Well, throw some more petrol on him, then."

➤ "Mum, Mum! I don't want to empty the compost heap." "Shut up and keep eating."

➤ "Mum, Mum! I don't want to go to Australia." "Shut up and keep swimming."

Kids are like husbands – they're fine as long as they're someone else's.

Marsha Warfield

➤ "Mum, Mum! I don't want to see Niagara Falls!" "Shut up and get back in the barrel!"

➤ "Mum, Mum! I keep running in circles." "Shut up or I'll nail your other foot to the floor."

➤ "Mum, Mum! Sally won't come skipping with me." "Don't be cruel, dear, you know it makes her stumps bleed."

↦ "Mum, Mum! The milkman's here. Have you got the money or should I go out and play?"

↦ "Mum, Mum! What happened to all that dog food Fido wouldn't eat?" "Shut up and eat your meatloaf."

↦ "Mum, Mum! What's a nymphomaniac?" "Shut up and help me get Gran off the doorknob!"

↦ "Mum, Mum! What's a vampire?" "Shut up and eat your soup before it clots."

↦ "Mum, Mum! What's a werewolf?" "Shut up and comb your face."

↦ "Mum, Mum! What's an Oedipus complex?" "Shut up and kiss me."

↦ "Mum, Mum! What's an orgasm?" "I don't know, dear, ask your father."

↦ "Mum, Mum! When are we going to have Aunt Edna for dinner?" "Shut up, we haven't finished your grandmother yet."

↦ "Mum, Mum! Why are we pushing the car off the cliff?" "Shut up, you'll wake your father."

↦ "Mum, Mum! Why can't I play with the other kids?" "Shut up and deal."

➤ "Mum, Mum! Why do I have to hop everywhere?" "Shut up or I'll chop off the other leg!"

➤ "Mum, Mum! Why don't I have a big thing like Dad's between my legs?" "Shut up, Lucy. You will when you're older."

➤ "Mum, Mum! Why is my hair so slimy?" "Shut up, you little snot."

➤ "Mum, Mum! Why do the singers rock left and right while performing on stage?" "Because it is harder to hit a moving target."

music

➤ A famous blues musician died. His tombstone bore the inscription "Didn't wake up this morning..."

➤ A musical reviewer admitted he always praised the first show of a new theatrical season. "Who am I to stone the first cast?"

➤ A musician dies of a heroin overdose, and finds himself in purgatory. There he meets an angel who is reading a large book with his name on the cover. The angel looks up at the newly-arrived spirit and says: "Hi, we've been expecting you." "Where am I?" asks the musician. "In purgatory," the angel answers. "I've been reading the book of your life, and your good deeds are evenly balanced by your bad deeds." "So, what's next?" "We've decided to let you pick where you are going – heaven or hell. And, to help you make up your mind, we're going to give you a glimpse of each." So saying, the angel motions the musician over to a curtain labelled 'Heaven'. The angel parts the curtain, and before them is a bucolic scene of eternal spring with angelic choirs singing praises to God. The musician surveys the scene, and says, "Well, I could hang with that. But...what's hell look like?" In response, the angel motions the musician over to a curtain labelled 'Hell'. Parting the curtain reveals a smoke filled room with well-dressed people happily talking and dancing, while a quartet is playing a rather good version of 'Have You Met Miss Jones?'. "Well, to tell you the truth," says the musician, "I've got nothing against heaven, but hell looks like a place that I could really dig." "No problem," answers the angel. With that, he pulls an unseen lever and the musician falls through a trap door. The musician lands with a large splash in a cauldron of boiling blood. There are screams of eternal agony in the distance. A horribly ugly demon begins poking the musician in the side with a large trident. "What's this?" cries the musician. "I've been tricked!" The demon answers, "Yeah, I know. But that thing up there sure is a top demo tape, eh?"

Musicals: a series of catastrophes ending with a floorshow.
Oscar Levant, 1906 – 1972

➻ Agnes Dei was a woman composer famous for her church music.

→ Band members do it in front of 100,000 people.

→ A tourist is sightseeing in a European city. She comes upon the tomb of Beethoven and begins reading the commemorative plaque, only to be distracted by a low scratching noise, as if something were rubbing against a piece of paper. She collars a passing native and asks what the scratching sound is. The local person replies: "Oh, that is Beethoven. He's decomposing."

→ Chandran, a classical Indian dancer of some standing, has complained about an upcoming Atomic Kitten concert scheduled to be held near certain ancient Indian sculptures. Her protest is that Atomic Kitten are "inappropriate for the locale." Rumour suggests she would think it far more suitable to have Atomic Kitten dropped into a pit and then stoned to death.

Music is the brandy of the damned.
George Bernard Shaw

→ Chord: usually spelled with an 's' on the end, means a particular type of trousers, e.g. 'he wears chords.'

→ Disco is to music what Etch-A-Sketch is to art.

→ Music sung by two people at the same time is called a duel.

→ Real musicians don't die, they just decompose.

➤ Semiconductors are part-time musicians.

➤ What do you get if Bach falls off a horse, but has the courage to get on again and continue riding? Bach in the saddle again.

➤ What do you get when you play a New-Age song backwards? Another New-Age song.

➤ What is the definition of a Soviet string quartet? A Soviet symphony orchestra after a tour of the USA.

➤ What's the difference between a trombonist and a man who plays alto and tenor saxophones? One's horny and one's bisaxual.

➤ Why don't they know where Mozart is buried? Because he's Haydn.

➤ Woodwind players do it in the reeds.

nuns

➤ A nun is undressing for a bath and while she's standing naked, there's a knock at the door. The nun calls, "Who is it?" A voice answers, "A blind salesman." The nun decides to get a thrill by having the blind man in the room while she's naked, so she lets him in. The man walks in, looks straight at the nun and says: "Uhhhh, well, hello there. Where would you be wanting the blinds fitted...?"

↔ A man is rushed to his nearest hospital in New York, Our Holy Mother of BeJesus, after a heart attack. The surgeon performs heart surgery and the man survives, no problem. Afterwards, the man is lying in his bed and one of the nuns is comforting him. "Don't worry sir, you'll be just fine, it's all over now," says the nun. "But we would like to know, sir, if you don't mind the asking, as to how you intend to pay your bill for the operation and the care. Would you be covered by an insurance policy?" "Well, actually sister, I don't think I am," the man replies. "Oh dear," continues the nun, "maybe you've got a load of money lying around and you'd like to pay by cash?" "Er, no, I don't think so sister," the man replies. "I'm not really a man of much material wealth." "Well," says the nun, "perhaps you've some close family who could help out?" "Well, not really, sister," the man replies, "I've just the one sister in County Kerry in the old country, but she's a spinster nun." The nun replies, "Nuns are not spinsters, sir, nuns are married to God." "In that case," says the man, "perhaps you could get my brother-in-law to foot the bill!"

↔ A nun and a priest were travelling across the desert and realized halfway across that the camel they were using for transportation was about to die. They set up a makeshift camp, hoping that someone would come to their rescue, but to no avail. Soon the camel died. After several days, they agreed that they were not going to be rescued. They prayed a lot (of course), and they discussed their predicament in great depth. Finally the priest said to the nun, "You know, Sister, I am about to die, and there's always been one thing I've wanted here on Earth – to see a woman naked. Would you mind taking off your clothes so I can look at you?" The nun thought about his request for several seconds and then agreed to take off her clothes. As she was doing so, she remarked, "Well, Father, now that I think about it, I've never seen a man naked, either. Would you mind taking off your clothes, too?" With a little hesitation, the priest also stripped. Suddenly the nun exclaimed, "Father! What is that little thing hanging between your legs?" The priest patiently answered, "That, my child, is a gift from God. If I put it in you, it creates a new life." "Well," responded the nun, "forget about me. Stick it in the camel."

↦ A nun gets into a taxi. As he drives her along, the taxi driver says he has a confession to make – he's always had a sexual thing about nuns. As he's just been told he has a terminal illness it would mean a lot to him if he could have sex with a nun just once before he dies. "Well, my son," says the nun, "in view of your tragic circumstances, it is my duty to do what I can for you. I will have sex with you on one condition – obviously I can't get pregnant, so I'll have to take it up the tradesman's entrance." The taxi driver gets in the back, lifts up the nun's habit and buggers her soundly. Afterwards, the taxi driver starts to cry. "I feel so guilty," he says. "I lied to you to get you to have sex with me. I don't really have a terminal illness at all." "That's all right," says the nun, "I lied to you as well – my name's Kevin and I'm on my way to a fancy dress party."

↦ A priest asks a nun if he can walk her back to the convent. She says, "Just this once." Upon arriving, he asks if he can kiss her. She replies, "Well, alright, as long as you don't get into the habit."

➻ A priest and nun were on their way back home from a seminary when their car broke down. The garage didn't open until the morning, so they had to spend the night in the village's only B&B. It only had one room available, though. The priest said, "Holy Sister, I don't think the Lord would object, under the circumstances, if we spent the night sharing this one room. I'll sleep on the sofa, and you can have the bed." "Yes, I think that would be fine," agreed the nun. They prepared for bed, said some prayers, and then each one took up their agreed place and settled down to sleep. Ten minutes passed, and the nun said, "Father, I'm terribly cold." "Okay," said the priest, "I'll get you a blanket from the cupboard." Another ten minutes passed, and the nun said again, "Father, I'm still terribly cold." The priest said, "Don't worry Sister, I'll get up and fetch you another blanket." Well, another ten minutes passed, and the nun spoke up again. "Father, I'm still terribly cold. I don't think the Lord would mind if we acted as man and wife just for this one night." "I think you're right," said the priest. "Get up and get your own damn blankets."

This agglomeration which was called, and which still calls itself, the Holy Roman Empire is neither Holy, nor Roman, nor an Empire.

Voltaire, Essai sur les Moeurs, 1694 – 1778

➻ Did you hear the one about the man who opened a dry-cleaning business next door to the convent? He knocked on the door and asked the Mother Superior if she had any dirty habits.

➥ It is Friday, and four nuns go to the priest at the local Catholic church to ask for the weekend off. They argue for a few minutes but finally the priest agrees to let them leave the convent for the weekend. "However," he says, "as soon as you get back on Monday morning I want you to confess to me what you have done over the weekend." The four nuns agree, and run off. Monday comes, and the four nuns return. The first nun goes to the priest and says: "Forgive me, Father, for I have sinned." The priest asks: "What did you do, Sister?" She replies: "I watched an X-rated movie." The priest looks up at heaven for a few seconds, then replies: "You are forgiven. Go and drink the holy water." The first nun leaves, and the fourth nun begins to chuckle quietly under her breath. The second nun then goes up to the priest and says: "Forgive me, Father, for I have sinned." The priest replies: "Okay, what happened?" She says: "I was driving my brother's car down the street in front of his house and I hit a neighbour's dog and killed it." The priest looks up to heaven for half a minute, then says: "You are forgiven. Go and drink the holy water." The second nun goes out. By this time, the fourth nun is laughing quite audibly. Then the third nun walks to the priest and says: "Forgive me, Father, for I have sinned." The priest asks: "Out with it. What did you do?" She says: "Last night, I ran naked up and down Main Street." The priest looks up at heaven for a full five minutes before responding: "God forgives you. Go and drink the holy water." She leaves. The fourth nun falls on the floor, laughing so hard tears run down her cheeks. The priest asks her: "Okay. What did you do that was so funny?" The fourth nun replies: "I pissed in the holy water..."

➥ Mother Superior: "Sister Maria, if you were walking through town at night, and were accosted by a man with bad intentions, what would you do?" Sister Maria: "I would lift my habit, Mother Superior." Mother Superior (shocked): "And what would you do next?" Sister Maria "I would tell him to drop his trousers." Mother Superior: (even more shocked) "And what then?" Sister Maria: "I would run away. I can run much faster with my habit up than he can with his trousers down."

➥ Sister Catherine is asking all the Catholic school children in the fourth grade what they want to be when they grow up. Little Sheila says: "When I grow up, I want to be a prostitute!" Sister Catherine's eyes grow wide and she barks: "What in the name of God did you say?" "A prostitute," Sheila repeats. Sister Catherine breathes a sight of relief and says: "Thank God! I thought you said a Protestant."

➥ The seven dwarfs are in Rome and they go on a tour of the city. After a while they go to the Vatican and Grumpy gets to meet the Pope privately. Grumpy, for once, seems to have a lot to say; he keeps asking the pontiff questions about the church, and in particular, nuns. "Your Holiness, do you have any really short nuns?" "No, my son, all our nuns are at least 5 feet tall." "Are you sure? I mean, you wouldn't have any nuns that are, say, about my height? Maybe a little shorter?" "I'm afraid not. Why do you ask?" "No reason." Pause. "Positive? Nobody in a habit that's about two feet tall?" "I'm sure." "Okay." Grumpy looks dejected at this news, and the Pope wonders why. So he listens to the dwarves as they leave the building. "What'd he say? What'd he say?" chant the other six. Grumpy says: "He said they don't have any." And the other six start chanting: "Grumpy fucked a penguin! Grumpy fucked a penguin! Grumpy fucked a penguin!"

➺ There are two nuns in a bath. The first one says: "Where's the soap?" The second one replies: "Yes it does, doesn't it?"

➺ Two nuns are shipped in from Ireland to the United States of America. As they are walking from the docks to the convent, they walk past a hot dog stand. "Well, would you look at that sister. I did not know that they ate dogs in this country. How weird," said one nun to the other. Her companion replied, "Yes sister, but now that we are to live here, should we not do as the Americans do? I think that we should at least try to eat some dog should we not?" Both of the nuns go over to the vendor and they buy a hot dog each. The vendor hands them each a foil-wrapped dog. The nuns walk off, unwrapping their food. The first nun stares at hers, and then leans over her friend's shoulder before asking, "Um, so, er, sister, which part of the dog did you get then?"

➺ Two nuns are walking down an alley at night. Two guys jump out and start raping them. The first nun looks to heaven and says, "Forgive them Father, for they know not what they're doing." The second nun looks up and says, "This one does."

➺ What is the definition of innocence? A nun working in a condom factory thinking she's making sleeping bags for mice.

➺ What kind of fun does a priest have? Nun.

➥ Two nuns walk into an off-licence and pick up the biggest bottle of whisky that they can find. When they get to the cash desk the salesman says, "I'm not sure that I can sell booze to you ladies, now, can I? I didn't think you were supposed to drink that stuff." "Don't be worrying yourself about that, now, will you?" replies one of the sisters, "it's not for lowly nuns like us, 'tis for the Holy Mother Superior – she has constipation!" "Oh well, sister," says the salesman, "I'm so sorry, in that case, have the bottle on the house and wish her my best." The nuns thank him and leave quietly. A couple of hours later the salesman shuts up the shop and leaves. As he is walking to the bus stop he hears laughing and sees the two nuns sitting on a park bench laughing their heads off, rolling around and drinking all the whisky he gave them. He is disgusted and runs over to them. "You lied to me, sisters!" he begins, "you told me that whisky was for the Holy Mother Superior's constipation." "And so it is," replies one of the nuns, "and so it is – when the Holy Mother Superior sees us in this state she's sure to shit herself!"

➥ What do you call a nun who walks in her sleep? A roaming Catholic.

➥ What do you call a nun with a sex change operation? A trans-sister.

➥ What is the definition of suspicious? A nun doing the splits in a cucumber field.

➥ What's black and white and red hot? A shapely young nun with pierced nipples.

nurses

↦ "Tell me nurse, how is that boy doing; the one who ate all those 5p pieces?" "Still no change, doctor."

↦ A doctor is having an affair with his young, enthusiastic, if a bit dumb, nurse. The nurse gets pregnant and the doctor, of course, doesn't want his wife to know. So he says to his mistress: "You go and lie low somewhere, say Italy, for a while, until the baby is due. When the baby is born, just send me a postcard with 'spaghetti' written on it and I'll know. By this time, I'll have spoken to my wife." "Why 'spaghetti'?" she asks. "Because you'll be in Italy, that's why," the doctor says, just on this side of panicking. Not finding anything logical to reply to that, the girl agrees and flies off to Italy. After nine months, the doctor receives a call from his wife, who tells him she has just received the strangest postcard. "Don't worry, honey," the doctor says. "I'm coming home and I'll explain everything." Back home, he picks up the postcard, wondering what he is going to say to his wife, reads it, stares at it for a second or two and then topples over and dies of a massive heart attack. Stunned, her wife re-reads the mysterious postcard through tears of grief. It says: "Spaghetti, spaghetti, spaghetti, spaghetti – three with sausage and meatballs, one with mussels."

↦ A new nurse spotted a couple of surgeons grubbing around in the flower-beds outside the front of the hospital. "Excuse me, doctors," she said, "Can I help at all? Have you lost anything?" "Oh, no, thank you, nurse," replied one. "We're prepping a heart transplant for a tax inspector, so we're just hunting for a suitable stone."

❥ A nurse walks into a ward to see patients early in the morning. "Well, nurse, it seems to me you got up from the wrong side of the bed this morning," says one patient. "Why do you say that?" "You're wearing the surgeon's slippers."

Jogging bra-less by the canal, she looked like the original inspiration for Barnes Wallis.

Ann Winter

❥ Did you hear about the nurse who swallowed a scalpel by mistake? She gave herself a tonsillectomy, an appendectomy and a hysterectomy, and circumcised three of the doctors.

❥ Four nurses decided to play jokes on the doctor they worked for, because he was an arrogant tosser. That evening, they all got together on a break and discussed what they had done. The first nurse said, "I filled his stethoscope with cotton wool so he won't be able to hear anything." The second nurse said, "That's nothing! I drained the mercury out of his thermometers and painted them so that they all read 106 degrees." The third nurse said, "Well, I did worse than that. I stabbed tiny holes in all his condoms; you know, the ones he keeps in his desk drawer." The fourth nurse just fainted.

❥ One afternoon, two new doctors from India were having an animated discussion in a corridor of an American hospital. "I say it's spelled 'W-H-O-O-M'," said the first Indian doctor. "No, you're mistaken: it is spelled 'W-H-O-M-B'," said the other Indian doctor.

A haughty American nurse passing by said smugly, "Excuse me: you are both wrong. It is spelled 'W-O-M-B'." "Thank you, nurse," said one of the doctors, rather coldly, "but we prefer to settle this argument ourselves. Besides, I don't think you're in a position to describe the sound of an elephant passing wind under water, are you?"

↦ Three nurses died and went to the Pearly Gates. St Peter asked the first one: "What did you do on Earth that you deserve to get in here? The first nurse replied, "I was an intensive care nurse and I saved hundreds of lives." "Welcome," said St Peter, "come right in. And what did you do?" he asked the second one. The second nurse replied, "I was an emergency room nurse and I saved hundreds of lives." "Welcome," said St Peter, "come right in. And what did you do?" he asked the third one. The third nurse replied, "I was a managed care nurse and I saved the taxpayer hundreds of thousands of pounds by getting people out of hospitals quickly." "Welcome," said St Peter, "come right in – but only for three days."

OFFICE SPACE

↦ A businessman was having a tough time lugging his lumpy, oversized suitcase on to the plane. Helped by a stewardess, he finally managed to stuff it in the overhead locker. "Do you always carry such heavy luggage?" she sighed. "Never again," the man replied. "Next time, I'm riding in the bag, and my partner can buy the ticket."

➟ After a two-year study, the National Association for Sports and Activities announced the following results on the USA's recreational preferences:

1. The sport of choice for unemployed or imprisoned people is basketball.
2. The sport of choice for maintenance-level employees is bowling.
3. The sport of choice for blue-collar workers is football.
4. The sport of choice for supervisors is baseball.
5. The sport of choice for middle management is tennis.
6. The sport of choice for corporate officers is golf.

Conclusion: The higher you rise in the corporate structure, the smaller your balls!

I find it rather easy to portray a businessman. Being bland, rather cruel and incompetent comes naturally to me.

John Cleese, on businessmen

➟ I'll share with you my own secret method for moving up the corporate ladder. It's called the Hind-lick Manoeuvre.

➟ Once overheard at the office water cooler: "The boss said that I would get a rise when I earned it. He's crazy if he thinks I'm gonna wait that long."

➟ Jack and Jill are both vice-presidents of the same company. One Friday, the president and CEO of the company calls them both into his office. "The company is going through some rough times right now", the president began. "We're having to cut costs where we can, and, as much as I hate to do this, the company cannot afford two vice-presidents, so I will have to let one of you go. You are both equally qualified and do your jobs well so I can't find any criteria on which to base this decision. What I will do is lay off the first one of you to leave your desk on Monday." Monday morning, the boss is there early, looking out his inter-office window waiting for his two vice presidents. Jack arrives almost 10 minutes early, flips through his rolodex and starts to make some phone calls. Jill had been out partying the night before, so she arrives right at 8, sits at her desk, and starts reading some documents and making notes. The two work for a couple of hours, but Jill is kind of hung over, so she gets up from her desk, goes to the water cooler and takes some aspirin. The boss sees this, and goes to the water cooler to talk to Jill. "Jill," he says, "You left your desk." "Yeah, so?" Jill replies. "Don't you remember the meeting on Friday?" the boss says. "We need to cut costs and I either have to lay you or Jack off." "So jack off," says Jill. "I've got a headache."

I come from an environment where, if you see a snake, you kill it. At General Motors, if you see a snake, the first thing you do is hire a consultant on snakes. Then you spend a year talking about snakes.

Ross Perot

↔ This executive was interviewing a nervous young women for a position in his company. He wanted to find out something about her personality so he asked, "If you could have a conversation with someone, living or dead, who would it be?" The girl quickly responded, "The living one."

➤ When angry, count to ten before you speak. If VERY angry, count to 100, and then go and shout at someone junior.

➤ I am writing in response to your request for additional information pertaining to my insurance claim. In block number 3 of the accident report form, I put "Trying to get the job done" as the cause of my accident. You said in your letter that you would like to have me explain more fully, and I trust the following details will be sufficient. I am a bricklayer by trade. On the day of the accident, I was working alone on the roof of a new six storey building. When I completed my work, I discovered that I had about 500 pounds of brick left over. Rather than carry them down by hand, I decided to lower them in a barrel by using a pulley which fortunately was attached to the side of the building at the 6th floor. Securing the rope at ground level, I went up to the roof, swung the barrel out, and loaded the bricks into it. Then, I went back to the ground and untied the rope, holding it tightly to ensure a slow descent of the 500 pounds of bricks. You will note in block number 7 of the accident report form that my own weight is 135 pounds. Due to my surprise at being jerked off my feet so suddenly, I lost my presence of mind and forgot to let go of the rope. Needless to say, I proceeded at a rather rapid rate up the side of the building. In the vicinity of the 3rd floor, I met the barrel coming down. This will explain the fractured skull and broken collar bone. Slowed only slightly, I continued my rapid ascent, not stopping until the fingers of my right hand were two knuckles into the pulley. Fortunately, by this time, I had recovered my presence of mind and was able to hold tightly to the rope in spite of the extreme pain. At approximately the same time, however, the barrel of bricks hit the ground and the bottom fell out of the barrel. Devoid of the weight of the bricks, the barrel now weighed about 50 pounds. I again refer you to my weight in block number 7. As you might imagine, I began a rapid descent back down the side of the building. In the vicinity of the 3rd floor, I met the barrel coming up. This accounts for the two fractured ankles and the lacerations on my legs and lower body. The encounter with the barrel slowed me enough to lessen my injuries when I fell onto the pile of bricks, and fortunately, only three vertebrae were cracked. I am sorry to report, however, that as I lay there on the bricks, in pain, unable to stand, and watching the empty barrel six storeys above me, I again lost my presence of mind, and let go of the rope...

➳ Once upon a time, an American automobile company and a Japanese auto company decided to have a competitive boat race on the Detroit River. Both teams practiced hard and long to reach their peak performance. On the big day, they were as ready as they could be. The Japanese team won by a mile. Afterwards, the American team became discouraged by the loss and their moral sagged. Corporate management decided that the reason for the crushing defeat had to be found. A Continuous Measurable Improvement Team of "Executives" was set up to investigate the problem and to recommend appropriate corrective action. Their conclusion: The problem was that the Japanese team had 8 people rowing and 1 person steering, whereas the American team had 1 person rowing and 8 people steering. The American Corporate Steering Committee immediately hired a consulting firm to do a study on the management structure. After some time and billions of dollars, the consulting firm concluded that "too many people were steering and not enough rowing." To prevent losing to the Japanese again next year, the management structure was changed to "4 Steering Managers, 3 Area Steering Managers, and 1 Staff Steering Manager" and a new performance system for the person rowing the boat to give more incentive to work harder and become a six sigma performer. "We must give him empowerment and enrichment." That ought to do it. The next year the Japanese team won by two miles. The American Corporation laid off the rower for poor performance, sold all of the paddles, cancelled all capital investments for new equipment, halted development of a new canoe, awarded high performance awards to the consulting firm, and distributed the money saved as bonuses to the senior executives.

OLD AGE

➼ A 75-year-old golfer comes back home after a game. "How was your golf game, dear?" asked his wife. "Well, I was hitting the ball pretty well, but my eyesight's gotten so bad I couldn't see where it went," the man said, sounding dejected. "You are 75 years old, Jack," said his wife gently. "I'll tell you what: why don't you take my brother Scott along?" "But he's 85 and doesn't even play golf anymore," protested Jack. "Yes, but he's got perfect eyesight. He could watch your ball for you," Tracy pointed out. The next day Jack teed off with Scott looking on. Jack swung, and the ball disappeared down the middle of the fairway. "Do you see it?" asked Jack. "Yup," Scott answered. "Well, where is it?" yelled Jack, peering off into the distance. "I forgot."

➤ A 92-year-old man went to the doctor to get a physical check-up. A few days later, the doctor saw the man walking down the street with a gorgeous young lady on his arm. A couple of days later, when the old man had an appointment with the doctor again, the doctor said, "You're really doing great, aren't you? You seem chirpy enough!" The man replied, "Just doing what you said, doctor: 'Get a hot mama and be cheerful,' and it works wonders." Horrified, the doctor said: "I didn't say that! I said, 'You've got a heart murmur. Be careful!'"

➤ A bloke gives his 85-year-old father a surprise visit from a whore as a birthday present. He answers the door, and she bubbles at him: "Hi, I'm here to give you super sex." He looks at her for a moment, and replies: "Um, thanks, I'll have the soup."

➤ A couple in their late sixties decide to marry (their respective spouses having died), and move to Bournemouth. In preparation for this they talk through the sharing of household expenses and various other matters. Jane asks Harold what they should do about their present houses. "Well, we ought to each sell our home and then we can each fund half the purchase price of our new home." Jane agrees. Harold then asks Jane what she'd like to do about the grocery bills. She suggests: "Neither one of us eats very much, so maybe we ought to split that bill on a monthly basis." Harold agrees. Then what about the utility bill? Again, they decide to share. Then Jane asks Harold what he wants to do about sex, to which he replies: "Oh, infrequently." Jane looks at him and asks: "Is that one word or two?"

➡ A couple of OAPs – a man and a woman – are sitting outside their old folks' home talking of the old days. All of a sudden an ice cream van pulls up at the gate with the tune playing. The woman says, "I'd love an ice cream, you know," to which the man replies, "Would you like me to get you one?" "Don't bother," the old dear says, "by the time you get to the van you'll never remember what I wanted anyway." "Don't be silly," says the man, "I won't forget. Now, come on: what do you want?" "Well, OK, then," says the woman, "I'll have a double-scoop of strawberry with chocolate sauce, nuts and a flake on top." "A double-scoop of strawberry with chocolate sauce, nuts and a flake on top coming right up," says the man and off he goes. Five minutes later he comes back carrying four hot dogs and two large Cokes. "Oh, my God," says the woman, "I knew I shouldn't have trusted you – where's the gravy?"

Growing old is like being increasingly penalized for a crime you haven't committed.

Anthony Powell

➡ A man goes to his doctor complaining that he cannot get his wife pregnant. The doctor is a little surprised because the man is 75. Not wishing to stand in his way, however, the doctor asks the man to provide him with a sperm sample and gives him a jar to place it in. Two days later the old man walks back into the surgery and gives the doctor the empty jar back. "What's that all about?" asks the doctor and the man begins his explanation. "Well, first of all, doc I tried with my left hand. That didn't work, so I tried with my right hand. That didn't work either, so I asked my wife to help. She's younger than me and she tried first with her left hand and then her right, but there was still no joy. Then she tried with her mouth – even between her teeth – but still nothing. As a last resort we called the neighbour over from next door. The woman tried, with both hands and then with the mouth, too, but it just really wouldn't work." The doctor was a bit shocked by this and asked, "Even your neighbour?" "Yes, doc," said the man. "We tried and tried and tried, but no matter what we did, none of us could get the lid off that bloody jar!"

➻ An elderly bloke goes to his doctor to get the results of some check-ups. He sits down, and notices that the doctor has a grave look on his face. "Some bad news, I'm afraid. The worst of it is that you have cancer, and only have six months to live." The elderly bloke is devastated. "Is there more, doctor?" "Yes, I'm afraid so," replies the doctor. "You have Alzheimer's." The elderly bloke's face lights up. "Thank God! I was sure I had cancer!"

I need another birthday like a hole in the head.

Dorothy Parker

➻ An elderly man tells the doctor he is planning to marry a women aged 30 and asks if he has any suggestions. "Yes," says the doctor, "I would advise you to take in a lodger." A year later, at his eightieth birthday check-up, the doctor asks how everything is going. The man says: "Fine, my wife is pregnant." The doctor remarks, "so you took my advice and took in a lodger?" "Yes, I did," comes the reply, "and she's pregnant as well."

➡ An old lady phones the fire brigade in the middle of the night. "Please come at once – a couple of big hairy bikers are outside, trying to climb up to my bedroom window." "Madam, we're the fire brigade – you need to call the police." "Why? I thought you were the ones with the ladders!"

➡ An old man marries a girl barely out of her teens. Needless to say, she's pretty horny, so when they get into bed on the wedding night she asks him: "So are we going to have rampant sex tonight?" The man responds by raising his hand and outstretching his fingers. "What? Five times?" asks the eager girl. "No," he replies, "pick a finger."

Experience is a good teacher, but her fees are very high.

WR Inge, 1860 – 1954

➡ How do you know when you're getting old? You can sleep with someone half your age without breaking any laws.

➡ How do you make four old ladies swear? Get a fifth old lady to shout "Bingo!"

➡ Two little old ladies are sitting outside their nursing home having a smoke because it's a no-smoking establishment. It begins to rain and one of them pulls out a condom, cuts the end off and puts it over her cigarette, keeping it nice and dry. The other lady asks her what that thing is. "It's a condom," the little old lady replies. "And where do you get them from?" her friend asks. "Any chemist will sell them to you," the lady replies. The next day, the woman's friend goes off to her local chemist and walks up to the counter. "I'd like some condoms, please, young man," she says to the man behind the counter. "Yes, ma'am," he says, giving her a funny look. "Would you like any particular brand?" "Not really," the little old lady replies, "as long as they'll fit a Camel!"

↠ What dominates the thoughts of men at different stages in their lives?

Age	Primary Concerns
0-3	Shitting and drooling
4-10	Shitting and drooling
11-15	Sex and beer
16-20	Sex and beer
20-40	Sex and beer
40-60	Sex and beer
60-80	Sex and beer
80-?	Shitting and drooling

↠ What dominates the thoughts of women at different stages in their lives?

Age	Primary Concerns
0-3	Shitting and drooling
4-10	Dolls and shopping
11-15	Periods and shopping
16-20	Sex and shopping
20-40	Shopping and shopping
40-60	Getting old and wrinkly, and shopping
60-80	The price of coal and shopping
80-?	Whingeing and shopping

➻ If you reach 90, you can help advance medical science. There isn't much we know about sex at that age. Rats don't live that long...

➻ Two elderly men are sitting at the bar, watching the young girls go by. One says to the other: "You know, I'm still sexually interested in women. In fact, I always get excited when I see the young girls walking by. The real problem is that at this age, I don't see so well any more."

➻ What has one hundred balls and screws old ladies? Bingo.

➻ What tells you that you are getting old? When your dreams stay dry and your farts get wet!

➻ You Know You're Getting Old When... you feel like the morning after but there was no night before.

I prefer old age to the alternative.

Maurice Chevalier, 1888 – 1972

➻ You Know You're Getting Old When...a fortune-teller offers to read your face.

➻ You Know You're Getting Old When...the gleam in your eyes is from the sun hitting your bifocals.

➻ You Know You're Getting Old When...you regret all those mistakes you made when you resisted temptation.

➻ You Know You're Getting Old When...your birthday cake collapses from the weight of the candles.

opera

➻ A soprano died and went to heaven. St Peter stopped her at the gate and asked: "Well, how many false notes did you sing in your life?" The soprano answers: "Three." "Three times, fellows," says St Peter, and along comes an angel and sticks the soprano three times with a needle. "Ow! What was that for?" asks the soprano. St Peter explains, "Here in heaven, we stick you once for each false note you've sung down on Earth." "Oh," says the soprano, and is just about to step through the gates when she suddenly hears a horrible screaming from behind a door. "Oh my goodness, what is THAT?" asks the soprano, horrified. "That," says St Peter, "is a tenor we got some time back. He's just about to start his third week in the sewing machine."

➻ Did you hear about the female opera singer who had quite a range at the lower end of the scale? She was known as the deep C diva.

There is a total extinction of all taste: our authors are vulgar, gross, illiberal; the theatre swarms with wretched translations and ballad operas, and we have nothing new but improving abuse.

Horace Walpole, 1717 – 1797

➻ How many altos does it take to change a light bulb? None. They can't get up that high.

➻ How many tenors does it take to change a light bulb? Six. One to do it and five to say, "It's too high for HIM."

➻ Opera is when a guy gets stabbed in the back and, instead of bleeding, he sings.

➻ Person 1: "It must be terrible for an opera singer to realize that he can never sing again." Person 2: "Yes, but it's much more terrible if he doesn't realize it."

ORAL SEX

➻ 69 + 69 = Dinner for four.

➻ A bloke went to the dentist to get his teeth checked. While he was sitting in the chair, the dentist asked him, "Have you performed oral sex recently?" Slightly uncomfortable, the bloke replied: "Yes, this morning. I suppose I've got a hair stuck in my teeth?" The dentist shook his head. "No. As a matter of fact, the tip of your nose is covered in shit."

➻ A boy's mother is pregnant, so she has to go off to hospital. The night before she goes, the boy chances upon her in the bathroom and sees hair between her legs. He asks, "What's that, Mummy?" and she tells him, "It's my washcloth, dear." A couple of weeks later the mother is back from hospital, but she had to have her pubic hair shaved during the birth. The boy chances in on her again and notices that her hair has gone. He asks, "What happened to your washcloth, Mummy?" and his mother replies, "I lost it dear." A couple of days later the boy is running through the house shouting "Mummy, I found your washcloth," so his mother stops him and says, "What do you mean, dear?" "I found your washcloth, Mummy," the boy says again. The mother finds this pretty odd, but decides to go along with it so she asks him, "And where did you find it, dear?" So the boy says, "The maid has it now, and she's washing Daddy's face with it!"

↣ A decent young man goes for dinner at his new girlfriend's house. He is very anxious and keen to impress his prospective in-laws. As the meal is served the family dog comes out of its basket, sits on the floor right beside the dinner table and proceeds to start licking its balls with a massively loud slurping sound. There is a shocked silence: nobody knows where to look or what to say. Driven to a state of wild nervousness, the man stutters, "Um, er, um...I er wish I could do that!" The girlfriend's family all look around in even greater shock and the mother says to him, "Well, if you gave him a biscuit I'm sure he'd let you!"

↣ A woman calls a male escort agency and asks for the most mind-blowing sex she's ever had. They say they'll send over their best stud, Ramon. A while later, the doorbell rings but when she answers the door, she sees a man with no arms and no legs down on the floor. "I am Ramon," says the man. "You?" says the woman, "How can you give me the most mind-blowing sex I've ever had? You've got no arms and no legs." "Listen, lady," says Ramon, "I rang the doorbell, didn't I?"

➻ A German is climbing in the Alps when he stops for a rest. He notices a bottle half-hidden in the pile of stones that he is sitting on. He uncorks it and WHAM! a genie pops out. "Thank you for releasing me, O Great One," the genie says. "I can grant you one wish – it can be anything you want." The man has a think, and eventually says, "I'm a big fan of schnapps and it's rather expensive. Could you arrange for me to piss schnapps?" "Your wish is my command, O Great One," says the genie, who waves his hand and then disappears. The man carries on with his walk and eventually gets home. That evening, after dinner, he goes to the toilet. As he is going, he thinks to himself, "I wonder if that genie was telling the truth...let's see, now that smells like schnapps, and it looks like schnapps, so..." And he pees a bit into a glass. He holds it up to the light and then tastes just a tiny bit. "Hurrah! It is schnapps, and good schnapps at that," he shouts, and drinks the entire glass. The man rushes out of the bathroom calling for his wife, "Helga, Helga, come quickly: it's a miracle!" Helga comes downstairs and he "pours" her a glass of schnapps. She is very apprehensive and it is not until he drinks some himself that she will try the liquid. She finds the taste fantastic as well, so the two of them get blasted on top-quality schnapps all night and have a great time. The next day after work the German tells Helga to take two glasses out of the cupboard because they will be having another party. She willingly agrees and the couple party the night away on the excellent schnapps that the man "produces". The next day after work the German tells Helga to take only one glass out of the cupboard because they will be having another party. "But, my love," she says, "why only the one glass?" The man fills his glass, lifts it to his wife and says, "Because tonight, my dear, you drink from the bottle!"

↦ A little boy comes home early from school one day and catches his parents having sex. In fact, the wife is giving the husband a blowjob. The boy asks, "Mummy and Daddy, what are you doing?" so the parents reply, "Making fish-sticks," because they figure he's only young and he's never going to know what they're up to, and what does he care anyway? A couple of nights later the boy walks in on them again and as they turn around he says, "Are you making fish-sticks again?" Both parents say "Yes." So the boy says, "Well. Mummy, you've got some tartare sauce stuck on your lip!"

↦ A man walks into a bar with a frog. He puts the frog on the bar and orders a pint and a packet of peanuts. Then he says, "Billy – catch!", and throws the peanuts to the frog, one at a time, who catches them in its mouth. "Wow," says the barmaid, "a performing frog!" "Yes," says the man, "This frog can do all sorts of tricks. It catches peanuts, it fetches a stick – and it gives the best cunnilingus in the world." The barmaid can't believe her ears, so the man says if she doesn't believe him, she can try it for herself. At closing time, the barmaid takes the man and the frog upstairs and lies naked on the bed. The man puts the frog gently down between her legs but the frog does nothing. "Billy – cunnilingus!" says the man. Still the frog does nothing. "Oh, for heavens sake Billy," says the man, "How many times do I have to show you?"

↦ How do you know if you have a high sperm count? If the girl has to chew before she swallows.

➻ A masked man runs through the door of a sperm bank. He is brandishing a shotgun. He leaps over the counter and points the gun at the receptionist. "Open the safe!" he barks at her. "What?" she says. "There's no money here: we're a sperm bank, not a money bank." "Just do it!" the guy continues. "Just open the goddamned safe and don't talk back. Don't make me hurt you, lady." So the lady leads him out back and opens the safe. It is just a big refrigerator full of sperm samples. "Now take a sample out," the guy snaps. The woman obliges. "Now, drink it," the guy says. "But it's sperm," the woman says. "Don't make me mad – just do it!" shouts the man. Fearing the worst, the woman pops the cap off the bottle and drinks the sperm. She chokes a couple of times but drains the bottle. "Another one," says the guy. She takes another bottle from the racks and drinks it. At that moment the man drops his gun and pulls off his mask. The woman cannot believe her eyes – the man who just had a gun at her head is her husband! "You see," he shouts at her, "it wasn't that bloody difficult, was it?"

Continental people have a sex life.
The English have hot-water bottles.

George Mikes

➻ A newly-married couple checked into a hotel, and while they were signing in told the attendant that they'd just got hitched. "Congratulations!" said the girl, looking at the bride. "You'll be wanting the Bridal, then." "Oh, no thanks," replied the wife. "I'll just hold his ears until he gets the hang of it."

↪ A sex therapist was doing research at the local college when one of the male volunteers told him: "When I get it in part-way, my vision blurs. And when I get it all the way in, I can't see a thing." "Hmmm...that's an interesting optical reaction to sex," said the researcher. "Would you mind if I had a look at it?" So the volunteer stuck out his tongue.

↪ A young newly-wed couple decide to have a romantic weekend away in the mountains in the winter: candlelit dinners, roaring fires and peace and quiet. They arrive in their winter cabin and the husband goes out to chop wood as the wife prepares their lunch. After a while he returns, saying, "Wow! It sure is cold. My hands are freezing." "Well", his wife tells him, "pop them between my thighs, baby: it's pretty hot down there, and sure to warm them up." He does so. After lunch he realizes they are low on wood again, so the husband goes out to chop some more. After a while he returns, saying, "Wow! It sure is cold. My hands are freezing." "Well," his wife tells him, "pop them between my thighs, baby: it's pretty hot down there, and sure to warm them up." He does so again. Later in the evening the husband goes out to chop wood again. After a while he returns, saying, "Wow! It sure is cold. My hands are freezing." But this time the wife says, "For goodness sake! Don't you ever get cold ears?"

↪ How do you eat a frog? You put one leg over each ear.

↪ How do you know when you've given a good blow job? He has to pull the bed sheets out of his arse.

↪ How do you tell the head nurse? She's the one with scuffed knees.

➳ Cinderella's going to the ball. "Dress – yes. Crystal carriage – yes. Handsome coachmen – yes. There's just one more thing I need, Fairy Godmother." "What's that, my dear?" "I don't have any contraception." The Fairy Godmother looks around and sees a pumpkin. With a wave of her wand, she turns it into a diaphragm. "Off you go, Cinderella, but remember – you must be home by midnight or your dress will turn back into rags, your carriage will revert to a coal scuttle, the coachmen will be mice again and – most important – your diaphragm will turn back into a pumpkin!" Cinderella promises to be back by midnight, pops the diaphragm in, and goes off to the ball. At five o'clock in the morning, Cinderella finally rolls in, dressed in rags, carrying a coal scuttle full of mice, but smiling happily. "Where have you been?" asks Fairy Godmother, "I told you to be back by midnight!" "I know," sighs Cinderella, "but I met such a nice man." "Prince Charming?" "No, his name was Peter Peter something..."

➳ Elton John was recently knighted by the Queen. Interviewed after the event, Sir Elton said that it felt odd to get down on his knees only to end up not swallowing the sword.

➳ Little Red Riding Hood is walking through the forest with her basket when out hops a little rabbit. "Oh, be careful, Little Red Riding Hood," says the rabbit, "The Big Bad Wolf is out hunting. If he catches you, he'll pull up your skirt, pull down your panties and shag you!" "Thanks for the warning," replies Little Red Riding Hood, "but I'll be ok." A little further along the path a squirrel pops out of a tree. "Oh, be careful, Little Red Riding Hood," says the squirrel, "The Big Bad Wolf is out hunting. If he catches you, he'll pull up your skirt, pull down your panties and shag you!"

"Thanks for the warning," replies Little Red Riding Hood, "but really, I'll be ok." After half a mile, the Big Bad Wolf jumps out of the bushes and confronts Little Red Riding Hood. "Now I've caught you," says the Wolf, "I'm going to pull up your skirt, pull down your panties and shag you!" Cool as anything, Little Red Riding Hood puts her hand into her basket and pulls out a gun. "I think not," she says, pointing her gun right at the Big Bad Wolf. "I think you're going to eat me, just like it says in the book."

➻ There was once a guy whose tongue was so long that when he stuck it out for the doctor, the nurse went, "Aaaaaahhh!"

Marry a German and you'll see that the women have hairy tongues.

Ruthenian saying

➻ There's a regular-drinking guy whose local is called Sally's Legs after an old song. One Friday he knocks off work early, planning to spend the entire evening there getting steadily drunk. Unfortunately he doesn't count on the bar not opening until after work time, so he is forced to sit and wait for the staff to show up. As he is parked outside, a suspicious policeman walks up to his window and raps on it. "Yes, officer?" he says, "what can I do for you?" "What do you think you're doing hanging around here at this time of day?" says the policeman. "Well, sir," says the man, "I'm just waiting for Sally's Legs to open so I can be the first in to get a drink!"

➻ What is the Chinese for a 69? Toocanchu.

↦ What did Cinderella do when she got to the ball? She choked!

↦ What do being in the military and getting a blowjob have in common? The closer you get to discharge, the better it gets.

↦ What do parsley and pubic hair have in common? You push them both aside and keep on eating!

↦ What do Santa's female reindeer do on Christmas Eve while the male reindeer pull his sleigh and deliver presents? They head into town to blow a few bucks.

↦ What do you call a woman who can suck an orange through a hose pipe? "Darling."

↦ What do you get if you cross a rooster with peanut butter? A cock that sticks to the roof of your mouth.

↦ What is 'egghead'? What Mrs Dumpty gives to Humpty.

↦ What was the smartest thing that ever came out of a woman's mouth? Einstein's dick.

↦ What would happen if the Founding Fathers had killed cats instead of turkeys? Americans would be eating pussy every Thanksgiving.

↦ What's better than roses on your piano? Tulips on your organ.

➤ What's the definition of trust? Two cannibals giving each other a blowjob.

➤ What's the difference between a dove and a swallow? One's the bird of peace and the other's the bird of true love.

➤ What's the difference between oral and anal sex? Oral sex makes your day; anal sex makes your hole weak.

➤ Why did the rag doll get thrown out of the toy box? She kept sitting on Pinocchio's face and shouting, "Lie to me, lie to me!"

➤ Why did the snowman drop his trousers? He heard the snowblower coming.

➤ A man and a woman were waiting at the hospital donation centre. Man: "What are you doing here today?" Woman: "Oh, I'm here to donate some blood. They're going to give me £5 for it." Man: "Hmm, that's interesting. I'm here to donate sperm, myself. But they pay me £25." The woman looked thoughtful for a moment and they chatted some more before going their separate ways. Several months later, the same man and woman met again in the donation centre. Man: "Oh, hi there. Here to donate blood again?" Woman: [shaking her head with mouth closed] "Unh unh."

ORGASM

↦ "Did you come on the bus, Grandma?" "Yes, dear, but I passed it off as an asthma attack."

↦ A husband asked his wife, "Has the postman come yet, dear?" "No," she replied, "but he's panting hard and sweating a lot."

↦ According to a recent survey, 85% of women masturbate in the shower and the other 15% sing. And do you know what they sing? Thought not.

Despite a lifetime of service to the cause of sexual liberation, I have never caught a venereal disease, which makes me feel rather like an Arctic explorer who has never had frostbite.

Germaine Greer

↦ Bob is having a drink with his friend Bill. "Do you know," says Bill, "there are four kinds of female orgasm: positive, negative, religious and fake." "How do you tell them apart?" asks Bob. "If it's positive, she shouts, "Oh yes, yes!", negative is when she shouts, "Oh no, no!" and "Oh God, oh God!" is the religious orgasm." "But what does she shout when it's fake?" asks Bob. "She shouts, 'Bob! Bob!'"

↦ Orgasm types:

Sex with a rower: oargasm
Sex after falling out of bed: floorgasm
Wet dream: snoregasm

Group sex: fourgasm
Sex for hours and hours: soregasm
Cheap sex: poorgasm
Noisy sex: roargasm
Nymphomaniac sex: Iwantmoregasm
Sex on the beach: shoregasm
Swedish sex: smorgasborgasm
Competitive sex: scoregasm
Sex with a pig: boargasm
Sex on holiday: tourgasm
Sex on the farm: tractorgasm
Sex with a Viking: Thorgasm

➤ What does the sperm clinic say to donors when they leave? Thanks for coming.

➤ What's bad about being a test tube baby? You know for sure that your dad was a wanker.

➤ What's sticky, white and falls from the sky? The second coming of the Lord Jesus!

PARROTS

➤ A punk rocker gets on a bus: he's pierced and tattooed, with multicoloured hair in a big Mohican. He sees an old man staring and asks, "What's the matter old boy – didn't you ever do anything wild in your life?" "Yes," says the old man. "I had sex with a parrot once, and I was just wondering if you were my son."

➻ A bloke was about to bring his new girlfriend home, so he warned his parrot not to make any offensive remarks; the parrot had a tendency to verbally abuse anyone who came into the house. The next night the guy walked in with his new girlfriend, and the parrot instantly began to insult her: "Who's a fat cow, then? Who's been hit by a truck, then?" The next day, the infuriated man decided to shove the parrot in the freezer to teach it a lesson. About two minutes later the parrot called out, "I'm sorry. I'm really sorry. I'm really, really sorry. I won't do it again!" The man let the parrot back out and said: "I hope you behave, otherwise it's back in the cooler!" For the next couple of months he didn't hear so much as a squeak out of the parrot. He couldn't believe how successful his freezer trick turned out to be. But finally one night the parrot got up enough courage to talk again. "Excuse me, please," the parrot said, very cautiously, "but what exactly did the chicken do?"

➻ A burglar has just made it into the house he's intending to ransack, and he's looking around for stuff to steal. All of a sudden, a little voice pipes up, "I can see you, and so can Jesus!" Startled, the burglar looks around the room. No one there at all, so he goes back to his business. "I can see you, and so can Jesus!" The burglar jumps again, and takes a longer look around the room. Over in the corner by the window, almost obscured by curtains, is a cage in which sits a budgie, who pipes up again: "I can see you, and so can Jesus!" "So what?" says the burglar, "you're only a budgie!" To which the budgie replies: "Maybe, but 'Jesus' is the Rottweiler!"

➻ A man gets on a plane and is surprised to be seated next to a parrot. He doesn't really say anything, but thinks it a bit odd. When the stewardess comes around to see if anyone wants drinks, she asks the man. He says he'd like a cup of coffee, and as he says this the parrot squawks, "And get me a whisky on the rocks, bitch!" The stewardess is visibly shaken and walks off. She comes back a few minutes later and hands the parrot his whisky, but she has forgotten the man's coffee. The man points this out and asks again. As he does so, the parrot squawks, "And bring me another whisky on the rocks, you slut!" The stewardess goes off again and comes back – again with the parrot's drink, but with no coffee for the man. The man is a bit sick of this so he decides to use the parrot's approach. So he barks, "That's twice I've asked you for coffee, you useless cow, what the hell do I have to do to get a friggin' drink around here?" The next thing the man knows he's been picked up by two huge stewards and thrown out of the plane. He has the parrot next to him and, as they both start their plunge to earth, the bird turns to him and says, "Phew-ee, for someone who can't fly, you sure are one gobby bastard!"

➡ A parrot has a habit of shagging chickens, so the farmer tells him that if he does it again he will pull out every feather on its head. The parrot jumps on the hens again, and his head feathers are duly pulled out. Meanwhile, the farmer's wife, who has pretensions to culture, is having a formal dinner. She appoints the parrot to be butler and to tell the guests where to put their hats and coats. The party proceeds without mishap, with the parrot announcing, "Ladies to the right! Gentlemen to the left!" Suddenly, two bald-headed men enter, and the parrot says: "You two chicken-fuckers come out to the hen house with me."

➻ A vicar wanted to buy a parrot. "Are you sure it doesn't swear?" he asked the storekeeper. "Oh, absolutely. It's a religious parrot," the storekeeper assured him. "Do you see those strings on his legs? When you pull the right one he recites the Lord's Prayer, and when you pull on the left one he chants the 23rd Psalm." "That's wonderful!" said the vicar, reaching for his chequebook, "and what happens if you pull both strings?" "I fall off my fucking perch, you piece of shit!" screeched the parrot.

You can make even a parrot into a learned political economist – all he must learn are the two words 'Supply' and 'Demand'.

Anonymous

➻ A woman goes to see her priest because she has a problem with the couple of female parrots that she owns – they just will not behave themselves. All they can say is, "Hello, we are prostitutes. Do you wanna have a good time?" The father agrees that that's a terrible situation, but he realizes very quickly that he, himself can provide a simple solution. He asks the woman to bring her two parrots over to his house, because he too has two parrots – his are male – and he has bought them up to read the Bible and to pray and all that sort of "good" stuff. He figures that his good parrots will be a very good influence on her "bad" parrots and that all will live happily together eventually. The next day, the woman brings her two female parrots over to the priest's house. She sees the priest's two parrots in their cage. They are praying, burning incense and fiddling with their rosary beads, all in a very devout manner. The woman puts her parrots down next to the priest's parrots and hers pipe up, "Hello, we are prostitutes. Do you wanna have a good time?" Upon hearing this, one of the priest's parrots turns to the other one and says, "Put the Good Book away my man, our prayers have been answered!"

↬ An elderly lady buys a pair of parrots, but she cannot identify their sexes. She calls the pet shop, and the man there advises her to watch them carefully and all will become clear in time. She spends weeks staring at the cage, and eventually catches them shagging. To make sure she doesn't get them mixed up again, she cuts a ring out from a piece of cardboard and puts it round the male parrot's neck. The following week, the local vicar calls in for a cup of tea. He's just making himself comfortable when the male parrot notices his dog- collar. "Eh up," leered the parrot, "Who did she catch you screwing?"

↬ Hillary Clinton goes into a pet shop and sees the most beautiful parrot she has ever seen. "Does it talk?" she enquires of the shopkeeper. "He sure does, ma'am," the man replies. "Well, how come he only costs fifty bucks when all the other parrots are at least five hundred?" "Well, ma'am, that's a good question, and the answer is that he's got a bit of a fruity vocabulary on him. He used to live in a brothel and some of the things he says would even make a tart blush!" Hillary, used to foul language and deeds, says, "Not a problem for me. I'll take him right now." She gets home and places the parrot in its new cage in the front room. The parrot turns to her as soon as the cover goes off the cage, looks her square in the eye and says, "New house, new madam!" Hillary laughs and carries on with her day. Later on, Chelsea arrives with a friend and they go over to pet the new bird. The parrot turns to them, looks them square in the eye, and squawks, "New house, new whores." They run off, giggling. Later that night, Bill comes home after a hard day's work. He walks up to have a look at the new bird. The parrot turns to him, and with the briefest glance says, "Hey, Bill!"

➻ Kath was expecting the plumber. He was supposed to arrive at ten o'clock. Ten o'clock came and went – no plumber. Eleven o'clock, twelve o'clock, and one o'clock sailed past, still with no plumber. She decided he wasn't coming, and went out to do some chores. Naturally, no sooner had she left than the plumber arrived. He knocked on the door and, from the lounge, Kath's parrot called, "Who is it?" Presuming the parrot to be the lady of the house he called back, "It's the plumber," and waited for her to come and let him in. When no-one opened the door, he knocked again. Again the parrot called, "Who is it?" Frustrated, he yelled, "It's the plumber!" He waited some more, and again no-one came to the door. He knocked again, long and hard. Again the parrot called, "Who is it?" and he shouted, "IT'S THE PLUMBER!" Once again he waited, and again she didn't come. Furious at the way she was taking the piss, he hammered on the door again and again. The parrot, who was having a great time, called, "Who is it?" innocently. It was too much for the plumber, who went berserk. With a loud scream he took a wrench to the lock, hammered it to bits and broke the door down. The excitement proved too much for the poor bloke, though, and he had a massive heart attack, dropping dead in the hall. When Kath got back an hour later she found the door ripped open and a corpse lying in the doorway. "Fuck!" she shrieked, "WHO IS IT?" Gleefully, the parrot howled "IT'S THE PLUMBER!"

➺ This bloke with a parrot is getting married. On the day of the wedding, he says, "Listen, I know you're always in that bloody window. My wife and I are coming back here to pack after the wedding, and no matter what you hear, do not turn around or I'll break your damned neck! We want some privacy!" The parrot reluctantly agrees. The happy couple then come back from the wedding and start packing, but they can't get the suitcase closed. "Get on top," says the bloke, "that'll do it." She gives it a shot, but despite much effort and grunting it doesn't close. His wife then says, "Look, you get on top, that'll be better." They heave away again, with no luck. Finally, the bloke says, "I tell you what, let's both get on top; that should fix it!" The parrot immediately turns around and says, "Neck or no neck, I have got to see this!"

➺ When her dishwasher packed up, Mrs Williams phoned the repair man. He couldn't accommodate her request for an after-hours appointment, and because she had to go to work she told him, "I'll leave the key under the mat. Fix the dishwasher, leave your invoice on the counter and I'll post you a cheque. By the way, I have a large Rottweiler called Fang, but don't worry, he's very well-trained and he won't bother you. I also have a large parrot. Whatever you do, no matter what he says to you, do not say anything to the bird!" Well, sure enough, the dog totally ignored the repair man, but the whole time he was there the parrot swore, yelled, screamed and just about drove the bloke mad. As he was getting ready to leave, he just couldn't resist saying to the parrot, "You stupid fucking mangy ball of feathers, shut the fuck up!" The bird went quiet for a moment, fixed him with a malicious glare, then shouted at the top of its voice: "Kill, Fang. Kill, boy!"

↦ What do you get when you cross a parrot with a centipede? A walkie-talkie.

Penises

↦ A bloke is in the toilet of his local pub taking a slash. He looks around, and notices this black guy also using the urinals, and he's got a huge cock. "Damn!" says the bloke, in awe, "I wish I had a cock like that." The black guy looks over at him, "Well, it's simple. All you have to do is whack your dick on the side of your bath tub every morning." "Really?" asks the bloke. "Really," answers the black guy. The following week the black guy sees the bloke in the pub again, so he walks over and says to him, "So, have you been following my advice?" The bloke nods. "Well," says the black guy, "I can't help you with the size, but at least you've got the colour right!"

↦ A bloke went to a private urologist and said, "Doctor, I have a problem. My penis is garishly red." The urologist replied, "Well, okay, let's have a look at the old fellow then. Hmm...yes, no problem. We'll have you sorted out in no time." He told the bloke to lie down, then fiddled about a bit with the bloke's prick, did one or two things and said, "Right. All done; that'll be £50." Sure enough, the bloke's penis was back to normal. Impressed, he paid up. A couple of weeks later, he was chatting to a friend of his who looked a bit shifty and said, "You know, I've got the same problem, but it's greenish, not red. That specialist sounds cheap – I'll go and try him out." So the next day the friend went to the same doctor. He showed the urologist his penis, and the chap said, "Hmm...well, we can sort you out, but it's going to cost you £4,100, I'm afraid, and we'll have to operate." The bloke looked at the doctor in horror. "£4,100 and an operation? You sorted my mate out for fifty quid!" "That's very true," nodded the doctor, "but he had lipstick smudges on his old chap. You've got gangrene!"

↦ A couple meet in a bar and end up back at his place. "You don't talk much," she says as he's undressing. "No," he says, "I do my talking with this." "Sorry," she says, "I don't do small talk."

↦ A guy goes to the doctor with a mysterious pain and tells the doctor, "Doc, Doc, my penis has been burning lately." And the doctor says reassuringly, "Don't worry, son, that just means someone is talking about it."

↦ A guy walks into the doctor's office and says, "D-d-d-doct-tor-r-r, I've b-been st-t-tuttering f-for y-y-years and I-I-I-I'm t-t-tired of it. C-c-can y-y-you he-he-help me?" The doctor examines him swiftly and says, "Well I think I know what the problem is." The guy says, "W-w-well, w-w-what is it, d-doc?" The doctor says, "Well, it's your penis, you see: it's about a foot long and all the downward pressure is putting a strain on your vocal cords." The guy says, "I d-d-d-didn't kn-n-n-n-now it c-c-c-could c-c-cause a p-p-p-p... p-p-p-p... p-p-problem. W-w-what c-c-can we d-do?" The doctor advises, "Well, I can cut it off and transplant a shorter one. The pressure will disappear and so will your stutter." The guy thinks for a minute then says, "D-d-do it!" He has the operation and, three weeks later, he returns to see the doctor and says, "Doc, you solved the problem and I don't stutter anymore, but I've only had sex once in the past three weeks. My wife doesn't like it any more. She liked it with my long one. I don't care if I have to stutter: I want you to put my long one back on." The doctor says, "N-n-n-no. A d-d-d-deal's a d-d-d-deal!!!"

↦ A Jewish boy was walking with his girlfriend in the grounds of his father's house. His father was a successful doctor, and was carrying out a circumcision in the on-site surgery. As they were walking, they heard a scream and a foreskin flew out of the window and landed at the girl's feet. "What's this?" she asked. "Taste it," he replied, "If you like it, I'll give you a whole one."

↦ A man goes into a party shop and says, "I'd like to hire a costume, I'm going to a fancy dress party as Adam." So the assistant gets out a fig leaf: "There you are sir, that's £5." "No, that's not big enough," he says, so she gets out a bigger one. "That one's £10." "Still not big enough," he says, so she gets out an even bigger one. "This one's £15," she says. "No, I won't fit into that," he says, so she gets out a hat that says "Esso". "There," she says, "wear this, sling it over your shoulder and go as a petrol pump."

↦ A man is having problems with his dick, which certainly has seen better times. He consults a doctor who, after a couple of tests, says: "Sorry, but you've overdone it the last 30 years, your dick is burned out. You won't be able to make love more than 30 times." The man walks home deeply depressed; his wife is already expecting him at the front door and asks him what the doctor said concerning his problem. He tells her what the doctor told him. She says: "Oh my God, only 30 times. We should not waste that; we should make a list." He replies, "Yes, I already made a list on the way home. Sorry, your name's not on it."

↝ A man went to a doctor to have his penis enlarged. Well, this particular procedure involved grafting a baby elephant's trunk onto the man's penis. Overjoyed, the man went out with his best girl to a very fancy restaurant. After cocktails, the man's penis crept out of his pants, felt around the table, grabbed a bread roll and quickly disappeared under the tablecloth. The girl was startled and exclaimed: "What was that?" Suddenly the penis came back, took another bread roll and just as quickly disappeared. The girl was silent for a moment, then finally said: "I don't believe I saw what I think I just saw...can you do that again?" With a strained smile the man replied: "Darling, I'd like to, but I don't think my arse can take another bread roll!"

> **You know Linford Christie? My genitals are**
> **like a sort of travel version of that.**
>
> *Frank Skinner. Linford Christie, a British athlete,*
> *is famed for his tight running gear*

↝ Did you hear the one about the blind circumciser? He got the sack.

↝ Have you heard about the couple who got married in a nudist colony? They wanted everyone to be sure who the best man was.

↝ How do you get some groovy lovin'? Use a corduroy condom.

↦ A Scots chap in England is walking home pissed from the pub, as usual, and decides to take a quick nap on a nearby bench, to provide stamina for the rest of the journey. While he's dozing, a couple of girls stroll by. One says to the other, "Hey, is it true that they don't wear anything beneath those kilts?" The other giggles and says, "Let's take a look." So, after finding that the chap is indeed naked under his kilt, the first one says, "We should leave something to let him know we were here." So saying, she removes a blue ribbon from her hair and carefully ties it around his bell-end. When he comes round a couple of hours later, the Scot nips behind a bush to relieve himself. He finds the ribbon, and in tones of awe murmurs, "I don't know where you've been, laddie, but I see you took first prize..."

↦ At the fairground, a man sees a sign outside a tent: "Make the horse laugh and win £100". So he goes in. After two minutes the sound of horse laughter comes from the tent, and the man comes out and collects his £100. Next year, the fair is back, but this time the sign outside the tent reads "Make the horse cry and win £100". The same man goes in again, and after two minutes horsy sobs are coming from the tent. As the £100 is being counted out, the horse's owner asks the man what his secret is. "Well, last year, I told that horse that my dick was bigger than his. That's why he laughed." "And this year?" "This year, I didn't just tell him, I showed him."

↦ Dad, Mum and little Jimmy decide to go to the zoo one day. Eventually they end up at the elephant house. Jimmy looks at the elephant, sees its penis, points to it and says, "Mum, what is that long thing?" His mother replies, "That's the elephant's trunk,

Jimmy." "No, at the other end." "That's the elephant's tail." "No, mummy," said Jimmy, "the thing under the elephant." A short embarrassed silence followed, after which she said, "Oh, that's nothing." Mum then went to buy some ice-cream and Jimmy, not being satisfied with her answer, asks Dad the same question. "Dad, what is that long thing?" "That's the elephant's trunk, Jimmy," replied his father. "No, at the other end." "Oh, that's the elephant's tail." "No, dad, the thing below," asked Jimmy in frustration. "Ah. That's the elephant's penis, Jimmy. Why do you ask?" "Well, mum said it was nothing," said Jimmy. Dad shook his head wryly and said, "I tell you, I spoil that woman..."

↠ If women had a penis for a day they would:

1. Measure it to see whether that really is six inches.
2. Pee standing up, without even trying to hit the toilet.
3. Get a blow job.
4. Fall asleep without saying thanks.
5. Wake up.
6. Repeat number 3.
7. Repeat number 3.
8. Repeat number 3.
9. Repeat number 3.
10. Repeat number 3.

↠ On the first evening of their honeymoon, they were sitting on the balcony of the hotel while the sun was setting. "Honey," she said, "now that we're married, will you tell me what a penis is?" He almost fell off the chair. Being her husband, he led her into their room and took his pants off. "This, my love, is a penis," he told her. "Oh!" she exclaimed, "it looks like a cock, only smaller."

➺ It was the night before Christmas and a rather lonely lady, who hadn't got laid in a very long time, was waiting for Father Christmas to come down the chimney at her house. When he did, she removed her shirt and said, "Oh, Santa, please stay a while." Santa said, "Ho ho ho, lady: I'd love to, but I've got toys to deliver to children around the world." So she dropped her skirt and says, "Oh Santa, please stay a while." Santa says, "Ho ho ho, lady, I'd love to, but I've got toys to deliver to children around the world." So she stripped naked and said, "Oh, Santa, please stay a while." So Santa said, "Well, I'm never going to get up the chimney with my dick in this state, so I guess I'd better stay a while!"

➺ John Wayne Bobbitt has turned to the church for solace, and been ordained as a minister in Las Vegas. Rumour has it, however, that his chapel has no organ...

➺ Mr Rennie was an old man and he lived in a nursing home. One day he walked into the nurses' quarters and told them his penis had died. None of them were shocked – this sort of thing happened all the time – and they just figured he was a bit bored and would get over it. A couple of days later, Mr Rennie bumped into one of the nurses walking down the corridor. His penis was hanging out of his trousers. The nurse said to him, "I thought your penis had died, Mr Rennie?" "It certainly did, young lady," he replied, "but today's the viewing!"

➺ Mr Smith hires a gardener who says he's got a huge penis – a foot long relaxed, over a yard erect. When Mrs Smith hears this she wants to see, so she tells her husband to get the gardener to show it to him while she hides in the shed. The next day, while Mr Smith and the gardener are cutting the hedge, Mr Smith asks to see the huge penis. They go to the shed, where Mrs Smith is hiding, and the gardener gets it out. Impressed, Mr Smith asks to see it erect, so the gardener rubs it till it grows to be a yard long. The gardener then asks to see Mr Smith's penis, so he gets his out – it's pretty small. Even when he rubs it, it's only a few inches long. That night, he says to his wife, "I hope you're satisfied. I was pretty embarrassed when he asked to see mine, too. It looked so small next to that monster." "You were embarrassed? I couldn't think of what to say to all my friends from work that were in the shed with me."

How the hell should I know, dahling? He never sucked my cock!

Tallulah Bankhead, when asked about Tab Hunter's rumoured homosexuality

➡ On a sunny, hot afternoon a man is sitting on his porch drinking iced lemonade in a deckchair relaxing and watching as his wife grunts, groans and struggles with the lawnmower. The next-door neighbour can't believe her eyes and she storms over to the porch. "You should be ashamed of yourself, you caveman, letting your wife mow the lawn on a day like this. You ought to be hung!" "I am," says the man with a smug smile, "and that's exactly why my wife is mowing the lawn."

➡ What do you call six nude blokes standing on each others' shoulders? A scrotum pole.

➡ There's this really vain surfer type. He jogs and he lifts weights and he stretches and he tones. He's admiring himself in the mirror one day and he notices that all of him looks great apart from his willy – it is the only part of him that doesn't have a tan. So he tries instant tan from all sorts of places and tanning booths, but nothing works. Eventually he goes to see a doctor who tells him that because of the sensitive nature of the skin, he will only be able to tan his willy in proper sunlight. So the man goes to the beach. Sadly, there are no nudist beaches near where he lives, so he goes to a normal one and tries to get himself a tan without anyone noticing. He can't manage it, so he develops a plan: he digs a hole big enough to hide in and buries himself, apart from his willy, which he leaves sticking out, and his mouth. He puts on suntan lotion and falls asleep. A few minutes later, a couple of little old ladies walk past and one of them notices the willy in the sand. She prods it a couple of times with her walking stick and gets it to wake up a little bit. Then she sighs and says to her friend, "There's no justice, is there?" "What do you mean, dear?" her friend replies. The lady says, "Well, I've spent my life being curious about willies, enjoying them, asking for them, tasting them, praying for more of them, hoping they'll get bigger, and now here I am, 80 years old – they grow wild on the beach and I can't even squat down!"

➡ This guy goes to the doctor for a vasectomy. Unlike the usual patients, he shows up in a Rolls Royce, and sits in the doctor's office in a tuxedo with black tie. The doctor says, "I've done a lot of these, but I've never seen a Rolls and tuxedo before. What's the story?" To which the fellow responds, "If I'm gonna BE impotent, I'm going to LOOK impotent."

↦ Two brothers are having a medical, and the doctor comments on the unusual length of their penises. "Yes, sir, we got them from our mother." "Your mother? Surely you inherited them from your father?" "No, sir. You see our mother only has one arm." "One arm? What's that got to do with the length of your penises?" "Well, she had to lift us out of the bath somehow."

↦ Two mates are out for an evening in a bar. They happen to go to the toilet at the same time. As they are standing there, John notices that Thomas is pretty well-endowed and he can't help mentioning the fact. "Yeah," says Thomas. "But it wasn't always like that, you know. I was sick of only having a small one, so I had a transplant from a doctor in Harley Street. It was pretty expensive – £10,000 – but it was really worth it." A few months later, the two mates find themselves next to each other in a toilet again. John says to Thomas "I thought about what you said last time, and I decided to get myself a transplant, too. You got well ripped off, mate – mine only cost a grand!" Thomas leans across the urinals and has a quick look. "Not surprising," he says. "They've given you my old one!"

↦ What do you get if you cross a penis and a potato? A dictator.

↦ What is the proper medical term for the circumcision of a rabbit? A hare cut.

↦ What matters is not the length of the wand, but the magic in the stick.

↦ What's the best thing to come out of a penis? The wrinkles.

↦ What's the definition of a man with a small penis? If he walks into a door with an erection he bangs his nose.

They think they can act like God almighty because they've got a cock and they can mend a flex.

Victoria Wood, on men

↦ What's the difference between embarrassment, worry and panic? Embarrassment is the first time a man can't get it up a second time. Worry is the first time he can't get it up for the first time. Panic is the second time he can't get it up for the first time.

↦ What's the difference between medium and rare? Five inches is medium, ten inches is rare.

↦ When John Wayne Bobbit's wife cut off his penis, she drove away with it and threw it out of the car window. Before it landed in the field, it hit the windscreen of another car and bounced off. In the car, a little girl was being driven home by her mother. "Wow!" said the girl, "What was THAT?" "Nothing, honey," replied her embarrassed mother, "just a fly." "Well," says the girl, "for a little fly, it had a huge willy."

↦ Who's the most popular girl on the nudist beach? The one who can eat the sixth doughnut.

↦ Who's the most popular man on the nudist beach? The one who can carry two cups of coffee and six doughnuts.

↦ Why are eggs frustrated? They only get laid once, eaten once, and you have to boil them if you want to get them hard!

↦ Why do women prefer a circumcised penis? Because anything with 10% off is always attractive.

↦ Why is being a penis not all it's cracked up to be? Because you have a head, but no brains. There's always a couple of nuts following you around. Your neighbour's an arsehole and your best friend's a complete pussy.

PERVERSION

↦ Women! You can't live with them, and you can't get them to dress up in a skimpy Nazi costume and beat you with a warm courgette.

↦ "Can you beat my total of 71 men?" asked Suzie. "Perhaps," replied Jane, "provided you supply the whips."

↦ "I'm worried," said the woman to her sex therapist. "I happened to find my daughter and the boy next door both naked, giggling and examining each other's bodies." "That's not unusual," smiled the therapist. "I wouldn't worry about it." "But I am worried, doctor," insisted the woman, "and so is my daughter's husband."

↦ A doctor lost his practitioner's license when he was caught having sex with one of his patients. It was a particular shame, as he had been the best mortician in town.

➼ A door-to-door salesman had suffered a really rough day and decided to try one more house before heading home. He knocked on the door, determined that this time he was going to make a sale. He could almost taste it. A boy opened the door and the salesman starts in with his sales pitch. The boy just stood there, speechless, staring at him and the salesman, seeing that he wasn't getting anywhere, asked the boy where his mother was. The boy didn't say a word, he just pointed upstairs. The salesman went up the stairs, opened the bedroom door, and found the boy's mother in bed, fucking a goat! Completely flabbergasted, the salesman slammed the door shut and charged down the stairs. He grabbed the little boy by the shoulders and yelled, "Don't you know what's in bed with your mother? Don't you know what they're doing? Doesn't it bother you?" The boy looked at him, then shook his head and answered, "Na-a-a-a-a-a."

➼ A man goes to a brothel and asks for the kinkiest girl they have. "I'm sorry, sir, all our girls are busy, but if you like you can have the pig." He thinks it's pretty kinky, so he has sex with the pig. Next week he's back, asking for the kinkiest girl they have. "I'm sorry, sir, all our girls are busy." "Well, can I have the pig again?" "No, sorry, sir, no pig, but if you like you can go into the room at the end and watch." So he goes into the room at the end and there are a dozen guys all masturbating, watching through a pane of glass while a woman licks melted chocolate off a man who is tied to the bed. "Wow!" he says, "That's pretty hot!" "You think this is good," says one of the other guys, "there was some pervert in there last week, having sex with a pig."

➼ A woman goes to a doctor with a problem. She's sitting on the chair next to the doctor, and she's very hesitant about describing her problem. Eventually, the doctor manages to discover that she thinks she may be sexually perverted. "What sort of perversion are you talking about?" asks the doctor. "Well," says the woman, "I like to be...Ohh...Ah...Ummm...I'm sorry, doctor, but I'm too ashamed to talk about it." "Come, come, my dear. I'm a doctor, you know; I've been trained to understand these problems. So what's the matter...?" So the woman again tries to explain, but gets so embarrassed that she just turns bright red and looks as though she might faint. Then the doctor has a bright idea. "Look," he says, "I'm a bit of a pervert myself. So if you show me what your perversion is, I'll show you what mine is. Okay? Is it a deal?" The woman considers the offer and after a short while agrees that it's a fair request. So after a slight pause, she says: "Well, my perversion is...my perversion...Oh...I like to be kissed on the bottom." "Shit, is that ALL," says the doctor. "Look, go behind that screen, take all your clothes off, and I'll come round and show you what MY perversion is." So the woman does as she is told and undresses behind the screen. She gets down on all fours thinking to herself, "Hmmmm, perhaps he might kiss me on the bottom." Anyway, 15 minutes pass and nothing has happened. So the woman peers around the side of the screen to see the doctor sitting behind his desk, his feet up on the table, reading a newspaper and whistling to himself. "Hey!" shouts the woman, "I thought you said you were a pervert?" "Oh, I am," says the doctor, "I've just crapped in your handbag."

↔ Heard about the transvestite who lost the high-heel-wearing contest? He suffered the agony of defeat.

↔ I wanted to be a streaker but I wasn't suited for it.

➡ A woman meets a German in a bar and goes back to his hotel room. He confides that he's a bit kinky, and would she mind dressing up? She says no, so he gets out a big costume, covered in feathers, with a duck's bill and big webbed feet. She thinks this is OK, so she puts it on and they start shagging. He then asks if she would mind putting something else on, and gets out four huge bedsprings. She says OK, so he straps them on her knees and elbows, she gets on all fours and soon they're at it, bouncing away, getting more and more excited. Finally, he asks her if she'll shout, "Quack! Quack!" As soon as she does this, they both have the most amazing orgasm. "How did you do that?" she asks, as soon as she can speak. "Four-sprung duck technique," he replies.

➡ An Englishman, an Irishman and a Scotsman are being interviewed for the priesthood and they're told they have to pass a celibacy test to see if they're capable of controlling their carnal urges. They stand naked in a room and a small bell is tied to each of their pricks to reveal the slightest arousal. A beautiful woman is then brought in and she starts to perform a striptease. "Ting-a-ling!" the Irishman's bell rings as his prick stirs uncontrollably. Then the naked woman approaches the Scotsman and starts to blow on his neck. "Ting-a-ling!" the Scotsman's bell rings. Now the two have huge erections, but the Englishman is not aroused at all. The woman runs her hands all over his naked body, but nothing – his bell remains silent. At last the priest says, "Enough! You have proved yourself worthy of the priesthood. As for you other two, your punishment shall be a severe caning." "Ting-a-ling!" goes the Englishman's bell.

❧ An old rancher marries a young wife, hoping she can help with the hard work, but soon it's clear that they need more help, so they hire a strapping young cowboy to help around the place. After a month the rancher's wife says to the rancher, "Hank's worked so hard, I think he deserves a night off. Let's tell him he can ride into town, and I'll wait up to let him in when he gets back." The rancher agrees, and Hank rides into town. When he gets back, the rancher's wife is sitting in the kitchen waiting for him. "Come in, Hank," she says, "now, I want you to take off my shoes." "Yes, Ma'am," says Hank, and he takes off her little button boots. "Very good, Hank. Now take off my skirt." So Hank slips off her skirt. "Now Hank, take off my stockings and my corset." So Hank takes off her stockings and her corset. "And finally, Hank, I want you to take off my panties." So Hank takes off her panties. "Very good, Hank. Now, if I ever catch you wearing my clothes to town again, you're fired."

Mr Lawrence has a diseased mind. He is obsessed by sex and we have no doubt that he will be ostracised by all except the most degenerate coteries of the world.

John Bull magazine, 1928, on DH Lawrence

❧ Arthur C. Clarke's proposed knighthood was postponed when a tabloid newspaper printed a story alleging that he was a paedophile, an accusation over which Clarke took the paper to court. Royal sources suggest that the Crown wants to be absolutely certain that he is a pervert before ennobling him.

➼ If I have sex with my clone, will I go blind?

➼ Patient: "Doc, Doc, you've got to help me. Every time I sneeze, I have an orgasm." Doctor: "Really? What are you taking for it?" Patient: "Black pepper."

➼ Some perverts like to watch a woman wrestle, but most men prefer to see her box.

➼ This American redneck walks into a bar and says, "Gimme a Coke." The landlord says "Nah, you want a beer, mate. Every night you come in, have three beers and leave." The redneck says "Yeah, but last night I had three beers here, then I went to the bar down the street and had ten more beers. Then I went home and blew chunks." The landlord says, "Well, don't worry, it happens to the best of us." The redneck says, "You don't understand. Chunks is my pit-bull!"

➼ This bloke went to the doctor to get the results of his tests. He was devastated to learn that he was HIV positive, and slumped over the desk in despair. "Fuck," he moaned, "you can't trust anyone any more. Not even your own bloody children."

➼ Three women are in the vet's waiting room with their dogs. "What a lovely Labrador," says one, "What are you bringing him in for?" "He is lovely", says the owner, "but he's a terrible chewer. He's chewed the furniture, my husband's shoes, but the final straw was when he chewed up my husband's golf clubs and left nothing but a pile of sawdust. So my husband said, either the dog goes, or he goes." "So you're having him put to sleep?" "I'm afraid so," says the owner. The second dog is a collie. "What a lovely collie, what are you bringing him in for?" "He is lovely but he's a terrible chaser. He chases cars, he chases bicycles, he even chases the postman. The final straw came when he chased my husband's mother down the drive and out of the gate. So my husband said, either the dog goes, or he goes." "So you're having him put to sleep?" "Yes, I'm afraid so." So they turn to the third dog. "What a lovely Great Dane." "He is lovely, but he's a terrible shagger. He'll shag anything – the sofa, the neighbour's dog, the vicar's leg. The final straw was when I was getting out of the shower. I bent over to pick up the soap and in no time he was on top of me, shagging away. It took my husband ten minutes to pull him off, and that was it – my husband said, either that dog goes, or I go." "So you're having him put to sleep?" "Oh no, I've just brought him in to have his claws trimmed."

He was like a eunuch. For one thing, he was a voyeur. Terrified of sex but dying to watch or peep. He was fat and squishy and the most asexual man I've ever known.

James Mason on Alfred Hitchcock

→ Two men are walking home from work one hot, sweaty Friday in London. The first man says, "First thing I'm going to do when I get home is rip my wife's knickers off!" "Steady on, mate," says the second. "You've got the whole weekend. Why are you in such a hurry?" The first man replies, "They've been chafing my groin all day!"

→ What do you get if you cross a pervert and a hamster? Letters from animal rights campaigners.

➡ What's the difference between a masochist and a mosquito? If you hit a mosquito, it'll stop eating you.

➡ What's the difference between sexy and kinky? Sexy is using a feather – kinky is when it's still attached to the chicken.

➡ What's a 72? It's a 69 with three people watching.

➡ Why did the pervert cross the road? His dick was stuck in the chicken.

➡ Why did the pervert fancy the chicken? He thought it was poultry in motion.

➡ Why did the sadist steal the batteries for the vibrator? Because he liked to take charge.

➡ Why do sadists take so long to get to the point? Because they're always beating around the bush.

PHOne messAGes

➡ Have you heard the disorganized girl's answering machine? It says: "Hello. I'm home right now but cannot find the phone. Please leave a message and I will call you back as soon as I find it."

➡ Have you heard the English Foundation's answering machine? It says: "This is the literacy self-test hotline. After the tone, leave your name and number, and recite a sentence using today's vocabulary word, 'supercilious'."

↦ Have you heard the hypnotist's answering machine? It says: "You're growing tired. Your eyelids are getting heavy. You feel very sleepy now. You are gradually losing your willpower and your ability to resist suggestions. When you hear the tone you will feel helplessly compelled to leave your name, number, and a message."

↦ Have you heard the lunatic's answering machine? It says: "Hi, I'm not sane right now, but if you leave your name, number and shoe size at the sound of the tone, I'll get back to you when and if I return to my senses."

Public telephones in Europe are like pin-ball machines. They are primarily a form of entertainment and a test of skill rather than a means of communication.

Henry Beard

↦ Have you heard the mad scientist's answering machine? It says: "The machine answering this message is connected to a 5,000-volt power supply and a relay, which is wired to this small kitten. (Sound of a kitten meowing). If you hang up before you leave a message, it will complete the circuit and fry the kitty. The choice is yours."

↦ Have you heard the MI6 agent's answering machine? It says: "This is John's answering machine. Please leave your name and number, and after I've doctored the tape, your message will implicate you in a serious crime and be brought to the attention of Scotland Yard."

↦ Have you heard the Psychic Hotline's answering machine? It says: "This is not an answering machine – this is a telepathic thought-recording device. After the tone, think about your name, your reason for calling, and a number where I can reach you, and I'll think about returning your call."

↦ Have you heard the suicidal bloke's answering machine? It says: "Sorry, I'm far too depressed to come to the phone. If you can be bothered, leave a message after the sound of the gunshot, and maybe somebody will call you, I guess..."

Pianos

↦ An eccentric lady was in need of a piano player for her forthcoming party. She placed ads and spread the word but could not find a suitable one. A bum knocked on her door and when she saw the state of his condition, she responded, "Go away." He said: "Please, won't you just give me a chance? I'm a piano player." She was desperate, so she let him in. After his performance, she couldn't believe her ears. "Wow! That sounded great – best I've heard in years. What was the name of that song?" The bum answered, "Oh, it's called 'I Love Me Wife So Much I Took A Big Dump'." "Oh," said the lady, "how unusual, would you play another?" He proceeded to play another tune and again she was astounded by the performance. "That was fantastic," she said. "What was the name of that tune?" "That one is called 'I Took My Wife From Behind And Made A Mess All Over That Carpet'." Again she commented: "How unusual," adding "you've got the job, but if anyone asks the names of your songs, please don't tell them. And do something about your clothes; you look terrible. Go and buy a tux for the party." The bum was happy about his new job and happy to buy a tuxedo but, as he had never bought one before, he wound up getting one that was three sizes too small. At the big party, the crowd was amazed at his performance. He bowed at the crowd back and forth and ripped out the whole rear end of his trousers. One lady stepped forward clapping and said, "Sir, you are a great piano player but do you know you have a hairy ass and your balls are hanging out?" With a smile, the bum replied, "Know it, lady? I wrote it."

Dancing with her was like moving a piano.

Ring Lardner

➤ What do you get when you drop a piano down a mine shaft? A flat minor.

PRe-menstRuaL Tension

Hollywood's first case of syphilis.

Bette Davis on Joan Crawford

➤ Have you heard about the new American radio station called WPMT? Each month, they play two weeks of love songs, one week of blues, one week of ragtime and two days of death metal.

➤ How can you tell which bottle contains the PMT medicine? It's the one with bite marks on the cap.

➻ What's the difference between a woman with PMT and a pit bull? Lipstick.

➻ What's the difference between mad cow disease and PMT? Nothing.

POETRY

There are two ways of disliking poetry. One is to dislike it; the other is to read Pope.

Oscar Wilde on Alexander Pope

➻ At the National Improvised Poetry Competition, there were two finalists. One was an Oxford graduate, the other a dustbin man from Suffolk. As a tiebreak they had two minutes to make up a poem containing the word 'Timbuktu.' The Oxford graduate read his poem first:

> We came across the desert,
> Miles across the sand,
> Both on camels, me and you,
> On our search for Timbuktu.

The audience cheered and thought the bumpkin would have no chance against so eloquent an effort. However, the dustbin man won hands-down with his effort:

> Me and Tom a-huntin' went
> Met three birds in a field in Kent

They were three and us but two
So I bucked one and Timbuktu!

POLICE

➥ A farmer is in court fighting for a large insurance claim following a serious road accident he didn't cause. He is being questioned by the insurance company's lawyer and is being given a hard time because of his conflicting statements. The lawyer asks, "So, Farmer Brown; you are trying to claim substantial damages from the person you claim caused the accident, yet I have a sworn statement from the police officer who was present at the scene claiming that when asked how you were feeling, immediately following the accident, you said, and I quote, 'I'm fine, officer; in fact, I've never felt better in my life!'" There is a gasp around the courtroom. "Now, is this or is this not true, Farmer Brown?" continues the brief. "Well, yes, but..." the farmer starts, but he is interrupted by the barrister: "Just a simple yes or no answer will suffice, Farmer Brown." "Yes," says Farmer Brown. After a while, it was the turn of the lawyer for the farmer's insurance to question him. "So, Farmer Brown, tell us the exact circumstances surrounding your statement of good health that my learned friend just made you discuss," the barrister says to the farmer. "Well, sir, as I was trying to say," Farmer Brown explains, "I had just had this horrific accident and I was lying in the middle of the road injured. My horse had been injured, too, and so had my dog. So, after a little while a policeman comes up to the horse, sees it struggling for life and shoots it. Then he walks over to my dog, hears it howling and shoots it. Then he walks over to me, bleeding on the ground, and says, 'How are you, sir?' Now what the hell would you have said in those circumstances?"

↦ A man gets himself an Audi TT with a share bonus windfall at work and takes Friday night to drive it around the M25. As he gets more used to the car, he starts to go faster and faster. Eventually he winds up at over 100 miles per hour. Just as the needle goes over the hundred, he sees flashing lights in his rear-view mirror and he pulls over. The policeman walks up to his window, leans in and says, "Look here, mate, I've had a rough day, I'm nearly off, so if you can give me an excuse I've never heard before I'll let you off the ticket, the fine and the driving ban." The man can't believe his potential luck and excitedly says, "Well officer, my wife ran away with a policeman last week and I was driving so quickly away from you 'cos I thought you were trying to give her back!" "You take it easy sir, and have a good weekend," said the policeman as he turned to go back to his car.

A vague uneasiness – the police. It's like when you suddenly understand you have to undress in front of a doctor.

Ugo Betti

↦ A mounted policeman was on patrol one day when he comes across a kid on a shiny new bicycle. The policeman leans down to the boy and says, "That's a nice shiny bike. Did Father Christmas bring it for you?" "He sure did," says the boy, all pleased with himself. Then the cop sits back up and writes the boy a £25 fine. "Next year, boy," he says, "ask Father Christmas to put a licence plate on it, too." The boy is really annoyed, so decides to get his own back. He looks up at the policeman and says, "That's a fine horse. Did Father Christmas bring it for you?" The policeman, thinking he will humour the boy, says, "He sure did," and is pretty pleased with himself. The boy then looks down underneath the horse and back up at the policeman before saying, "Next year, officer, perhaps you could ask Father Christmas to put the prick underneath the horse instead of on top!"

The Metropolitan Police Force is abbreviated to the 'Met' to give more of its members a chance of spelling it.

Mike Barfield

↠ What's the difference between cinema snacks and pictures of naked policewomen? One's popcorn and the other's cop porn!

↠ What's the only animal with an arsehole in the middle of its back? A police horse.

POLITICS

↠ A fool and his money are soon elected.

↠ A president of a democracy is a man who is always ready, willing and able to lay down your life for his country.

➼ A well-known politician dies and goes to heaven. At the Pearly Gates he is met by St Peter and led in. St Peter speaks: "Well, you committed a few teeny-weenie sins while you were alive, didn't you? Lying is something we're a bit hot on at the moment, and, as a politician..." "Say no more," says the politician, "you've got me there." "Right, then, since you did so much good generally for your country, we're prepared to let you in, but you'll have to do penance for two years. You will have to spend that time with this woman." At this, the most hideously deformed, smelly, gossiping woman appears. The politician appears to blanch slightly, but says: "Fair enough; I guess it's worth it for eternity in paradise." "Good man, this way now." St Peter leads them through a door into a vast chamber, filled with white-robed couples, chatting and laughing with each other. Sweet music and the aroma of rose blossom fill the air, and angels and cherubs flutter about. Suddenly, the politician notices his old rival, whose death had preceded his by a matter of weeks. Amazingly, this man is arm-in-arm with a beautiful model. "What the hell is this?" storms the politician. "That man was the worst thing to happen to my country for 200 years. He destroyed everything I stood for, and was totally dishonest in doing it. How come I get two years with this hag, while he gets to cavort with a beautiful model?" "Steady on," says St Peter, "let me explain. That's not your rival doing his penance, it's the model doing hers."

➼ Ex-President Bill Clinton dies and goes to Hell. Satan, who's been waiting for him at the gate, greets him warmly. Now it turns out that Hell is a bit full at the moment, so Bill will be replacing some lucky person, who will get to go up to "the other place" instead. The good news for Bill is that he gets to choose who he can replace. Satan tells Bill to follow him as he leads him to three doorways. Satan opens the first door and Bill sees a man chained to the wall, smashing big rocks into smaller ones with a big hammer. At the sight of this, Bill goes pale and says, "Oh, no, I couldn't handle that: no way." Satan opens the second door and Bill sees a man up to his neck in mud, just able to breathe and keeping his head above water. At the sight of this, Bill goes even paler, and says, "Oh, no, I couldn't handle that, no way." Satan opens the third door and Bill sees a man tied to a pole, totally naked. Kneeling in front of him is Monica Lewinsky, giving him a blowjob. At the sight of this, Bill gets a bit of colour back in his cheeks. "Well, I think I could handle this," he says. "Great choice," says the Devil. "Monica – you can go now."

➤ First man: "There's a guy who lives up the street from me who used to work in construction. One day last year his hand got run over by a bulldozer. Whatever those doctors did, it's really amazing – today he's a concert pianist." Second man: "That's nothing. I knew a guy in college – laziest bum I ever knew. He was really fat and out of shape. He was trying to hitch a ride one day and got hit by a truck. Broke nearly every damn bone in his body. Somehow they put him back together better than he was before. Now he's a triathlete and he's planning to try out for the Olympics." Third man: "Yeah, well I knew this poor retarded kid. He couldn't do a whole lot, but someone at the dynamite factory got charitable and gave him a job as a stock boy. He was working in the warehouse one day and got locked in. It was dark and he couldn't find the door. Not being too bright, he lit a match to try to find his way. The whole place exploded. All they could find of him was a few fingers and his eyebrows. From that little bit they were able to put him back together and today that kid is the president of the USA."

➝ Between the pigeons and the politicians, it's hard to keep the courthouse clean.

➝ Diplomacy is the art of saying "Nice doggy" until you find a large enough rock.

Politicians are the same all over. They promise to build a bridge even where there is no river.

Nikita Khruschev, 1894 – 1971

➝ George Tenet, Director of the CIA, was once called before the American Congress to explain why US intelligence forces were unaware that India and Pakistan were both about to start detonating nuclear weapons. Reports suggest that Tenet blamed the lapse on the workload involved in finding and killing all of Bill Clinton's former business associates, adding, "We've got most of them now, though, so soon it'll be business as usual."

➝ It has been discovered that lawyers are the larval stage of politicians.

➝ Japanese state visitors on a historic trip to Britain recently expressed their regret over the horrific suffering experienced by prisoners of war during World War II. Gordon Brown later expressed some confusion as to whether the Japanese had actually apologised or not, saying, "Well, we're not sure. What does 'Velly Solly' mean?"

↔ Nappies and government ministers need to be changed frequently, and for much the same reason.

↔ Notoriously stupid American politician Jeb Bush has announced that he will be following in his brother's and father's footsteps, and standing for president, but he has yet to decide when. One colleague close to Jeb Bush has said campaign officials are praying that it happens to be a year when there's going to be an election.

↔ Recent discoveries of ancient primate remains suggest that humans evolved in several different places at the same time. That fits predictive models based on the British political system – a close look at Whitehall, the Houses of Parliament, Downing Street and Buckingham Palace clearly shows that there is all sorts of monkey business going on all over the place.

↔ Reports from military intelligence sources discovered some years ago that Iraqi president Saddam Hussein placed his wife under house arrest, and forbid her to leave the palace. The presidential compound contained over 100 rooms, a bowling alley, indoor and outdoor pools and three satellite dishes. Civil liberties groups in the UK immediately condemned Hussein for subjecting his own wife to a regime even worse that than suffered by British convicts.

↔ Unemployed French citizens occupied government buildings recently as part of a protest movement demanding greater social security benefits. The disturbance was quickly settled however, when the French government appealed to the Germans to send the tanks back in.

•• Rumour has it that both Tony Blair and Paddy Ashdown are left-handed...That's peculiar for politicians because they are all, without exception, under-handed.

•• The May Day parade in Moscow is the largest, most important military parade of the year. For the 1993 parade, Yeltsin and Gorbachev invited Bill Clinton to come and watch it with them. The parade commenced with a battalion of tanks, followed by a division of infantry, followed by armoured personnel carriers and mobile artillery. They had mobile ballistic missile launchers, electronic jamming vehicles, and throughout the entire time the formations were overflown by squadrons of the most advanced interceptors, fighters, and long-range strategic bombers. Clinton was suitably impressed. Then he noticed that, way back at the end of the parade, there was a disorganized, messy bunch of men in rumpled suits tagging along behind the last artillery pieces. "Who are they?" he asked. "Ah," said Yeltsin, "those are our economists." "But I thought this parade was military..." said Clinton, confused. "Mr Clinton," said Gorbachev, "have you SEEN the damage those men can do?"

•• This bloke was in Devon, walking along a country path, when he noticed a young lad over to one side busy making something. He took a closer look, and was horrified to see that the boy was playing with cow manure. A bit taken aback, he went over and said, "What on earth are you doing, lad?" The boy looked up and said, "I'm making David Cameron." Amazed, and unable to think of anything sensible to say, he asked "Cameron? Why are you making David Cameron? Why not Gordon Brown?" The boy looked at him seriously and said, "Oh no, I could never make Gordon Brown." "Really?

Why's that?" asked the man. The lad shrugged, and replied, "Come off it. There's not enough bullshit in all of Devon to make Gordon Brown."

Politics and the fate of mankind are shaped by men without ideals and without greatness. Men who have greatness within them don't go in for politics.

Albert Camus, 1913 – 1960, Notebooks

↦ What do you call a feeding ground for corrupt Scottish sharks? Westminster.

↦ We need either less corruption or more chance to participate in it.

↦ What do you call a man who ignores doctors' advice? The Health Secretary.

↦ What do you get when you cross a lesbian Rottweiler with a perverted draft dodger? Chelsea Clinton.

↦ What is a politician's seven-course dinner? A piece of essential vote-winning employment for catering staff.

POO

↦ What's brown and sits on a piano stool? Beethoven's First Movement.

➡ This bloke is really desperate for a shit, so he nips into a nearby crowded pub. He looks around and sees that the toilets are upstairs, so he pops up there. When he gets up to the first floor, though, he can't find the damn things anywhere. Eventually, after several minutes of hunting around, he finds a hole in the floor and decides it's better than dumping on the floor, so he craps into it. When he's finished up, he goes back downstairs thinking he'll have a quick beer. To his amazement, the place is deserted; just the landlord standing behind the bar. "Where is everyone?" he asks. The landlord looks at him in amazement. "Where the hell were you when the shit hit the fan?"

A pile of shit in a silk stocking.
Napoleon Bonaparte, 1769 – 1821, on Talleyrand

➡ Two men are changing after a sweaty game of squash. One notices that the other has a cork up his arse. He says, "Um, I couldn't help noticing, but how the hell did you get that cork up your arse?" The other man says, "Well, um, yes: it's a bit embarrassing, really. I was walking along a beach barefoot when I trip over this old bottle. I pick it up, take the cork out and whoosh! Out pops a huge red man with a turban on his head, floating in space in front of me. He says 'I am a genie. I grant you one wish. What will it be?' So I – rather foolishly, upon reflection – said, 'No shit!'"

➡ What's brown and sticky? A stick!

➡ What do you call a vegetarian with diarrhoea? A salad shooter.

➻ What do Eskimos get if they sit on ice for too long? Polaroids.

PORNOGRaPHY

➻ A husband and wife went to see a poncy European art movie at their local cinema. It was pretty strong stuff and involved a lot of graphic sex – all in the name of art, of course, nothing porno about it. The husband thought it was great, but the wife was a bit disturbed by the content, particularly by a scene of people masturbating which left nothing to the imagination. As the couple were having a drink afterwards, the wife said to her husband, "You know dear, I find it very difficult to deal with masturbation in the movies," to which the husband replied, "Oh, sorry love, I'll stop doing it then!"

> **In adolescence, pornography is a substitute**
> **for sex, whereas in adulthood sex is a**
> **substitute for pornography.**
> *Edmund White*

➻ How do you know when a male porn star is in your petrol station? Just before the petrol tank's full, he pulls out the hose and sprays petrol all over the car.

➻ What's the difference between a Pussycat Dolls video and a porno? The porno has better music!

PRIESTS

➻ A drunk staggers into church and manages to make his way into one of the confessionals. He sits there in silence. The priest coughs once to get the man's attention, but the man just ignores him and sits there. The priest can see that the man isn't asleep so he coughs again, only this time louder. The man still ignores him. The priest then knocks on the divider in a last attempt to get the man to speak. This seems to have the desired effect, and the man shouts to the priest, "It's no use knocking, there's no bloody paper in this one, either!"

> **Whatever a theologian regards as true must be false; there you have almost a criterion of truth.**
>
> *Friedrich Nietzsche, 1844 – 1900, The Antichrist*

➻ A man goes to confession. In the booth he says, "Forgive me, Father, for I have sinned. I... almost... had an affair with a woman." "Almost? What do you mean 'almost'?" says the priest, not really understanding what the man is going on about. "Well, Father," the man continues, "we got undressed and rubbed against one another, but then we both thought better of it and so we stopped." "Very good," says the priest, "but rubbing up against it is just the same as putting it in. You must not go near that woman again. You must say five Hail Marys and you must put £50 in the donation box by the door." The man thanks the priest and walks to the door of the church. He stops by the donation box, pauses and then starts to leave. The priest runs up to him and says, "Oi, I saw that – you didn't put anything in the donation box did you?" "Well no, I didn't Father," the man says, "I rubbed up against it, and as you say, that's the same as putting it in!"

➼ A priest is shopping in the local town when he returns to his car and discovers he has been given a parking ticket. The traffic warden is still writing out the ticket when he arrives. The priest asks, "Oh, you couldn't waive the ticket could you now son?" But the traffic warden replies, "Oh, Father, I'm so sorry, but I've begun to write it and I'm not allowed to stop halfway through. If you'd just been a minute quicker..." "Oh well," says the priest, "I'm terrible with parking, I never remember what the time is or where I've parked, to be sure." "That's very decent of you, Father," says the traffic warden, "quite often when this happens us traffic wardens get given a whole load of abuse." "Oh my goodness, that's awful," says the priest, "after all you're only doing your job aren't you? Now, there's a tea party at the abbey this Sunday, would you like to come over?" "Well, Father, that's very nice of you to ask, I'd love to. And thanks again for being so understanding," says the traffic warden. "And perhaps you'd like to bring your father and your mother, too," says the priest, "I could marry the pair of them while I'm at it!"

Why do born-again people so often make you wish they'd never been born the first time?

Katherine Whitehorn, in the Observer newspaper

➤ A priest thinks his sermons need modernizing a bit, so he decides to preach on windsurfing instead of the usual fire and brimstone, or condemnation of sex. He tells his wife, who thinks it's a great idea, despite the priest's inexperience with the subject matter, but is sorry she won't be able to hear his new-style sermon because she has a sick friend to see. On his way to church the priest has second thoughts. "I don't know a thing about windsurfing and I can't relate it to anything," he said to himself. "I'll just stick to what I know," and proceeded to preach his usual sermon on the sinfulness of sex. After the service, and before the priest gets home, one of the lay readers walks past the priest's house. The priest's wife is back and out doing some gardening. "Great sermon today," says the lay reader. "That's a surprise," said the wife, "because he only tried it twice, and he fell off both times!"

➤ There are two priests who ride bicycles to their parish church every week. One day one of the priests shows up to 'work' without his bicycle. The other priest says to him, "Where has your bike gone, Father Michael?" to which Father Michael replies, "I'm not really sure, but I think it's been stolen!" The other priest tells him to read out the Ten Commandments at the next sermon he gives, and by the time he gets to "Thou Shalt Not Steal", someone will own up to stealing the bicycle from him. The next time the two priests see each other they are both on bicycles again. The other priest asks Father Michael, "So you made the thief own up, then, did you father?" Father Michael says, "Well, not really. I took your advice, sure enough, and I was reading out the Ten Commandments. I got to 'Thou Shalt Not Commit Adultery', when I all of a sudden remembered where I'd left my bike!"

PRISON

•• An accountant is thrown in prison for fraud and is seriously worried to see that his cellmate is a huge body-builder type with no hair and covered in tattoos. His new cellmate says, "Don't worry, little man, I'm in here for white collar crime as well." The accountant says, "Phew, that's lucky, I'm in for insider dealing and tax evasion. What about you?" The cellmate replies, "I murdered three priests!"

•• It was a busy day for the electric chair. Three men were up for their death sentences. The first man was a political scientist from Oxford. He was strapped into the chair and asked if he had any final comments. He replied, "I had a promising career in politics until...I was framed, I tell you – framed!" His tirade was interrupted by the flick of the switch, but nothing happened. As was the custom at this particular prison, the Oxford man was taken from the chair and allowed to live after the failed execution attempt. The second man was a computer scientist from Cambridge. His final words were, "I had a promising career in computing, but I didn't think that tampering with the national air traffic control system would crash that many planes..." Again, the electrical switch was flipped and again nothing happened. The man was released from the chair and allowed to live. The third man was an electrical engineer, named Kev, from Loughborough University. Kev was strapped into the chair and asked if he had any final words. He says, "I had a promising career as an electrical engineer, but... Hey, wait a moment....If you cross that red wire over there with that blue wire, this thing will work."

➥ A cowboy and a biker are on Death Row, and are to be executed on the same day. The day comes, and they are brought to the gas chamber. The warden asks the cowboy if he has a last request, to which the cowboy replies: "Ah shore do, warden. Ah'd be mighty grateful if'n yoo'd play 'Achy Breaky Heart' fur me bahfore ah hafta go." "Sure enough, cowboy, we can do that," says the warden. He turns to the biker, "And you, biker, what's your last request?" "That you kill me first."

A reader senses that Joan Crawford, idol of an age, would have made an exemplary prison matron, possibly at Buchenwald. She had the requisite sadism and taste for violence.

Harriet van Horne, 1921 – 1998, on reading a biography of Joan Crawford

➥ An inmate went to see the prison doctor, and was dismayed to be told that he needed to have one of his kidneys removed. "Look," said the prisoner, "You're already whipped out my tonsils, my adenoids, my spleen and my gall-bladder, and now you want my kidney? I only came to you in the first place to see if you could get me out of here!" The doctor was unruffled. "And that's exactly what I am doing," he replied, "bit by bit..."

PSYCHIATRISTS

➥ "Doctor, I keep thinking that I'm a deck of cards." Psychiatrist: "Sit over there and I'll deal with you later."

↦ "Oh, doctor," moaned the woman to the psychiatrist. "Everyone calls me a nymphomaniac." "I understand," said the doctor, "but I'll be able to take better notes if you'll let go of my penis."

↦ "Doctor, I don't understand what's going on with me. It's really strange, sometimes I feel like a tepee." The doctor thinks about it for a while and then urges the man to continue. So, the man continues, "Other times, I feel like a wigwam." To which the doctor says: "I wouldn't worry about it, Fred, you're just two tents."

Forget about smacking children, when are we going to start hitting child psychologists?

Julie Burchill

↦ A child psychologist for a school is asked to see a pupil who draws all his pictures with black and brown crayons. He talks to him. Nothing obvious. He gives him projective tests. Nothing shows up. Finally, in desperation, he gives him some paper and a box of crayons. "Oh goody," says the boy, "I got an old box in school and only black and brown were left."

↦ A man walked into a psychiatrist's office, sat down and took out a pack of cigarettes. He removed a cigarette from the pack, unrolled it, and stuffed the tobacco up his nose. The shrink frowned and said, "I see you need my help." The guy said, "Yeah doctor. Got a match?"

➡ A man walked into the psychiatrist's office with a bit of buttered toast on his head, fried eggs on each shoulder, a sausage in his left nostril and a strip of bacon tied to each eyebrow. The psychiatrist looked at him, then calmly asked, "What seems to be the problem, sir?" The man looked at him, and replied, "Well, I'm really worried about my brother."

➡ A man walks into the office of an eminent psychiatrist and sits down to explain his problem. "Yes, well, you see, I've got this problem," the man says. "I keep hallucinating that I'm a dog. A large, white, hairy Dulux dog. It's crazy. I don't know what to do!" "Ah, a common canine complex," said the doctor soothingly. "It's all right: we can cure this together if we work hard and concentrate. Come over here, lie down on the couch and tell me more about it." "Oh no, doctor," the man says, horrified, "I'm not allowed on the furniture."

**Psychiatrists have a financial interest in
being wrong; the more children they can disturb,
the larger their adult clientele.**

Geoffrey Robertson

➡ A psychiatrist, who was just starting out, advertised his clinic as follows: "Satisfaction guaranteed or your mania back."

➡ After years of battling with himself, John finally went to a psychiatrist. "Doc," he said, "I've got trouble. Every time I get into bed, I think there's somebody under it. If I get under the bed, I think there's somebody on top of it. I know there's no one in my bed or under my bed, but it doesn't matter, I have to check. You have to help me, it's been going on for years and I am going mad." "It's all in your head. Just put yourself in my hands for two years," said the shrink. "Come to me three times a week, and I'll cure your fears." "How much do you charge?" asked John, suspiciously. "£50 per visit." "£50, three times a week, for two years?" chokes John. "No way!" and he storms off. Six months later the doctor meets John on the street. "Why didn't you ever come to see me again?" asked the psychiatrist. "£50 a visit? A bartender cured me for the price of a beer." "Is that so?" says the doctor scornfully, "How?" "He told me to cut the legs off the bed!"

↪ Be a better psychiatrist and the world will beat a psychopath to your door.

↪ Hypnotist: "Alright, Mr Henry, when I say wake up you will no longer be shy but full of confidence and be able to speak your mind... Wake up." Patient: "Right, you! How about giving me a refund, you money-grabbing old quack?"

↪ I had to kill my psychiatrist. He helped me a lot, but he just knew too much.

↪ I think, therefore I am confused.

↪ Patient walks into a doctor's office. Patient: "Doc, Doc, people ignore me." Doctor: "Next."

↪ Patient: "Doc, Doc, I can't stop stealing things." Psychiatrist: "Take these pills. They should help you." Patient: "But what if they don't?" Psychiatrist: "Then I'll take a wide-screen TV off you."

↦ Patient: "Doc, Doc, I keep thinking I'm a billiard ball." Psychiatrist: "Get to the end of the queue."

↦ Patient: "Doc, Doc, I keep thinking I'm a dustbin." Psychiatrist: "Don't talk such rubbish."

↦ Patient: "Doc, Doc, I keep thinking I'm a pair of curtains." Psychiatrist: "Pull yourself together."

↦ Patient: "Doc, Doc, I keep thinking I'm invisible." Psychiatrist: "Who said that?"

↦ Patient: "Doc, Doc, my wife thinks I'm crazy because I like sausages." Psychiatrist: "Nonsense! I like sausages too." Patient: "Good, you should come and see my collection. I've got hundreds."

I refuse to endure months of expensive humiliation only to be told that at the age of four I was in love with my rocking-horse.

Noel Coward on psychology

↦ Patient: "Doc, Doc, my wife thinks she's a refrigerator." Psychiatrist: "Don't worry, it will pass." Man: "But, doctor, when she sleeps with her mouth open, the damn light keeps me awake."

↦ Patient: "Doc, Doc, people tell me I'm a wheelbarrow." Psychiatrist: "Don't let them push you around."

➟ Patient: "Doc, Doc, you must help me. I'm under such a lot of stress, I keep losing my temper with people." Doctor: "Tell me about your problem." Patient: "I just did, you stupid bastard."

➟ Psychiatrist: "What's wrong with your brother?" Sister: "He thinks he's a chicken." Psychiatrist: "I see. And how long has be been acting like a chicken?" Sister: "Three years. We would have come in sooner, but we needed the eggs."

➟ Three patients in a mental institution prepare for an examination given by the head psychiatrist. If the patients pass the exam, they will be free to leave the hospital and go back to a normal life. However, if they fail, the institution will detain them for another five years. The doctor takes the three patients to the top of a diving board looking over an empty swimming pool, and asks the first patient to jump. The first patient jumps headfirst into the pool and breaks both arms. The second patient, who has just witnessed what has happened, jumps enthusiastically into the empty pool and breaks both legs. The third patient looks over the side and backs off from the diving board. "Congratulations! You're a free man. Just tell me, why didn't you jump?" asked the doctor. "Well, doc, I can't swim!"

➟ Wife: "Doc, Doc, my husband thinks he's a horse." Psychiatrist: "He is just probably a little stressed out and needs some rest." Wife: "But he kicks chairs and eats grass and doesn't even sleep in the bed." Psychiatrist: "Well, in that case, it looks like he may need a lot of help, but it may cost quite a lot of money for prolonged treatment." Wife: "Oh, you don't have to worry about the money part. Last Sunday he won the Grand National."

➜ Psychiatrist: "What's your problem?" Patient: "I think I'm a chicken." Psychiatrist: "And how long has this been going on?" Patient: "Ever since I was an egg."

PUNS

➜ A crushingly poor farmer was down to his last meal. The only thing he had in the world, apart from his mud hut and the rags he wore, was his talking mule. This particular talking mule had a snappy line in comedy, and a great stand-up routine with a dry, understated type of humour, so the farmer was reluctant to sell up, but there was no choice. With much regret, he set off to the city to sell the mule. Relying on the mule's natural talents, he stopped at a street corner and let the mule go for it. Well, the mule was so funny that within five minutes he had a whole crowd around, rolling in the street with laughter. One guy near the front said, "Look, I'm a talent agent, and I've got to have that mule." "What will you offer?" asked the farmer. "I don't have any cash," said the man, "but I'll tell you what. Here is my key-ring, my Porsche, my flat in town, my house in the country — they're all yours. These people here can bear witness to the deal." "Alright," said the farmer, and they made the exchange. The agent walked off with the mule, and most of the people followed, while the farmer adjusted to the idea of being a wealthy property-owner. "That didn't take long," he mused. "Ahh," replied a guy who hadn't left the area, "A mule that is funny is soon bartered..."

➡ A frog goes into a London bank and approaches the teller. He can see from her nameplate that the teller's name is Patricia Whack. He says, "Ms Whack, I'd like to get a loan to buy a boat and go on a long vacation." Patti looks at the frog in disbelief and asks how much he wants to borrow. The frog says £30,000. The teller asks his name and the frog says that his name is Kermit Jagger and that it's OK, he knows the bank manager. Patti explains that £30,000 is a substantial amount of money and that he will need to secure the loan. She asks if he has anything he can use as collateral. The frog says, "Sure. I have this," and he produces a tiny pink porcelain elephant, about half an inch tall. It's bright pink and perfectly formed, but of no obvious visible value. Very confused, Patti explains that she'll have to consult with the manager and disappears into a back office. She finds the manager and reports: "There's a frog called Kermit Jagger out there who claims to know you, and he wants to borrow £30,000. He wants to use this as collateral," she says, holding up the tiny pink elephant. "I mean, what the heck is this?" The bank manager looks back at her and says: "It's a knick-knack, Patti Whack. Give the frog a loan. His old man's a Rolling Stone!"

➡ A young guy had a job bagging groceries at the supermarket. One day, the shop got a flashy new machine for squeezing the juice out of fresh fruit. Because of the potential danger, someone from the shop would have to work the machine. Intrigued, the guy asked if he could switch jobs, but his request was denied. The store manager shook his head sadly, and said, "Sorry lad, but baggers can't be juicers."

➻ A rich bloke decided to have himself cloned. After a long and expensive developmental process a clone was created and specially matured. Unsurprisingly, it turned out to be an exact physical duplicate of the man. Mentally, however, something went wrong, and all the clone could do was spew forth the most vile language and filthy profanities. After a couple of weeks of putting up with this torrent and trying to find out if the clone could respond or be somehow healed or repaired, the bloke decided to cut his losses. He took the clone up into the mountains, went to the edge of a steep cliff and pushed the clone over the edge. A policeman popped out from behind a tree and said, "I'm afraid you're under arrest, sir. I'm going to have to ask you to come with me." The bloke sighed, "Look, officer, it isn't what it looks like. I didn't murder anyone; that wasn't a real person." The officer shook his head. "I didn't say anything about murder, sir. I'm arresting you under suspicion of making an obscene clone fall."

There's many a man hath more hair than wit.

William Shakespeare, The Comedy of Errors

➻ A team of scientists were nominated for the Nobel Prize. They had used dental equipment to discover and measure the smallest particles yet known to man. They became known as "The Graders of the Flossed Quark..."

➻ A three-legged dog walks into a saloon in the Old West. He slides up to the bar and announces: "I'm looking for the man who shot my paw."

➥ Deep in the jungles of Africa lived two tribes, and they hated each other. One tribe lived at the foot of a gigantic mountain. They panned for gold in the river and mined for gold in the mountain. There was lots of gold in the area, and they were extremely rich. The other tribe lived in a swampland area and lived on crocodiles and fish, and they had nothing. They were extremely poor. The tribes never visited each other except to raid each others' grass huts and plunder them. There wasn't much gain for the rich tribe in raiding the poor tribe, but they did it out of a sense of vengeance for the poor tribe's raids, and to try to get their stuff back. One day the Chief of the rich tribe got wind of a raid planned for the following day. The poor tribe were going to sneak in and steal his golden throne. The Chief was furious. Determined not to let them get away with it, he called his wise man over to advise him. The wise man told him, "Chief, you will have to make your throne disappear. Get some men to stick long wooden poles into the grass roof. Then, using ropes, your strongest men can hide the throne up in the roof of your grass palace. The raiders will never think to look up there." The Chief thought this was a great idea, and immediately ordered it to be done. The next day, as expected, the poor tribe attacked and swept through the village, searching everywhere. They didn't find a thing. The rich tribe were hiding in the mines in the mountains, and all the valuables were safely hidden away on top of the throne. When the raiders had gone the tribe came out and went back down to their village, and had a great celebration. The Chief stood in the centre of his palace, looked up at the roof, and gloated, "We fooled those idiots! Right over their heads, and they missed it!" Suddenly there were several tremendous bangs. The wooden poles supporting the gold throne snapped. Two tons of gold came crashing down on top of the Chief, and killed him stone dead — which just goes to show you that people who live in grass houses shouldn't stow thrones.

➻ An old farmer had spent his life collecting tractors. Whenever one finally broke down or became hopelessly out of date, he refused to sell it, instead keeping it in a large barn. He even bought tractors that were no longer any use from other farmers. He tidied up the bodywork and polished them, treating them like museum exhibits. Eventually, when it was time for him to retire, he decided to sell off his massive collection so that he could live comfortably with his wife in a nice country cottage. So he put advertisements in local and national papers, inviting offers. He didn't have long to wait. A few days later, he received a letter from a businessman whose company had built some of the tractors mentioned in the advert many years before, and who had an interest in old vehicles himself. The two men arranged to meet in the farmer's local pub on the following Sunday. The day came and the businessman arrived. Despite the heavy clouds of pipe smoke, the two passed an hour in most pleasant conversation, and turned out to have much in common. "Well," sighed the farmer eventually, "I haven't had such a good natter for a long time, but I suppose it's about time we got down to business, eh?" "Yes, I suppose so," replied the other, "but maybe we could go somewhere else? I'm finding it hard to think in such a smoky atmosphere." The farmer grinned, and said "Ah, there's no need for that. Watch this!" He then proceeded to take an amazingly long, deep breath, and sucked in every last wisp of smoke in the room. He then turned to the window behind him and blew all the smoke out of the pub. "Wow! How the hell did you manage that?" asked the businessman, astonished. "Oh, it was nothing," replied the farmer, "After all, I am an ex-tractor fan."

➤ In days of yore, a doughty knight was on a vital quest. The life of the King hung in the balance, for unless he was able to rush a special potion back to the palace that very day the King would surely die. He was still about a hundred miles from the palace when his horse, exhausted from the rate at which the knight was pushing it, became lame. Well, through the woods he could see a small inn, so he ran and ran up to the inn as fast as he could. He headed straight for the stables, found the inn's stable-keeper, and shouted, "I must have a horse! The life of the King hangs in the balance, for he will surely die unless I can get a special potion back to him this very day." The stable-keeper shook his old, grizzled head regretfully, and said, "Ahh, I'm dreadful sorry, Sir Knight. We haven't got any horses in the stable today. Patrons are a bit light on the ground at this point in the season, what with the crops and all." The knight was distraught. "This is disastrous! Oh, evil chance! You must have some steed, good man — a pony, a donkey, even a mule? Please?" The stable-keeper shook his head again, lank grey hair flying everywhere. "No, Sir Knight, we've not got anything at all. Well...no. No, nothing." The knight's eyes lit up. "You had an idea! What? Whatever it is, I'll take it and pay well." The stable-keeper sighed and said, "Well, it's not pretty, but we do have a specially-trained shaggy war-mastiff." "A war-mastiff?" asked the knight, "A dog? Show me!" So the stable-keeper escorted the knight into one of the stables. Inside was a dog like none the knight had ever seen. It was a giant, as tall at the knight himself. It also stank. It was the dirtiest, hairiest, mangiest, sorriest-looking dog that the knight had clapped eyes on in his entire life. He was revolted, but duty called..."It'll do," said the knight with resignation, "Saddle it up, stout stable-keeper." The stable-keeper nodded and headed over to the wall, where a saddle was hanging. As he reached for it, however, he started coughing so hard he convulsed. He fell on to the floor and lay there for 30 seconds, gasping, while the knight looked on impatiently. He recovered, got to his feet again, and reached for the saddle. Again, he was seized by coughing and convulsions, and he fell over. Finally, he struggled to his feet, looked at the knight regretfully, and said "I'm most dreadful sorry, sir knight, but I can't do it." "What?" asked the knight, thunderstruck, "Why not?" The stable-keeper shook his head. "I can't do it. I can't send a knight out on a dog like this."

→ June 3, 1861. Out here, at the frontier, it's very easy to wonder if maybe those old missionaries weren't right all those centuries ago, and I have actually come to the edge of the world. There's no other white man — or woman, damn it — for 100 miles in any direction. I devote my time to reading my copy of the Bible and tending my patch of cucumbers. This outpost was supposed to hold back the Indians, but that's a joke, and it seems to be unnecessary, anyway. June 11, 1861. I was excited this morning by an interesting, if silent, visitor. One of the Indians from the tribe that lives nearby stood at the top of the hill and watched me perform my chores for over an hour, and then left without a word. Contact with the local natives is a thrilling prospect, and I have resolved to do nothing to scare them away. June 19, 1861. Breakthrough! I have finally managed to convince the Indians to make proper contact. I taught them the word for "fort", which seemed like a simple enough place to begin. They in turn taught me the Indian word "toitonka", which refers to a mysterious device, a tiny horseless carriage made of metal. I envy these people their simplicity. June 22, 1861. Today I was greatly flattered to be taken to the Indians' village. It is built on one of the many flat-topped plateaux, or mesas, in the area. As the buffalo herds decline, this noble tribe too will face a decline of its own. They need a fighting chance, so I will try to teach them agriculture. Their name for themselves is "Waatch," which, as far as I can make out, means "The people known as the Waatch" in their language. I am known to them — it seems that they've been observing me closely — as "Stinchapocla" which means "he who has bodily odour."

July 8, 1861. Today I received a rude awakening; I have been foolish. The Indians are in fact fully aware of agriculture, and have nothing to do with the buffalo. That makes sense, I suppose — no nomads would build a village on a mesa. Unfortunately, they are suffering from a drought, as they have no rivers on top of the mesa, and the rainfall has been poor recently. I can help at last! I have told them to dig a ditch from near the stream that runs past my fort, up the cliff, to their mesa-top fields. They seem doubtful, but they are desperate, and their shaman, Bahnee, has told them to go ahead. In the meantime, I am pickling my youngest cucumbers.

July 20, 1861. The drought is getting critical, but the ditch is complete and my pickles are now ready. I have lined the ditch with pickles. The Waatch are nervous, but I have promised them results in the morning.

July 21, 1861. Success! The stream has been diverted, and is flowing up the cliff-face to the Waatch fields. I have gained much status by what they see as a feat of magic. The shaman asked about my powerful medicine, but I came clean and told him that I was simply making use of a common fact in my world. After all, everyone knows that Dill Waters run Steep.

➹ Mama Weevil gave birth to two identical twin weevils. They grew up together, but there came a time when they had to discover the world on their own, and tearfully they separated, each to go its own weevil way. One was very successful in Hollywood, got tons of girlfriends and money, while the other didn't have much luck in its life and ended up broke, alone and miserable. He was, therefore, known as the lesser of two weevils.

**Look, he's winding up the watch of his wit;
by and by it will strike.**

William Shakespeare, The Tempest

➹ One day a snail got fed up with his reputation for being slow. He decided that he should get himself a fast car to compensate. After checking out the markets, he decided to go for the new Japanese Nissda 950-Z, which was clearly the best buy on the market, doing 0-60 in just 4.3 seconds. He went down to a car showroom, and asked about availability. The dealer was only too happy to help, after seeing the snail's platinum credit card, and assured him that he could have the car ready the following day. "Okay," said the snail, "it's a deal. But can you rebadge it for me as a 950-S? Change the paint-work to include an S, and modify the badge at the back." "Well, I guess so," said the salesman, "but it'll cost extra. Why do you want it done?" The snail smiled, "I don't mind about the price. 'S' stands for 'snail'. It's really important to me that everybody who sees me roaring past knows who's driving." The salesman thought "Fair enough", and the deal was concluded. The snail picked his car up the next day, and could be found blasting down roads and motorways happily for the rest of his life. Whenever he shot past, the people saw him zoom by and said, "Wow! Look at that S-car go!"

➻ The Russians had been purchasing huge quantities of grain from the NATO countries. This placed Russia in a weak, dependent position so they instigated a research program and invested heavily. After a year or so Russian scientists discovered a new type of grain, called Krilk, that was good to eat, yielded twice as much as normal wheat and ripened in just half the time. The only catch was that it required special treatment during milling in order to provide usable flour. Well, that was OK, and huge prairies of Krilk sprung up all over Russia, along with super-secret milling stations, highly protected black buildings that took Krilk in one side and churned bags of flour out the other. The CIA teamed up with MI6 to discover the secrets of Krilk, either to appropriate it for the West or to find a way to stop production, because Russia was no longer dependent on the NATO countries. Either way, the key was the milling process. Teams of highly-trained infiltrators tried to get into the Krilk mills, but they all failed. Gorgeous femmes fatales attempted to seduce Krilk millers, but got nowhere; the pretty-boy gigolos did no better. Spy satellites could see the outside of the buildings, but not the milling process. Nothing worked. Someone even suggested offering to purchase the information through normal channels, but that suggestion was quickly squashed. One morning the Russian representative at the United Nations sent an offensive little note to the American and British representatives about the matter, which read, "Stop wasting your money and our time. The new super-grain will remain Russian secret. There is no use spying over milled Krilk."

➻ There are two businessmen, whose names happen to be Mr Turtle and Mr Carrot and, one day, as they were coming back from lunch, Mr Turtle says to Mr Carrot: "You know, you're getting fat." To which Mr Carrot says, "You're not so slim yourself." So Mr Turtle says, "Okay, we'll see who is the least fit; race you back to the office." So the race starts and they have only got about a hundred yards down the street when Mr Turtle crosses the road in front of a car and gets knocked down. Mr Carrot sees that he's in a pretty bad way, so he rushes to the phone and calls Mr Cabbage, the ambulance driver. Mr Cabbage duly arrives and piles Mr Turtle into the ambulance and rushes to a hospital. Mr Turtle follows and as soon as he gets to the hospital he asks the nurse, Miss Cauliflower, whether he will be alright. "Miss Cauliflower, Miss Cauliflower, will Mr Turtle be alright?" She replies, "Well, I couldn't really say, you'll have to ask Dr Bean." So he rushes over to Dr Bean and says, "Dr Bean, Dr Bean, will Mr Turtle be alright?" And the doctor says, "Well, I wouldn't like to say, you'd best ask the specialist, Dr Pea." So of course, Mr Carrot rushes over to Dr Pea and says, "Dr Pea, Dr Pea, will Mr Turtle be alright?" And Doctor Pea says, "I've done all I can for him, it's all in the hands of the surgeon, Dr Turnip." So Mr Carrot waits outside the surgery for three hours until they have finished the operation and rushes up to Dr Turnip and says, "Dr Turnip, Dr Turnip, will Mr Turtle be alright?" Dr Turnip turns to him and says, "We did all we could, but I'm afraid he'll be a vegetable for the rest of his life..."

His wit's as thick as Tewksbury mustard.

William Shakespeare, Henry IV pt II

➻ There was a bloke who was famous across the world for the quality of the tulips that he grew. People used to come from all around to admire them, and to try and get the secret of how he grew them out of him. He was very cagey, and would only say, "I just put the bulbs in, and they come up perfectly." No one believed him, of course, but no one could discover what it was that he used to turn ordinary bulbs into the most beautiful tulip blooms that had ever been grown. There were whole fields of them, ranks and ranks, all identical and all perfect. Eventually, a friend of his of long standing decided to get the secret out of the tulip-grower and, if it was a simple enough trick, to maybe turn a few quid on the side. He invited his horticultural friend over one evening; they settled down to watch the football and have a few tins of beer, and once the grower started to relax, they moved on to Scotch; eventually, the friend started to gently steer the conversation towards tulips. Well, by now the grower was drunk, and his guard was down. They chatted for a while about tulips, with the friend congratulating the grower on his skill, and eventually, when the friend asked, "So, how do you get them so good, anyway?" he tapped the side of his nose and announced, "Hamsters!" Well, the friend was taken aback, and peered at the grower suspiciously to see if he was taking the piss, but he looked sincere. "Don't be daft," said the friend, "how can hamsters make ordinary tulip bulbs produce flowers the quality of yours?" "Well," said the grower, "On my other plot of land, I breed hamsters. Not just one or two, mind you, but thousands of the little buggers. God! They don't half stink out a place, I can tell you. It's appalling. Anyway, when they become adults I wait until the evening, when they're asleep, then run over them all with a huge turbo-charged steamroller that I got especially for the purpose. It's a beauty — 12,000cc of growling monster, thundering around at 40mph. When they're all accounted for, I bulldoze the mush into a machine which cans them into barrels, which I store in a big warehouse. At the start of the growing season, I go out at night with the old fertilising machine, filled up from the tins of course, and spread the mess all over the fields. Then I then get the tractor out, and plough and plough until it's all thoroughly worked into the ground. The next day I plant the bulbs, and you've seen the results for yourself." The friend paused for a moment and thought it over, then said, "Well I suppose it must work, but I really can't see how!" The tulip-grower grinned at him. "Obvious, isn't it? I copied the idea from the Dutch flower-growers, 'cos they're the real experts when you get down to it. I grow tulips from hamster jam!"

➻ There was once a wise, sensitive guy (no, really!) who loved a beautiful girl. She lived in the middle of nowhere, in a marsh where his car always got stuck. To make matters worse, her father had a gun and disliked the guy. Although the girl was fond of him, he could only get to see her by fooling her father into thinking he was someone else. However, he had a rival — a more energetic suitor. This second guy wasn't as wise or sensitive, but he was more persistent, so he bought a set of amphibious tyres for his car and, one night when her father was asleep, drove up and sneaked away with her. The moral of this is, of course, that treads rush in where wise men fear to fool.

➻ There was an organic farmer who didn't want to use a tractor on his small fields, so instead he had a pair of Shire horses to pull his plough and his wagons. Unfortunately, a group of small birds had made nests inside the horses manes, weaving the hairs together, which prevented him from hitching the reins properly. He tried everything he could think of to get rid of the birds, but no matter what he did, they just came back again. He tried lotions, potions, shields and notions. He kept the stable colder, and he kept the stable warmer. He went to horse doctors, he went to bird specialists, he went to his local MP, he went to the vet, and he even called the MAFF. He trimmed the manes down as much as he could. He tried loud bangs, cats, and little horsehair scarecrows. Nothing would make the birds leave his horses alone. Finally, he took advice from a bloke down the pub and went to see a supposed wise-woman at the end of the village. The wise-woman listened to his story, nodded, and gave him some vile-smelling yeast extract to rub into the manes. To his delight and amazement, it worked. Within two days, all the birds had gone and the horses could get back to work. The farmer was extremely pleased, but puzzled. He went back to the wise woman, and asked her "Well, you're obviously very wise, but how come your yeast extract was able to solve a problem that nothing, not even vets and bureaucrats hadn't been able to?" She smiled, and said "Ah, it's simple. Yeast is yeast, and nest is nest, and never the mane shall tweet."

PUT-DOWNS

➥ A drunken bum is sitting on a bar stool when a really high-class bird sits down next to him. He immediately turns around and says to her, "Hey, darlin'. How's about you and me getting together for a bit of how's your father? I've got a couple of Euro and you look like you could do with a little cash!" The woman looks at him coldly before replying, "What makes you think I charge by the inch?"

↠ "Are you an optical spanner? Because every time you look at me I feel my nuts tighten." "Lucky you've got nuts because you're not getting a screw."

↠ "Can I buy you a drink?" "Can I just have the money?"

↠ "Can I give you my number?" "Yes, I'll call you when my dog's on heat."

↠ "Did you know light travels faster than sound?" "That's why you seemed quite bright till you opened your mouth."

↠ "Do you always use contraception?" "Yes..." "Good, so you learned from your parents' mistake."

↠ "Do you come here often?" "No, it's just the way I laugh."

↠ "Do you like it doggy style?" "Yes – you can beg all you like, but I'll roll over and play dead."

↠ "Go out with you? Sorry, I was about to call Greenpeace and tell them to come and float you off the beach."

↠ "Go out? Yes, we could go to the zoo. They must be wondering where you've been."

↠ "Have you thought of blind dating? Then you'd only frighten them off with the smell."

↠ "Haven't I seen you before?" "Yes, I'm the receptionist from the VD clinic."

→ "Haven't I seen you somewhere before?" "Yes, that's why I stopped going there."

→ "I bet when you call one of those telephone sex lines, the woman on the other end gets an earache."

→ "I bet you're not a virgin." "You're right – not all men are as ugly as you."

→ "I didn't know they did condoms in cheese-and-onion flavour! Oh, sorry, you haven't put one on yet..."

→ "I heard you're nobody's fool. Never mind, maybe someone will adopt you."

Thou art violently carried away from grace. There is a devil haunts thee in the likeness of an old fat man; a tun of man is thy companion. Why dost thou converse with that trunk of humours, that bolting hutch of beastliness, that swoll'n parcel of dropsies, that huge bombard of sack, that stuff'd cloakbag of guts, that roasted Manningtree ox with the pudding in his belly, that reverend vice, that grey iniquity, that father ruffian, that vanity in years?

William Shakespeare, Henry IV pt I

→ "I seem to have lost my phone number, can I have yours?" "No, there's no need, I've already got your number."

→ "If I throw a stick, will you leave?"

↠ "I wish you were a door – I could bang you all day." "I doubt it; you haven't got a key that would fit my lock."

↠ "I'd like to get into your pants." "I already have one arsehole in my pants, thanks."

↠ "I'd like to leave you with one thought... It'd be one more than you've had all evening."

↠ "I'd love to fuck your brains out, but it looks like someone else got there first."

↠ "I'm an expert in mouth-to-mouth resuscitation – want a demonstration?" "I'd have to be completely dead before I let you get that close."

↠ "I've got a telepathic watch. It tells me you're not wearing any underwear." "You wish. I'm wearing underwear." "Damn, the thing's an hour fast again."

**I never forget a face – but in your case,
I'll be glad to make an exception.**

Groucho Marx, 1890 – 1977

↠ "If I blindfold my dog, I might get it to hump your leg."

↠ "If I bought you some underwear, would there be anything in it for me?" "Yes, the knowledge that you'd made my boyfriend very happy."

↦ "If I could see you naked, I could die happy." "Yeah? If I saw you naked, I'd die laughing."

↦ "If we are what we eat, I could be you by tomorrow morning." "No, by tomorrow morning you'll be 18 pints of lager and a kebab."

↦ "If you took an IQ test the results would come back negative."

↦ "Is your name Ex-Lax? Because you're irritating the shit out of me."

↦ "Just because you have a prick, it doesn't mean you have to act like one."

↦ "My dog wouldn't fuck you – not even if you had a pork chop tied round your neck."

↦ "Save your breath – you'll need it to blow up your regular lay."

↦ "Sorry, I'm not your type – I'm not inflatable."

↦ "Tell me everything you know – I have 20 seconds to spare."

↦ "Want to come back to my place?" "Will both of us fit under one rock?"

↦ "Want to suck it?" "Sorry, I choke on small bones."

⤷ "We could be having wild sex by midnight tonight." "I suppose it's possible – but not with each other."

⤷ "What's a nice girl like you doing in a place like this?" "If I were a nice girl, I wouldn't be in a place like this."

⤷ "What's the best position to make an ugly baby?" "I don't know." "Well, call your mum, because she certainly does."

⤷ "What's your sign, baby?" "No Entry."

⤷ "Where did you meet your last girlfriend? Battersea Dogs' Home?"

⤷ "Where have you been all my life?" "Outside your window, in the bushes, with the binoculars."

After all the nice things I've said about that hag! When I get hold of her, I'll tear every hair out of her moustache!

Tallulah Bankhead, 1903 – 1968, irritated by Bette Davis

⤷ "Where have you been all my life?" "Right where I'll be the rest of your life – in your wildest dreams."

⤷ "Why is a beautiful girl like you still single?" "Just lucky, I guess."

⤷ "Why not chat up someone your own size – like the QE2?"

➤ "Will you miss me?" "Go away and we'll find out."

➤ "You know, I like an intelligent woman." "Yeah, I heard opposites attract."

➤ "You know, you have the body of a god – Buddha."

Barbara Cartland's eyes were twin miracles of mascara and looked like two small crows that had crashed into a chalk cliff.

Clive James

➤ "You must be a man of rare intelligence – or perhaps completely extinct."

➤ The top ten rejections used by men, and what they really mean, are:
10. I see you as a sister. (You're ugly.)
 9. There's too big a difference in our ages. (You're ugly.)
 8. I don't think about you in 'that' way. (You're ugly.)
 7. My life is too complicated right now. (You're ugly.)
 6. I've already got a girlfriend. (You're ugly.)
 5. I don't go out with women from work. (You're ugly.)
 4. It's not you, it's me. (You're ugly.)
 3. I'm concentrating on my career. (You're ugly.)
 2. I'm celibate. (You're ugly.)
 1. Let's be friends. (You're hideous.)

➤ "You'd better get in training – I hear that 'ugly' is going to be an Olympic sport."

↔ "Your place or mine?" "Both – you go to yours and I'll go to mine."

RELIGION

↔ A dishevelled man, stinking like a distillery, flopped onto a bar stool next to the local Catholic vicar. His tie was tattered, his face was covered with lipstick prints and a half-empty bottle of gin was sticking out of his coat pocket. He pulled a newspaper out of his coat and began reading. After a few minutes, the dishevelled bloke turned to the vicar and asked, "Tell me Father, what causes arthritis?" The priest looked at the chap for a moment or two, and then disapprovingly said: "Actually, it's caused by loose morals, cavorting with cheap, wicked women, drinking excessive quantities of alcohol and having contempt for your fellows." "Well, I'll be damned," the drunk muttered, returning to his paper. The vicar thought about what he had said for a few moments, then nudged the man and apologised. "I'm sorry, I didn't mean to be so heavy with you. How long have you had arthritis?" The dishevelled bloke shook his head, and said, "I don't have arthritis, Father. I was just reading here that the Pope does."

↔ A Jew, a Hindu and a Baptist acquire a time machine. They decide that their first trip will be back to Bethlehem to witness the birth of Christ. They manage to arrive a little later than planned and find that there is only one room left at the inn and it has only one narrow bed. "It's perfectly alright," says the Hindu, "material things are unimportant. I will go and sleep in the stable." He leaves, but ten minutes later there is a knock on the door. It is the Hindu. "I'm sorry, but there is a cow in the stable. Cows are sacred and it would be quite improper for me to stay there." "Alright," says the Jew, "you are, in a manner of speaking, my guests here. I will sleep in the stable." He leaves, but ten minutes later there is a knock on the door. It is the Jew,. "I'm sorry, but there is a pig in the stable. I cannot possibly stay there." "Ah my friends," says the Baptist, "was not our Lord Jesus unafraid to stay in poor lodgings? I will sleep in the stable," and he leaves. A few minutes later there's a knock on the door. It's the pig and the cow. The cow says: "Excuse me but there's a Baptist in the stable..."

↔ A man in the Middle Ages became fed-up with humanity and decided to spend the rest of his life in a monastery. The abbot warned him that he would have to take a vow of silence and live the rest of his life as a scribe, to which the man replied, "No problem. I'm sick of talking." Ten years went by, and the abbot called for the man. He told him that he was a model monk and perfect scribe, and that they were very happy to have him. As per their tradition, he was allowed to say two words. Asked if he had anything to say, the man nodded and said: "Food cold." The abbot sent him on his way. Ten years later, he was brought before the abbot again and once again told how pleased they were with his performance, and that he was again allowed two more words if he so chose. The man said: "Bed hard," and was sent back to work. Another ten years went by and again the abbot sent for the man, telling him that he was the best monk they had ever had, and that he was allowed another two words. The man nodded and said: "I quit." To this, the abbot replied in a disgusted tone: "Doesn't surprise me. You've done nothing but whinge since you got here."

> **To be a moral thief, and unblushing liar, a**
> **supreme dictator, and a cruel, self-satisfied monster,**
> **and attain, in the minds of millions, the status of a**
> **deity, is not only remarkable, but a dismal reflection**
> **on the human race. She had much in common with**
> **Hitler, only no moustache.**
>
> *Noël Coward on Mary Baker Eddy, founder of the*
> *Church of Christ Scientist*

➡ A man is walking along a remote beach on the south coast of England. After about 20 minutes he hears a deep, booming voice say, "DIG!" He looks up, down, left and right, but he cannot see where the voice could possibly have come from, so he carries on. "I SAID DIG!" says the same deep, booming voice. The man figures that the sensible thing to do under these circumstances is to do as he's told, so he starts digging in the sand at the point where he first heard the voice. After about ten minutes he digs up a little metal box, about one foot square. On the front of it is an old rusted padlock. He hears a deep, booming voice say, "OPEN!" so he pulls and pushes and tweaks and bends until the padlock breaks. Inside, the box is full of gold coins. The deep, booming voice says, "TO THE CASINO!" so the man packs up the box, puts it in his car and drives to the nearest casino. He's had a right result so far, he reckons, so he may as well carry on. He changes the coins for a big stack of chips and starts to wander round the casino when the deep, booming voice says, "ROULETTE!", so he goes to the roulette table. There are a few people playing, but he has no problem getting in on the game. Just then, the deep, booming voice says, "TWENTY-SEVEN" so he puts a couple of chips on that number. "ALL OF IT," the deep, booming voice says so the man loads all the rest of the chips on to number 27. The croupier spins the wheel and rolls the ball. The crowd gathered around the table is silent as the ball spins. And spins. And spins. Eventually, it stops on... number 26. And the deep, booming voice says, "SHIT!"

➻ A Rabbi was visiting his old friend, a Priest. The Rabbi had never seen the practices in the church so he asks his friend if he could attend one of his sermons. The father says "OK." After the sermon the confessions begin. The Rabbi asks if he could sit behind and listen to the confessions. The Priest agrees. A young man steps in the confessional and says "Bless me Father for I have sinned." "What did you do my son" the Priest asks. "I slept with three women during the past week." "Are you married?" "No" "You have committed a great sin but I can help you. Pray to the lord, sing gospels and Hail Marys and donate £100 to the church." After a few minutes another man enters the confessional and says the same things. The Priest asks him to the do the same things and tells him to donate £100 to the church. At this point the Priest gets a phone call and has to leave. Before leaving he asks the Rabbi if he could take over the duties for a few minutes and Rabbi says "Don't worry. It's a piece of cake." A few minutes later a young woman enters the confessional. "Bless me Father for I have sinned". "What did you do my child?" asks the Rabbi. "I slept with a married man." "How many men did you sleep with?" asks the Rabbi, "Just one." "Are you sure you did not sleep with three men?" "Yes , I am sure." The Rabbi thinks for a minute and says; "You have definitely committed a sin but I will help you. Pray the Lord, sing gospels and Hail Marys and donate £100 to the church and now the church owes you two fucks."

↣ A Nuncio, where they exist, has the rank of an ambassador. While in Paris, Roncalli once said: "You know, it's rough being a Papal Nuncio. I get invited to these diplomatic parties where everyone stands around with a small plate of canapés trying not to look bored. Then, in walks a shapely woman in a low-cut, revealing gown, and everyone in the whole place turns around and looks – AT ME."

↣ A pastor was addressing the children during the Christmas service. "Who is the mother of Jesus?" he asked them. Without hesitation, dozens of tiny voices chorused back "Mary." "That's right. Now who can tell me who is the father of Jesus?" There was quiet and fidgeting. After all, no one had told them there was going to be a quiz. Then a young girl spoke up. With assurance, she boldly announced: "I know. It's Virg." After two more seconds of silence the entire community erupted in laughter. Of course – we all know it was Virg an' Mary.

We always like our pop stars to be like Greek gods: bigger, better and uglier than us. We hate the bores, Jesus Christ and the Dutch. Especially the Dutch.

Malcolm McLaren

↣ A pious man lived right next door to an atheist. While the religious one prayed, day in, day out, and was constantly on his knees in communion with his Lord, the atheist never even looked twice at a church. However, the atheist's life was good; he had a well-paying job and a beautiful wife, and his children were healthy and good-natured. The pious man's job was strenuous and his wages were low, his wife was getting fatter every day and his children wouldn't give him the time of day. So one day, deep in prayer as usual, he raised his eyes towards heaven and asked: "Oh God, I honour you every day, I ask your advice for every problem and confess to you my every sin. Yet my neighbour, who doesn't even believe in you and certainly never prays, seems blessed with every happiness, while I go poor and suffer many an indignity. Why is this?" And a great voice was heard from above: "BECAUSE HE DOESN'T BOTHER ME ALL THE TIME!"

** A priest and a rabbi found themselves seated together on a long trans-Atlantic flight. They started talking and became quite friendly. The priest slyly said to the rabbi: "Tell me the truth rabbi. Have you ever tried a ham sandwich?" The rabbi confessed that he had once tried a ham sandwich. Then the rabbi asked the priest: "You chaps are supposed to be celibate. Have you ever had sex with a woman?" The priest confessed that he had. "Beats the hell out of a ham sandwich, doesn't it?" said the rabbi.

** A Swedish bishop was getting ready to visit America. Some of his close associates advised him to be careful when responding to reporters on his arrival in New York. The bishop, however, was overconfident and paid little heed to the advice. During a press conference, held on his arrival at JFK Airport, one reporter asked the bishop if he was planning on visiting any nightclubs in New York. The bishop replied "Are there any nightclubs in New York?" suggesting that he was ignorant of anything like night clubs in New York. To his surprise, the next morning's papers had the following banner headlines: "While still on tarmac at JFK, Swedish bishop asks, 'Are there any nightclubs in New York'?"

➥ A woman fell off her balcony on the 23rd floor, and as she fell, she prayed, "Oh God, please give me a chance to live!" Suddenly a man leant out from his balcony and caught her in his arms. Before she had a chance to thank him, he asked her, "Do you suck?" "Of course not!" she shouted, thinking this can't be what God intended. So the man let go and she fell again, hurtling towards the ground. Suddenly a second man put out his arms and caught her. "Do you screw?" he asked. "No!" she shouted, wondering what the hell God was playing at, sending all these perverts to catch her. So the man dropped her and she continued to fall. Just as death seemed certain, a third man put out his arms and caught her. Before he could say a word, the woman shouted, "I suck! I screw!" "Slut!" cried the man, and dropped her to her death.

➥ After the PLO and Israel shook hands and said that everything was fine, the President invited the Israeli Prime Minister back to the Oval Office. The Prime Minister looked at the President's desk and noticed that he had three phones, a black one, a red one, and a white one. The Prime Minister asked, "What is the red phone for?" the President said, "It's a direct line to Russia. Got to keep up with them." "What about the black one?" "That's to the Pentagon." Then the Prime Minister asked, "What's the white one for, then?" the President said, "That's a direct line to God. Did you know that it's a $5,000,000 a minute phone call to him?" The Prime Minister just nodded and went on with the tour. Weeks later, the President took a secret trip to Israel and, while he was there, toured the Prime Minister's office. He noticed that the Prime Minister had three phones just like his. He asked, "What's the red phone for?" The Prime Minister replied, "It's a direct line to Russia." "How about the Black one?" "Mossad." The President nodded and then asked, "What's the white one for?" The Prime Minister replied, "It's a direct line to God." the President said, "How can a poor country like yours afford such an expensive phone call?" The Prime Minister said, "Oh, well, from here it's local rate."

Whenever we read the obscene stories, the voluptuous debaucheries, the cruel and torturous executions, the unrelenting vindictiveness, with which more than half the bible is filled, it would be more consistent that we called it the word of a demon than the Word of God. It is a history of wickedness that has served to corrupt and brutalise mankind, and for my own part, I sincerely detest it, as I detest everything that is cruel.

Thomas Paine, 1737 – 1809, The Age of Reason, on the Bible

➥ Brother William is on his way back from teaching children at a local school. It is late at night and the Abbey's car that he is travelling in breaks down. He knows that he hasn't run out of petrol because he's just filled up, so he opens up the bonnet and starts to have a look at the engine. A few minutes later a car pulls up next to him and the window is wound down. A red-faced man pops his head out and says, "Hello, old chap, what's the matter with you, then?" "Piston broke, I think," says the monk, to which the man in the car replies, "Me too, but what's up with the motor?"

➥ How can you make God laugh? Tell Him your plans for the future.

↦ How do you get a nun pregnant? Dress her up as an altar-boy.

↦ Jesus returned and ended up by the side of the River Severn in Worcestershire. He confronted an old boy who was sat there fishing. "I am Jesus – I have come to save all from the horrors that be," exclaimed the great one. "Sod off, you're scaring the fish," answered the old one. "No, you don't understand – I have returned to save the Earth, now tell me, where should I start?" The old boy thinks for a while and tells him to perform a miracle, then he will believe that this is truly The Lord. "Walk across the river," he tells Jesus. So Jesus starts walking across the river, and the water is lapping round his ankles – then around his shins, then his knees. This starts worrying him, but he continues, knowing that he can do it. The next thing he knows, he slips and disappears under the water, and nearly drowns. He manages to claw his way back to the shore, and the old man says to him: "There you are, see, you're not Jesus, you can't walk across water." Jesus responds, "Well, I used to be able to do it until I got these nail holes in my feet."

↦ So this bloke walks up to a Buddhist hot dog vendor and says, "Make me one with everything..."

↦ The Pope was in the middle of an audience when his principal advisor whispered in his ear: "Your Holiness, I hate to interrupt, but the Messiah is on the phone and he wants to talk to you." The Pope excused himself so he could take the call in private. A few minutes later he came back out with a sombre expression. He said, "I have some good news and some bad news. The good news is that the call was from the Messiah, the Lord Jesus, our saviour, and the time of the second coming is at hand. The bad news is that He was calling from Salt Lake City."

➤ Two navvies were digging a ditch across from a brothel, and one noticed a rabbi walk into the place. One said to the other, "It's a sad day when men of the cloth walk into a place like that." After a little while, the other man saw a minister walk into the brothel. He stood up and said to his partner, "Did you see that? It's no wonder the children today are so confused with the example that the clergy are setting for them." After about another hour, the first man saw a Catholic priest walk in. He promptly stood up and proclaimed to his partner. "Aye, that is truly sad. One of the poor lassies must be dying."

> **Theologians are all alike, of whatever religion or country they may be; their aim is always to wield despotic authority over men's consciences; they therefore persecute all of us who have the temerity to tell the truth.**
>
> *Frederick the Great, 1712 – 1786, private correspondence*

➤ What did Adam say to Eve? "Stand back: I'm not sure how big this thing gets!"

➤ What do you get when you cross a devil worshipper with a Jehovah's Witness? Someone who goes from door to door telling people to go to hell.

➤ What do you get when you cross a Mafia soldier with a Jehovah's Witness? Lots of converts.

↦ What does an atheist miss during orgasm? Somebody to shout to.

↦ What's the difference between Jesus and a picture of Jesus? It only takes one nail to hang up the picture.

↦ Who is the most constipated man in the Bible? David – on the throne for 40 years.

↦ Who is the most elastic man in the Bible? Balaam. He tied his ass to a tree and walked two miles into town.

↦ Why did the Mormon cross the road? To get to the other bride.

↦ Why were most of Jesus' apostles fishermen and not cabinet-makers? If they were cabinet-makers, Jesus would have had to say: "Drop your drawers and follow me."

Restaurants

↦ A bloke in a café late one evening called the waitress over and said, "You're really cute. I'd love to shag you." The waitress looked at him and said, "Oh, for God's sake. Look, I've been stood on my feet all day. I'm exhausted." The bloke shrugged, and said, "Great, let's go and lie down..."

↦ A customer was bothering the waiter in a restaurant. First, he asked that the air conditioning be turned up because he was too hot, then he asked it be turned down because he was too cold, and so on for about half an hour. Surprisingly, the waiter was very patient. He walked back and forth and never once got angry. So finally, a second customer asked him why he didn't throw out the pest. "Oh, I don't mind," said the waiter with a smile, "we don't even have an air conditioner."

↔ A man in a restaurant orders chicken noodle soup. He starts to eat the soup and chokes on a hair in it. After gagging for a minute, he calls the waitress. "I'm not paying for this soup. There was a hair in it." The waitress and customer get into a bit of an argument over the problem. The man ends up storming out of the restaurant without paying. The waitress sees him go across the street to a house of ill repute. The waitress's shift finishes and she hurries over to the house, finds out where the man is and interrupts his evening of pleasure. As she walks in, she sees the man with his face in the hooker's business area. "You wouldn't pay for the chicken noodle soup because you found hair in it. Now look where your face is." The man pulls his face out of the muff, turns to the waitress and says, "And if I find a noodle in there, I won't pay this lady, either."

↔ A Polish couple went into a restaurant and ordered their food. When it was served a few minutes later, the husband started tucking in ravenously while his wife just watched, not touching her food. After a little while the waitress came over and asked, "Is something wrong?" "I'm waiting for my husband to finish," said the woman. The waitress looked at her and said: "But your dinner's getting cold. You don't need to wait." The woman nodded vigorously. "Yes, I must. It's his turn to go first with our false teeth."

↦ An Indian chef was sacked for being divisive after a week in his new job. He keep favouring curry.

↦ Did you hear about the Irish restaurant that hired dwarf waiters and waitresses to make the portions look bigger?

↦ Did you hear about the restaurant that had a sign in the window reading "Now Serving Food"? You really have to wonder what they used to serve...

Surrounded with cold, white fat, the rabbit legs looked like maps of Greenland, and tasted like a dryad's inner thigh.

Clive James

↦ One day, Bill and Tom went to a restaurant for dinner. As soon as the waiter brought out two steaks, Bill quickly picked out the bigger steak for himself. Tom wasn't happy about that, asking: "When are you going to learn to be polite?" Bill replied "If you had the chance to pick first, which one would you pick?" Tom said: "The smaller piece, of course." Bill sneered: "What are you mumbling about then? Then the smaller piece is what you want, right?"

↦ There was a restaurant that had a sign in the window which read, "Eat now – pay waiter."

↦ This bloke was in a curry house, flicking through the menu and idly munching on poppadoms. After a few minutes he called the waiter over. "Waiter, could you possibly explain something on the menu to me?" "Oh, most certainly, sir," replied the waiter cheerfully. "I know Indian food pretty well," said the bloke, "but I've never heard of this dish here, Lamb Tarka. Surely you mean Lamb Tikka?" The waiter shook his head and said, "No sir, we mean Lamb Tarka. It is indeed similar to Lamb Tikka, you are most correct, but it's just a little 'otter."

➡ There's a small snack-bar next to the atomic accelerator at CERN. It's called "The Fission Chips Café"!

➡ This Polish guy walked into a restaurant. "What would you like?" asked the waitress. "You know what I like," replied the man, "but first we eat, yes?"

➡ We reserve the right to serve refuse to anyone.

sales

➡ A travelling salesman stops at a petrol station to take a crap. The toilet has two stalls and there's a man already there using one of them. The two men acknowledge each other and go about their business. The salesman finishes first and, as he pulls his trousers up, some coins drop into the toilet bowl. He looks at it, thinks for a moment and throws a £20 note into the bowl. The other man, astonished, asks: "Why the hell did you do that?" The salesman says: "You don't expect me to put my hand in there for 35 pence do you?"

➠ "I'd like to buy some gloves for my wife," the young man said, eyeing the attractive salesgirl, "but I don't know her size." "Will this help?" she asked sweetly, placing her hand in his. "Oh, yes," he answered. "Her hands are just slightly smaller that yours." "Will there be anything else?" the salesgirl queried as she wrapped the gloves. "Now that you mention it," he replied, "she also needs a bra and knickers."

➠ A door-to-door vacuum cleaner salesman manages to bullshit his way into a woman's home in outback Australia. "This machine is the best ever," he claims, while pouring a bag of dirt over the lounge floor. The woman says she's really worried it may not all come off, so the salesman says: "If this machine doesn't remove all the dust completely, I'll lick it off myself." The woman says, "Do you want ketchup. We're not connected to the electricity yet."

➠ A man walks into a department store, finds the manager and says, "I really need a job; how about giving me a chance?" The manager says, "Certainly, but you have to sell these 500 toothbrushes in a week to get the job." Our hero takes the toothbrushes and leaves. Next week, he comes back with the toothbrushes and finds the manager. "I didn't get any of these sold, but please, please, give me another chance." The manager says, "OK, but you have to take another 500 toothbrushes." Our man takes the toothbrushes and tries his luck again. Again our man comes back with the 1,000 toothbrushes, talks to the manager, gets another 500 toothbrushes and tries his luck. So he comes back in a week, not with 1,500 toothbrushes but with a bag of money. The manager gives him the job and wants to know his trick. Our hero says: "Well, the idea came to me a couple of days ago. I set up a table on a busy street corner with a bowl of chips, a bowl of shit, and a sign saying 'Free Chip and Dip'. Someone would come along, dip the chip, and say, 'Yuck! That tastes like shit.' and, of course, I would reply, 'Yeah. So, want to buy a toothbrush'?"

➡ A man was walking down the street one day and he saw a "Salesman Wanted" sign in a window. He went in the store and the owner asked, "Can I help you?" "I'I'IIII w'w'waannnttt j'j'jjoooobbbb," said the man. "I don't know if this job would suit you because of your speaking problem," said the owner. "I'I'III h'h'avvee a'a'a wif'f'fe annd si' si' six k'k'ids a'a'ndd I'I n'neeeed th'th'e j'joobb," said the man. "Okay, here are three Bibles. Go out and sell them," said the owner. So the man went out and came back an hour later. "H'here'sss your mm'money," said the man. The owner was impressed, so he gave the man a dozen more Bibles and sent him out. The man came back in two hours and said, "H'here'sss your mm'money." The owner said, "This is fantastic. You sold more Bibles in three hours than anyone has sold in a week. Tell me, what do you say to the people when they come to the door?" "W'welll," said the man, "III r'r'ing the d'd'oor b'b'ell a'a'nd s's'say 'M'M'aaddammm, d'd'o y'y'ou w'w'ant t'to b'buy t'this B'Bible o'o'rrr d'd'o y'you w'w'w'ant m'me t't'o read it to you?'"

Consultants are people who borrow your watch to tell you the time and then walk off with it.

Robert Townsend

➻ A very large department store chain in the UK is very low on sales. The head of personnel, Mr Jones, informs the head of each department store that they are to send all employees over the age of 60 out on early pension. The early pension plan is implemented. After three months Mr Jones, in going over store reports, notices that the Croydon store has an employee over the age of 60. Mr Jones calls Mr Smith at the Croydon branch to find out why Mr Green is still with the firm. Mr Smith explains to Mr Jones that Mr Green is the best salesman that the store has ever had. He brings hundreds of thousands of pounds into the shop a year – to let him go would be a real loss. The following week, Mr Jones goes to the shop and down to the sales floor to secretly watch Mr Green in action. Mr Green says to a customer: "You know, with that new fishing rod that you bought, you should really have some new fishing clothes." The customer is convinced and Mr Green outfits him in hundreds of pounds'-worth of new fishing clothes. Mr Green continues: "You know, you are going to look so spiffy in that new outfit with your new fishing rod that it would be a pity not to be seen. Instead of just standing on the bank of the river, you should be seen in a new fishing boat." The customer is convinced and Mr Green sells him a new fishing boat. Mr Green is so convincing that he also sells the customer a new boat trailer and a new car to go along with the new boat, new outfit, and new fishing rod. By the time the sale is rung up, Mr Green has sold thousands and thousands of pounds'-worth of merchandise. Mr Jones is absolutely astounded. He tells Mr Smith to give Mr Green a raise. He says to Mr Smith, "I have never seen such an outstanding selling job in my life. It is unbelievable that the customer came in for a simple fishing rod and Mr Green sold him thousands of pounds'-worth of merchandize." Mr Smith says: "That's not even the beautiful part. That customer didn't even come in for a fishing rod. He came in to buy his wife a box of tampons. Mr Green convinced him that since his weekend was already shot, he might as well go fishing..."

→ It has been reported in a magazine that a certain cosmetics company has more than 36,000 sales representatives in the Amazonia region of Brazil, with sales growing at 50% a year. The company representatives in Amazonia sell the complete range of products, from lipstick, moisturizer and mascara to men's bikini briefs, and accept for payment almost any barterable items, such as fish.

→ The merchandizing manager of a large food chain was on holiday. While driving through rural Norfolk he developed a headache and decided to stop in the next town and buy some aspirin. Stopping at a small grocery store, he went in and got his aspirin. While in the store, more out of habit than anything, he walked around to see how it was merchandized. To his amazement, only about two of the ten aisles in the store were devoted to the basic staples and the other eight aisles were filled with salt. He had never seen anything like this in his life and wondered what caused this huge demand for salt in a small rural town in Norfolk. Seeing the proprietor in the rear of the store, he said, "My God, you sell a lot of salt." At which the owner said: "Who, me? Wurr, boy. I don't 'ardly sell any salt at all, but that fellow that sells me salt, does he know how to sell salt."

➻ There were two grocers, Smith and Jones, in the same street. Smith had a sign in his window, "Avocados, 20 pence a pound." A woman goes in and asks for some. "Sorry, love", said Smith, "I haven't got any in just now. Come back on Wednesday." So she goes on up the street to Jones' shop. His avocados are £2.50 a pound, but at least he has them in stock. "That's a bit steep, isn't it? Smith's are only 20 pence a pound." "Yeah," says Jones, "so are mine when I'm out of stock."

science

➻ A somewhat advanced society has figured how to package basic knowledge in pill form. A student, needing some learning, goes to the pharmacy and asks what kind of knowledge pills are available. The pharmacist says: "Here's a pill for English literature." The student takes the pill and swallows it and has new knowledge about English literature. "What else do you have?" asks the student. "Well, I have pills for art, history, biology, and world history," replies the pharmacist. The student asks for these, and swallows them and has new knowledge about those subjects. Then the student asks: "Do you have a pill for maths?" The pharmacist says, "Wait just a moment," goes back into the storeroom, brings back a whopper of a pill and plonks it on the counter. "I have to take that huge pill for maths?" inquires the student. The pharmacist replied, "Well, you know maths always was a little hard to swallow."

➻ Descartes walks into a pub. "Would you like a beer, sir?" asks the landlord politely. Descartes replies, "I think not" and ping! he vanishes.

↦ Did you hear about the scientist whose wife had twins? He baptized one and kept the other as a control.

Sir, I have tested your machine. It adds a new terror to life and makes death a long-felt want.

Sir Herbert Beerbohm Tree on an early ancestor of the record player

↦ Three agricultural scientists were determined to discover how much a pig could eat before it just had to take a shit. To this end they procured a Yorkshire sow and pushed a large cork into her arse. After six weeks of force-feeding, the sow was the size of the Goodyear airship and threatening to burst. Being humane types, the scientists agreed that the cork must now be removed. No one wished to volunteer for the job, however, so in true scientific tradition, they decided to train a monkey for the task and swiftly put a small gibbon through a crash course in cork-pulling. The day came and the pig was airlifted out to the desert for safety's sake. Special equipment was set up to monitor the event. Picture the scene: in the middle of the desert, the pig. Behind the pig, the monkey. One mile behind him, the first scientist with a video camera. One mile behind that scientist are the other two scientists with a seismometer. Finally, the monkey reaches up and pulls out the cork. SPLAT! When the massive geyser has subsided, the two scientists find themselves knee-deep in pigshit. Grabbing shovels, they wade forward and dig out the first man who has been buried up to his neck. When they free him they find that he is laughing hysterically. "What's so funny?" they ask. "You should have seen the monkey trying to get the cork back in!"

→ Does fuzzy logic tickle your brain?

We have genuflected before the god of science only to find that it has given us the atomic bomb, producing fears and anxieties that science can never mitigate.

Martin Luther King

→ Pessimists have already begun to worry about what is going to replace automation.

→ Scientists say that 92% of all ten-pound notes carry germs. That's not true. Not even a germ could live on a tenner.

senses

→ A man is talking to the family doctor. "Doctor, I think my wife's going deaf." The doctor answers, "Well, here's something you can try on her to test her hearing. Stand some distance away from her and ask her a question. If she doesn't answer, move a little closer and ask again. Keep repeating this until she answers. Then you'll be able to tell just how hard of hearing she really is." The man goes home and tries it out. He walks in the door and says: "Honey, what's for dinner?" He doesn't hear an answer, so he moves closer to her. "Honey, what's for dinner?" Still no answer. He repeats this several times, until he's standing just a few feet away from her. Finally, she answers: "For the eleventh time, I said we're having MEATLOAF."

sex

↦ A businessman goes on a trip to Japan. As is traditional, he and his associates all go out with their Japanese equivalents and get totally drunk. Then they send the American upstairs with a prostitute. As he begins to have sex with her, she starts to moan, "Nai com chai, nai com chai!" He has no idea what it means, but the moaning sounds pretty good, so the businessman feels quite pleased with himself. The next day, he is out playing golf with his associates when one of his Japanese hosts slices the ball horribly to one side and in frustration shouts, "Nai com chai!" The American businessman says to him, "What does that mean?" The Japanese businessman replies, "Wrong hole!"

↦ A fly was hovering over a lake. A fish, swimming below the water, saw the fly and said to itself, "If that fly would just drop six more inches, I could get it." In the woods beside the lake, a bear was watching the fish and said to itself, "If that fly would just drop six more inches, the fish could get that fly and I could get that fish." Deeper in the woods, a hunter, sitting eating a sandwich, saw the bear and said to himself, "If that fly would just drop six more inches, that fish could get that fly, that bear could get that fish and I could get that bear." Just behind him a mouse was watching. The mouse said to itself, "If that fly would just drop six more inches, that fish could get that fly, that bear could get that fish, that hunter could get that bear and I could get that sandwich." Behind the mouse was a cat, watching intently. It said to itself, "If that fly would just drop six more inches, that fish could get that fly, that bear could get that fish, that hunter could get that bear, that mouse could get that sandwich and I could get that mouse!" Suddenly, the fly dropped six inches. The fish leaped up and snapped it up. The bear grabbed the fish, and the hunter jumped up and shot the bear. The mouse leaped for the sandwich and the cat jumped for the mouse, but was too excited, so shot past it and landed in the lake. The moral of the story? When a fly drops six inches, a pussy gets wet!

➻ A girl takes a guy home. When he takes his pants off, he's got the biggest cock she's ever seen – it reaches down past his knees. "You want a blow job?" she says, but he replies, "I'd rather fuck, I can do blow jobs myself."

➻ A Hell's Angel drops his motorbike off to be mended, and is walking home. On the way he remembers that he's meant to be picking up some things at the hardware shop for the Hell's Angel Clubhouse. "Ah, yes," says the shopkeeper, "Here you are," and he gets out a bucket, an anvil, a goat, an axe and a black cockerel. "How am I meant to carry this lot without my bike?" says the Hell's Angel. "Well," says the shopkeeper, "You could put the cockerel under one arm, the anvil under the other arm, put the axe in the bucket and hold it in one hand, then lead the goat with the other hand." So the Hell's Angel does as the shopkeeper suggests and starts walking back to the Clubhouse. A few yards down the road, he's stopped by a little old lady. "Excuse me, young man," she says, "Can you tell me the way to the chapel?" "It's right next to our clubhouse," says the Hell's Angel, "So come with me and I'll show you the way. It's just down this alley." The old lady looks at him very suspiciously. "Young man," she says, "You are a tall, hairy, muscular man and I am a helpless old woman. How do I know you won't get me half way down that alley, push me roughly against the wall, pull down my panties and take me roughly till your wicked desires are sated?" "Madam," he replies, "I have a bucket in one hand with an axe in it, a goat on a string in the other hand, an anvil under one arm and a cockerel under the other arm, how could I possibly push you roughly against any wall?" So the old lady says, "Put the cockerel down, put the bucket over the cockerel and the anvil on top of the bucket, lay the axe on the ground and I'll hold on to the goat."

Mr. Shaw was born old... He was rumoured to be neutral about sex. Shaw would have made a perfect priest, except he happened to be an atheist.

Estelle Winwood on George Bernard Shaw

→ A man goes to a hypnotherapist to get help for his impotence. While he's hypnotized, the therapist tells him that next time he hears the words "1-2-3" he'll get a huge hard on. When he hears the words "1-2-3-4" it will go down again. The man wakes up and the therapist explains that all he needs to do is say the numbers to control his erection. Very excited, the man can't wait to get into bed with his wife. She's preparing to go straight to sleep as usual when he slips between the sheets and murmurs, "1-2-3." Immediately, he starts to swell and gets a huge erection. Just as he's about to get amorous, his wife rolls over and asks, "What did you say 1-2-3 for?"

→ A really arrogant bloke was shagging a really arrogant bird. "God, aren't I tight, baby?" she moaned. "Nope," he grunted, "just stretched."

➥ A young wife was frustrated by the lack of spice in her and her husband's sex life, so she decided to see what she could do about it. Straight after work she went shopping and bought herself a pair of crotchless panties in a sex shop. She ran home and put on her new panties, along with a particularly short skirt. When her husband came home from work she fixed him a drink and sat across from him as he drank it. "Now you've had some of that, sugar..." she cooed as she slowly spread her legs, "...perhaps you'd like some of this?" "God, no!" screamed the husband. "Look what it's done to your underwear!"

➥ An Italian, a Frenchman and an Irishman are all chatting about their love-making prowess. The Italian begins by saying, "When I have feeneesh make-a love with my-a wife, I just stroke her-a buttocks and she-a float seex eenches above-a tha bed in total ecstasy." The Frenchman continues, "Zat's noseeng. When I av-a feeneeshed to make ze lurve wiz my wife, I leek ze solez of 'er feet and she float 12 eenches above ze bed in total ecstasy!" So the Irishman says, "Well, when I've screwed da woife, I git out da bed, wipe me dick on da curtins and she hits da fukkin' roof!"

➥ Did you hear about the Morning After Pill for men? It disguises your DNA!

➥ Did you hear about the streaker who was thinking of retirement? He decided to stick it out for one more year!

➥ Have you heard about the new mint-flavoured birth control pill for women that they take immediately before sex? They're called Pre-dickamints.

⟶ Have you heard about the new super-sensitive condoms? They hang around and talk to the woman after you've rolled over, farted and fallen asleep.

⟶ How do married couples use Vaseline to help with their sex lives? They put it on the bedroom doorknob to keep the kids out.

⟶ How do you find a blind man in a nudist colony? Keep looking – it's not hard.

⟶ How do you know when you're in bed with a blacksmith? He hammers away for hours and then he makes a bolt for the door.

⟶ How do you know when you're in bed with a fireman? He comes when you're hot and leaves you soaking wet.

⟶ How do you know when you're in bed with a mathematician? He divides your legs and then he subtracts his root so you don't multiply.

⟶ How do you know when you're in bed with a policeman? He asks you to blow into his breathalyzer.

⟶ How do you know when you're in bed with a postman? He doesn't come when he's supposed to, and half the time it's in the wrong box.

⟶ How do you know when you're in bed with a takeaway chef? You ask for 69 and he gives you egg-fried rice.

➻ How do you know when you're in bed with an archaeologist? They'll date anything.

➻ How do you know when you're in bed with an astronaut? The equipment is huge, but there's no atmosphere.

➻ How do you know when you're in bed with an explorer? He goes deeper into the bush than any man has ever been.

➻ How do you make two kilos of fat look good? Stick a nipple on top.

➻ How many newspapers can a woman hold between her legs? One Post, two Globes and as many Times as you can.

➻ If mothers have Mother's Day and fathers have Father's Day, what do bachelors have? Palm Sunday.

➻ Love is a thousand miles long, but comes in six-inch instalments.

➻ My latest Freudian slip came just as my wife arrived back from a week-long business trip. As she grabbed her luggage and we headed off, she asked, "Did you miss me?" I replied quite innocently, "It's been so hard without you."

➻ One night a guy had a few too many at his local and decided to drive home very slowly, taking the "clever" route to avoid any policemen or other snoopers. As he did so, he passed a field full of pumpkins. Having been drinking, the man was feeling pretty horny so started to think about how pumpkins are soft, and how no one need ever know, and how it wouldn't really do any harm, would it? So he pulled over and picked out a nice soft pumpkin, cut the right-sized hole in the side and began to have a go. He really started getting carried away and before he knew it he was sweating away, oblivious to the world: so oblivious, he didn't even notice a police car turn up right behind him. The two policemen walk up behind him and one of them shouts, "Hey sir, sir, do you realize you're fucking a pumpkin?" The man jumps, realizes he's been rumbled and starts thinking. Quick as a flash, he says, "A pumpkin? Is it midnight already, officer?"

➠ The night before her wedding, a young woman had a talk with her mother. "Mum," she started, "I want you to teach me how to make my new husband happy." The mother took a deep breath, steeled herself, and began, "When two people admire, honour, and respect each other, love can be a very beautiful thing..." "I know how to fuck, mum," the young woman interrupted. "I want you to tell me how to make that wonderful lasagne you do."

➠ There are five types of sex involved in a marriage. The first is Smurf Sex. This happens during the honeymoon; you both keep doing it until you're blue in the face. The second is Kitchen Sex. This is at the beginning of the marriage; you'll have sex anywhere, any time. Hence, also in the kitchen. The third kind is Bedroom Sex. You've calmed down a bit, perhaps have kids, so you have to do it in the bedroom. The fourth kind is Hallway Sex. This is where you pass each other in the hallway and say: "Fuck you!" The fifth kind is Courtroom Sex. This is when you get divorced and your wife fucks you in front of everyone in court.

↦ Sex is a three-letter word which needs some old-fashioned four-letter words to convey its full meaning.

↦ Sex is like snow; you never know how many inches you are going to get or how long it is going to last.

↦ Think how much fun you could have with the doctor's wife and a bucket of apples.

↦ Three young female students all lived together in a flat and one night they all had dates at the same time. Around midnight they all got back and started comparing notes. The first girl says, "You know what? You can tell a good date when you come back home and your hair's all messed up." And the second girl says, "You know what? You can tell a good date when you come back home and your make-up's all smeared." The third girl says nothing, but just reaches under her skirt, removes her knickers and throws them against the wall. They stick there. "You know what? That's a good date," she says.

↦ Two cowboys are sat having a drink in a bar. One asks his friend if he's heard of the latest sexual position. Apparently it's called 'the rodeo.' The other says no and asks what you do. "Well," says the first cowboy, "first you mount your wife from the back, reach around her front and cup both breasts with your hands. Then you whisper softly in her ear, 'Oh baby, these are almost as nice as your sister's!' Then you see how long you can hang on for!"

↦ What do a toilet seat and a pussy have in common? They both feel good, but you wonder who was there before you.

↦ What do a virgin and a balloon have in common? One prick and it's all over.

↦ What do a woman and a computer have in common? Both can take a 3.5-inch floppy.

↦ What do women and police cars have in common? They both make a lot of noise to let you know they're coming.

↦ What do you call a virgin lying on a waterbed? A cherry float.

↦ What do you do if your girlfriend starts smoking? Slow down and lubricate.

The French are particularly well-known for their arrogance and, following on the heels of their promiscuity, they are also known for their spectacular sexual diseases.

Billy Wilder

↦ What do you do in case of fall-out? Put it back in and take shorter strokes!

↦ What do you do with 365 used condoms? Melt them down, make a car tyre and call it a "Goodyear."

↦ What is better than a cold Bud? A warm bush.

↦ What's the definition of eternity? The time between when you cum and she leaves.

↣ What's the best thing about sex with a bank clerk? The bigger the deposit and the longer you leave it in, the more interest you get. And the worst thing? He's not so keen on withdrawals.

↣ What's the best thing about sex with a clown? Great big feet – you know what they say about men with big feet. And the worst thing? Infidelity: you'll catch him having sex with the contortionist behind her back.

↣ What's the best thing about sex with a despatch rider? He's dressed completely in leather and he's really, really dirty. And the worst thing? He's always slipping into narrow spaces where he's not meant to go.

↣ What's the best thing about sex with a taxi driver? He's never in a hurry to get from A to B. In fact he'll usually take as long as he can. And the worst thing? You can never tell when he's going to pull out.

↣ What's the difference between a child car seat and a condom? One stops kids in the back seat causing accidents, the other stops accidents in the back seat causing kids.

↣ What's the difference between a girl snowman and a boy snowman? Snowballs.

↣ What's the difference between a pussy and a grill? Nobody minds if you stab their sausage with a fork before you put it in your grill.

↣ What's the difference between a woman and a fridge? A

fridge doesn't make a squelching noise when you pull your meat out!

↔ What's the difference between an unlucky mouse and a lucky cock? Nothing – they both end up inside a satisfied pussy.

↔ What's the difference between pink and purple? Grip!

↔ What's the difference between sin and shame? It's a sin to put it in, but it's a shame to pull it out.

When I met him, I wondered how he could possibly be qualified to direct this movie.

John Carradine, on Woody Allen directing "Everything You Always Wanted To Know About Sex (But Were Afraid To Ask)"

↔ What's the difference between northern girls and southern girls on a date? Southern girls say, "Alright, I'll go to bed with you." Northern girls say, "Alright, I'll go to bed with all of you."

↔ When men say, "Do you have any fantasies?" they mean, "Can we try anal sex / you dressing up as Batgirl / a threesome with your sister?" When women say, "Do you have any fantasies?" they mean, "I'm so bored that, frankly, I'll try anything."

↔ When men say, "Who else do you fancy?" they mean, "I fancy your sister." When women say, "Who else do you fancy?" they mean, "you fancy my sister, don't you?"

↦ Who's the world's greatest athlete? The man who gets gold and silver medals in the masturbation contest.

↦ Why did God create alcohol? So ugly people would get to have sex.

↦ Why did the Avon Lady walk funny? Her lipstick.

↦ Why is a one-night stand like a newsflash? It's unexpected, brief and probably a disaster.

↦ Why is air a lot like sex? Because it's no big deal until you aren't getting any.

↦ Why is sex just like KFC? You start with breast, work your way down the thigh, and all you're ever left with is a greasy box to put your bone in!

↦ Women who love only women may have a good point.

SEX PILLS

↦ A man comes to a doctor and, twitching his fingers and stuttering, finally manages to say, "Doctor, I have a... er... sexual performance problem. Can you help me?" "Oh, that's not a problem for us men any more!" announces the proud physician with a broad wink. "This new pill just came out – a new wonder drug called Viagra. That does the trick! You take a few of these and it's the end of your problems!" So the doctor gives the man a prescription for a packet of Viagra and sends him on his merry way. A couple of months later, the doctor runs into his patient on the street. "Doctor, doctor!" exclaims the man excitedly, "I've got to thank you! This drug is a miracle! It's wonderful!" "Well, I'm glad to hear that," says the physician, rather pleased with himself. "And what does your wife think about it?" "Wife?" the guy said with a silly grin on his face, "I haven't been home yet!"

➻ A woman walks into her sex therapist's office. She tells the therapist that her husband is not a very good lover, and they never have sex any more, and she asks what to do about it. The therapist tells her that there is an experimental drug that might do the trick. She tells the woman to give her husband one pill that night and come back in the morning and tell her what happens. The next day, the woman comes in, ecstatic, telling the therapist that the pill worked and that she and her husband had the best sex ever. She asks her therapist what would happen if she gave her husband two pills and the therapist says she doesn't know, but to go ahead and try it. The next day, the same thing happens, the woman comes in telling the therapist that the sex was even better than the night before and what would happen if she gave him five pills? The therapist says she doesn't know, but to go ahead and try it. The next day, the woman comes in limp but happy, and tells the therapist that the sex just keeps getting better and what would happen if she gave her husband the rest of the bottle? The therapist says she doesn't know; it's an experimental drug and she doesn't know what a full bottle could do to a person. Anyway, the woman leaves the therapist's office and puts the rest of the bottle of pills in her husband's morning coffee. A week later, a boy walks into the therapist's office and says: "Are you the dick-head who gave my mother a bottle of experimental pills?" "Why, yes, young man, I did. Why?" "Well, Mum's dead, my sister's pregnant, my arse hurts, and Dad's sitting in the corner going 'Here, kitty, kitty, kitty'..."

➥ Early reports suggest that at least six men have already died after using the new anti-impotence drug Viagra. Ironically, sales of the drug have been increased. One customer said that the fact it could keep men stiff indefinitely was a huge plus.

➥ How do you know when a truckload of Viagra has fallen in the river Thames? Tower Bridge stays open for hours.

➥ Man goes into a chemist and asks, "Do you sell Viagra?" "Yes," says the chemist. "And does it work?" "Yes," says the chemist. "And can you get it over the counter?" "Yes, if I take two."

How do you like them? Like a pear, a lemon, a la Montgolfier, half an apple, or a cantaloupe? Go on, choose, don't be embarrassed.

Collete, on breasts

➥ Old Farmer Giles got a hefty loan from the bank to buy an expensive bull. A few days later the banker dropped by and asked, "So, how's the new bull doing?" Giles looked downcast and said, "The bull ain't doing none too good, see. I got him out there in the pasture with a lovely bunch of young heifers and he don't want nothing to do with 'em." The banker frowned and said, "You'd better call the vet, and I'll come back in a few days." A week later the banker came back and asked, "Well, Giles, how's that bull doing now?" Smiling, Giles said, "A whole bushel better, he be. He's had his way with all of my cows, jumped over the fence, and he's working his way through Silas's cows next door." The banker was much relieved and said, "Great! What did the vet give him?" Giles said, "He gave him some pills." The banker said, "What kind of pills were those?" Giles said, "I don't rightly know, but they had a strange lemony taste."

➻ A farmer is having trouble with his prize stud bull, which has a herd of 300 cows to sort out. It won't do what is required of it, so the farmer takes it to the vet. Without even examining the animal, the vet hands the farmer a small bottle of pills and says, "Grind one of these into its feed, stand back and watch it go!" Two weeks later, the farmer returns to the vet and says, "Veterinary, that was truly incredible. I did what you said and as soon as he'd eaten the feed he leaped over the fence and screwed all 300 cows in less than an hour!" The vet says, "So what's the problem then – why are you back?" The farmer says, "Well, I was wondering: it's a bit personal, but I've got a hot date with a 21-year-old tonight and I could really do with one of those tablets. I'm not really the man I used to be, after all." "Well, I can't really let you have a whole one," says the vet, "but I guess a quarter of a pill wouldn't do much harm!" So he gives a quarter-pill to the farmer, who goes off to prepare for his date. A few days later, the farmer is back at the vet's again. "What is it this time?" asks the vet. "Well, the pill worked fine – 40 times that one night," says the farmer. "So what's up, then?" asks the vet. "Well, now I need something for my wrist," says the farmer. "She never showed up!"

➥ Heard about the new Viagra eye drops? They make him look really hard.

➥ What do theme parks and Viagra have in common? They both make you wait hours for a two-minute ride.

➥ What's the difference between a bankrupt and a man who takes Viagra? They're both hard up, but the bankrupt can't spend any more.

➥ What's the difference between Niagara and Viagra? Niagara Falls.

➥ Why is it dangerous for a man to take Viagra and iron tablets? Every time he gets an erection he ends up pointing North.

➥ Why is Viagra like an amusement park? They both make you wait two hours for a three-minute ride.

SHeeP

➥ A cowboy goes out to seek his fortune on the frontier of the Old West. He finally settles on a ranching town near the edge of civilisation. It's so near the edge, in fact, that there aren't any women to be found, not for love nor money. Well, he's young and full of hormones, and after a month or so he starts getting randy, so he goes to the saloon to ask around. After a couple of nervous, whispered conversations, it comes out that everybody uses the sheep. He isn't particularly happy about this, but he's really desperate. He buys a bottle to provide some Dutch courage, goes and finds the nearest flock and decides that if he's going to do it at all, he's going to do it right. He spends most of the afternoon picking out the prettiest sheep in the flock. He shampoos her, ties ribbons around her neck and even puts a little bell on her collar. He's also getting pretty drunk. By evening he's finished cleaning up the sheep, and he's not thinking particularly clearly. He's so proud of the way the sheep looks, he decides to take her in to town to show her off at the saloon. When he walks in with the sheep, the room goes quiet. Everybody stares at him. They're not just staring either, but recoiling in shock and horror. He's mortally ashamed, but he's very drunk, so he slurs out, "Whassamada? I thought ever'body went out to the sheep?" Finally, one old timer pipes up. "Yeah, boy, but you got the sheriff's girl."

A sheep in sheep's clothing.
Winston Churchill on Clement Attlee

↦ Two shepherds are flying their flock to a new farm. Suddenly the engine fails and the plane begins to plunge quickly to the ground. "Quick!" shouts one, "Grab a parachute and jump!" The other one blinks. "What about the sheep?" The first shepherd stares at him. "Eh? Fuck the sheep!" The second one pauses for a moment, then asks him "Do you think we have time?"

↦ Why do Welsh sheep farmers like to screw sheep on the edge of cliffs? Because they scrabble backwards so charmingly.

➻ What's a shepherd's favourite love song? "I only have eyes for ewe!"

➻ Why do Scotsmen wear kilts? So the sheep won't hear the zip.

➻ Nikos, a Greek man, was sitting in a bar talking to a young tourist. "So," he says, "you see that wall out there in that field?" He points to a huge stone wall separating two fields. "Can you see how well it's built? I spent a year of my life moving stones from down in the valley up to those pastures and carving them so they fitted. That's the strongest fence between here and Athens! And do they call me Nikos the wall-builder? No; they do not!" Then he continues, "So, you see the bar here? The one you are leaning on right now?" and he raps it with his knuckles. "Can you see how well it's built? I spent a year of my life cutting and sanding and waxing this bar. This is the finest bar between here and Athens! And do they call me Nikos the bar-builder? No, they do not!" Then he continues, "So, you see the pier out there in the water?" He points to a long, solid pier that stretches out into the deep, deep water. "I spent a year of my life putting that pier together. I cut down the trees, I nailed the boards and I dug the holes for the poles. It almost killed me, and it is the finest pier between here and Athens! And do they call me Nikos the pier-builder? No, they do not!" Then he looks around and checks the bar before he continues, "So I fuck one lousy sheep...!"

➻ Why do sheep-shaggers wear green wellies? So they can stick the sheep's back legs down them.

SKIING

➤ A beautiful young woman is trying out skiing. By the fourth day, she feels confident enough to take the lift with her husband to the top of a gentle slope. While on the lift, stress takes its toll and the desire to visit the bathroom builds up, until it becomes unbearable. Unfortunately, on top of the slope, there is nothing as far as powder rooms go, so the husband, seeing that she desperately needs to go, suggests that she just uses the nearby thicket to do her business: her all-white suit would provide adequate camouflage. The woman weighs up her options and realizes that this is the only solution she has if she doesn't want to pee in her suit, so off she goes. The woman is quite a novice at skiing, however, and doesn't really know the position to leave her skis in and, slowly, inexorably, starts sliding down the slope. Gathering speed, she somehow manages to stay on her skis, her bottom bare and her undies wrapped around her ankles. "And this is what happened, doctor," a young man, laying on a hospital bed said to the surgeon. "I was on the lift when I saw this gorgeous woman sliding backwards, half naked and her pants around her ankles. I bent over to get a better view and I fell off the seat and broke my leg." "I see," the surgeon said. "But tell me, how did you break your arm?"

**I get my exercise acting as a pall-bearer to
my friends who exercise.**

Chancey Depew, 1834 – 1928

➤ Three blokes arrived late at the ski resort, and when they got to the hotel found that they'd have to share a room until the morning, because nothing else was available. When they got up there they found it just had one large bed. "It's just for one night," they thought, and went to bed. The next morning, the one on the far right said, "I had a really odd dream last night. I kept dreaming that I was wanking like a furious donkey, but I couldn't feel my hands." "That's really strange," said the bloke on the far left, "because that's what I dreamt, too. Exactly the same. Eerie." "You lads!" laughed the guy in the middle. "I just dreamt I was skiing..."

snappy

↔ A Polish restaurant was in the habit of putting buckets of shit around the edges of the dining-room to draw the flies away from the diners. The air was so polluted anyway that the smell didn't really make an impact. They had to stop, though. They found that their customers kept getting drunk and eating everything in sight...

↔ A truck carrying copies of Roget's Thesaurus overturned on the highway. The local newspaper reported that onlookers were "stunned, overwhelmed, astonished, bewildered and dumbfounded."

↔ How did the priest cross the road? He painted another line, from pavement to pavement.

↔ How do you tell if you have acne? Blind people can read your face.

➻ I broke a mirror in my house. I'm supposed to get seven years of bad luck, but my lawyer thinks he can get me five.

➻ I was engaged once. To a contortionist. But she broke it off.

➻ If you cloned Henry IV, would he be Henry V, or Henry IV Part II?

➻ One good turn gets most of the duvet.

➻ One of those days? I'm having one of those lives.

**I like long walks – especially when they are taken
by people who annoy me.**
Fred Allen, 1894 – 1957

➻ So this baby seal walks into a club... What a fucking tragedy.

➻ Sow your wild oats on Saturday night – then on Sunday, pray for crop failure.

➻ The other day, I was walking my dog around my building... on the ledge. Some people are afraid of heights. Not me. I'm afraid of widths.

➻ The unemployment rate is so bad in Birmingham that when a post office posted a notice reading, "WANTED for Armed Robbery", 25 people responded.

↦ What did the cannibal do after she dumped her boyfriend? Wiped her arse.

↦ What do the letters 'DNA' stand for? National Dyslexics' Association.

↦ What do you call three days of filthy weather followed by bright sunshine? A bank holiday.

↦ What do you find in a clean nose? Fingerprints!

↦ Where did Prince Charles spend his honeymoon? Indiana.

↦ Why did the one-handed man cross the road? To get to the second-hand shop.

↦ Your family is so poor that when I went over to visit you at your house I stepped on a cigarette butt and your momma said, "Who turned off the heating?"

soccer

↦ A bloke was walking his three-legged greyhound through a park when he spotted something in the undergrowth. Going for a closer look he found that it was a lamp, so he gave it a quick buffing on the off-chance and out popped a genie. "Oh, hello," said the genie. "I suppose you want a wish?" The bloke nodded, too surprised to speak. "Well, you can have the one." "Alright," said the bloke. "Um...can you fix it so my dog will win all six races one evening at the dog races? They'll put ludicrous odds on it, because he's three-legged, and I can put my life savings on and be a rich man." The genie looked doubtful and said, "Well, I dunno. I mean, a three-legged dog winning six races is a pretty obvious sign of supernatural intervention, and things are supposed to be more subtle than that, according to the Codes and Regulations For Supernatural Semi-Divinities Act 1941. Can't you think of anything else?" "Well, I suppose so," said the bloke. "I'm a Southampton fan, so could you fix it so we get back into the Premiership this year?" The genie sighed. "About that dog of yours..."

↦ A man was walking down a street in Brazil when he heard a woman screaming and noticed a smell of burning. He ran round the corner to find a huge crowd of people watching a building burn and wringing their hands. On the eighth floor, a woman was leaning out of a window screaming for someone to save her baby. The man stepped forward and called, "Throw down your baby. I'll catch her." The woman yelled back, "No! You'll drop her, and she'll die!" "No, I won't," shouted back the man. "I'm the goalkeeper for the Brazilian national team. I've played every international for ten years. I've never missed a match, and I've never let in a goal. I'm not going to drop your baby." The woman was incredulous. "You've never let in even one goal?" "No, never," he calls back. "I am the greatest goalkeeper the world has ever seen. Throw down your baby." And with that he went into a crouch, legs bent, body angling forward, arms ready. The woman looked at the flames licking up the building, realised she had no choice, shouted, "Okay, here she comes!" and with a shriek threw her baby down.

Unfortunately, as she did so, she knocked her elbow against the window frame, jerking it, and the baby went flying, tumbling wildly off-course. The crowd gasped, the woman screamed, but the man never took his eye off the baby. He stayed dead still as the child fell, watching it tumble and spin, until it was just feet from the pavement. Suddenly, like a panther, he leapt across the street, a jump of 25 feet, snatched the child from the air, rolled and came up with the baby clutched to his chest. He looked around at the crowd, acknowledged their admiration, and lifted an arm to the woman in a salute. Then he turned and, in one swift motion, drop-kicked the baby through a plate-glass window and into the back of a hardware shop.

A bad soccer team is like an old bra – it has no cups and little support.

Anonymous, on Soccer

➼ A very rich bloke wanted to give his sons presents, so he called them to him and asked them what they wanted. The oldest son asked for a train set, so his father purchased London Underground for him. The second asked for a CD player, so his father bought him Virgin Radio. The final son wanted a cowboy outfit, so his father gave him Everton.

➼ An evil-tempered old farmer died and went down to Hell. A couple of weeks later the Devil checked up on him and noticed that he didn't seem to be suffering like the rest of the damned souls. He checked the gauges and observed that the room was set to 80% humidity and a temperature of 28 degrees, so went in and said to the farmer, "What are you so cheerful about?" The farmer grinned and said, "I like it here. It's just like ploughing my fields in June." Well, that pissed the Devil off, so he went back to the controls and turned it to 90% humidity and a temperature of 32 degrees. He then went back to check the farmer again, who was standing around happy as a sandboy. "Oh, honestly," thought the Devil. "What are you so damn cheerful about now, then?" he asked the farmer. "This is even better," replied the farmer. "It's like tugging weeds out of the fields in July, except that my back's not breaking." Well, the Devil was even more pissed off, so he went to the controls and reset them yet again – 99% humidity and 40 degrees. When he looked in, the farmer was still grinning broadly. With a sinking feeling, the Devil asked him what this reminded him of. "Oh, it's just like spending the day in the grain silo in the middle of August," replied the farmer. Suddenly the Devil had a brainwave, thought, "I'm going to sort out this smug little sod," and went to the controls, where he turned the temperature to minus ten degrees. Well, sure enough, at that humidity it started snowing. "We'll see what happy summers this reminds the old bastard of now!" thought the Devil. He went back, only to find the farmer leaping up and down and shouting for joy. "Yes! Away the Saints! Southampton have finally won the Premiership!"

↦ The manager of Reading Football Club was woken up by a call from his local police station. "I'm afraid the club has been broken into, sir." Horrified, the manager asked, "Did they get the cups?" "No, sir," replied the policeman, "they didn't go into the kitchen."

➻ Sleeping with a woman never harmed any professional footballer. It's staying up all night hunting for a woman to sleep with that does the damage...

SPORT

➻ "When you go diving," warned the Caribbean instructor, "always take a friend with you. If you run out of air, your friend can help you. If you forget which way the surface is – I know it sounds silly, but it's easy – your friend can help you. If you have equipment problems, your friend can help you. Most important of all, though, is that if a shark turns up, your chance of survival is 50%, not 0!"

➻ "He's great on the court," a sportswriter said of a college basketball player in an interview with his coach, "but how's his scholastic work?" "Why, he makes straight As," replied the coach. "Wonderful!" said the sportswriter. "Yes," agreed the coach, "but his Bs are a little crooked."

➻ A London mortician has a new apprentice who is learning the art of embalming. One day, after a particularly eventful post-match session at Highbury, the cadaver of a Manchester United fan ends up lying on the table of the embalming room. The mortician notes to his apprentice that he is to start the procedure while he finishes filling in a report. The apprentice nods, gathers the tools of his trade and begins examining the body. He rolls it over and, to his amazement, finds a cork in its rectum. Mystified, he pulls it out and immediately hears the 'Glory Glory Man United' song come out of the guy's arse. Startled, he shoves the cork back into the cadaver's butt and runs up the stairs to find the mortician: "Sir, you've got to come down and help me, you won't believe what I saw!" Slightly annoyed by the naivety of his assistant, the mortician follows him downstairs. "There, look at the cork in the arse of that body, I couldn't imagine what it was doing there so I pulled it out. You do it." The mortician is a bit surprised to see the cork, too, so he walks to the table and removes it as instructed. The 'Glory Glory Man United' song starts playing again out of the dead guy's arse. Sighing, he replaces the cork in its appointed position, turns to his assistant and says: "What's so surprising about that? I've heard thousands of arseholes sing that song."

↪ A parachutist who always carried his parachute as hand luggage had checked in for a commercial flight to the States and was entering the departure lounge. At the X-ray machine, the inspector did not recognise the 'chute, and insisted that the bloke unpack it to prove he wasn't hiding anything in there. They argued over it for a while, and eventually the supervisor came over, calmed the bloke and the inspector down and let the bloke go on his way. Later, on the plane, he found that he was sitting next to an old couple who had seen him at the X-ray machine. The old boy turned to his wife and said, "Ellie dear, that young man has a parachute in his backpack," and pointed to where the bloke had placed his 'chute under the seat. The old woman looked doubtful, turned to the parachutist and asked, "Is that really a parachute?" Still irritated by the inspector, the bloke turned to her and said, "Yes, of course. Did you not get yours?"

➺ After spending all day watching rugby, Harry fell asleep in front of the TV and spent the whole night in the chair. In the morning, his wife woke him up. "Get up dear," she said, "it's twenty to seven." He awoke with a start and said, "To who?"

➺ BASE jumping is an excellent way to relax. It really takes your mind off your problems...

➺ Did you hear about the moron who went elephant-hunting? He got a hernia carrying the decoys.

➺ Do you know that sport in the Olympics where you track through deep snow, stop to shoot your gun, and then continue? Most of the world calls it the biathlon. In America though, they refer to it as 'winter'...

The game is too long, the season is too long, and the players are too long.

Jack Dolph, on basketball

➺ Have you ever thought about which game came first? Tennis has often been suggested, because the Old Testament states, "Joseph served in Pharaoh's Court." Others prefer the cricket hypothesis, because Genesis itself starts with "In the big Inning." There's no doubt about the last game that will ever be played, though. It's bridge. At the end of the world, we are told, "Gabriel will play the last trump..."

➺ If at first you don't succeed, skydiving is not your sport.

↔ Man with unchecked parachute will leap to conclusion.

↔ Marry not a tennis player. For love means nothing to them.

↔ Remember the days when sex was safe and skydiving was dangerous?

↔ Tennis players have fuzzy balls.

↔ The Irish parachutist realised that he had problems when his snorkel wouldn't open.

I was watching Sumo wrestling on the television for two hours before I realised it was darts.

Hattie Hayridge, on the weight of some darts players

↔ What's the difference between a hockey game and all-in wrestling? In a hockey game, the fights are real.

↔ Why do mountain climbers rope themselves together? To prevent the sensible ones from going home.

↔ You know you've made the right decision to take up jogging if, on your first try at it, you have more jiggle than jog.

SUPERSTARS

➻ After her operation, the famous lady soap-opera star was propped up in bed in her private room, as the doctor did his rounds. "Tell me, how are you feeling now?" he asked. "A lot better, thank you," purred the star in reply. "But one thing does bother me. When will I be able to resume a normal sex life?" "Oh, that's rather hard to say," said the doctor, "I've never been asked that after a tonsillectomy before."

➻ "Ol' Blue Eyes" died in the late 90s. Frank Sinatra, who thrilled millions world-wide with his voice, is now known as "Ol' Shut Eyes." Then-President Clinton saluted Sinatra, saying that the famous entertainer "really did do it his way." Clinton vowed that he too would try to follow Sinatra's sterling example, adding that he would be endeavouring to keep his Mafia links secret and saying, "I'm sure going to smack that bitch Hillary around next time she starts getting lippy, too."

He is every other inch a gentleman.

Noël Coward on an anonymous novelist

➻ "What is it, Lassie? A boy fell down a mine shaft and broke his ankle and is diabetic and needs insulin? Is THAT what you're trying to tell me?"

➻ Elizabeth Taylor, the legendary actress, was recently hospitalised following a fall in which she injured her hip. Doctors said that Miss Taylor was extremely fortunate, and that her injuries would have been much worse if her fall had not been cushioned by her revoltingly saggy tits.

➻ Did you hear about the "OJ Simpson Special Deal" from Hertz? When you rent a white Bronco, you get a free police chase, TV helicopters and a 'Get Away With Murder For A Small Fortune' card.

➻ Did you know that Cher is re-forming the Spice Girls? She's going to be Old Spice.

➻ How do you train King Kong? Hit him with a rolled-up newspaper building.

➻ M sends James Bond on a secret mission to heaven. When M doesn't hear from Bond for over a day, he gets worried and calls up heaven. The Virgin Mary picks up the phone and says, "Virgin Mary speaking." M asks her if Bond has reached there yet. She replies that he hasn't. M waits another few hours and calls heaven back again. "Virgin Mary speaking," comes the response. "Is James there yet?" asks M. Again the answer is no. M is really worried by this time, but he waits for a few more hours and then calls heaven back again. "Hello, Mary speaking..."

➻ Sources indicate that Madonna, the bad girl of rock and roll, has started studying the Qaballah, an ancient form of Jewish mystical occultism. One commentator expressed no surprise, saying, "After you hit 40, have a kid and lose your interest in sex, becoming Jewish is the next logical step."

➻ Superman is flying through the skies of the city feeling horny and looking for opportunities to score. Suddenly he sees Wonder Woman sunbathing naked on the top of a building. "Aw, she won't mind; and besides, I'll be so quick she'll hardly notice!" he says to himself. He swiftly flies down, fucks her in quadruple-quick time and shoots off. Wonder Woman jumps up and says, "What the hell was that?" to which the Invisible Man replies, "I don't know, but my bum sure hurts!"

➻ The Lone Ranger rides into town during the hottest part of summer. He stops outside a saloon and tells Tonto to run in circles around Silver, waving his poncho to keep a nice breeze on the horse while he goes in for a drink. A couple of minutes later, a man dressed in black swaggers into the bar and says, "You the Lone Ranger?" "Yes, I am," the Lone Ranger replies. "Well," says the man in black, "Did ya know ya left your injun runnin'?"

➻ Two men are drinking together in the bar on the top floor of the Empire State Building. The first one says to the second, "You know what? I bet you a hundred bucks I can jump out of that window and not hurt myself." "Bullshit – you're on," says the second man and the first man walks over to the window, opens it and jumps out. Two seconds later – whoosh! – and he is thrown back in. The second guy admits that this is incredible but thinks it must be a fluke, so he offers double or nothing if the first guy can somehow do it again. The first guy takes him up on the bet and walks over to the window, opens it and jumps out again. Two seconds later – whoosh! – and he is thrown back in again. The second guy is amazed again, but now he figures that there must be one of those freak gusts of wind that you get around tall buildings. So he says to the first guy, "How about this, then: double or quits again, but this time I jump out of the window?" "You're on," says the first guy and the second guy walks up to the window, opens it and jumps out. Five seconds later – whoosh! splat! – he is squashed flat and dead on the sidewalk, 70 floors below. The barman pours another drink and says to the remaining man, "You can be a real wanker when you've been drinking, Superman!"

I must decline your invitation owing to an engagement that I am just about to make.

Oscar Wilde

→ What did Bill Clinton say to Monica Lewinsky? "I didn't, say 'Wreck my election', I said ...".

→ What did OJ Simpson say to Ronald Goldman when he found the bloke with his ex-wife? "Hey, buddy; mind if I cut in?"

→ What happened to the Pope as he went to Mount Olive? Popeye nearly killed him!

→ Why are Monica Lewinsky's cheeks so puffed up? She's withholding evidence.

→ Why did King Kong join the Army? He wanted to know about gorilla warfare.

↦ Word has it that Michael Jackson, the world's first trans-racial, is about to release a new book. The working title (allegedly) is, "The Ins and Outs of Child Rearing."

Terms and Definitions

LAWS:

> **Our laws make law impossible, our liberties destroy all freedom, our property is organised robbery, our morality is an impudent hypocrisy, our wisdom is administered by inexperienced or malexperienced dupes, our power wielded by cowards and weaklings and our honour false in all its points. I am an enemy of the existing order for good reasons.**
>
> *George Bernard Shaw, Major Barbara*

↦ Sod's Law: The thing you have been hanging around waiting for so long for will happen at exactly the moment that it becomes most unhelpful.

↦ Murphy's Law: Anything that can go wrong will go wrong.

↦ Cole's Law: Finely shredded cabbage and carrot in a thin mayonnaise.

SEXUAL:

All American writing gives me the impression that Americans don't care for girls at all. What the American male really wants is two things: he wants to be blown by a stranger while reading a newspaper, and he wants to be fucked by his buddy when he's drunk. Everything else is society.

WH Auden, 1907 – 1973

↦ Biodegradable: likes to be humiliated by lovers of either sex.

↦ Combination: to achieve orgasm in order of nationality.

↦ Deferred: shaved pubic hair.

↦ Erectile: to be turned on by flooring.

↦ Gaggle: sound made by someone trying to laugh while wearing a gag.

↦ Hamstring: what Hollywood stars do with a small rodent.

↦ Hermitage: when the woman wears gloves.

↦ Hertz: sadistic sex.

↦ Liposuction: a blow job.

↦ Mathematical model: 36-24-36.

- Mathematical check: The remuneration received by a mathematical model.

- Megahertz: really sadistic sex.

- Multitude: oral sex with lots of partners.

- Mystical: a dominatrix with a feather duster.

- Negligent: a man who likes to wear frilly nightwear.

- Permitted: wearing gloves while dressed as Catwoman.

- Referred: pubic hair grown back.

- Stalemate: wife-swapping.

- Tourist liaison: a pair of handcuffs.

OFFICE:

They are not fit to manage a whelk-stall.

Winston Churchill, on the British Labour Party

- Blamestorming: Sitting around in a group discussing why a deadline was missed or a project failed and who was responsible.

- Body Nazis: Hardcore exercise and weightlifting fanatics who look down on anyone who doesn't work out obsessively.

↔ Chainsaw Consultant: An outside expert brought in to reduce the employee headcount, leaving the top brass with clean hands.

↔ Cube Farm: An office filled with cubicles.

↔ D-word: Four-letter words used by programmers in a state of confusion.

↔ Ego Surfing: Scanning the Net, databases, print media and so on, looking for references to one's own name.

↔ Elvis Year: The peak year of something's popularity: Survivor's Elvis Year was 1993.

↔ Mouse Potato: The on-line generation's answer to the couch potato.

↔ Prairie Dogging: Something loud happens in a cube farm, as people's heads pop up over the walls to see what's going on.

↔ SITCOM: Stands for Single Income, Two Children, Oppressive Mortgage.

↔ Stress Puppy: A person who thrives on being stressed-out and whiny.

↔ Tourists: Those who take training classes just to take a vacation from their jobs – "We had three serious students in the class; the rest were tourists."

↦ Xerox Subsidy: Euphemism for swiping free photocopies from a workplace.

MUSICAL:

Wagner's music is better than it sounds.

Mark Twain on Richard Wagner

↦ Beat: what music students do to each other with their musical instruments. The down beat is performed on the top of the head, while the up beat is struck under the chin.

↦ Crotchet: it's like knitting, but faster.

↦ English horn: a woodwind instrument so called because it is neither English nor a horn. Not to be confused with the French horn, which is German.

↦ Gregorian chant: a way of singing in unison, invented by monks to hide snoring.

↦ Metronome: a dwarf who lives in the city.

↦ Quaver: beginning violin class.

↦ Refrain: Don't do it. A refrain in music is the part you had better not try to sing.

➻ Rhythmic drone: the sound of many monks suffering with crotchet.

➻ Rubber band: Group of musicians who believe in safe sex.

➻ Tempo: this is where a headache begins.

➻ Trombone: a slide whistle with delusions of grandeur.

➻ Vibrato: the singer's equivalent of an epileptic seizure.

COMPUTING:

Garbage In, Garbage Out.

Computer jargon (acronymically known as GIGO) to refer to user errors that cause confusion

➻ 404 – Someone who is clueless, from the World Wide Web error message "404 Not Found", meaning the requested document couldn't be located: "Don't bother asking him, he's 404."

➻ Bit: The increment by which programmers slowly go mad.

➻ Branch instruction: Advice from a district office.

➻ Chaining: Method of attaching programmers to desks until output speeds up.

↦ Character density: The number of very weird people in the office, divided by the floorspace.

↦ Checkpoint: Where a programmer draws his salary from.

↦ Computer: A device designed to speed up and automate errors.

↦ Constant: A type of pressure felt by programmers.

↦ Core storage: A receptacle for the centre section of apples.

↦ Debugging: Removing the needles from the haystack.

↦ Default directory: Black hole. Default directory is where all files that you need disappear to.

↦ DSE: Dedicated Solitaire Engine (any PC computer).

↦ Error: Someone else's non-satisfaction with your computer output.

↦ External storage: Wastebasket.

↦ File: A document that has been saved with an unidentifiable name. It helps to think of a file as something stored in a filing cabinet – except that when you try to remove the file, the cabinet gives you an electric shock and tells you the file format is unknown.

↦ Garbage: Highly aromatic computer output.

↦ Hardware: The parts of a computer which can be kicked.

↦ Help: The feature that assists in generating more questions. When the Help feature is used correctly, users are able to navigate through a series of Help screens and end up where they started from without learning anything.

↦ High-speed printer: Wife writing cheques.

↦ Input/Output: Information is input from the keyboard as intelligible data and output to the printer as unrecognizable junk.

↦ Input: Food, whisky, beer, Nurofen.

↦ Internal sort: The stomach, liver and kidneys keep changing positions.

↦ Keyboard: An instrument used for entering errors into a system.

↦ Language: A system of organizing and defining error messages.

↦ Low-order position: The programmers' place in the chain of command.

↦ Machine-independent program: A program which will not run on any machine.

⊷ Macro: The last half of an expression: for example "Holy Macro."

⊷ Memory dump: Immediate amnesia after a glimpse of a normal life.

⊷ Microcomputer: One millionth of a computer.

⊷ Microsecond: The amount of time required for a program to hang.

⊷ Null string: The result of a four-hour database search.

⊷ Off-line: Failure to pass a sobriety test.

⊷ On-line: Full of alcohol, but not drunk.

⊷ Output: Four-letter words.

⊷ Overflow: The result of drinking too much alcohol.

⊷ Parameter: The absolute limit before the secretary yells for help.

⊷ Printer: A printer consists of three main parts: the case, the jammed paper tray and the blinking red light.

⊷ Program library: An organized collection of obsolete programs.

⊷ Reference manual: Object that raises the monitor to eye level. Also used to compensate for that short table leg.

⊷ Uninstalled – Euphemism for being fired.

➻ Users: Collective term for those who stare vacantly at a monitor. Users are divided into three types: novice, intermediate and idiot.

Texas

In America any boy may become President, and I suppose that's just one of the risks he takes!

Adlai Stevenson

➻ A white Texan, a black Texan and a Mexican are walking along a beach. The Mexican spots an old oil lamp, picks it up and rubs it. A genie immediately appears and says that since there are three of them, they can each have one wish. The black Texan thinks for a bit and says, "I wish that my brothers and sisters world-wide were all free of American oppression and back in our ancestral homelands, living happy, successful, wealthy, contented lives." The genie grants his wish, and the black guy vanishes. The Mexican says, "Yeah, that would be nice," so he makes the same wish, but for all Latin Americans, and he too vanishes. The genie then turns to the white Texan, and asks if he too wants freedom and contentment for himself and his fellow-Caucasians. He looks around slowly, grins, and says "Nope. Reckon I'll just have me a beer, boy. It don't get much better than this..."

➻ The Hindenburg was in fact very similar to Waco in Texas. When push came to shove, both proved to contain flammable compounds.

➻ David Koresh had a lot of wives, it's true, but they were all excellent matches.

➡ Two Texas Longhorn students and a catering student were driving through the Texas countryside when their car broke down. Luckily, they were near a farmhouse. So they knocked on the door and asked the gruff old farmer if they could stay the night. The farmer agreed, but only on one bizarre condition. He told them to go out into his field, pick any fruit or vegetable they could find, then return to the farmhouse. Some time later, the two Longhorns found themselves dead and in line at the Pearly Gates. St Peter was there, listening to their tale. "Okay," said St Peter, "you went out and found some fruits and vegetables. How did you die?" "Well," continued one of the Longhorns, "my friend here returned first with a cherry. Then the farmer pointed his gun at him and commanded, 'Stick that cherry up your ass, and if you laugh I'll shoot you.'" "And?" prompted St Peter. "He laughed, and the farmer shot him." "Why did you laugh?" St Peter asked the second Longhorn. "It tickled," he said. "Then it was my turn," continued the first Longhorn. "I had also brought a cherry, and the farmer pointed his gun at me and told me the same thing. I laughed and he shot me." "And why did you laugh?" St Peter asked. "I saw the catering student coming up the walkway with a watermelon."

TRUCKERS

➡ A truck stops to pick up a female hitchhiker. The driver opens the door and says: "Come on in. I'm not like the other ones that only let the good-looking girls have a ride."

➻ A hippy, long-haired youth was on a hitch-hiking holiday through the southern states. In Georgia he got a ride from a really nasty-looking trucker in a check shirt and dungarees. After 30 miles of scorched earth, the youth said to the trucker, "Well, aren't you going to ask me?" "Ask you what?" drawls the trucker. "If I'm a boy or a girl," answers the youth. "Don't matter none to me," says the trucker, "I'm going to screw you anyhow!"

He didn't care which direction the car was travelling, so long as he remained in the driver's seat.

Lord Beaverbrook, 1879 – 1964, on Lloyd George

➻ Why did the lumber truck stop? To let the lumber jack off.

TV and Radio

➻ In 1969 the Apollo 11 mission went to the moon and sent back live images of Neil Armstrong and Buzz Aldrin bouncing around on the surface. More recently, in 1997, a special probe to Mars passed back images of the red planet's surface live as scientists sent the little buggy around the place. Why the hell then can Channel Five not get a signal from the transmitter down the road to my house?

The only 'ism' Hollywood believes in is plagiarism.

Dorothy Parker, 1893 – 1967

➻ Pol Pot, the evil Cambodian dictator, is finally dead. The leader of the Khmer Rouge, his reign saw the murder of more than a million intellectuals and urbanites in an attempt to turn Cambodia into a nation of farmers. He eventually realised his mistake and repented after being forced to listen to 12 hours of The Archers non-stop.

UNIVERSITY

➻ "If there are any idiots in the room, will they please stand up," said the sarcastic lecturer. After a long silence, one freshman rose to his feet. "Now then, mister, why do you consider yourself an idiot?" enquired the lecturer with a sneer. "Well, actually I don't," said the student, "but I hate to see you standing up there all by yourself."

➻ A friendly young doctor from a college town treated a lot of college-age girls. One day, one of them came in for a routine check-up. She took off her T-shirt to reveal a big, but faint, "H" shape on her chest. How curious, he thought, so asked her how she got it. "Oh that," she giggled. "That's Harvey, my boyfriend. He was so proud of getting into Harvard that he never takes his Harvard T-shirt off, even when we're in bed." The next day, another college girl came in for her check-up. She took off her T-shirt, and there was a big, but faint, "Y" shape on her chest. How curious, the doctor thought again, so asked her how she got it. "Oh that," she giggled, "that's Youssef, my boyfriend. He was so proud of getting into Yale that he never takes his Yale T-shirt off, even when we're in bed." The next day, a third college girl comes in for her check-up. She takes off her T-shirt, and there is a big but faint "M" on her chest. "Don't tell me – you have a boyfriend at Michigan," the doctor says. "No, but I have a girlfriend at Wisconsin!" the girl replies.

↦ A philosophy professor stands at the front of the classroom with the following final exam question written on the blackboard: "How do you plan to make a living with a philosophy degree?"

↦ A professor is one who talks in someone else's sleep.

↦ A professor was grading the essay finals he had just given his class and opened the exam book of a failing student to reveal blank pages and a £100 note. The only thing written in the book was "£100 = 100% – I get an A." A month later, the student approached the professor. "I don't understand," he said, "I failed the course. Didn't you read my final?" The professor handed the student the exam book. The student opened it to reveal £50 and the phrase "£50 = 50% – you fail!"

↦ A professor was known for being a generous marker. The grades he gave for one of his courses were based solely on two exams, and the stuff on the exams was covered entirely in the textbook. As word of the course spread, each term there was a larger group of students who turned up infrequently, or not at all, just showing up for the exams. Finally, it got so bad that one term, about half of the students never turned up at all until the exams. On the day of the first exam, the students sat down and a graduate assistant handed out the papers, explaining, "The professor is ill, so I'll be taking the exams." When they opened the booklet, the students discovered just one question. It listed twenty grainy staff photos, and the instructions read, "Circle the picture of the professor who teaches this course."

➻ A student who changes the course of history is probably taking an exam.

➻ An economics lecturer had a strict policy that the fortnightly examinations were to be completed in exactly one hour and anyone who kept writing on their paper after the bell would get a zero. Well, one session a student kept writing on his exam paper for a moment or two after the bell and then confidently strode up to turn it in. The professor looked at him and said, "Don't bother to hand that paper in... you get a zero for continuing after the bell." The bloke looked at him and said, "Professor, do you know who I am?" The professor replied, "No, and I don't care if your father is Tony Blair... you get a zero on this exam." The bloke, with a enraged look on his face, shouted, "You mean you have no idea who I am?" The professor responded, "No, I've no idea, and I couldn't care less." The bloke grinned, then said, "Good!" quickly whipped his exam into the middle of the stack, and sprinted out.

➻ If you took all the students that fell asleep in class and laid them end to end, they'd be a lot more comfortable.

➻ In a huge psychology lecture class, a professor took great pains each lecture to read a chapter of his weighty textbook, written by his good self, to the class. One student made a point of sitting in the front row, right in front of the podium, and knitted while the professor read the text. It irritated the professor no end, so after about five weeks of this, the professor paused mid-lecture, looked at the young lady, and said, "Miss, are you aware that Freud considered knitting to be a form of masturbation?" The student looked up and retorted, "You do it your way Professor – I'll do it mine."

➺ One can pity the father with three kids at university. He tells his wife that they are getting poorer by degrees.

➺ One day, a very attractive undergraduate visited the professor's office. She pulled the chair closer to the professor, smiled at him shyly, bumped his knee 'accidentally', and so on. Finally, the undergraduate said: "Professor, I really need to pass your course. It is extremely important to me. It is so important that I'll do anything you suggest." The professor, somewhat taken aback by this attention, replied: "Anything?" To which the undergraduate cooed: "Yes, anything you say." After some brief reflection, the professor asked: "What are you doing tomorrow afternoon at 3pm?" The student lied: "Oh, nothing at all, sir. I can be free then." The professor then advised: "Excellent! Professor Palmer is holding a help session for his students. Why don't you attend that."

➺ Student: "What's your opinion on the paper I submitted last week?" Professor: "It's absolute drivel." Student: "I know, but let's hear it anyway."

➡ The graduate with a science degree asks, "Why does it work?" The graduate with an engineering degree asks, "How does it work?" The graduate with a management degree asks, "How much will it cost?" The graduate with an arts degree asks, "Do you want fries with that?"

We are told that Mr. Ruskin has devoted his long life to art, and as a result is Slade Professor at Oxford... A life passed among pictures does not make a painter – else the policeman in the National Gallery might assert himself... Let not Mr. Ruskin flatter himself that more education makes the difference between himself and the policeman.

James Whistler on John Ruskin

➡ University is like a gorgeous woman. You try really hard to get in, then, nine months later, you wish you had never come.

➡ When professors want your opinion, they'll give it to you.

➡ There was a story around Oxford that the final exam on a maths degree always read: "Make up an appropriate final exam for this course and answer it. You will be graded on both parts." Then one year, a student answered as follows: "The exam question is: 'Make up an appropriate final exam for this course and answer it. You will be graded on both parts.' The answer is: 'Make up an appropriate final exam for this course and answer it. You will be graded on both parts.'" His reasoning was that since that was the best exam the professor could write, it certainly ought to be good enough for a student. He got an A. The professor specifically prohibited that answer from then on.

↦ University – the fountain of knowledge where everyone goes to drink.

vaginas

↦ If men had a vagina for a day they would:

1. Wonder what the little pink button next to it does.
2. Lie in bed all morning with a hand mirror.
3. Get up and go shopping for cucumbers.
4. Go to church and pray for breasts as well.
5. Secretly worry about whether it was bigger than everybody else's.
6. Lie in bed all afternoon with a home video camera.
7. Finally find that damn g-spot that all the fuss is about.
8. Get picked up in a bar without even trying.
9. Have an orgasm – then have another one without needing a nap first.
10. Repeat number 9.

Giving birth is like sitting on top of the Eiffel Tower and spinning.

Ruby Wax

→ A mother walked into the bathroom one day and was shocked to find her son scrubbing away furiously at his cock using a toothbrush and toothpaste. "Oh, my God: what on earth's going on?" she said. "Don't try and stop me, Mum," the boy said. "I'm doing this three times a day because if you think I'm going to end up with a cavity that looks as bad as my sister's you've got another think coming!"

venereal disease

→ A bloke walked into a bar, whipped out a big syringe and told everyone, "Give me all your money, watches, jewellery and anything else of value, or I will inject you with AIDS." One by one, everyone handed over their valuables, apart from one man at the end of the bar. "I told you to hand over all your stuff or I'll inject you with AIDS," shouted the robber. The man at the bar said "Go ahead. I'm wearing a condom."

→ A van driver is driving along when he sees a woman dressed in a PVC suit hitch-hiking. He stops to give her a lift and after a couple of miles she asks if he wants sex. They're going at it in the back, and she starts shouting, "Spank me, spank me!" So he spanks her and she gets more and more excited. Then she starts shouting, "Whip me, whip me!" "I haven't got a whip," he protests. "Well, there must be something you can use – why not pull the radio aerial off and use that?" So he pulls the aerial off the van and whips her with that. Afterwards she's really sore, so she goes to the doctor and shows him the marks on her bottom from the whipping. "Did you get these marks having sex?" asks the doctor. "Yes, I did," she says. "I thought so. This is the worst case of van-aerial disease I've ever seen."

Rock Hudson surrounded himself with fellow closet queens, horrible, selfish, self-loathing older men. The day after Rock died of AIDS, one of them went on national TV to say that Rock had died of anorexia, and another went on TV to deny that Rock was gay! This was all by way of saving their own silly skins, staying in that closet forever...

Peter Allen, 1944 – 1992, on Rock Hudson

⟶ If there's one thing worse than your doctor telling you that you have venereal disease, it's your dentist telling you.

⟶ New tests have revealed that survivors of the bubonic plague that swept through England and the rest of Europe in the Middle Ages may have passed on a genetic resistance to the HIV virus to their modern ancestors. The researchers have however warned people at risk from AIDS not to test for the immunity by stuffing live rodents into their rectal cavities.

⟶ Two village idiots are discussing safe sex: "So, matey, how do you protect yourself from AIDS?" says the first. "I wear a condom constantly," says the second. "Don't you ever take it off?" says the first. "Of course! When I go to the bathroom and when I have sex!" says the second.

➤ What do you get when you cross a male chicken with a flea? An itchy cock.

➤ What is meaner than a pit-bull with AIDS? Whatever gave it AIDS in the first place.

➤ What is the difference between a clever midget and a venereal disease? One's a cunning runt...

➤ What's the difference between love and herpes? Love is not forever.

VETS

He looked like a horse who, in addition to having a secret sorrow, had laryngitis as well.

PG Wodehouse

➤ Did you hear about the doctor who had his licence taken away because he was having affairs with his patients? Yes, it's a shame because he was one of the top veterinarians in the country.

➤ Howie had been feeling guilty all day long. He kept trying to put it out of his mind, but he couldn't: the sense of betrayal was overwhelming him. Every so often his soothing inner voice would try to rally his defences, saying reassuringly, "Howie, don't worry. You aren't the first doctor to sleep with a patient, and certainly you won't be the last." Invariably, though, the sneering voice of guilt would interrupt, accusing, saying, "Howie Reed, how can you call yourself Basingstoke's top vet?"

↦ There was a country doctor who was the only doctor for miles around. He wanted to go on a fishing trip , so he called the vet and asked him to look after things while he was gone. The vet asked: "Is anything happening?" The doctor replied, "Mrs Jones is about due, but I don't think the baby will come before I get back. Anyway, if it does, just deliver it. This is her third and the first two went really easily." The vet said "Okay", and the doctor went on the fishing trip. When he returned, he called the vet. "How did things go while I was gone?" "Pretty good." "Did Mrs Jones have her baby?" "Yes, it was an eight-pound boy. Everyone's doing fine." "Did you have any trouble?" "Well, there was just one little problem." "What was that?" "I had a terrible time getting her to eat the afterbirth."

↦ What did the vet say to the dog who kept licking his balls? "Thanks, darling."

VIOLINS

↦ "Haven't I seen your face before?" a judge demanded, looking down at the defendant. "You have, your Honour," the man answered hopefully, "I gave your son violin lessons last winter." "Ah, yes," recalled the judge. "Twenty years!"

↦ How can you tell if a violin's out of tune? The bow is moving.

➻ This guy says to his wife, "Oh, baby. I can play you just like a violin." His wife says, "But I'd rather have you play me like a harmonica."

➻ What is the difference between a violin and a viola? The viola holds more beer.

waiter, waiter

➻ "Tea or coffee, gentlemen?" asked the waiter. "I'll have tea," said one bloke. "Me, too," said his mate, "and make sure the glass is clean." The waiter returned shortly afterwards, saying, "Two teas. Which of you asked for the clean glass?"

➻ "Waiter, there is a mosquito in my soup." "Yes sir, I'm afraid we've run out of flies."

It is a silly place.

*Lloyd Grossman, on Le Gavroche restaurant, London,
possibly citing Monty Python...*

➻ A bloke reading the menu in a small café called the waiter over. "Are you ready to order, sir?" asked the waiter. "I have a question," said the bloke. "Why do two hard-boiled eggs cost twice as much as a three-egg omelette?" "Ah," said the waiter, "Well, you can't count the eggs in an omelette..."

↦ A bloke was eating in a Polish restaurant when to his horror he found a dead cockroach at the bottom of his soup. He screamed for the waitress, "There's a cockroach in my soup!" She smiled, and said: "Eat. We have more. I bring you fork."

↦ This bloke was in a café. He took a big swig out of his mug of coffee and spat it out. "Waiter!" he called, "This is disgusting. This coffee tastes like soap." The waiter rushed over. "I'm dreadfully sorry, sir! I've given you a mug of tea by mistake! I'll bring you a coffee at once. It tastes like glue."

↦ This bloke was in a restaurant and the waiter brought him his meal in a nosebag. "What's the meaning of this?" asked the man indignantly. "Oh, sorry, sir," said the waiter, "I must have misunderstood. The chef told me that you come in every Tuesday and eat like a horse."

↦ This woman was ordering a meal. "I'd like the lamb chops, please – and make them lean, would you?" "Certainly, madam," replied the waiter. "In which direction?"

WALES

↦ A 12-year-old boy comes up to the Welshman and says, "I was looking in your bedroom window last night and I saw your wife giving you a blow job. Ha ha!" The Welshman answers, "The joke's on you, Ivor. I wasn't even home last night."

➻ A city man, completely ignorant of country life, was visiting Wales. He stopped at an educational farm, had a look around and went to chat with the farmer. "Nice pigs you've got there," he said. "How big are they?" The pig farmer puts one of the pig's tails in his mouth and bobbed his head up and down. "30 pounds," he said to the city guy. "What? I can't believe that's the way you weigh pigs! You're having me on!" "No, I'm not," the farmer said. He then called his son over and asked him to weigh the pig. The son put the pig's tail in his mouth, bobbed his head a couple of times and said the pig weighed 30 pounds. As the city guy still couldn't believe this was the way to weigh a pig, the farmer asked his son to go and get his mum so that she could weigh the pig, too. The boy left and came back alone a few minutes later, saying: "Mum can't come, she's busy weighing the postman."

➻ A guy breaks down while driving through Wales. Luckily, a farmer stops and offers him a lift to the nearest town, only about 20 miles away. They set off, and after a few minutes they pass by a field full of sheep. All of a sudden the farmer slams on the brakes and leaps out of the van. He hops over the fence, grabs a sheep, sticks its head in the fence and begins to hump it from behind. The guy jumps out and walks up to the fence. "What the hell are you doing?" he asks the farmer. "What the hell does it look like? Why, do you want some?" moans the farmer. "Sure do," says the guy, "but not if you're going to do that with my head."

➻ A travelling salesman has an audience with the new Pope, David, and, not quite knowing what to say, tries to break the ice with a joke... "Have you heard the one about the two Welsh priests, Holy Father?" "But I am Welsh, my son." There followed a pregnant pause while the salesman thought quickly..."That's okay, Holy Father, I'll tell it to you slowly."

➡ A ventriloquist is on a walking holiday in Wales and getting pretty bored. During one of his walks he stumbles across a farm and there, leaning on a gate, is a farmer, so the ventriloquist decides to have a bit of fun. "Hey, cool dog you have here, sir. Mind if I speak to him?" "My dog doesn't talk," the farmer says, surprised. "Hey, dog, how's it going?" the ventriloquist asks the dog. "Doin' alright." the dog says. The farmer stares at his dog in total disbelief, as he can't believe man's best friend can talk. "This is your owner, right?" the prankster asks the dog, pointing at the farmer. "Yep," says the dog. "How is he treating you?" "Real good. He walks me twice a day, feeds me great food and takes me to the lake once a week to play." The farmer is still shocked, starting to feel bad over rubbing his dog's nose into his own poop after last week's potty incident. "Mind if I talk to your horse?" the ventriloquist then asks. "Hey?" blurts the farmer. "My horse doesn't talk." The ventriloquist approaches the horse: "Hey, horse, how's it going?" "Cool," says the horse. "Is this your owner?" "Yep," says the horse. "How's he treating you?" "Pretty good, thanks for asking. He rides me regularly, brushes me down often and keeps me in the barn to protect me from the elements." By this time, the farmer is completely amazed and his eyes are bulging out of their sockets. The ventriloquist approaches the gate and says: "Mind if I talk to your sheep?" The farmer coughs loudly and says quickly: "Sheep lie!"

↔ A Welshman goes to a whorehouse. The madam is out of women but, since the guy is Welsh, she thinks she can get away with a blow-up doll and he will never know the difference. Being a bit nervous because she has never tried this one before, the madam waits outside the door. The Welshman comes out in five minutes. "How was it?" says the madam. "I don't know," says the Welshman, "I bit her on the tit and she farted and flew out the window."

The earth contains no race of human beings so totally vile and worthless as the Welsh. I have expended in labour, within three years, nearly eight thousand pounds amongst them, yet they treat me as their greatest enemy.

Walter Savage Landor, 1775 – 1864

↔ A Welshman is hired to paint the lines on the road. On the first day he paints ten miles, and his employers are amazed. But the second day he paints just five, and on only the third day, he paints only a mile of the road. Disappointed, his boss asks what the problem is. The Welshman replies, "Well sir, every day I have to walk farther and farther to get back to the paint bucket."

↔ A Welshman is shipwrecked after a big storm and ends up on a desert island with only an Alsatian and a sheep for company. There is enough food for them all and there is plentiful fresh water, too. The weather is great and they all have a pretty good time. After a few months, the three of them get into the habit of walking up into the hills to watch the sun go down every night. One particularly balmy night, everything is just beautiful: the sea can be heard gently lapping in the distance, the cool breeze carries the sound of the crickets chirping and everyone is happy. The Welshman looks over at the sheep and the sheep looks back. They glance into each other's eyes and the Welshman starts to feel warm inside. The sheep continues to look at him, so he reaches out and puts his arm around the animal. As soon as he does this, the Alsatian begins to growl, and doesn't stop until the arm is removed. The three of them continue to watch the sunset, but there is no more funny business. After a few more weeks there is a huge storm and a beautiful woman is washed up on the beach. She is pretty ill and has to be tended night and day for weeks before she even has enough strength to talk. After a few months of tender, loving care the woman is perfectly well again and the four of them all get along fine. The Welshman, the sheep and the Alsatian introduce the woman to their nightly ritual of watching the sun go down, and one night they are all there and it is just magical. As before, they can hear the sea, smell the scented air and see the most beautiful sunset of their lives and as before, romance is most certainly in the air. The Welshman is getting his warm feeling inside so he turns to the beautiful, scantily-clad maiden at his side and just nuzzles his mouth up next to her ear. She tips her head to one side to hear what he has to say, as he whispers, "You wouldn't take the dog off for a walk, would you?"

→ A Welshman was suffering from constipation, so his doctor prescribed suppositories. A week later the man complained to the doctor that they didn't produce the desired results. "Have you been taking them regularly?" the doctor asked. "What do you think I've been doing," the man said, "shoving them up my ass?"

➻ A Welshman saw a priest walking down the street. Noticing his collar, he stopped him and said, "Excuse me, but why are you wearing your shirt backwards?" The priest laughed, "Because, my son, I am a Father." The Welshman scratched his head. "But I am a father too, and I don't wear my shirt backwards." Again the priest laughed. "But I am a father of thousands." To which the Welshman replied, "Well then you should wear your shorts backwards."

➻ A Welshman wanted to learn how to sky-dive. He got an instructor and started lessons. The instructor told the Welshman to jump out of the plane and pull his rip cord. The instructor then explained that he himself would jump out right behind him so that they would go down together. The Welshman understood and was ready. The time came for the Welshman to jump and the instructor reminded the man that he would be right behind him. The Welshman jumped from the plane and, after being in the air for a few seconds, pulled the rip cord. The instructor followed by jumping from the plane but when he pulled his rip cord the parachute did not open. The instructor, frantically trying to get his parachute open, darted past the Welshman. The Welshman seeing this yelled as he undid the straps to his parachute, "So you wanna race, eh?"

The ordinary women of Wales are generally short and squat, ill-favoured and nasty.

David Mallet, 1705 – 1765

➻ A Welshman was walking down the street, carrying a brown paper bag. He ran into one of his friends, who asked,

"Hey! What do you have in the bag?" The man told his friend that he had some fish in the bag. His friend said, "Well, I'll make you a bet. If I can guess how many fish you have in the bag, you'll have to give me one." The man says, "I'll tell you what. If you tell me how many fish I have in this bag, I'll give you both of them."

The land of my fathers – and my fathers can have it.

Dylan Thomas, 1914 – 1953, on Wales

↦ A Welshman went to a carpenter and said: "Can you build me a box that is two inches high, two inches wide, and 50 feet long?" "Hmm," mused the carpenter, "it could be done, I suppose, but what would you want a box like that for?" "Well, you see," said the Welshman, "my neighbour moved away and forgot his garden hose."

↦ A Welshman, an Englishman, and a Frenchman are running away from the German soldiers when they come up to a forest and they decide to hide by each climbing a tree. When the Germans arrive, they go to the first tree where the English guy is, and shout, "We know you're up there; come down." The English guy, thinking fast, says, "Twit, twit, twit..." The Germans, thinking that it's a bird, move on to the next tree where the French guy is and once again shout, "We know you're up there; come down." The French guy, thinking fast, says, "Woo, woo, woo..." The Germans, thinking that it's an owl, move on to the next tree where the Welsh guy is and once again shout, "We know you're up there; come down." The Welsh guy thinks for a while and then says, "Moo, moo, moo..."

➻ An Englishman is walking down the street when he sees a Welshman with a very long pole and a yardstick. He's standing the pole on its end and trying to reach the top of it with his yardstick. Seeing the Welshman's ignorance, the Englishman wrenches the pole out of his hand, lays it on the sidewalk, measures it with the yardstick, and says, "There, ten feet long." The Welshman grabs the yardstick and shouts, "You idiot! I don't care how long it is, I want to know how high it is."

➻ An Englishman, a Frenchman and a Welshman are captured and thrown into prison. However, the guard is rather kind towards them, and says, "I am going to lock you away for five years, but I'll let you have anything you want now before I lock you away." The Englishman says: "I'll have five years' supply of beer." His wish is granted, and they lock him away with his beer. The Frenchman says: "I'll have five years' supply of brandy." His wish is granted, and they lock him away with his brandy. The Welshman says: "I'll have five years' supply of cigarettes." His wish is granted, and they lock him away with his cigarettes. Five years later the prisoners are released. First, they release the Englishman, who staggers out totally drunk. Then, they release the Frenchman, who also rolls out rather inebriated. Then, they release the Welshman, who comes out and says: "Has anyone got a light?"

➻ As the new Welsh assembly gets ready to take over administrative affairs, a new white paper has been tabled suggesting that housing benefit could be extended to same-sex couples. Farmers are likely to be disappointed at the paper, which requires that the couples still have to be the same species.

↦ This Welshman came home one day from work, hung up his coat, took off his hat and walked into his bedroom shouting, "I'm home, darling." What should he see but his best friend in bed with his wife. Infuriated, he rushed to the cupboard, pulled out his gun and put it to his own head. His wife started laughing. "Don't laugh," he screamed, "you're next."

↦ Three men are travelling in the Amazon; a German, an Englishman, and a Welshman, and they get captured by some Amazons. The head of the tribe says to the German, "What do you want on your back for your whipping?" The German responds, "I will take oil." So they put oil on his back, and a large Amazon whips him ten times. When he is finished the German has these huge welts on his back, and he can hardly move. The Amazons haul the German away, and say to the Welshman, "What do you want on your back?" "I will take nothing," says the Welshman, and he stands there straight and takes his ten lashings without a single flinch. "What will you take on your back?" the Amazons ask the Englishman. He responds, "I'll take the Welshman."

↦ Two American tourists were travelling through Wales. As they approached Llangollen, they started arguing about the pronunciation of the town's name until they stopped for lunch. As they stood at the counter, one tourist asked the counter girl, "Could you settle an argument for us? Would you please pronounce where we are very slowly?" The girl leaned over and said, "Burrrrrrrgurrrrrr Kingggg."

↦ Two Welsh hunters were driving in the US, bear hunting. They came upon a fork in the road where a sign read "BEAR LEFT". They went home.

➺ Two Welsh hunters were out looking for pheasant when they came upon the local farmer's daughter, sitting naked on a fence, sunning herself. The first hunter asked, "Are you game?" She replied, "I sure am, baby." The second hunter shot her.

➺ Wales sent its top team of scientists to attend the international science convention, where all the countries of the world gathered to compare their scientific achievements and plans. The scientists listened to the United States describe how they were another step closer to a cure for cancer, how the Russians were preparing a space ship to go to Saturn and how Germany was inventing a car that runs on water. Soon, it was the Welsh scientists' turn to speak. "Well, we are preparing a space ship to fly to the sun." This, of course was met with much ridicule. They were asked how they planned to deal with the sun's extreme heat. "Simple; we're going at night."

weddings

Wedding, n: a ceremony in which two persons undertake to become one, one undertakes to become nothing, and nothing undertakes to become supportable.

Ambrose Bierce, The Devil's Dictionary

➺ A bloke was at the altar getting married. The priest asked him to take his vows, and then he said, "I do." Immediately, his wife-to-be snapped, "Oh, no, you don't! I do!"

❧ A little boy at a wedding turns to his father and says, "Daddy, why is the girl wearing white?" His father replies, "The bride is in white to show that this is the happiest day of her life, son." The boy thinks about it, and then says, nervously, "Well then, why is the boy wearing black...?" His father nods slowly, and says, "You're catching on, son."

❧ A newly-wed couple are getting undressed for the first time, and the husband says, "Darling, your body is so beautiful – let me get my camera and take a picture." "Why?" asks his wife. "So that I can keep it with me always and remember how beautiful you are," he says. Then he takes his clothes off and she says, "Darling, I must also take a photograph of you." "Why?" asks her husband. "So I can get it enlarged," she replies.

❧ A woman was getting married. She entered the church wearing a black wedding gown that surprised everyone. The pastor was a bit annoyed and asked her: "Why are you dressed up in black?" The woman replied: "Well, that's because I'm not a virgin."

❧ A young couple met their priest to set a date for their wedding. When he asked whether they preferred a contemporary or a traditional service, they opted for the contemporary. On the big day, a major storm forced the groom to take an alternate route to the church. The streets were flooded, so he rolled up his trouser legs to keep them dry. When he finally reached the church, his best man rushed him into the sanctuary and up to the altar, just as the ceremony was starting. "Pull down your trousers," whispered the priest "Er, Reverend, I've changed my mind," the groom responded. "I think I want the traditional service."

➥ On their wedding night, a devout young man entered the bridal suite and found his wife lying languorously on top of the covers, naked. "I expected to find you on your knees by the side of the bed," he said disapprovingly. "Well, if I must," she replied, "but sucking cock always gives me hiccups."

➥ What's a shotgun wedding? It's a wife-or-death situation.

➥ Why do brides always wear white? Aren't all kitchen appliances that colour?

➥ Why does a bride smile when she walks down the aisle? She knows she's given her last blowjob.

Marriage is a good deal like a circus – there is not as much in it as represented in the advertising.

Edgar Watson Howe

women

➥ "I'd like my wife to be beautiful, well-behaved, smart and rich," the bachelor said. "Oh, well," his friend replied, "then you have to get married four times."

➥ A beggar walks up to a well-dressed woman who is shopping in Knightsbridge and says: "I haven't eaten anything in four days." She looks at him and says: "God, I wish I had your willpower."

↝ A lady is a woman who never shows her underwear unintentionally.

↝ A successful man is one who makes more money than his wife can spend. A successful woman is one who can find such a man.

↝ Adam was created first to give him a chance to say something.

There is one woman whom fate has destined for each of us. If we miss her, we are saved.

New York Times newspaper, 1948

↝ An ideal wife is one who remains faithful to you but tries to be just as charming as if she weren't.

↝ An obviously drunk bloke staggers into a pub and seats himself at the bar. After being served, he notices a woman sitting a few stools down. He motions the landlord over and says "Landlord, I'd like to buy that old douchebag down there a drink." Somewhat offended, the landlord replies, "Sir, I run a respectable establishment, and I don't appreciate you calling my female customers douchebags." The man looks ashamed for a moment and says "Yes, you're right, that was uncalled-for... please allow me to buy the woman a cocktail." "That's better," says the landlord, and he goes over to the woman. "Madam, the gentleman at the bar there would like to buy you a drink. What would you like?" "How nice!" replied the woman, "I'll have a vinegar and water, thanks."

↦ A man needs a mistress, just to break the monogamy.

↦ Anybody who claims that marriage is a 50/50 proposition doesn't know the first thing about women – or fractions.

↦ Being a woman is of special interest to aspiring male transsexuals. To actual women it is simply a good excuse not to play football.

↦ Do you know what the Oxford English Dictionary definition of a menstrual period is? A bloody waste of fucking time.

↦ How do you confuse a female archaeologist? You give her a used tampon and ask her what period it's from.

↦ How do you know when your wife is dead? Your sex life remains the same but your dirty clothes basket overflows.

↦ How do you make your girlfriend scream out loud while you're having sex? Phone her to let her know what she's missing!

↦ How does an older woman keep her youth? By giving him money.

↦ How is a woman like a laxative? They both irritate the shit out of you.

↦ How many men does it take to open a beer bottle? What the hell? It should be open when she brings it to you!

➻ If you want to resist the feminist movement, the simple way to do it is to give them what they ask for and let them defeat themselves. Today, you've got endless women in their twenties and thirties who have no idea whether they want to be a mother, have lunch or be Secretary of State.

➻ If your wife keeps coming out of the kitchen to nag you, what have you done wrong? Made her chain too long.

➻ In which month do women talk the least? February, of course. It's the shortest.

➻ Marriage has driven more than one man to sex.

➻ My wife has a split personality, and I hate both of them.

➻ Never argue with a woman when she's tired...or when she's rested.

➻ No man should marry until he has studied anatomy and dissected at least one woman.

➻ What do the small bumps around a woman's nipples represent? Braille for "Suck here."

➻ What do women and rocks have in common? The flat ones get skipped.

➻ What do you do if your dishwasher stops working? Shout at her.

➻ What does a 75-year-old woman have between her breasts that a 25-year-old doesn't? Her navel.

➻ What happened to the guy who figured out what it was with women? He killed himself before he could tell anybody.

➻ What is it when a man talks dirty to a woman? Sexual harassment. What is it when a woman talks dirty to a man? Two euro a minute.

➻ What is the definition of making love? Something a woman does while a man fucks her.

➻ What is the difference between a woman and a washing machine? You can bung your load in a washing machine and it won't call you a week later.

➻ What's good about having a homeless girlfriend? You can drop her off wherever you want!

➻ What's six inches long, two inches wide and drives women wild? Cash.

➻ What's the difference between a sumo wrestler and a feminist? A sumo wrestler has a feminine side.

➻ What's the difference between your pay cheque and your penis? You don't have to beg to get your wife to blow your salary!

↦ What's the difference between your wife and a wheelie bin? You only need to take a wheelie bin out once a week.

↦ What's the difference between your wife and your job? After five years your job will still suck.

↦ What's worse than a male chauvinist pig? A woman that won't do what she's told.

↦ When the lights are out, all women are beautiful.

↦ Why are hangovers better than women? Hangovers will go away eventually.

Twenty million young women rose to their feet with the cry "We will not be dictated to!", and promptly became secretaries.

GK Chesterton

↦ Why are women's feet small? So they can stand closer to the sink.

↦ Why are Wonderbras so called? When a woman takes one off, you wonder where her tits went!

↦ Why did God give men penises? So they'd have at least one way to shut a woman up.

↦ Why did God give women arms? Do you know how long it would take to lick a bathroom clean?

↦ Why did God make Man first? He didn't want a woman looking over his shoulder.

↦ Why did the woman cross the road? Who cares? How did she get out of the kitchen?

↦ Why didn't the man report his stolen credit card? The thief was spending less than his wife.

↦ Why do men die before their wives? To get some peace and quiet.

**Women are like elephants to me: I like to look
at them, but I wouldn't want to own one.**

WC Fields

↦ Why do they name hurricanes after women? Because they're wild and wet and noisy when they come – and when they go you lose your house and your car.

↦ Why do women change their minds so often? To keep them clean.

↦ Why do women have 2% more brainpower than cows? So that when you pull their tits they won't shit on the floor.

↦ Why do women like to have sex in the dark? They can't stand seeing a man have a good time.

➼ Why do women paratroopers always wear tampons? So they don't whistle as they make their way down.

➼ Why do women pierce their belly-buttons? Gives them somewhere to hang air freshener.

➼ Why do women prefer elderly gynaecologists? Shaky hands!

➼ Why do women wear black underwear? Mourning – for the stiff they buried the night before.

➼ Why don't women need to wear watches? There's a clock on the stove!

➼ Why don't women fart as much as men? Because they can't shut their mouths long enough to build up the pressure.

➼ Why haven't we sent a woman to the moon? It doesn't need cleaning.

➼ Why is a laundrette a bad place to pick up chicks? If she can't afford a washing machine, she'll never be able to support you.

➼ Why is the space between a woman's breasts and hips called a waist? Because there's enough room for another pair of tits in there.

➼ Women are one of the Almighty's enigmas, created to prove to men that He knows more than they do.

➻ Women! If you want to know why they are called the 'opposite sex', express an opinion.

➻ Women! You can't live with them, you can't do most positions without them.

➻ Yesterday scientists in Canada announced that beer contains small traces of female hormones. To prove the theory, they fed 100 men 12 pints of beer and observed that 100% of them started talking nonsense and lost the ability to drive.

➻ Your dog is barking to be let in the back door and your wife is barking to be let in the front door. Which do you let in first? The dog – once he's in, at least he shuts up!

WORK

Of the best rulers, the people know only that they exist; the next best they love and praise; the next they fear; and the next they revile; but of the best, when their task is accomplished, their work done, the people all remark 'We have done it ourselves'.

Lao Tzu, c.604 – 531BC

➻ A new employee was habitually late. Finally, the foreman called him in. "Don't you know what time we go to work here?" he shouted. "No, sir," was the reply, "I haven't been able to work it out yet, because the rest of you are always here."

You rise to play, and go to bed to work.

William Shakespeare, Othello

↦ A speaker was getting tired of being interrupted. He grabbed the microphone and said loudly, "We seem to have a great many fools here tonight. Would it be advisable to hear one at a time?" Someone in the back of the room said, "Yes. Get on with the speech."

↦ A woman goes to the hospital to visit a girlfriend who is about to have a heart transplant. She's worried about the friend so she speaks to the doctor. Girlfriend: "I'm worried about my friend, doctor. What if her body rejects the organ?" Doctor: "Well, she's 36 years old and healthy. How long has she been in business?" Girlfriend: "She's been working since she was 19 years old but what does that have to do with anything?" Doctor: "Well, she's been working 17 years and hasn't rejected an organ yet."

↦ How long have I been working at that office? As a matter of fact, I've been working there ever since they threatened to sack me.

↦ When I first started working, I used to dream of the day when I might be earning the salary I'm starving on now.

↦ Why didn't the mime artist feel too guilty about his career? At least he wasn't a lawyer.

↦ You know it is going to be a bad day at work when the gypsy fortune-teller offers to refund your money.